FRONTENAC : THE COURTIER GOVERNOR

FRONTENAC

THE COURTIER GOVERNOR

W. J. Eccles

Introduction by Peter Moogk

UNIVERSITY OF NEBRASKA PRESS

LINCOLN AND LONDON

⊗

First Nebraska paperback printing: 2003

Library of Congress Cataloging-in-Publication Data
Eccles, W. J. (William John)
Frontenac: the courtier governor / W. J. Eccles; introduction by Peter Moogk.
p.   cm.
Includes bibliographical references and index.
ISBN 0-8032-6750-9 (pbk.: alk. paper)
1. Frontenac, Louis de Buade, comte de, 1620–1698.   2. Governors—Canada—
Biography.   3. Canada—History—To 1763 (New France)   4. New France—
Biography.   5. France—Court and courtiers—Biography.   I. Title.
FI030.F9276   2003
971.01'63'092—dc22
2003015327

PETER MOOGK

INTRODUCTION

Written history is always imprinted with the character of its author, and in the case of Bill Eccles, the bold revisionism in his historical publications reflects his combative nature. He began life as a rebel against authority and became a formidable authority himself, dispensing categorical opinions and scathing judgments. Like Jupiter, Bill cast thunderbolts upon historians, other writers, and the unlucky students whose efforts fell short of his high standards.

I met Bill in 1963 when I arrived at the University of Toronto as a third-year transfer student from the University of Saskatchewan. I was his research assistant at McGill University from 1966 to 1967 and one of his graduate students from 1965 to 1973. He supervised my doctoral dissertation. Many of the quotations and memories that I include here were collected during our long association, despite Bill's resistance to being recorded, which was not because he was humble; he was just an extremely private man. He recognized that historians are the products of their upbringing and times without, evidently, applying that rule to himself.

Thanks to his defiant self-reliance, Bill reshaped Canadians' understanding of their country when it was a French colony. His independence was probably strengthened by a solitary childhood, and for a physically small boy, assertiveness may have been a necessity. He was born in England at Thirsk, Yorkshire, on 17 July 1917, the son of John and Jane Ellen (Thorpe) Eccles. Bill was their second child, born ten years after a daughter, Louise. At the time of Bill's birth John Eccles was a farmer-landowner performing wartime service as acting railway stationmaster of South Otterington, Yorkshire.[1]

As a child, Bill was willful and mischievous. He once found some railway warning "torpedoes" in an unlocked shed and laid them on the track, halting the Flying Scotsman express train—a historic first, he believed. When he was seven his father died of cancer. His mother was a strong-willed woman who took her then eleven-year-old son to Canada to escape scrutiny by the parsimonious solicitors administering her late husband's estate. Louise was left behind in England. The separation hurt Bill because he had felt much closer to his sister than to either of his parents.

Far from most of his family, Bill retained a nostalgic affection for his birthplace, and he came to know England better when he was stationed there during the Second World War. Later trips back to Britain were frequent enough to keep the link with his homeland alive. He retained only a hint of a British accent in his nasal voice, as when he inveighed against "rank *armateurs* who couldn't *marster* the basics of the subject." He wore tweed jackets, ate kippers, shopped at Marks and Spencer stores, and was fond of the word "whilst." He was once very pleased when an Italian waitress recognized him as an Englishman. Such was the unlikely background of a man who became a champion of French Canada.

While living at Senneville on Montreal Island during the 1930s, Bill could have shared the condescension of his fellow Protestant English-speakers toward Roman Catholicism and French-Canadians. When he and his mother were invited to their French-Canadian gardener's home, they were apprehensive but then charmed by the warmth and openness of their hosts. This illiterate but wise gardener taught Bill to speak French, which had the added attraction of being a language his mother did not understand. Bill was also entranced by French Canada's history. In a 1984 letter to one of my students, he wrote that as a teenager his youth "was spent at Senneville at the western tip of the island of Montreal. There I paddled my canoe to fish at the Ile aux Tourtes. . . . Across from it were the ruins of Fort Senneville. Standing there, one could easily imagine the fleets of canoes sweeping down the Lac des Deux Montagnes and the local settlers watching warily. Were they the Outouais [Ottawas] coming to trade or the Iroquois?"[2] Later, when working with French-speakers as a log driver, he witnessed a worker arguing ineffectually with an Anglo-Canadian supervisor over pay. Bill's instinctive sympathy for the underdog began to evolve into a partisanship for French Canada.

The need to perform manual labor was the result of a rupture with his mother. After his first year at McGill University, she made further payment of his tuition conditional upon his doing things her way. He characteristically dropped out of the university rather than submit to her will. She returned to England, leaving him in Canada. Thereafter they had so little contact that when she died in the 1950s, Bill's English relatives were forced to call upon the Royal Canadian Mounted Police to help locate and inform him of her death.

In the late 1930s Bill held a variety of jobs, from swineherd to office clerk. At a Montreal stockbroker's office he outraged his employer by reading—on company time—Thorstein Veblen's *Theory of the Leisure Class* and various works by Samuel Butler. The outbreak of the Second World War and his service in the Royal Canadian Air Force (RCAF) provided an escape from the tedium of civilian life during the Great Depression. Bill and his friends knew that appeasement of the fascist powers was merely delaying the conflict, and they greeted with relief the 1939 declaration of war against Nazi Germany by Britain and Canada.

In the RCAF Bill was a navigator on a Hudson bomber flying anti-submarine patrols out of Trinidad. He was later transferred to Bomber Command and, after spending the winter of 1942–43 in Wales, joined an RCAF squadron of Lancaster bombers based in Lincolnshire. He became a radio and radar operator and from that assignment retained a souvenir of anti-aircraft shrapnel that had lodged in a radar set just before it would have hit him.

Bill loathed military discipline and objected to the bombing of the old Hanseatic ports of Luebeck and Rostock, cities that had little strategic military value. Fellow airmen called their insubordinate companion "Hitler's secret weapon." His wartime experience bred a contempt for military officers, as was evident when he advised his son Peter not to join the army cadets: "If you join the army you'll have to take orders from idiots." Yet his disdain for superiors did not prevent him from becoming a flight sergeant. It is not surprising that Governor-General Buade de Frontenac's role as commander of troops in New France invited Bill's demolition of Frontenac's reputation; Generals Montcalm and Wolfe fared no better at his hands. The reputations of these "great men" celebrated by nineteenth-century historians were prey to Bill's critical eye and caustic pen.

As a returning war veteran, Bill's university tuition was paid by the Canadian government. At McGill University he met and married Jean Low, another student who had served in the RCAF. While there, Bill also came under the spell of Edward Robin Adair, a professor of British history who had ventured into the study of French-Canadian history and, after carefully reviewing the primary evidence, had exploded the myths of Quebec's conservative nationalists. Adair showed that the chivalrous Dollard des Ormeaux, who in 1660 reputedly sacrificed himself and his companions to save Montreal, was an inept freebooter who intended to waylay Iroquois fur traders coming down the Ottawa River but was trapped by them instead. Dollard and his companions had been Canada's equivalent of Leonidas and the Spartans, who died opposing Persian invaders at Thermopylae Pass in 480 B.C.

Bill admired Adair's iconoclasm, his insistence on well-documented judgments, and his high literary standards. As a teacher and scholar, Bill modeled himself upon his mentor, whose picture was later placed over his desk at home. Adair, he recalled, had a "fearsome reputation as an extremely demanding teacher, never satisfied with whatever they [his graduate students] did."[3] Other students wilted under Adair's brutal criticism, but Bill rose to the challenge. This professor made the history of New France exciting whereas, wrote Bill, "the history of English Canada [after 1800] seemed unutterably dreary." In imitation of his teacher, the student typed a corrective note about an article in a volume of the *Bulletin des Recherches Historiques* and tipped it into the volume in McGill's Redpath Library, where I found it in the late 1960s. The note pointed out that the article's author was wrong, explained why, and was signed "William J. Eccles, BA."[4]

Bill's master's thesis on intendant Jean Bochart de Champigny (McGill University, 1951) introduced him to the subjects of war, politics, and diplomacy in late seventeenth-century Canada, when Frontenac served as governor-general. As Bill read the transcribed French documents in the Public Archives of Canada at Ottawa—before the modern reproduction techniques of microfilming and photocopying were widely available—his view of the period changed: "Before long a view of events and personages at the end of the seventeenth century began to emerge that was markedly at variance with the accepted interpretation. This was particularly true of Frontenac who had been made a legendary, heroic figure, first by [Francis] Parkman, then by . . . Henri Lorin."⁵ A statue of Governor-General Frontenac, defiantly pointing to the mouth of his cannon in response to Sir William Phips's 1690 demand for surrender, adorned the façade of Quebec's legislature. Frontenac, like Dollard, has been misrepresented as the embodiment of French martial valor to counter the impression of Gallic military inferiority created by the British conquest of New France in 1759–60.

Professor Adair advised Bill to go to France to see for himself the original versions of the official correspondence that had passed between colony and mother country as well as other documents that had not been transcribed for the Canadian archives. A year in Paris at the Sorbonne in 1951–52, thanks to a French government fellowship, convinced Bill of the importance of knowing "Old Regime" France in order to understand New France. The colony, he realized, was an overseas extension of the parent state and not an entity whose affairs were entirely determined by local forces, local residents, or the North American environment. Bill was convinced that the social, legal, and political institutions; cultural values; religion; and language transferred from seventeenth-century France "really dominated the lives of Canadians."⁶

Bill's 1955 doctoral thesis, which became the award-winning *Frontenac: The Courtier Governor* (1959), presented Frontenac as an arrogant noble who had accepted the governorship of New France to escape his creditors and had misused his powers to enrich himself from the fur trade. In defiance of explicit orders from the king of France and the minister responsible for the French colonies, Frontenac had acquired a territorial empire whose defense was beyond French resources. The legendary "fighting governor" spent more time fighting other administrators and the bishop of Quebec than he did fighting the British and the Iroquois. His disobedience did not receive the retribution it deserved, according to Bill, because of Frontenac's persuasive pen, his courtier's charm, and his personal and familial connections with the minister.

Francis Parkman's earlier portrayal of Frontenac as the savior of New France who had cowed the Iroquois set the tone for most later historians.⁷ The myth of Governor-General Buade de Frontenac as the liberal opponent of theocratic priests and the masterful warrior-diplomat was based on a credulous reading of the governor's self-promoting dispatches. Bill believed that because the general histories of the period were so inadequate, he was compelled to provide the context for Frontenac's career in North America. Canadian historians have excelled in writing life-and-times biographies, and this mode of history would have been familiar to him.

When Bill arrived at the University of Manitoba in 1953 to take up his first teaching post, the history department's head asked him why he wanted to write about New France because Francis Parkman had supposedly said all there was to say on the subject. Parkman had indeed shaped the American and Anglo-Canadian view of the French Regime as an era of autocratic government and religious fanaticism with a feudal economy.[8] In June 1954 when Bill presented his paper, "Frontenac: New Light and a Reappraisal," at the Canadian Historical Society convention, he was accused of "debunking" one of the nation's heroes.

When *Frontenac: The Courtier Governor* was published in 1959, the reaction was more temperate. The external examiner at his thesis defense, Guy Frégault, assessed the book for the *Canadian Historical Review* and praised the author's erudition, his careful accumulation of evidence, and the lucid case he presented in support of his indictment of Frontenac. Only the book's introductory sketch of Canadian society in Louis XIV's reign was criticized for being "superficial" and "too traditional."[9] Grace Lee Nute, in the *American Historical Review*, acknowledged that the author had "done an excellent job of debunking the Frontenac myth," yet she simultaneously judged the book's condemnation of its subject as too harsh. Nute was not convinced by the explanation of the governor's ability to escape punishment for his insubordination and suggested that Frontenac must have been linked to a powerful faction in the French court. She felt that Bill had neglected the British sources that would have thrown more light on Frontenac's dealings with the Iroquois and the English colonies.[10] Nevertheless, the American Historical Association's Pacific Coast Branch awarded its 1959 prize to the book.

At the University of Toronto we students, who were already predisposed to regard politicians as knaves and generals as fools, were a receptive audience for Bill's iconoclastic viewpoint. In a graduate seminar Bill once told us that he regarded Frontenac as, in the parlance of the day, "a fink." But Bill must have felt a trace of envy because when I helped to identify and organize his research notes, which were on cards and slips of paper stored in shoeboxes, I found penmanship exercises in which Bill had practiced writing Frontenac's signature.

In his later books, such as *Canada under Louis XIV* (1964), *The Canadian Frontier* (1968), and *France in America* (1972), Bill argued that France had provided Canada with an "aristocratic welfare state" in no way inferior to the British colonies' system of government. Military ideals—not commercial values—dominated colonial society, he said. Having disposed of some of the much-celebrated leaders of the period, Bill paid homage to the colony's nameless settlers and rehabilitated the Native peoples, who were to Parkman brutal savages. In war and trade, according to Bill, the French were the dependents of their aboriginal allies, whose diplomatic skills confounded Europeans. These ideas are tame stuff today, yet at the time when they were first published, they presented a radically new view of Native peoples. The French, he wrote, expanded and subsidized the fur trade in the 1700s not for commercial reasons but to cement military alliances with the aboriginal peoples. In the 1980s Bill enthusiastically acted as a historical witness for the Temagami Anishinabeg (Ojibwas) in their land claim case against the Province of Ontario's government. When the judge ruled against the claim, Bill publicly denounced the decision as bad history and worse justice.

Bill's life was a series of paradoxes: he was a Briton who championed French Canada and a self-styled "exile from Montreal," who voluntarily spent thirty-five years of his life in Toronto—even his retirement years—all the while expressing contempt for the place. He had moved to Toronto in 1963 from the University of Alberta, where he had gone to teach after serving as a sessional lecturer at the University of Manitoba. He was an intensely private man with a very public life; he refused to be interviewed about his own past but would talk freely about North American history. He liberated the history of French North America from the censorious and unsympathetic perspective of Francis Parkman. When admirers came forth to shower him with praise, Bill was embarrassed, and he once told me, "I try to get away as soon as possible."

As scholarly opinion shifted in Bill's direction—because his views were well-grounded in the evidence—he had fewer targets for his verbal cannonades. He then turned his guns on the academic icons of the past, such as Canada's famous political economist Harold Adams Innis. In 1979 when he attacked Innis's book *The Fur Trade in Canada* as an exercise in economic determinism riddled with errors, a frisson of horror rippled through the ranks of Canadian nationalists. Bill liked to shock people, and he delighted in argument. His attitude was that if you have the evidence, then you should stand your ground and defend it. To the end of his days he relished a good argument, and thanks to an extraordinary memory, he could seemingly pull facts out of the air to sustain his interpretation. He had to have the last word. I think he enjoyed being an embattled heretic and was uncomfortable when his opinions became the new orthodoxy, which in turn was attacked by younger scholars for being too flattering to the institutions of New France. After retiring from the University of Toronto in 1983, he missed the lively give-and-take he had experienced with mature students. Even though it meant traveling far from home and was a strain on his health, he continued to preside over seminars at the College of William and Mary, McMaster University, and the University of Western Ontario.

Though small in stature, Bill, with his belligerent, owlish expression—eyebrows projecting over the frame of his glasses—and his acerbic tongue intimidated other historians. He maintained a prickly exterior and kept new acquaintances at a distance, yet he was tenderhearted and exceedingly loyal to his three children and to those of us who were his graduate students. He encouraged us and lobbied others to find jobs for us. We shared the gourmet meals and fine wines to which he was accustomed.

Our relationship to him was always clear: as disciples to the master. Our inheritance was the same that he had received from Edward Robin Adair: intellectual independence. We were taught never to accept an interpretation without first examining its evidentiary basis, to think for ourselves, and, after reconstructing events from the best available evidence, to defend our point of view.

Bill was a tireless researcher and had just finished a third revision of his authoritative survey, *The French in North America*, when he died in Toronto on 2 October 1998. The cause of death was a pulmonary embolism—possibly as a consequence of his smoking French Gitane cigarettes for years. Those at his funeral sang the hymn "He Who Would Valiant Be," in which these lines appear: "I'll care not what men say, I'll labor night and day, . . . There's no discouragement shall make him once relent, his first avowed intent, to be a pilgrim." It was a fitting recessional for a disputatious life.

NOTES

1. John was judged unfit for military service because of a leg tendon that had been damaged by a reaper. He was six feet two inches tall, as were his brothers, which made Bill all the more conscious of his own modest stature: about five feet seven inches. He once said, "I was a seven months' baby and the runt of the family."

2. Letter to Susan R. Woods of Vancouver BC, 16 October 1984. The letter was in response to her question about why Bill chose to study the history of New France.

3. Eccles, "Forty Years Back," in *William and Mary Quarterly* 41.3 (July 1984): 411. This autobiographical sketch of Bill's scholarly and academic career was reprinted as the introduction to his *Essays on New France* (Toronto: Oxford University Press, 1987). It is a personal and selective recollection which, for example, does not mention his guest lecturership at Beirut's American University in 1967.

4. When I visited the library in 1992 to find and photocopy this note, I discovered that the original volumes of the BRH had been replaced by cleaner copies. The much-thumbed original, with the inserted note, was probably discarded.

5. Eccles, "Forty Years Back," 411.

6. Eccles, "Forty Years Back," 417.

7. Since the late 1930s Father Jean Delanglez had been chipping away at Frontenac's inflated reputation, but this Jesuit's criticism of the anticlerical Frontenac may have been discounted. Delanglez died prematurely in 1949.

8. Realizing that discrediting Parkman was necessary to get English-speaking readers to accept a new version of the French Regime in North America, Bill wrote "The History of New France According to Francis Parkman," *William and Mary Quarterly* 18.2 (April 1961): 163–75. In the article Bill argues that Parkman, regardless of his literary merits, had forced the historical evidence into his a priori view that the struggle between the French and British empires in North America was, to quote the 1874 edition of *The Old Regime in Canada*, one of stultifying "French Roman Catholic [royal] absolutism" against "Anglo-Saxon Protestant liberty—which was the hallmark of Progress." Naturally, New France had to be destroyed for the sake of political and intellectual progress. In one seminar Bill eagerly asked us (his students) if we had read Parkman and, to his dismay, learned we had not. In reality, we had imbibed Parkman's ideas from later popularizations of his work.

9. *Canadian Historical Review* 40.4 (December 1959): 344–46.

10. *American Historical Review* 65.2 (January 1960): 371–72.

THERE have been to date only two studies made of Frontenac and his régime, based on original source material. The one by the American historian, Francis Parkman, entitled *Count Frontenac and New France under Louis XIV*, was first published in 1877; the other, by the French historian, Henri Lorin, entitled *Le comte de Frontenac*—and more a panegyric than a critical historical study —appeared in 1895. Their versions of this period in Canadian history, and more particularly Francis Parkman's version, have been accepted almost without question by all but a very few later historians and writers. Thus, the lapse of time and the advances made in historical methods during these intervening years seemed to be justification enough for a new study of Frontenac and New France in the late seventeenth century.

It will quickly be apparent to the reader that the present work is not a full-scale biography of Frontenac, nor is it a complete study of the history of New France under his government. Not enough evidence dealing with the first fifty years of Frontenac's life is available to write his biography; moreover, very little original work has been done on this period by modern scholars. Thus, in order to explain clearly Frontenac's actions, some aspects of the general history of New France in the age of Louis XIV had to be treated in detail, but limitations of space made it impossible to treat of them all. I have, then, been obliged almost to write two books rather than one, and this work pretends to be a reappraisal and a point of departure for future studies, nothing more.

I freely extend my apologies to scholarly critics for the deplorable fact that the reference notes are placed at the back of the book and not at the foot of the page, but their number and present-day costs of publication made this unavoidable. Explanatory notes, as distinct from references to source material, have, however, been placed at the foot of the page. These notes are indicated by an asterisk. In the text no attempt has been made at consistency in the use of the particle *de*; instead, I have tried to adhere to seventeenth-century usage and modern euphony. For example, de Frontenac has an awkward ring to the English attuned ear, but Meulles without the *de* seems equally awkward; Duchesneau is used rather than Chesneau, but Vaudreuil and Callières seemed better without the particle. Wherever English documents are cited in the notes, old-style dates during the months January to March inclusive are cited thus: 1689/90.

In the preparation of this work many people and institutions have been of great assistance in many ways. Had it not been for a scholarship granted me by the French government, it would have been impossible for me to spend a year in France consulting the original documents in the various archives. Grants in aid of research from the Humanities Research Council of Canada, and from the Staff Research Fund and the Ewart Foundation Fund of the University of Manitoba enabled me to consult the documents in the archives at Ottawa, Quebec, Boston and Albany. A generous grant by the Canada Council was of great assistance in making the publication of this work possible. The staff of the Public Archives of Canada were always exceedingly helpful to me in my research; in particular I would like to thank Miss Norah Story, Mr. W. G. Ormsby, Miss Juliette Bourque, Mr. L. Croteau, Mr. T. E. Layng and Mr. R. La Roque de Roquebrune, the Canadian archivist resident in Paris. In France, the officials of the Archives Nationales, Bibliothèque Nationale, Archives du Ministère de la Guerre, Archives du Ministère des Affaires Etrangères and the Bibliothèque Mazarine, once they had satisfied themselves that I could be trusted to handle the documents in their keeping with due care, were all most obliging. I must also thank M. Pierre Thilliez, chief archivist of the *département* of Indre and M. Jean Massiet du Biest, chief archivist of the *département* of Indre-et-Loire, for the trouble they took in searching for certain elusive documents on my behalf. Mr. C. M. Cross, Chief of the Tidal and Current Survey, Canadian Hydrographic Service, Ottawa, was of great assistance and went to much trouble to supply me with information concerning the time and rate of rise and fall of the tide at Quebec in October 1690. M. Jules Turcot of the Quebec Seminary Archives, Mr. Leo Flaherty of the Massachusetts State Archives, Dr. Albert B. Corey, State Historian of New York, and Miss Edna Jacobsen of the manuscript room at the New York State Archives provided every assistance during my researches among the documents in their charge. One of the pleasures of this craft is to have associations with such obliging and courteous people.

The book has been read in manuscript by Mr. A. M. Terroux, Professor W. L. Morton, Mr. Robert M. Dawson, Colonel C. P. Stacey, Professor Marcel Trudel and Dr. Wallace Farnham. Their comments and criticism have greatly improved the quality of this work and have saved me from innumerable errors of omission and commission; for this I am deeply grateful.

University of Alberta,
October 1958.

CONTENTS

MAPS

CHAPTER ONE

CANADA AND THE CANADIANS UNDER LOUIS XIV

IN the mid-seventeenth century the survival of New France was in doubt. The Company of One Hundred Associates was responsible for the administration of the colony, in return for which it had been granted a monopoly on colonial trade. When first founded by Richelieu, the Company had begun its work with considerable enterprise and enthusiasm. No sooner had it begun, however, than war intervened to cause the loss of most of the Company's capital, a blow from which it never fully recovered. The Associates became first discouraged, then indifferent, towards New France. And in the colony itself, cabals, intrigue, malfeasance and strife of one sort or another increasingly disrupted the administration. In addition, the colonists were under almost continual attack from the powerful Iroquois confederacy. During most of this period the government in France was unable, even if it had been so inclined, to take any great interest in the affairs of a handful of French subjects in far-off Canada; the Thirty Years War, followed by the turmoil of the Fronde, prevented it.

Then, in 1661, all this changed. Upon the death of Cardinal Mazarin, Louis XIV began to rule as well as to reign over his kingdom, and under him he had some of the ablest administrators France has ever known. One of these—and perhaps the greatest—was Jean Baptiste Colbert, minister of marine. In 1663 Louis withdrew the charter of the Company of One Hundred Associates and made New France a royal province under the jurisdiction of Colbert's Department of Marine. Just as Louis XIV was determined to master Europe in the military and diplomatic fields, so Colbert was determined that France should match her rivals in the economic sphere. Whereas Louis XIV's main aim in life was to gain power and military glory, Colbert regarded wars as good only in so far as they aided in the expansion of French commerce or harmed an economic rival; military adventures which did not have these ends in view he strongly deprecated. He saw clearly that England and the Netherlands had built their great commercial strength on colonies and overseas trade; he therefore determined that France should do likewise, and in this scheme he intended that Canada should play an important role. His first aim was to bring New France as quickly as possible to the point where it could stand on its own feet without depending on military and economic support from France. Once this had been accomplished, the colony would be able to fulfil its proper function in a mercantilist economy; that is, to supply the mother country with needed raw materials and to absorb her surplus manufactured goods.

No time was lost by Colbert in reorganizing the colony's administrative framework. A Sovereign Council was instituted at Quebec, modelled after the *Parlement de Paris*. This body, primarily a judicial court of appeal, also had administrative functions, and, in some degree, legislative powers. The membership was composed of the governor, the bishop, the intendant, five councillors, an attorney-general and a recording clerk. The five councillors were at first appointed jointly by the bishop and the governor. Perhaps Colbert's most important measure was the appointment of an intendant for New France who was made responsible for the civil administration of the colony, for ensuring that the people received swift and impartial justice, and for the disbursement of the royal funds. In France the office of intendant had proved to be an efficient instrument for the strengthening of the royal power in the provinces. The men appointed to these posts were skilled administrators, well educated and with a sound legal training; almost invariably they were recruited from among the *noblesse de robe*,* usually after they had given evidence of their ability in lesser posts. They were essentially career men, whose prospects in the royal service depended not so much on influence at the Court as on their ability to satisfy the minister that their past record merited their being promoted.

Despite the importance of the intendant, the governor still remained the most imposing figure in the colony. He retained complete jurisdiction over military matters and foreign affairs—

* *Noblesse de robe* (nobility of the robe) was the order of nobility to which entrance was gained by the acquisition of certain high offices, the title going with the office. The long robe of the legal profession was the distinguishing mark of many of these offices, hence the name, which distinguished the members of the *noblesse de robe* from the descendants of the feudal aristocracy, known as the *noblesse d'épée* (the nobility of the sword).

if such the latter can be called, since they consisted of nothing more than the colony's relations with the Indian tribes and, to a lesser extent, with the European colonies to the south. Although he was forbidden to meddle in those spheres delegated to the intendant and the Sovereign Council, these latter officials were obliged to obey the governor in all things and if he trespassed on their preserves they could merely point his offence out to him and then, if he persisted, report the matter to the minister of marine.[1] The reason for this semi-autocratic system was that the governor represented the king's person, and Louis XIV could not tolerate any apparent check to his authority, even by proxy. In effect this meant that when a dispute arose between the governor and the intendant or the Sovereign Council they had to wait nine months to a year, and even longer, before receiving the minister's decision in the case. In the meantime the dispute sometimes had either clarified itself or else worsened to such an extent that the minister's decision, when received, was no longer applicable.

In the final analysis, however, all authority rested with the king and the minister of marine; it was they who decided on all questions of policy. The officials in New France could not make any important decisions on their own initiative; except in cases of the direst emergency they had to refer everything to the Court. This meant that the governor and the intendant were little more than civil servants and that the actual seat of government lay, not at Quebec, but in the office of the minister of marine in Paris or Versailles. Every autumn the governor and intendant sent lengthy dispatches to the minister, recommending this or that policy, asking for the minister's decision in pressing matters and generally informing him in the greatest detail of all that had occurred during the previous twelve months. When the dispatches arrived at the Court an undersecretary drew up abstracts of these lengthy documents for the perusal of the minister, who scribbled his terse comments and decisions in the margin. From these marginal notations the undersecretary drafted the minister's replies. It can readily be seen that with such a system the minister might not always be too well informed on what was going on in the colony, and it is only when this is taken into account that certain events in the history of New France become explicable. As it is in our system of government today, where the deputy ministers draft a great deal of the legislation submitted to Parliament by the cabinet, so it was in Louis XIV's day. Unfortunately it is extremely difficult to discover very much about these shadowy officials who carried out the routine work of drafting policies, supplying the minister with the pertinent information upon which he based his decisions, making concrete suggestions on these matters, and, at times, reminding the minister that a decision could not be deferred much longer.

The king also sent a lengthy memoir each year to the governor and intendant containing instructions in more general terms, and lending the weight of his greater authority to that of the minister. In actual practice, however, it was not the king who composed these dispatches, but the minister of marine; marginal notations in Colbert's minuscule hand on the abstracts of the dispatches from Canada and on the initial drafts of the king's dispatches indicate that it was he, rather than Louis, who drafted them. Very probably it was the king's first secretary, M. Rose, who then wrote or dictated the king's dispatch from the minister's draft and added the royal signature.* Louis sometimes had the dispatches from Canada read to him, and no doubt Colbert discussed the colony's affairs with him at the meetings of the Council of State before making any far-reaching decisions.

Before Colbert's ambitious plans for Canada could be implemented, one main obstacle to any economic development in the colony had to be removed, namely, the constant attacks by the Iroquois. For the previous twenty-five years they had been ravaging the colony in an attempt to divert the fur trade of the Hurons and the Ottawas from New France to Albany, with themselves making the middle-man's profit. At the same time, however, that the eastern Iroquois were attacking the French settlements, they themselves were being attacked by the Mohicans, a powerful tribe on their eastern flank, and the three western nations were being hard pressed by the Andastes who occupied the lands to their south.†

* Louis XIV had four private secretaries, the senior among them *avait la plume.* This meant that he was a skilled forger and could write with a hand and style indistinguishable from that of Louis. He wrote most of the letters and memoirs from Louis XIV to generals and other high dignitaries, even to other monarchs, and legally forged Louis's signature to them—this to save Louis time and fatigue. M. Rose held this post for fifty years, until 1701, and was, understandably, a man of great influence in the highest circles. He had been secretary to Cardinal de Retz, then to Mazarin, was extremely discreet and treated the courtiers, even the great nobles, with quiet disdain.

† The Five Nations of the Iroquois confederacy were, moving from east to west the Mohawks, Oneidas, Onondagas, Cayugas and Senecas.

4

New France—The Compact Colony

In 1665 Colbert sent out the Carignan-Salières regiment, numbering nearly thirteen hundred officers and men. In three quick campaigns they invaded the Mohawk country, burning their villages and destroying their crops. Although the Mohawk warriors fled at the approach of the French and suffered no appreciable losses, this show of force was enough to make them sue for peace. The Oneidas asked for a treaty of peace at the same time. The Senecas, although they had always been neutral toward the French, upon hearing of these French attacks on the Mohawks, also sent ambassadors to Quebec to have their tribe included in the treaty and to solicit French aid in their war with the Andastes.[2] Thus, so long as the Five Nations were at war with the Mohicans and the Andastes, the French, with their recent great increase in military strength, held the balance of power. A firm hand and the mere threat of force were all that was needed to keep them in submission, and the governor, the Sieur de Courcelles, exercised these in a masterly fashion.

The security of the colony now assured, Colbert wasted no time in putting his plans into effect. Most of the officers and men of the Carignan-Salières regiment were induced to take up land and remain in New France. More troops and hundreds of settlers were sent out, as many as five hundred in one year landing at Quebec. In addition, young women to provide wives for the soldiers were sent, and a few "young ladies sufficiently well brought up" for the officers. They all found husbands quickly enough. As a natural consequence of this calculated policy, seven hundred children were baptized in 1671 alone, and the bishop estimated that there would be eleven hundred the following year.[3] Thus it is hardly surprising that by 1672 the population was approaching the six-thousand-seven-hundred mark, whereas ten years earlier it had been a mere two thousand five hundred.[4]

With this great influx of settlers the forest was rapidly pushed back from the river banks until there was an almost continuous stretch of cleared land on both sides of the St. Lawrence from below Quebec up to Montreal. As one contemporary account puts it:

> Formerly, the Iroquois kept us hemmed in so closely that we did not even dare to till the ground that lay beneath the cannon of the forts, far less to voyage afield to discover the benefits that

one can expect from land which differs hardly at all from that of France.

But now, since the fear of His Majesty's arms has filled these barbarians with terror, and has compelled them to seek our amity instead of molesting us with bloody wars as they used to, during this period of calm we can find out what the wealth of this country might be and the extent of the benefits which we can hope to gain from it.[5]

It was not long before land with river frontage became scarce; those who had been granted large concessions in the past and who had cleared only parts of them had to give up half their lands to the new immigrants. The desire on the part of the settlers to have land bordering on the St. Lawrence fixed once and for all the form of settlement in New France. The farms became narrow strips running back from the river, each with its house by the waterfront and well separated from its neighbours. This isolation of the individual farms posed a serious problem; it made them dangerously vulnerable to attack by the Iroquois. Colbert was particularly anxious that the *habitants* should live in villages, as in Europe, mainly for reasons of military security, but partly because it would be easier for the authorities to keep an eye on them.[6] But the geography of the country and the independent spirit of the Canadians defeated the project.

Although the land along the river banks was very fertile, this was not an unmixed blessing, as it resulted in many of the *habitants* completely neglecting to replenish the soil with manure, or even letting their fields lie fallow every few years. As a result, by the 1680's much of the land put to the plough twenty years earlier was completely exhausted, being reduced to little more than sand.[7] Wheat was the principal crop grown and, although neither the climate nor the soil was particularly suitable for this grain, it was claimed during the 1660's that the yield was as high as in France and quite often a glut resulted.[8] Peas were another crop that flourished and the intendant encouraged the settlers to raise hemp and flax as cash crops—but with slight success, it must be added. The livestock imported from France thrived in the colony, and in 1671 the minister was informed by the intendant that there was no need to send any more.[9] Tobacco was also grown in the colony with promising results, but Colbert quickly banned its cultivation lest it should compete with the tobacco from the French West Indies.[10] So far as food was concerned the people of New France were, if anything, better off than those of old France; they raised all the essential foodstuffs and they could vary their diet with the fresh fish teeming in the rivers and the wild game in the forest.

Such things, however, as salt, wine, cloth, metal goods, paper and manufactured wares of àll kinds had to be imported from France, and to pay for these imports the colony had to export something. Prior to 1663 the only export worth mentioning had been furs, and Colbert was far from satisfied with this state of affairs; he wanted to see the colony's economy widely diversified and no longer dependent on furs alone. He wanted to see fishing and lumbering industries established, overseas trade developed and the colony's mineral wealth exploited. In this last connection, he instructed the intendant, Jean Talon:

> Continually strive to discover and establish iron, lead, copper and tin mines and consider this task as the most important that can be done for the increase of Canada, particularly since these mines will bring such prosperity that in a little while the country will be populated to such a point that it will easily be able to support itself and become a great and powerful kingdom; this being the end which His Majesty desires to achieve by all the attention which, with such generosity, he devotes to Canada.[11]

Colbert was very distressed over the fact that out of some twenty thousand merchant ships trading to and from Europe, fifteen to sixteen thousand were Dutch, three to four thousand English and only five or six hundred French. To rectify this situation he tried to stimulate the export of ship masts and timber from Canada to supply the French shipyards. It was hoped that this would make France no longer dependent on the Baltic timber merchants. He was also very anxious to establish a ship-building industry in New France itself, and to emulate the English colonies by creating a three-way overseas trade between Canada, the French West Indies and France. Canadian ships were to take cargoes of barrel staves, timber, dried fish and other foodstuffs to the French West Indies and exchange these commodities for sugar and tobacco. These would then be carried to France and cargoes of French manufactured goods brought back to Quebec. To stimulate this commerce

Colbert even went so far, at Talon's suggestion, as to reduce the duties on sugar for Canadian ships transporting it from the Antilles to France.[12]

Urged on in this fashion, Talon, with the energy of a born *entrepreneur*, quickly began exploiting the colony's natural resources. To raise the necessary capital he took full advantage of his official position. He was permitted to import a certain quantity of goods for his own use free of duty, freight and insurance charges, and he stretched this privilege to the limit. He imported large quantities of merchandise, sold it to the settlers, and used the proceeds to finance his various commercial ventures. The colony's merchants, who had to pay a ten per cent duty on the goods they imported, complained bitterly of this, regarding it as unfair competition, and they declared openly that the king's efforts to develop the colony were being diverted to enrich Jean Talon.[13]

Regardless of the means he used to raise his capital, or his motives in so doing, Talon certainly put his opportunity to good use. He had timber cut both for export to France and for ship building in the colony; ship masts were made ready for transport to France and barrel staves for the West Indies. By 1667 one ship had been built in the colony, another was ready to be launched, and Talon, in partnership with a Quebec merchant, was shipping salted fish, peas, planks and whale oil to the Antilles. The manufacture of tar and potash, of shoes and hats, was also begun. Perhaps the most famous of all Talon's enterprises was his brewery. In addition to profits for Talon, it was hoped that it would achieve three main results : provide a market for the colony's surplus grain, reduce the amount of drunkenness in the colony by providing a milder beverage than brandy, and keep some of the money in New France that normally flowed out to pay for imported wines and spirits. That Colbert could countenance an enterprise that might reduce a market for the products of the French vineyards is a measure of his genuine desire to see the colony's economy strengthened. Even more striking is the fact that he allowed, and even encouraged, free trade between Quebec and Boston.[14]

The maintenance of an adequate currency supply in the colony was always a problem, owing to the adverse balance of trade and to the fact that the funds for the colony's administration were sent over in the form of merchandise. At one time it was proposed to issue special coins for use only in New France, but Colbert later decided against this.[15] Thus beaver skins became a principal medium of exchange and foreign coins were much in circulation. Everything, however, was reckoned in terms of *livres, sols* and *deniers*, there being 12 *deniers* to the *sol* and 20 *sols* to the *livre*; but any similarity to English sterling ended there, the French *livre* being worth about one shilling and sixpence or two shillings at this time.[16] The Canadian *livre* was at a twenty-five per cent discount in relation to the French *livre*.[17] Other coins in use were the *pistole*, worth 11 *livres* 2 *sols* in Canada, and the gold and the silver *ecu*, the former being worth 6 *livres* and the latter 3 *livres* 2 *sols*.[18] To try to translate the Canadian *livre* of the latter half of the seventeenth century into present-day Canadian currency is an extremely difficult task. The closest approximation that could be arrived at is that it had the buying power of approximately one dollar by 1958 standards, this estimate being based on the seventeenth-century prices of such commodities as bread, flour, wheat and wine, on the pay of the troops and the colonial officials, the rate of exchange with sterling, and the estimate that the latter currency has depreciated to something like one-fifth of its late-seventeenth-century value. However, it must be admitted that this estimate is little more than an enlightened guess.

So far as taxes were concerned, the Canadian settlers were more favoured than the people of France. The only taxes they paid were indirect ones: ten per cent on certain goods coming into the colony, the proceeds of which went to pay off the debts contracted by the colonists with merchants in France prior to 1663; and the *quart* on beaver and the *dix* on moose hides, twenty-five per cent of the purchase price of beaver and ten per cent of that on moose hides being deducted by the agents of the *Compagnie de l'Occident* at Quebec.[19] In addition, the Company also had a monopoly on the fur trade at Tadoussac, and out of these combined revenues it paid the administrative costs of the colony, which Colbert decreed were not to exceed 36,000 *livres* a year.[20] In 1675 the right to purchase all beaver pelts and moose hides in New France was sub-let to a certain M. Oudiette and his associates for ten years in return for an annual payment to the Crown of 350,000 *livres*.[21] It is apparent that during these years at least the colony was a source of profit to the Crown.

Although it was the fur trade that actually supported the colony, Colbert was very reluctant to allow the colonists to engage in it— for fear that they would neglect their farms and live in idleness a good part of the year. Prior to 1665 Colbert had little cause for concern on this score; very little fur of any sort was coming down to the colony from up country owing to the Iroquois attacks both on the colony proper and on the Indian allies of the French, who were loath to risk the trip to Montreal. But once the Iroquois had been quelled, the fur trade quickly revived and the western nations from as far as five or six hundred leagues away began coming down to Montreal to trade. Remote tribes who had never before had dealings with the French began to appear, and in 1667 furs to the value of 550,000 *livres* were shipped to France.[22] It was not long before the more enterprising merchants of Montreal managed to engross the best part of this profitable trade; but if the road was open for the Indians to bring their furs down to the colony, by the same token there was nothing to stop the more adventurous of the French from going up country to trade in the Indian villages and so forestall these merchants. Soon the merchants themselves were hiring *coureurs de bois* to go up country as their agents. Once begun, the practice grew apace, and more and more Canadians voyaged ever farther afield; living among the Indians for years on end; acquiring their languages; and coming to understand their mentalities, anticipate their reactions and have great influence in their councils. They established trading relations with the most distant tribes, became embroiled in their wars, and at the same time advanced the territorial claims of France into these distant lands.

The intendant Jean Talon has been blamed for the emergence of the *coureurs de bois* as a distinct group. Some of his near-contemporaries claimed that the parties sent out by Talon, ostensibly to explore the western water routes and search for minerals, were actually far more concerned with the furs they garnered *en route*. Certainly, Talon made no secret of the fact that he was engaging in the fur trade at Montreal, and he blandly informed Colbert that his exploration parties were being financed by the ingenious method of first taking possession of the lands occupied by the Indians in the name of the king of France, then graciously allowing the resident Indians to continue to occupy these territories. In return for this great privilege the new subjects of Louis XIV were expected to pay homage in the shape of a few packets of beaver pelts.[23] Although Talon may have stimulated the increase in the numbers of *coureurs de bois*, positively by example and negatively by neglecting to take strong action to curb their activities, it was inevitable that the French would expand into the west in search of furs for the simple reason that there was nothing to stop them and the profits to be made were great.

By 1672 the Canadian social scene had assumed the pattern that it was to retain down to the end of the French regime. At the top of the social scale were the royal officials: the governor, the intendant and the senior officers of the military, men sent out from France who expected to return there sooner or later. Beside them were the clergy. The bishop was the spiritual head of the colony and also a member of the Sovereign Council. Until 1675 he shared with the governor the privilege of appointing members of the Council as vacancies occurred; thus he could, if he so desired, exert some influence in civil matters. At the same time the Crown had far more authority over the clergy than does the state today. Although there were several spirited clashes between the secular officials and the clergy between 1663 and the end of the century, they were caused mainly by the strong, conflicting personalities of the dignitaries involved, and can hardly be regarded as a struggle between church and state for dominance. After 1663 there was never any real doubt that the state was supreme in New France.

Beneath the bishop's direct authority were the secular clergy who cared for the spiritual needs of the colonists. There were too few of these men for most of the parishes to have their own resident *curé*; the priests had to travel by canoe, on horseback, or on foot from settlement to settlement, and many of the outlying districts were, therefore, inadequately served by the church. In 1668 Mgr Laval founded a seminary at Quebec to train Canadian youths for the priesthood, but the demand continued to exceed the supply until well beyond the end of the century. Assisting the regular clergy were the Recollets at Quebec and the Jesuits. The latter order, however, devoted most of its attention to missionary work among the Indian tribes and to teaching at its college in Quebec. At Montreal the Messieurs de St. Sulpice, who were the seigneurs of the island, cared for the spiritual needs of the people and also gave the children some schooling. At Quebec the Ursulines looked after the education and religious instruction of the young girls, and the sick were cared for at the Hôtel Dieu. At Montreal there was also an Hôtel Dieu, as well as the Sisters of the Congregation, a teaching order that was also established in several of the rural parishes. For the most part the clergy of New France, in comparison with those in the mother country, were singularly well educated and many of them were persons of exceptionally strong character. In the seventeenth century they tended to be too puritanical for the liking of both the Canadian people and the royal officials. With the arrival of the regular troops in 1665 the colony received a strong leavening of men hardened to the rough conditions of campaign life and of officers too familiar with the easy ways of the Court for the liking of the clergy. In 1667 a Jesuit remarked: "Canada's first ball was held at the Sieur Chartier's. God grant that it has not set a precedent." The clergy had their thoughts and aspirations fixed more on the next world than this; thus they always remained a class apart.

Of the purely Canadian social groups, the members of the Sovereign Council were accorded the first rank, but the dignity of their office was never very high for the simple reason that their salaries were very low. The senior councillor and the attorney-general received 500 *livres* a year and the ordinary councillors only 300 *livres*,[24] and consequently they had to devote much of their time to commercial activities or working their land. The seigneurs were on a somewhat lower social plane than the members of the Sovereign Council. Most of them led lives that differed little from those of their *censitaires* and, as far as their dress and standard of living were concerned, they were barely distinguishable from the *habitants*. But some of these seigneurs adopted the airs and graces of the nobility while lacking the financial means to justify such pretensions. Instead of improving their land, they spent their time in hunting and fishing, they dabbled in commerce, sent their sons off to trade in the Indian villages and generally lived in a shiftless hand-to-mouth fashion. Many of the officers, who had been granted seigneuries on the understanding that they would remain in the colony permanently, quickly tired of a life that offered few rewards for anything but hard work, and began drifting back to France. By 1673 only six captains and as many junior officers still remained in the colony, despite a strict order from Colbert that no one was to quit the colony in this fashion.[25]

The main causes of this rather deplorable state of affairs were the French social system and the lack of careers in the colony. In France the nobility had the choice of only two careers, the army or the church; trade and industry were barred to them and a social stigma was attached to these occupations. The ambition of the rising French middle class was to study law and then obtain an administrative post of some sort. In Canada the opportunities for the sons of the seigneurs were more restricted; there was no standing army in the colony, nor any legal profession, and the civil-service posts were few and meagrely paid; they could enter the seminary at Quebec and become secular priests, but this had a very limited appeal. Members of the nobility in New France were, however, allowed to engage in commerce and industry, but for the most part, those who succeeded in these fields of activity had not been born into the nobility; they became nobles only after they had achieved wealth and position through trade. Moreover, it required capital to succeed in this activity and it could not be obtained working the land. Thus, for the more adventurous and those with initiative who wanted more out of life than could be gained from the struggle to convert virgin forest into arable soil, the free life of the *coureur de bois* held great attractions. The implications of this situation were fully appreciated by the Marquis de Denonville when he came to New France as governor in 1685. He stated it was absolutely essential that suitable employment be found in the king's service for Canadian youths, preferably in the King's Guards, for they were, he said, "well built and courageous men, very ingenious but frivolous and poorly disciplined."[26] And when the war with the Iroquois and the English began, both he and Frontenac recommended that no more officers be sent from France to serve in the colony but that Canadians be commissioned in their stead, as they were far superior for the type of warfare waged in the forests of Canada.[27]

In the towns of Quebec and Montreal there was a middle class, composed for the most part of merchants and subordinate officials. Whether or not tavern keepers could be included in this group is a moot point; if so, then the ranks of the middle class would thereby be swelled considerably. As for the merchants, they were of two varieties: the *marchands forains* who came out to the colony, disposed of the merchandise they had brought with them, then returned to France; and the merchants who were permanent residents. Of the latter group, only five or six were at all prosperous. The intendant Duchesneau blamed this on the vanity of their womenfolk and their own fecklessness, which caused them to spend their money as fast as they got it, living in a hand-to-mouth fashion so that they never became well established.[28]

13

Throughout this period there was a chronic labour shortage in the colony which enabled the labourers, skilled or otherwise, to demand high wages and to suit themselves, rather than their employers, as to hours and conditions of work. When the construction of fortifications at Quebec was being contemplated, Denonville informed the minister that workmen would have to be sent out from France and their wages stipulated on a yearly basis beforehand. To employ local labour, he warned, would cost "an infinite amount" since an ordinary mason demanded $3.60 (1 *ecu* 10 *sols*) a day and a carpenter $4.50 (4 *livres* 10 *sols*).[29] Frontenac, upon his arrival in the colony, stated that there was an urgent need for all types of skilled tradesmen and labourers. He himself was unable to obtain the services of a lackey for love nor money; he claimed that the workmen had their heels on the necks of the *habitants* and that jobs cost three times what they should, which was ruinous for the colony.[30] Efforts to import a labour supply from France were far from successful; skilled workers were very loath to come out to Canada and would only do so for a limited time and upon being guaranteed much higher wages than they were accustomed to receive in France.[31] A partial solution was eventually found when the Troupes de la Marine arrived in the colony. They were allowed to work as tradesmen and day labourers, thereby earning far more than their army pay, which they were quite content to let their captains pocket in return for leave of absence from their military duties. Once begun, this system, with its deplorable effects on the discipline and effectiveness of the troops, could not be halted. During the Iroquois war it frequently resulted in the *habitants* being called out for campaigns while the regular troops continued in their "civilian" occupations.

In fairness to the Canadian workmen it should be pointed out that prices for commodities were much higher in the colony than in France owing to freight and insurance charges, and also to profiteering on the part of the merchants of La Rochelle who had been granted a monopoly on the trade with the colony.[32] In normal times, wine, which cost 10 *livres* the hogshead in France, cost 50 to 70 *livres* in Canada, and clothing was double the French price.[33] Moreover, at this time the old medieval theory of the just price was in the discard and the theory of the free market was beginning to prevail; thus Canadian labour can hardly be blamed for charging all that the traffic would bear.

The group that appears to have been the best off of all was that of the ordinary peasant, or *habitant* as he was always called in Canada. Having no vain pretensions to gentility, he enjoyed in many ways a much better life than did his counterpart in France. The intendant Jean Bochart de Champigny declared in 1691 that the *habitants* who were satisfied to work their land were relatively rich, or at least lived very comfortably.[34] But not all the sons of the *habitants* were content to live on the land, particularly when the men who had made trips to the Ottawa country returned with money jingling in their pockets and tales of the great distances they had travelled, the hardships they had endured and the stirring sights they had seen among the forest tribes. And when the women-folk or the *curé* were not within hearing distance, doubtless they told other tales of the ardour of the eager Algonquin and Huron girls, who had never known any inhibitions where men were concerned. When the more spirited of the youth in the colony compared such a life as this to struggling with the primeval forest for possession of a few more acres of cleared land, it is small wonder that so many of them abandoned the axe and the plough for the canoe-paddle and the musket.

Thus it was that the one group which dominated the Canadian social scene more than any other was that of the *coureur de bois*. This group was purely Canadian in character, owing as much to the influence of environment as to French heritage. By roaming the forest and sharing the Indian's nomadic life, these men not only acquired the Indian's skill with paddle and snowshoe, his mastery over the forces of nature, but they also acquired certain traits of the Indian temperament. Their native Latin exuberance was tempered by the Indian's stoicism, their Christian morality by the Indian's natural penchant for cruelty. They not only learned to endure intense physical pain and hardship without flinching, but they also learned to inflict it on their foes.

For their trips to the Ottawa country with a canoe-load of trade goods they were paid 1,000 *livres* by the merchants who hired them,[35] and they usually managed to make something extra by trading a few jugs of brandy on their own account. When they returned to Montreal a year or two later and received their pay, many of them could not get rid of it quickly enough. Bedecking themselves in the most gaudy clothes on the merchants' shelves, they roistered about the taverns until their money was all gone;

then they signed on again with a merchant, exchanged their silks and lace for buckskin, moccasins and the canoe-paddle and once more began the long voyage to the Ottawa country. A life such as this could be endured only by the most hardy. When the numbers of the *coureurs de bois* increased to five or six hundred out of a total population of less than ten thousand, the shortage of able-bodied men in the colony became acute and seigneurs began to complain to the intendant that their fields were uncultivated because they could not find men to work them.[36] Colourful though these *coureurs de bois* may seem to the modern eye, to the seventeenth-century intendant charged with the administration of the colony they were little more than an economic and social liability.

The French were always a quarrelsome race, not given to compromise. In an attempt to curb this characteristic, Louis XIV and his ministers prescribed order, regularity and discipline as the qualities to be most esteemed in all aspects of life. Everything from literature to horticulture, architecture to religion, was regimented and reduced to conformity with established principles. Louis XIV succeeded in enforcing these concepts to an astonishing degree and this largely explains the great accomplishments of his reign; he succeeded in harnessing and directing the tremendous energies of the French people as no one before or—with the notable exception of Napoleon—since. But New France was far removed from the restraints of the Sun King's overpowering personality, and here the French penchant for aggressive individualism was given free rein. From 1665 down to the end of the century, and beyond, the government of the colony was continually disrupted by squabbling among those in authority. The governor fought viciously with the intendant, the local governors of Montreal and Trois Rivières fought with their junior officials; the officers of the Troupes de la Marine were continually duelling and brawling among themselves. Even the clergy were not immune; the Recollets and the regular clergy were frequently at loggerheads with their bishop, and the Sulpicians and the Recollets with the Jesuits. The correspondence to the Department of Marine is filled with the complaints of one official, or one group, against another; officers in the Troupes de la Marine were forever informing the minister of the shortcomings of their superiors, the governor and intendant accusing each other of all manner of crimes. Dissension was the normal condition among those in authority.

16

If the Canadians were excessively litigious and hard to govern it is not to be wondered at with such examples constantly before them. Moreover, frontier conditions left their impress on the Canadian character. Whereas in the English colonies the frontier was a definite line at the outer edge of the settlements, a line that could be traced on the map, in New France no such line could be drawn. Here the frontier was on the doorstep of every house of every seigneury in the colony, and this produced a decided frontier mentality among the Canadians. The French officials in the colony frequently complained of this. To them, the Canadians were possessed of a far too independent spirit. The governor and intendant could thunder as they liked, the *habitants* paid little or no attention. Edicts that did not please them they ignored; and when an attempt was made to enforce these edicts, those who objected too strongly merely loaded a canoe and slipped away to swell the ranks of the *coureurs de bois*.

Of the Canadians, the Marquis de Denonville, shortly after his arrival in the colony, had this to say : "[they] are all big, well built and firmly planted on their feet, accustomed whenever necessary to live on little, robust and vigorous, very obstinate and inclined to be dissolute, but quick witted and vivacious."[37] They were a unique product of their racial temperament and their environment : quarrelsome, impulsive, quick to resentment, headstrong, with amazing powers of endurance, sometimes cruel; but yet generous, with an easy-going attitude towards life and, from all accounts, possessed of a native courtesy and dignity that impressed everyone newly arrived from the Courts of Europe.

CHAPTER TWO

THE BACKGROUND OF LOUIS BUADE, COMTE DE FRONTENAC

FRONTENAC, like his father and grandfather before him, was a soldier and a courtier. His grandfather, Antoine de Frontenac, had been a companion of Henri IV and an associate of the Vicomte de Turenne, the father of the famous soldier. After serving as the king's personal equerry for several years Antoine de Buade was appointed to the coveted post of *premier maître d'hôtel du Roi*. In 1619 he was made a Knight of the Order of St. Esprit. Little else is known of him except that he was reputed to be insatiably avaricious: [1] he loaned money at high rates of interest and in 1606 he acquired the barony of Palluau by the time-honoured method of foreclosing the mortgage.[2] By such means he managed to bequeath a considerable estate to his sons.

Antoine de Buade's influential position at the Court is evidenced by the fact that the Constable Montmorency and Mlle de Vendôme stood as godfather and godmother to his son Henri, who eventually entered the army and obtained the rank of colonel of the regiment of Navarre.[3] With great perspicacity Antoine arranged a marriage between Henri and Anne Phélypeaux, a member of the very influential Pontchartrain family, whose father and uncle were both secretaries of state. When, in May, 1622, a son was born to Henri de Buade and Anne Phélypeaux it was Louis XIII who stood as the child's godfather and gave him his own name.[4] Thus, Louis de Buade, Comte de Frontenac et de Palluau, grandson of one secretary of state, grand-nephew of another, and godson of the king, began life under quite auspicious circumstances.

He was raised in the atmosphere of the Court and apparently he received as good an education as the times afforded, attending for several years the same college as the Abbé Tronson, who later became superior of the Messieurs de St. Sulpice.[5] For a person of his background only two careers were open, the church or the army. Being the son and grandson of soldiers, Louis de Buade naturally enough chose the latter and while still in his teens served with the French armies in the Netherlands. He is reputed to have seen action in several campaigns during the Thirty Years War, and at the age of twenty-three he obtained the rank of colonel of the regiment of Normandy.[6] It was while serving with this regiment at the siege of Orbitello in 1646 that he was severely wounded, his right arm being crippled for life. As compensation for his wound he was appointed a *maréchal de camp*,[7] this being equivalent to the rank of brigadier in the present-day Canadian army.

In the seventeenth century, military activity virtually ceased during the wet winter months, and the opposing armies retired into winter quarters. Many of the officers in the French forces then took up residence at the Court. Such a mode of existence was excessively expensive, and Frontenac soon found himself running heavily into debt; by 1648 his acknowledged debts amounted to at least 66,000 *livres*.[8] Mlle de Montpensier, "la grande Mademoiselle," comments in her memoirs on Frontenac's expensive tastes and what she regarded as his colossal vanity. In the summer of 1653 she spent a few days at his château at l'Îsle Savary, which she describes as being "fine enough for a man such as he." Frontenac showed her the plans he had drawn up for the embellishment of the château and for the formal gardens that he proposed to lay out. "One would have to be minister of finance in order to execute them," she tartly commented. On another occasion she depicts him as affecting to hold a court at St. Fargeau, one of the royal châteaux where she resided during her exile from the Court, and of his expecting to be treated as a *grand seigneur* by all who came to dine with him, this being a pretence which she found utterly ridiculous. She then went on to say: "Frontenac praised everything that he owned; he never came to dinner or supper without talking of some dish or new preserve that he had been served, crediting it to the excellence of his staff. Even meat, according to him, had a different taste at his table to what it had elsewhere. . . . Everyone who came to St. Fargeau he took to see his stable and in order to please him one had to praise his very indifferent horses; in short, he is like that in all things."[9]

When the disturbances of the Fronde first broke out, Frontenac was serving in the guards of Monsieur, the king's eldest brother.[10] He does not appear to have played a very active role in the struggle between the Court and *Parlement*; instead he waged a private

Fronde of his own against a certain *maître des requêtes* * named de Neufville de la Grange. The trouble between them began when de Neufville adamantly refused to countenance Frontenac as a son-in-law, despite the latter's great personal charm and his influential connections at the Court. De Neufville, a man of considerable wealth and narrowness of mind, regarded this as an impossible match which it was his duty as a parent to prevent by every available means.

His daughter, Anne de la Grange, was possessed of a rare physical beauty, a very imperious temperament, and a quick biting wit.[11] Moreover, apart from her father's estate, reputed to be worth some 200,000 *écus*, she stood to inherit a considerable fortune in her own right, left in trust for her by her mother until she came of age.[12] Frontenac, though not a member of one of the *grandes familles*, moved in that charmed circle of Court society which attracted girls of Anne de la Grange's gifts and temperament as a honey pot attracts bees, and to which, owing to her bourgeois background, she could never hope to gain an entrée except through marriage. In addition, Frontenac was desperately in need of money, a condition which Anne de la Grange would be in a position to remedy once a marriage settlement had been arranged. But her father would have none of it; he regarded Frontenac as a penniless fortune hunter. As he explained in a letter to the Comte de Chavigny: "I saw as clear as day that far from having twenty-five, or twenty thousand *livres* income, he did not have even five, once all his expenses and debts were paid; and this not including his commission which is completely mortgaged and a source of nothing but expense."[13] So strongly did he feel about this, he had Anne de la Grange immured in the convent of Ste Marie in the Faubourg St. Jacques to keep her out of Frontenac's way.[14]

For the next four months Frontenac tried desperately to get de Neufville to relent and to agree to the drawing up of a marriage settlement. Finally, in April, 1649, realizing that the only thing which would incline de Neufville to look favourably on his suit was

* *Maître des requêtes:* This was a venal office, costing some 300,000 *livres* to purchase and carrying a salary of only 1,000 *livres* a year. The number of office-holders was increased from eighty to eighty-nine in 1689 and the office was eagerly sought after, since the holders were entitled to sit in the king's Privy Council and it was from amongst their number that the senior posts in the administration were filled.

the one thing above all else that he could not provide, namely, evidence of his being solvent, Frontenac produced from up his sleeve what he believed to be a trump card. He blandly informed the Sieur de Neufville that he and Anne de la Grange were actually married. To add insult to injury, they had been secretly married the previous October, six weeks and more before de Neufville had had his daughter placed in the convent.

De Neufville was beside himself with fury when he heard this. He threatened, despite his age, to take desperate measures, being resolved to perish rather than suffer such an injury without obtaining satisfaction. He immediately attempted to have the marriage annulled, but without success.[15] He thereupon disowned his daughter out of hand and vowed that he would remarry as soon as possible in order to have other children to whom he could leave his estate.[16] Since there was no legal justification for retaining the Comtesse de Frontenac in the convent, she was now released.[17]

Frontenac himself was extremely anxious to obtain control of his wife's estate, while de Neufville was equally determined that he should never touch so much as a penny of it, and this he succeeded in doing by means of legal red tape. Lawyers were retained by both parties to the dispute, and for over a year they were engaged in legal wrangling. Finally, in September, 1650, almost two years after his marriage, Frontenac admitted defeat. A settlement was arranged whereby he was prevented for thirty years from touching his wife's estate without first obtaining her father's consent.[18] Previous to this, in June, 1649, de Neufville had made good his threat to remarry by taking a widow, Françoise Chouayne, as his wife. In his marriage contract he settled a large part of his estate on her and the remainder he bequeathed to the future issue of the marriage.[19] The Dame Chouayne de Neufville is reputed to have complained that her embittered husband was virtually killing her in his determined efforts to have another heir.[20] Be that as it may, she did manage to survive him; but before he died in 1654 she bore him a daughter[21] who effectively removed whatever faint hope Frontenac might still have had of ever obtaining some easing of his financial problems from that quarter.

In May, 1651, the Frontenacs had a son, François Louis,[22] and shortly afterwards they parted company temporarily. The child was left in the care of servants, this being the usual procedure in that age. Mme de Frontenac then joined the entourage of Mlle de

Montpensier, the turbulent *Grande Mademoiselle*, grand-daughter of Henri IV, and took an active part with her in the siege of Orléans in support of the Frondeurs. For this and for her conduct during the siege of Paris by the royal forces, Mademoiselle was exiled from the Court to a château in the provinces. She chose Mme de Frontenac as one of her ladies-in-waiting, much against the wishes, she later remarked, of the Queen Regent, whom she quotes as saying: "My niece selects a lady-in-waiting who has neither the rank nor the reputation to be such."[23] Frontenac himself joined the followers of Gaston d'Orléans, uncle of Louis XIV, who had the well earned reputation of being the most treacherous man in France. Some years earlier Gaston had occupied himself with plotting against the king and then betraying his fellow conspirators; in his declining years he confined himself to scheming to deprive his daughter of the lands left her by her grandfather. Mademoiselle subsequently became convinced that the Frontenacs were intriguing against her in her father's interests and she dismissed Mme de Frontenac from her establishment.[24]

The Frontenacs then took up residence in their Paris house in the Rue des Tournelles. Shortly afterwards Gaston d'Orléans and his daughter effected a temporary reconciliation and she was now permitted to reappear at the Court. At this Mme de Frontenac tried to regain the favour of Mademoiselle, but to no avail, and the Frontenacs now went out of their way to cause her as much petty annoyance as they could. She tried to have them excluded from the Court, but without success, owing to her father's continuing to lend them his support. Finally, their continued annoyance of Mademoiselle became so flagrant that Mazarin felt obliged to intervene and to appeal to the Queen Mother to have a stop put to it.[25] If nothing else, these petty squabbles and backstairs intrigues indicate that the Frontenacs had a great deal of influence in Court circles and were not to be crossed, even by a member of the royal family, with impunity.

By this time their financial position was in a most deplorable state. In 1653 Frontenac had given up his colonelcy of the regiment of Normandy.[26] The following year Mme de Frontenac's father died and they immediately entered into litigation with her stepmother to obtain her inheritance which her father had deeded, apparently in a spirit of vindictiveness, to his child by Françoise Chouayne. The lawyers retained by both parties appear to have decided that this was far too good a thing for them to allow it to be settled quickly, and so the litigation dragged on for over eight years, while lawyers' fees and legal expenses mounted steadily.[27] At the same time, the Frontenacs were living well beyond their means, borrowing money and running up bills on all sides. By 1664 their acknowledged debts amounted to over 325,878 *livres*, plus 17,530 *livres* 16 *sols* 10 *deniers* in accrued interest. This large sum represented some, but not all, of the debts which Frontenac had contracted between the years 1643 and 1663. He justified his sorry financial plight by claiming that, owing to his birth and social condition, he had been obliged to expend large sums of money for equipment in order to maintain his military rank with honour during several campaigns, and also to keep up appearances at the Court. He also pointed out that he had had to borrow considerable sums in order to defend his wife's interest at law during the lengthy litigation with her step-mother.

Needless to say, Frontenac's creditors were pressing him hard during this time. He held several discussions with one group of them and finally, in September, 1664, made a contract with them whereby they agreed not to dun him for four years, while he, at the end of that time, was to settle all his debts in full. He agreed, in the meantime, to pay them approximately 3½ per cent a year interest—this being a remarkably low rate—and he also guaranteed that his other creditors, not included in the terms of the agreement, would be prevented from touching any part of the properties he had assigned to the discharging of the debts named in the contract. And finally, he solemnly declared that he would not, under any circumstances, obtain letters of state or a decree of the royal councils to break the terms of the agreement. On December 12, 1664, this notarial contract was homologated by the *Parlement de Paris*.[28]

Despite his having received such accommodating terms from his creditors, Frontenac failed to honour them. He made no attempt to realize on his assets in order to repay the principal; he did not even pay his creditors so much as a *sol* of the interest on their money. As one of this long-suffering group later phrased it: "He has been granted delays of all kinds of three and of four years, during which we inconvenienced ourselves in order to accommodate him and to give him time in which to settle his affairs, and he has always broken his word in such a way that no one could trust him any longer."[29]

Some eight months after the expiry of his agreement with his creditors, Frontenac left France for Crete, accompanied by his son. Since 1646 this island had been besieged by the forces of the Ottoman Empire, and when the pope called upon the Christian powers to assist the Venetians, Louis XIV, for reasons of prestige, could not abstain, despite the long-standing tacit alliance of the French with the Grande Porte. Moreover, in 1668 Louis XIV had concluded his war in the Spanish Netherlands; thus large numbers of French officers on half pay and young gentlemen eager for excitement were available. A force of some six thousand such volunteers was quickly raised, and on June 5, 1669, this army, commanded by the Duc de Navailles, sailed from Toulon under the banner, not of France, but of the church.[30]

Frontenac, although he sailed with this force, was not actually a member of it, for he had obtained a commission as lieutenant general with the Venetian forces. The reason why he was selected for this post is very obscure. Francis Parkman has stated that a Venetian embassy, in begging for aid in Crete, "offered to place their own troops under French command, and they asked Turenne to name a general officer equal to the task. Frontenac had the signal honour of being chosen by the first soldier of Europe for this arduous and most difficult position. He went accordingly. The result increased his reputation for ability and courage."[31] In making this statement Parkman was gravely in error. There is no evidence that the Venetians offered to place their own troops under French command; Frontenac was not chosen by Turenne for any such mythical position *; and his actions in Crete do not appear to have enhanced his reputation in any way. The Venetians already had one French officer, the Marquis de St. André Montbrun, serving on their general staff; why they accepted the services of another is not clear.

But whatever the reason for his appointment, immediately upon receipt of his commission he demanded that the terms of service be altered. The commission was couched in the usual rather general

* Turenne's only connection with Frontenac's appointment appears to have been to make certain suggestions as to changes which Frontenac desired made in the terms of his commission. Later, in his defence before the Doge and Senate of Venice, Frontenac made much of the fact that Turenne had written these suggested changes in his own hand in the margin of the commission. Had Turenne selected Frontenac for the post it is inconceivable, under the circumstances, that Frontenac would not have laid great stress on this point in his defence. But he did not make any such claim.

24

terms, but one of its clauses stated that Frontenac would hold the rank of lieutenant general and be subordinate to the Venetian representatives, the Marquis de St. André Montbrun, and the officers holding the rank of general. Frontenac objected strenuously to this, and here he received the support of Turenne; he demanded that he be treated as subordinate only to the Venetian representatives and the Marquis de St. André, and that he be given his own command. He also demanded that his two aides-de-camp be put on the Venetian establishment and a fully-manned barque be placed at his disposal to transport his supplies. The Venetian ambassador in Paris sent these demands to the Senate, but Frontenac did not wait for a revised copy of his commission; accompanied by his son, he left for Crete armed only with a letter from the ambassador to the general in command of the Venetian forces, stating that the revisions had been requested and asking this general to honour them.[32]

Francesco Morosini, the Venetian captain general, was, however, not at all impressed by this letter, and even less so by Frontenac. Troops from many European nations were serving under the Venetian command and Frontenac soon began quarrelling with the other general officers. He became highly incensed when Morosini refused to order the Comte de Valdeck and his troops to obey his, Frontenac's, commands; he was even more enraged when Morosini tried to exclude him from the meetings of the council of war. Eventually Frontenac did gain access to the council meetings, whereupon he immediately became embroiled in a squabble with another general, Monsieur de Spar, about who was to have precedence. Morosini opposed Frontenac in this issue too, and, according to Frontenac, habitually treated him with little more than contempt.[33]

At this time relations between the French forces and those under Venetian command were far from cordial. The campaign was not going well. In their first assault on the Turkish positions the French were severely mauled, losing five hundred men, including their commanding officer, the Duc de Beaufort. The Turks continued to receive reinforcements, the position of the defenders steadily worsened, and mutual recriminations between the allies grew more intense. Finally, the French decided to withdraw their forces from the island, leaving the Venetians no recourse but to ask the Turks for terms. This was a very bitter pill for them to swallow after having defended the island valiantly for twenty-four years at a total cost to Venice of 126,000,000 *ducats*.[34] A few days before the commander of the French army gave the order for his troops to leave, a meeting of the principal officers in the Venetian forces was held at the headquarters of one of their commanders, General Bataille. At this meeting the assembled officers expressed their feelings very forcibly on the subject. Some harsh phrases were uttered, and General Bataille was reputed to have said that it would be more correct to say that the French were fleeing from the field rather than withdrawing. Word of this rapidly reached the ears of the intendant of the French forces, and at a joint council of war held three days later he accused General Bataille of having insulted the honour of the French army. He threatened to report this, and similar incidents that had been brought to his attention, to Louis XIV who, he claimed, would most assuredly demand satisfaction from the Venetian Senate. The incident was eventually smoothed over, but it was quite obvious that someone who had been at the earlier council of war had carried these tales to the intendant. Captain General Morosini became convinced that the person was Frontenac.

Shortly after this incident, Frontenac put in a request for a payment of two or three hundred *pistoles* on his salary. He was curtly informed that the Captain General had ordered not only that he was to receive a mere two hundred *piastres*,* but that his two aides-de-camp were to be struck off the establishment. This staggered Frontenac, particularly since none of the other officers of his rank had been deprived of their aides-de-camp. He immediately went to the Captain General's headquarters in the château of Candia and, according to his version of events, politely requested Morosini to revise his orders in these matters. Morosini refused to do anything of the sort and dismissed Frontenac's request out of hand. Messieurs de Spar and Kiemansueck and several other officers entered the room at this point and in front of them Frontenac complained at being treated in such a shabby fashion. Morosini sharply retorted that, far from this being the case, he had received much better treatment than he deserved and accused him point-blank of having betrayed the secrecy of the council of war to the intendant of the French forces. Frontenac denied this vehemently and was brusquely ordered out of the room by Morosini. Frontenac replied that he would leave in his own good time, then had to beat a hasty retreat

* The Spanish *pistole* was worth 21 *livres* 10 *sols*, the *piastre* only 6 *livres*.

to escape being forcibly thrown out by Morosini's guards. A few hours later he was relieved of his military duties and the following day he received his dismissal from the Venetian forces. He and his son left the island the following morning.[35]

Five months later, on February 7, 1670, Frontenac appeared before the Doge and Senate of the Republic of Venice to answer the charges brought against him by Francesco Morosini. What these actually were can be only partially deduced from Frontenac's defence, and in so appearing he apparently had three main objects in view: to justify his actions in Crete, to obtain payment of the 450 *ducats* a month salary mentioned in his original commission, and to be retained in the Venetian service. In his defence he presented a lengthy memoir narrating all that had transpired in Crete between Morosini and himself. Much of it consists of an attack on Morosini's military abilities and an extolment of his own; but in answer to what appears to have been the principal charge against him, namely, that he had reported General Bataille's remarks to the intendant of the French forces, he asserted that the intendant had been informed of what had been said at this council before he, Frontenac, had even left the chamber, and that it could not have been he who had betrayed the secrecy of the council.[36] Unfortunately, the reception which this defence received is not known, but Frontenac's desire to be retained in the Venetian service does not appear to have been gratified.

Nothing more is heard of Frontenac until two years later when, in the spring of 1672, he obtained the appointment of governor of New France.* Several theories have been advanced to explain why he received this appointment, some of them more colourful than credible. The Duc de Saint-Simon states in his memoirs that Frontenac's friends obtained the position for him in order that he might

---

* The only other contender for the post was M. de Grignan, Mme de Sévigné's son-in-law, who was reputed to be of a very extravagant nature, too susceptible to flattery and heavily in debt. When she learned that Frontenac had received the appointment, Mme de Sévigné wrote to console her daughter: ". . . it is a sad thing to reside in a new country and to leave that which one knows and loves in order to live in another clime amongst people whom one would be ashamed to associate with in this. 'One belongs to every country'; that is from Montaigne; but he was at his ease in the comfort of his own home when he said it." (See *Lettres de Madame de Sévigné à Madame de Grignan*, Hachette, Paris, 1862, III, 7–8, letter dated Paris, April 6, 1672.) It would be interesting to speculate on —among other things—the light that Mme de Sévigné's correspondence might have thrown on Canadian affairs had her son-in-law been appointed governor.

be kept from starving, and also to relieve him of his wife's company.[37] Since Saint-Simon was writing some thirty-five years after the event, he was obviously recalling rather ancient Court gossip. It is, however, true that Mme de Frontenac did not accompany her husband to Quebec and he did obtain, along with his commission, "letters of the Council of State" lifting the seizure that his creditors had placed on his properties and deferring his legal obligation to repay his debts.[38] Meanwhile, at the end of May, Colbert de Terron, the intendant at Rochefort, was impatiently awaiting the arrival of the newly appointed governor in order that a waiting convoy could leave for Canada. Frontenac finally arrived, complete with some eighteen bales of personal baggage, after having collected his year's salary of 12,000 *livres* plus another 3,000 *livres* to defray his travelling expenses, and on June 28, 1672, the convoy set sail.[39]

This, then, is as much as is known of Frontenac's early career. Admittedly, the evidence is very scanty and what there is does not show him in a very favourable light. With the exception of the odd letter pertaining strictly to routine regimental matters, none of his personal correspondence during this period has survived. It has frequently been claimed that he had had a distinguished military career before his appointment as governor of New France. It may well be that he had, but unfortunately there is no evidence to substantiate such statements. It has also been claimed that his relations with his wife were far from amicable; but this is based largely on the evidence contained in the memoirs of Mlle de Montpensier, who was notorious for the vehemence of her attachment or hostility to people. Moreover, although Mademoiselle states that on one occasion Mme de Frontenac had displayed a marked aversion for her husband, refusing to share his bed, she makes it plain that on subsequent occasions no such aversion existed. Mademoiselle also relates that she inadvertently intercepted a *billet doux* from Frontenac to Louis XIV's mistress, Madame de Montespan, of whom, she adds, Frontenac was "fort amoureux."[40] Tallemant des Réaux, in his scurrilous tales of Court life in the age of Louis XIV, recounts a piece of doggerel verse that was going the rounds at this time:

> Je suis ravy que le roy nostre sire
> Aime la Montespan;
> Moy, Frontenac, je m'en creve de rire,
> Scachant ce qui lui pend.

Et je diray sans estre des plus bestes,
Tu n'as que mes restes,
Toy,
Tu n'as que mes restes.[41]

Réaux also states that Louis XIV himself at one time pursued Mme de Frontenac and that the Queen Mother had to intervene. But, considering its source, such backstairs gossip need not be taken very seriously. That Mme de Frontenac did not accompany her husband to New France is not surprising; she would not have been happy there and she could be of far greater help to Frontenac at the Court than as the châtelaine of the governor's residence at Quebec. And throughout his entire career in Canada, Mme de Frontenac did a great deal to advance his interests and protect him from his enemies; certainly Frontenac himself counted on her support, and his salary was paid directly to her.[42] All in all, considering the age in which they lived and the milieu in which they moved, their marital relations seem to have been quite normal.

Frontenac's heavy debts indicate clearly enough that he was very extravagant, but he lived in an extravagant age. His creditors, of course, were highly incensed when they learned that they were unable to collect what he owed them. The Comte de Crécy, French ambassador at Cologne, had loaned Frontenac some 6,300 *livres* fourteen years previously and he protested bitterly to Colbert the injustice of Frontenac's being allowed to bilk his creditors in such a fashion. He was particularly irate because his own creditors were pressing him hard; moreover, he had recently been instrumental in obtaining the colonelcy of a Münster regiment for Frontenac's son, who died shortly afterwards.[43] * However, no social stigma was attached to Frontenac's bankrupt condition, nor were the means he used to defraud his creditors looked at askance—except by those whom he had defrauded—for such things were everyday occurrences in Court circles. In fact, the Comte de Crécy, outraged though he was by Frontenac's actions, two years later himself obtained a decree of the Council of State to prevent his own properties being seized by his creditors.[44]

When all this has been said, however, the fact remains that

---

* The exact date and causes of the death of Frontenac's son are not known. It may be that he died before Frontenac left France, for in his correspondence from Canada he gives no hint whatsoever that he has suffered such a loss.

Frontenac's career previous to his appointment as governor of New France does not seem to have been very distinguished. The defects in his character are all very obvious ones : he was excessively vain, unscrupulous and quick to resentment; his attitude towards money was a mixture of cupidity and extravagance, he cared little what means he used to get it, and spent it faster than he got it. What is not so obvious from the nature of the evidence is the fact that he was undoubtedly possessed of great personal charm. The art of the courtier was the art of knowing how to please the right people, and Frontenac must have been highly skilled at this, otherwise his influence at the Court would have been negligible. Certainly in his correspondence it is plain that he was a man very skilled in the use of words, of making circumstances redound to his personal credit; and the literary style makes his dispatches a pleasure to read. Moreover, the very nature of his debts would seem to indicate that he was possessed of this elusive quality, charm, to a considerable degree. His known debts were all for relatively modest sums, varying from 2,000 to 24,000 *livres*, borrowed from some thirty-six different people.[45] Anyone who could borrow that much money from that many people must have had great persuasive powers. Charm is a very powerful, and sometimes dangerous, thing; it is also one that is not easy to detect in written documents, particularly those of an official nature. Yet without it, Frontenac's career is inexplicable.

CHAPTER THREE

HIGH AND MIGHTY LORD

IT was not until early autumn that Frontenac arrived in Canada. The voyage across the Atlantic had been long and tedious; for weeks, contrary winds kept his ship cruising back and forth off the coast of France. With his customary wit he remarked in a letter to the minister that there need have been no fears for the security of this coast, since he had been acting as an involuntary coastguard for what had seemed an interminable time. The crossing was also marked by a succession of mishaps which Frontenac attributed to a disinclination on the part of some of the ships' captains to heed his instructions and orders.[1] Although he was greatly impressed with the site of Quebec, the town itself did not impress him very favourably. In Upper Town there were few buildings but churches and religious houses. In Lower Town the houses, all built of wood, had been erected wherever their owners' fancies dictated, and this haphazard arrangement offended Frontenac's sense of symmetry.[2] Accustomed as he was to the extravagant splendours of the Court, it is hardly surprising that this small frontier town on the edge of the Canadian wilderness should seem anything but prepossessing; but it did have its compensations : he was almost a viceroy, the only check to his authority was Colbert on the other side of the Atlantic, and his creditors could not touch him. When he arrived in New France the framework of the royal administration had already been firmly established. During the preceding seven years great advances had been made in the colony in almost every field of activity, and there was the promise of greater things to come. Courcelles left the colony at peace; he bequeathed no great problems to his successor, who had only to carry on where he had left off.

Frontenac had been at Quebec only a very short time when he began making innovations in the colony's administrative system. Some of these were probably intended to achieve a greater degree of efficiency; but his first such innovation was clearly an attempt to introduce the pomp and ceremony of the Court to Quebec, and little more. In his commission he had been instructed to "have the three orders of the country—clergy, nobles and commons—as well as the local governors and officers of the Sovereign Council, swear a new oath of fealty." [3] This was merely one of those cant phrases beloved by the clerks who drew up such documents. It appeared in the commissions of all the governors, before and after Frontenac, but he was the only one among them who took it at all seriously. He set about organizing a colonial Estates General. He had no difficulty in obtaining a hall for his assembly; the Jesuits offered him their recently completed church for the occasion. The forming of the three estates posed a rather more difficult problem. The clergy were available, but the colony could boast of little by way of nobility, so Frontenac had to be satisfied with three or four "gentlemen" and the officers of his guards; the syndic of the Quebec *habitants*, along with the leading merchants of the town, sufficed for the third estate; the members of the Sovereign Council and the lower law courts were placed in a separate "legal estate." [4] The intendant declined to have anything to do with the affair, excusing himself on the grounds that he was a little indisposed. [5] Two days later, however, Talon was sufficiently recovered to attend the meeting of the Sovereign Council. [6]

On October 23 the assembly took place and was attended, at Frontenac's estimate, by over a thousand persons. This represented a feat of no small proportions, deserving to rank almost with the miracle of the loaves and the fishes, for the outside dimensions of the Jesuit church were only one hundred feet by thirty. [7] Frontenac opened the proceedings with a speech from the throne which was obviously calculated to appeal to an audience on the other side of the Atlantic, for he larded it heavily with flattering references to Colbert and the undying glories of the king. [8] Following this, the oath of fealty was administered.

At least one group were suitably impressed by the proceedings; a party of Hurons who happened to be present asked the governor the following day to go through the ceremony again for their benefit, and in all seriousness Frontenac informed the minister that he had been pleased to do so. [9] It was perhaps fortunate that Colbert read only abstracts of the Canadian dispatches, for had he read Frontenac's glowing description of these assemblies, particularly the second one, he would very probably have concluded that such a performance brought the Crown dangerously close to ridicule. As it was, he informed Frontenac that since it was royal policy not to call meetings of the Estates General, but to allow this institution to wither on the vine lest it in some way detract from the king's absolute authority, no more such meetings should be convened in Canada.[10]

Francis Parkman, looking at New France through his Whig-coloured glasses, has stated: "Like so many of his station, Frontenac was not in full sympathy with the centralizing movement of the time, which tended to level ancient rights, privileges, and prescriptions under the ponderous roller of the monarchical administration. He looked back with regret to the day when the three orders of the state, clergy, nobles, and commons, had a place and a power in the direction of affairs." [11] To ascribe these motives to Frontenac is to misunderstand both his character and the age in which he lived. He himself denied ever having entertained such notions, for in answer to Colbert's mild rebuke he wrote: "I never claimed thereby to form bodies that should subsist, knowing well of what consequence that could be." [12] Frontenac's entire career demonstrates his firm belief in autocratic government. There can be little doubt that he held his assembly for no other reason than to create an impression on the people of Quebec.

In his dealings with the subordinate officials, from the moment that he first took over the reins of government, Frontenac made it plain that he required complete subservience. But here it must be remembered that most of his life had been spent in the army, where he had been accustomed to giving orders and having them obeyed on the instant without question. Military men in positions of civil authority frequently find it difficult to tolerate disagreement with their ideas of how things should be done, and Frontenac was certainly no exception. He could not comprehend such a thing as division of authority between himself, the intendant and the Sovereign Council. Whereas his predecessors, in the records of the Council, had always been referred to simply as "monsieur the governor," he insisted on being termed "high and mighty lord." [13] Talon had always presided over the meetings of the Sovereign Council in his capacity of *intendant de justice*; although Frontenac's instructions were rather vague as to who was actually to perform the functions of president of the Council, he personally had no doubts whatsoever on this score, and consequently he was soon involved in a violent dispute with Talon.[14] He also resented the intendant's jurisdiction over the general administration of the colony, his granting of land concessions, and the fact that passports to go out of the colony, either to France or to the Ottawa country, had to be countersigned by this official. Frontenac requested the minister to remove these restrictions to his authority before a new intendant was appointed on the grounds that "as long as a governor here lacks the power to grant any favours and is almost without a function . . . he cannot gain much influence or esteem." [15]

In mid-November the last ships of the year sailed from Quebec and Jean Talon sailed with them. Bishop Laval had left for France the year before. Frontenac now ruled supreme. In his instructions he had been told that he was not to interfere in any way with the Sovereign Council except to preside over its meetings. If the Councillors failed to perform their duties in an honest and competent manner, he could warn them to mend their ways, but if anything more serious developed he had to report the circumstances to the king, nothing more. [16] Frontenac interpreted this to mean that the members of the Council were to be free only to comply with his wishes, their freedom of action equivalent to that of a soldier on parade, and he made it quite plain to them that they held office only during his good pleasure. [17] In his early dispatches to the minister he praised them in a rather condescending manner, stating that within the limits of their experience and intelligence they tried to discharge their duties in an efficient and honest fashion. [18] A year after his arrival he suggested that their number should be increased from five to seven to obviate the necessity of calling in judges from outside the ranks of the Council to hear criminal cases. [19] This was a very sensible proposal; five judges were required to hear criminal cases, which meant that whenever a member of the Council was unable to attend or had to withdraw owing to his being related to the defendant—as often happened—someone outside its ranks had to be brought in to make up the requisite number.

When Talon departed from the colony he left a very awkward gap in the administrative machinery, and Colbert had neglected to give any instructions on who was to exercise the extremely important powers of the intendant. These could have been performed only by the governor or by the Sovereign Council, or by the governor acting in concert with the Council. Frontenac appears never to have doubted for one moment that it was he who should perform these functions, and under the circumstances, he did have some grounds for so acting. Unfortunately he was far from circumspect in the way he went about it. He immediately began dispensing justice personally, having cases brought before him and rendering summary judgement. His reasons for doing this were that he believed he could dispense justice far more efficiently and equitably than could the established courts, and he informed the minister : "Thus, without proceedings, without expense and without records, I settle in one day more cases than the chief judges and the Council try in a month." [20] And in the legislative field, he began encroaching on the authority of the Sovereign Council. He claimed, and probably not without cause, that once the ships sailed for France in the autumn, taking the itinerant French merchants with them, the merchants of Montreal and Trois Rivières raised the prices of their goods to exorbitant heights. To put a stop to this, Frontenac issued an *ordonnance* fixing price ceilings on certain essential commodities.[21] There was nothing novel about this; three years earlier the Sovereign Council had taken similar steps to curb this abuse.[22] Frontenac, however, was acting by virtue of his own authority, without consulting the Sovereign Council.

He also took it upon himself to reorganize the Quebec butcher and bake shops and the general market, fixing the prices at which commodities could be sold. He went about this last in a fashion which, at first sight, smacked suspiciously of democracy. The more well-to-do men in Quebec were called before him and informed of his intentions; this, as he put it, "so that by giving them some share in that which I intended to do, the execution of which depended in part on their efforts and their pockets, they would be more willing to undertake it." These men were required merely to approve Frontenac's proposals, not to discuss them or offer suggestions, but they were expected to elect the *échevins* who were to see that the proposals were carried out. Frontenac was, however, at pains to assure the minister that the confirmation of the popular choice and the distribution of office would be entirely dependent on the governor's will; moreover, the appointees would be required to swear fidelity to the governor.[23] Actually, this involved procedure merely gave Frontenac a certain amount of patronage to dispense, and when he had his proposals registered by the Sovereign Council he encountered some opposition which he attributed to the subversive activities of certain people, notably the lieutenant-general of Quebec and his son, who happened to be deputy attorney-general of the Sovereign Council. This opposition stemmed, Frontenac claimed, from the quarrelsome attitude of a certain group in the colony who were opposed to order and efficient administration lest it should interfere with their own vested interests.[24]

One official who earned Frontenac's displeasure was summarily dismissed from his post. This man, the Sieur de Villeray, had been a member of the Sovereign Council, but had been removed from office by Courcelles who had regarded him as a troublemaker. Some of the leading *habitants* in the colony had protested at this and had declared their intention of petitioning the king for Villeray's reinstatement once Courcelles left the colony.[25] Villeray had also been appointed collector of the ten per cent import duty by Talon. Tax collectors are rarely popular and Frontenac's statement that some of the merchants had complained of the manner in which Villeray performed his functions may well be true. Frontenac maintained also that Villeray was a tool of the Jesuits and entirely unsuitable for any position on the Sovereign Council.[26]

Upon receipt of all this information the minister curtly informed Frontenac that he was to leave things as they were, allowing Villeray to continue collecting the tax, and that when a suitable person had been found to fill the vacancy of intendant this official would look into the matter.[27] Previously, Colbert had solicited the opinion of Patoulet, who had been Talon's deputy in Canada, on Villeray's character. Patoulet had recommended that in order to uphold the royal authority vested in Courcelles, the king should issue a decree of the Council of State confirming Villeray's exclusion from the Sovereign Council and then reappoint him as senior councillor, since he was the only man in the colony with the talent and training required for judicial work. As for Villeray's suspected association with the Jesuits, Patoulet dismissed this with the left-handed comment: "The bishop of Petrea and the Jesuit fathers conform in all things to the intentions of the king, he cannot be suspect any longer on this account."[28] However, by the time that Frontenac had received the minister's order, he had already dismissed Villeray from his post and appointed the Sieur de Peiras, Courcelles's ex-secretary, in his stead. Frontenac informed Colbert that he had taken this action because the tax funds were not safe in Villeray's hands and that he was nothing but a troublemaker. Expressing confidence that the minister would concur in this, he did not reinstate Villeray but waited for Colbert's further instructions.[29]

When Frontenac received the dispatches from the Court in the summer of 1674 he was considerably taken aback to learn that Colbert had disallowed all his innovations. Colbert informed him that he had greatly exceeded his authority and that he had no right whatsoever to establish *échevins* or to issue regulations for the civil government of Quebec. Nor did he have any right to meddle in matters pertaining to justice; this was the sole responsibility of the established courts. Colbert warned him to treat the judges of these courts with great discretion and to allow them complete freedom of action. Only in exceptional cases, where the peace and security of the people were imperilled, could he take any action and even then only when the parties involved requested him to do so of their own free will. Colbert tersely gave Frontenac to understand that it was, in fact, a form of benevolent despotism that was required in New France, and he added, ". . . that proper liberty which you grant will bestow a high opinion in this kingdom of the justice of your government and by this means a great many people will be persuaded to go there."[30]

Most humiliating of all, Frontenac was ordered to reinstate Villeray as collector of the ten per cent import duty and he was informed that the king had been pleased to appoint Villeray senior councillor of the Sovereign Council. At the same time the membership of the Council was increased from five to seven, as Frontenac had suggested; but, without consulting the governor, Colbert had appointed the Sieur de Lotbinière as a councillor and the Sieur d'Auteuil as attorney-general. Frontenac was enraged by this. He had just succeeded in cowing thoroughly the members of the Sovereign Council; during the past year two vacancies had occurred in its ranks and he had appointed men of his own choosing who could be counted on to give him their unswerving support. But now, with Villeray as senior councillor and d'Auteuil as attorney-general, he could expect to meet with considerable opposition. He complained to Colbert that the minister seemed to place no faith in what he wrote him and that he might just as well have appointed the father superior of the Jesuits to the Council as Villeray and d'Auteuil.[31]

He did swallow his pride sufficiently to give Villeray the commission as tax collector, but he availed himself of a technicality in order to exclude him from the senior councillor's post. Commissions had been sent for the new members of the Sovereign Council, Lotbinière and d'Auteuil, by Colbert's assistant, Bellinzany, but he had omitted to send a commission for Villeray, most likely thinking that a new one was not required since Villeray had previously been a member of the Council. On the strength of this omission Frontenac chose to believe that the minister might have had second thoughts about giving the senior appointment to Villeray. Therefore he allowed Villeray to occupy only the last place in the Council until the minister had made his wishes clear in the matter.[32] In this way Frontenac managed to avert temporarily the full impact of this blow to his prestige. Certainly he was hard pressed to salvage something from the debacle in which he now found himself, for the closing paragraph of the minister's dispatch could hardly have been better contrived to destroy Frontenac's peace of mind. Colbert wrote: "His Majesty also orders me to recommend to you particularly the person and interests of the Sieur Perrot, governor of Montreal and nephew of the Sieur Talon."[33] This seemingly innocuous request could not have come at a more unpropitious moment. A few months earlier Frontenac had thrown the Sieur Perrot into gaol and had kept him there ever since.

A great many things led up to the arrest of Perrot and it was to have important consequences, not only for those chiefly concerned, but also for the administrative system of New France. The first act in the drama began with Frontenac's establishment of his fort at Cataracoui—at the eastern end of Lake Ontario, where the city of Kingston now stands—in the summer of 1673. The founding of this trading post, which marked Frontenac's active entry into the fur trade, was bitterly resented by the people of Montreal. The local merchants, with the exception of Le Ber, who was in partnership with Frontenac in this undertaking, saw that the post would deprive them of the Great Lakes fur trade, might well be a means to forestall the furs that normally came down from the Ottawa country, and consequently had shown great hostility to its foundation. The local *habitants* were also very resentful because Frontenac had obliged them to supply the canoes for the expedition and had ordered them out on *corvée* to provide the labour needed to transport the materials and build the fort.[34] Usually, *corvées* were of short duration, a few days a year for work on roads, bridges and suchlike in the settled areas; but this particular *corvée* had lasted over a month and others had followed to transport supplies to the new post. The *habitants* who had been obliged to spend the best part of the summer in this forced labour were under no delusions as to who

38

would reap the profits from the post; consequently the people of Montreal, humble and well-to-do alike, were in an ugly mood. Frontenac was well aware of this sullen hostility and he was determined to show these people at the head of the colony who was master.[35]

Owing to its remoteness, Montreal had been little troubled in the past by the authorities at Quebec. François Marie Perrot, a young man of thirty-two, had received the appointment of governor of the district from the Sulpician order, the seigneurs of the island, through the influence of his uncle, Jean Talon.[36] In character he was arrogant, overbearing, not in the least reluctant to use his authority arbitrarily in order to serve his personal interests and as a result highly unpopular with the people of Montreal. He was very active in the fur trade and if he did not openly oppose Frontenac's establishment of a post at Cataracoui he did little to help; in fact, a *habitant* later stated that had it not been for Perrot there would have been many more such *corvées*.[37] Under these circumstances, old frictions were temporarily forgotten and the people under Perrot's government suddenly discovered he had hitherto unsuspected qualities.

Upon his return from Lake Ontario in 1673 Frontenac immediately took steps to prevent any interference with his fur-trade ventures. He began by restricting Perrot's authority to the island of Montreal proper, appointing the Sieur de Chambly, one of his own following, as commander of the south shore of the St. Lawrence from Rivière-du-Loup-en-Haut * to above Montreal.[38] Shortly after receiving this appointment Chambly was named governor of Acadia by Colbert. This left Perrot still supreme at the head of the colony. Shortly afterwards a *coureur de bois* named Dupas obtained a permit from Frontenac—at a cost of 25 *pistoles*, it was alleged [39] —to hunt at the Natouan river and winter there with three companions. Instead of going to the area designated on the permit, Dupas and his men went some ten leagues above Montreal with a canoe-load of brandy which they traded with the Indians. When two of Dupas' men returned to Montreal to obtain more brandy, Perrot had them arrested for disobeying the king's edicts against trading outside the confines of the colony. Later, Dupas himself returned to Montreal to find out what had happened to his men,

* Rivière-du-Loup-en-Haut is the present-day city of Louiseville, between Montreal and Trois Rivières.

whereupon Perrot confiscated his hunting permit and ordered him not to leave Montreal.[40]

Perrot, rightly enough, insisted that all licence holders had to show their permits to him before leaving Montreal, and when a *coureur de bois* named Le Duc left without doing so, he had him brought back and confiscated his permit for failing to report before leaving and for taking three men with him when the licence specified only one. But while he was preventing the holders of Frontenac's permits from abusing their privileges, his own lieutenant, the Sieur de Brucy, was operating a trading post on Île Perrot and supplying *coureurs de bois* with trade goods. Perrot later pointed out the Île Perrot was beyond the confines of his jurisdiction since Frontenac had limited his authority to the island of Montreal proper. He was thus able to claim that even had he wanted to, there was nothing he could legally do about this situation.[41]

In the face of this, Frontenac now set about provoking an incident that would serve as an excuse to remove Perrot from office and enable him to install his own appointee as governor of Montreal. His first step was to issue secret instructions to a judge in Montreal, who had suffered at the hands of Perrot some time earlier,[42] to arrest any *coureurs de bois* lacking his, Frontenac's, licence. This judge subsequently learned that two *coureurs de bois* were at the house of a Sieur Carion, a retired officer of the Carignan-Salières regiment, and he sent a bailiff to arrest them. When the bailiff arrived at the house and tried to execute his orders, he was ignominiously put to flight by Carion's wife and the *coureurs de bois* at once made good their escape. Frontenac now had the excuse he had been looking for. He immediately sent a lieutenant of his guards—a man named Bizard who had been one of his aides-de-camp in Crete—to Montreal with three men to arrest Carion. From the way that Bizard went about this, it is abundantly clear that he acted as little more than an *agent provocateur*. Upon arriving at Montreal, Bizard should first have shown his warrant to the local governor; instead, he went directly to Carion's house and placed him under arrest, leaving one of his men there as guard. Then he proceeded to the house of Le Ber, at that time an associate of Frontenac's in the fur trade, and awaited developments.[43]

Perrot knew full well that Frontenac was searching for some excuse to remove him from office; he later remarked with contempt that Frontenac all along had acted "*plustost en homme* *d'affaires qu'en homme de guerre**."[44] Consequently he was relatively circumspect in his actions. But he did feel obliged to seek out Bizard and demand to know why he had arrested Carion without first reporting to the local governor and showing his warrant. According to Perrot, Bizard was drunk and behaved in a most insolent manner, leaving no choice but to place him under arrest, since not to have done so would have been an affront to his dignity as governor of Montreal.[45] Bizard was indeed a notorious drunkard. Frontenac himself, however, admitted that there had been nothing to stop his disregarding Perrot's order and walking out of the house, since he had two of his own men with him and Perrot had left only one man to guard them. He stated that Bizard "nevertheless believed, with an exactitude a little too religious, that he ought to obey promptly the instructions that he had been given and to do without any resistance everything that he was told, provided that he executed the order that he had been given. He therefore allowed himself to be held prisoner in order to see how far this violence and carrying on, which is perhaps quite without precedent, would go."[46]

The next day Perrot released Bizard and sent him back to Quebec, allowing him to take his prisoner, Carion, with him. He also gave him a scathing letter to Frontenac, which stated that if the Governor General was anxious to punish those who contravened the king's edicts against trading in the bush, he need look no further than the holders of his own so-called hunting permits.[47]

Two things are clear here: Perrot had not prevented Bizard's arresting Carion, nor had he prevented Bizard returning to Quebec with his prisoner; at the same time, Bizard's refusal to show his orders to Perrot and his insolent, provocative attitude throughout had given Perrot little alternative but to place him under house arrest. The incident did, however, serve the purpose that Frontenac had intended; he maintained that Perrot had defied his authority, which was true, and since this was the equivalent of defying the king's authority, he then had no alternative but to arrest Perrot. He was further persuaded of the necessity for this, he claimed, because he feared that the Iroquois, upon hearing of the dissension in the colony, would seize the opportunity to break with the

---

* This phrase defies translation. Literally, it means "more like a business man than a soldier". But in the seventeenth century to call a noble of the old aristocracy an *homme d'affaires* was a gross insult, akin today to calling a lady a streetwalker.

French.[48] Since at this particular time the Iroquois were mainly concerned with keeping the French from breaking with them, there was no danger from that quarter whatsoever. Moreover, at the same time that Frontenac made this statement, in his other dispatches he declared that he had cowed the Iroquois and had them practically eating out of his hand.

To find some justification for the arrest of Perrot was one thing, but effecting it, like putting the bell on the cat, was something else again. Frontenac later informed the minister that he had intended to go down to Montreal himself and place Perrot under arrest, thereby demonstrating that the authority of the governor of New France was not lightly to be questioned, but that Perrot had made this course of action unnecessary by obeying an order to come to Quebec to answer for his actions.[49] He conspicuously failed to mention, however, how it was that Perrot came so meekly to Quebec when summoned. This was certainly in strong contrast to Frontenac's account of his earlier rebellious attitude. In fact, Frontenac effected it by means of a subterfuge.

Perrot was led to believe by Frontenac that were he to go to Quebec the entire incident would be smoothed over without difficulty.[50] At the same time that he wrote to Perrot, Frontenac sent a letter to the Abbé Fénelon, a member of the Montreal seminary, requesting him to use his good offices to persuade Perrot to go to Quebec to settle the affair.[51] This Fénelon did. Perrot then agreed to go and the Abbé Fénelon accompanied him. On the evening of January 28 they arrived at Quebec. The following afternoon Perrot presented himself at the Château St. Louis. Frontenac had laid the scene very carefully for his reception. When the governor of Montreal entered the hall he found Frontenac, along with some twenty of his followers, assembled and waiting expectantly. Perrot immediately realized that he had walked into a trap, but before he could utter a word Bizard stepped forward, demanded his sword, and placed him under arrest. He was then conducted to the cells in the château and orders were given that no one was to be allowed to see him.[52]

The next day Frontenac brought Perrot's case before the Sovereign Council. The members of this body knew full well what to expect if they did not comply with his wishes; just a few weeks earlier he had reminded them that they could be removed from office at any time that he saw fit.[53] The Council dutifully appointed the Sieurs Dupont and Tilly to cross-examine Perrot. For the next eight months the Council was concerned with little else but this case. Meanwhile, Frontenac dismissed the town-major of Montreal from his post and appointed one of his own following, the Sieur de La Nouguère, in his stead.[54] La Nouguère was now the acting governor of Montreal and any opposition to the fur-trade activities of Frontenac's associates, or opposition of any other kind, could be quickly and effectively quelled.

The Abbé Fénelon, upon hearing of Perrot's arrest, pleaded with Frontenac to release him, but to no avail. Frontenac even refused to allow him to see Perrot in his cell.[55] Fénelon now became convinced that Frontenac had used him as a dupe to lure Perrot into the trap and he apparently feared that Perrot would regard him as having been a partner to the deed. This is most likely the explanation for his subsequent rash actions. He was a member of the order of St. Sulpice, an order that prides itself on the fact that its members are gentlemen; consequently, feeling that his honour was at stake, he now set about making it quite clear to all concerned that he, as well as Perrot, had been tricked by Frontenac. He went about this in rather too determined a fashion for his own good. Upon his return to Montreal he lent his support to Mme Perrot, who had drawn up a petition stating that the signatories had no complaints against her husband and were well satisfied with his government. Many people on the island signed the petition willingly enough.[56] When Frontenac heard of it he charged that it was nothing less than sedition,[57] and certainly such things were so regarded in France at that time.

Fénelon then made matters worse at Easter by preaching in the Montreal parish church a sermon which Frontenac's supporters claimed was a direct attack on the governor. In this sermon Fénelon, speaking in general terms, listed several things that would constitute an abuse of authority on the part of a temporal ruler, things such as forcing the people to perform corvées which served only his private interests, oppressing those who refused to grant him a part in the profits of their commerce, persecuting royal officials on feeble pretexts because they opposed his private undertakings, and surrounding himself with sycophants. La Salle, who was to become one of Frontenac's most ardent supporters, rose to his feet in the church as Fénelon was speaking and began gesticulating to draw the attention of his friends to what Fénelon was saying. Others in the congregation saw nothing amiss in Fénelon's remarks; in fact, from their subsequent statements, it looks suspiciously as though some of them had slept through most of the sermon. Some of the priests at the Seminary stated that this sermon could have been preached in any church in France without its causing any critical comment. But since some, if not all, of the abuses mentioned by Fénelon were ones recently committed by Frontenac, other members of the Seminary expressed the fear that the governor would consider that the cap fitted.[58] La Salle and his friends immediately fanned the feeble sparks given off by the sermon into a great conflagration; they lost no time in giving Frontenac their version of what Fénelon had said. The governor sent his secretary to Montreal to demand a copy of the sermon, but Fénelon refused to oblige. He argued, rather casuistically, that he was under no legal compulsion to do so, but that if he were provided with a copy of the charges and evidence against him he would then decide what action to take; for if he were innocent of the charges there was no case against him, and if guilty, which he strongly denied, then no one had the legal right to demand that he should assist in his own condemnation.[59]

Frontenac then sent two members of the Sovereign Council to Montreal to conduct an inquiry into the sermon and the petition that had been circulated by Mme Perrot and Fénelon. The purpose of this inquiry was to accumulate evidence against the abbé so that charges could be laid against him. Fourteen persons were interrogated and from the testimony of nine of them it is clear that Perrot enjoyed considerable popular support in his conflict with Frontenac; moreover, they stated that Fénelon had said nothing in his sermon to which Frontenac could justly take exception. The other five persons questioned were all members of Frontenac's following. La Salle and Le Ber were closely associated with him in the fur trade, Bellefontaine was an officer of Frontenac's guards, La Nouguère had recently been appointed town-major of Montreal by Frontenac, and the Sieur Migeon, the seigneur's attorney of Montreal, was no friend of Perrot's, having recently been imprisoned by him. From their testimony it is obvious that they made their depositions from a previously prepared statement which they had drawn up among themselves; they did not even trouble to vary the wording of their separate statements.[60] The testimony of all those questioned indicates clearly enough that had it not been for La Salle and his following, Fénelon's sermon would have aroused little comment; but it was on the basis of the evidence brought to light during these interrogations that Frontenac ordered Fénelon to appear before the Sovereign Council to be tried on a charge of sedition, the punishment for which was death.

When Fénelon appeared he denied, in an arrogant manner, the authority of the court to try him. As an ecclesiastic he claimed immunity from the civil courts unless his bishop ordered him to submit to such a trial. Since Bishop Laval was in France, this was out of the question. Several times the abbé was brought before the Council, each time his answer was the same, and Frontenac became more and more infuriated. When other members of the clergy were ordered to testify against him, they too refused on the same grounds. This posed a serious problem and the Sovereign Council, having no precedent to refer to, found themselves completely at a loss what to do about it.[61]

They soon found themselves in a similar predicament in Perrot's case. Throughout the spring and summer the Sieurs Dupont and Tilly, coached by Frontenac, kept plying Perrot with all manner of leading questions in an attempt to obtain something that could be used as evidence against him. But the more they questioned him the worse the case began to look, not against Perrot but against Frontenac. He maintained that since he held his commission as governor from the king, neither Frontenac nor the Sovereign Council could try him without thereby affronting the king's authority. He further claimed that since Frontenac was his accuser and his sworn enemy, he could not sit in judgement in the case, and since Frontenac could and would remove any councillor who earned his serious displeasure, they were merely his agents and therefore could not act as judges. He maintained that the dispute was a personal one between himself and Frontenac, who had plotted to remove him from office in order to appoint one of his "tools" to govern Montreal.[62]

Although Perrot was under close guard and allowed to see no one except his interrogators, he was somehow kept informed of all that went on concerning his case, both at Montreal, where Frontenac was intimidating anyone thought likely to give evidence in Perrot's favour,[63] and at meetings of the Sovereign Council. Moreover, he received surreptitious legal counsel from the Sieur de Villeray; at least, the evidence indicates that it must have been Villeray who acted as Perrot's adviser. Frontenac's earlier treatment of Villeray was sufficient motive for him to aid Perrot; also, it had to be someone in the Sovereign Council, and Villeray was the only member with sufficient knowledge of the law to have enabled Perrot to use the arguments that he now began to submit to the Council—such as his claim that de Vitre and Peiras had not been properly appointed as councillors since, by virtue of edicts of Francis I in 1535 and Charles IX in 1566, all prospective councillors had to be examined in the law before being appointed.[64]

Any accused person had the right to challenge the judges in his case and have them replaced should he demonstrate that they were interested parties, but when Perrot did succeed in submitting a petition to the Council, stating why its members could not legally hear the case and explaining why it could be adjudicated only by the king, it was summarily dismissed.[65] At the end of August he submitted another petition challenging the right of Frontenac and the Sieurs de Tilly, Peiras and de Vitre to remain as judges.[66] In this document his arguments were all well taken and were couched in legal terms. Frequently such phraseology has a rather unnerving effect on those without legal training—particularly when they are in a position where such knowledge is a prerequisite. Some members of the Council now began to feel uneasy about the entire proceedings and to entertain serious doubts as to the legality of their actions. Perrot—or Villeray—played on their fears very cleverly and conducted a veritable war of nerves from the prison cell. Needless to say, Frontenac was infuriated by this. When Perrot's second petition was read at the Council meeting he flew into a blind rage, seized the offending document, and tore it to shreds.[67] Perrot immediately sent another petition to the Council. Once again he explained at length all the legal reasons why his case could be heard only by the king. He maintained that the real issue was whether or not Frontenac could send an officer to arrest someone in the government of Montreal without notifying the local governor first. The remainder of this lengthy document explained in detail all the legal reasons why the members of the Sovereign Council, individually and collectively, could not hear the case. He particularly stressed their lack of legal training, maintaining that for this reason alone they were incompetent to judge a case such as this. He also pointed out that no matter how much Frontenac might bully and threaten them, they would eventually regret it if they submitted to his threats, for when the affair was brought before the king, as it most assuredly would be, one word from Louis XIV would be sufficient to draw Frontenac's fangs and they themselves would then have to answer to Louis for their actions. He therefore advised them to consider very carefully before proceeding any further.

When this petition was read in the Sovereign Council the members became even more uneasy. To earn Frontenac's displeasure could have unpleasant consequences, but the prospect of earning Louis XIV's displeasure was too frightening to contemplate. They were now completely out of their depth. Perrot's claim that they lacked the legal training necessary to judge the case had been very well taken. The Sieur de Tilly was the first to crack under the strain; he voiced the fears of them all when he openly admitted at a meeting of the Council that he was terrified every time Perrot's case came up for discussion. He admitted that he understood nothing of the legal aspects of the affair and would like nothing better than to remove himself from it entirely. This damaging admission enraged Frontenac. He bellowed that he would dismiss them all if they took that attitude. Tilly replied that he would be only too glad to resign his office. This brought Frontenac up short. He suddenly realized that he was on very dangerous ground. His only effective means of bending the Sovereign Council to his will was the threat of dismissal; if that failed there was no telling what might happen. He was now forced to humble his pride and plead with Tilly to remain on the Council.[68]

Realizing that he must step very warily, Frontenac agreed that he and the three councillors challenged by Perrot as being interested parties in the case should retire from the Council meetings until it could be determined whether or not the accused had valid grounds for challenging them. But at the same time he took it on himself to select five judges from outside the ranks of the Sovereign Council to join the remaining councillors in deciding this question. Perrot then challenged the new judges on the grounds that Frontenac, as his accuser, had no more right to appoint these judges than he had to act as a judge himself. Frontenac did manage to get his appointees to reject Perrot's objection, but it availed him nothing. The newly constituted court concluded that the case was too dangerous for them to handle, and they therefore decreed that it should be sent to the king.[69] This was the last thing that Frontenac wanted to happen. His whole purpose in bringing Perrot before the

Sovereign Council had been to cloak his arrest and imprisonment of the governor of Montreal with a semblance of legality. Were Perrot to be convicted by this court, then Frontenac could ship him back to France with the expectation that the king would accept the court's verdict, or at worst, place the onus on the Council rather than on Frontenac. Upon hearing the court's decision he stormed that they would either sit in judgement and render a verdict in the case or else suffer heavy fines. But the time was now past when threats and bluster had much effect on these men. Perrot had succeeded in defeating Frontenac by implanting in the councillors' minds the fear of earning the king's displeasure. The Council persisted in its decision to refer Perrot's case to the Court and at the same time they decided to send Fénelon's case to the king as well.[70] Frontenac now had no choice but to send both Perrot and Fénelon to France, without their having been condemned by the Quebec court. With them he sent his secretary to present his version of events to the minister.[71]

Another ten months then had to elapse before anyone in the colony could know what had transpired at the Court. But the following September, when the ships arrived from France, Frontenac must have felt rather uneasy as he broke the seals on the dispatches. Colbert had, as usual, drafted both his own and the king's dispatch, and at first glance Frontenac appeared to have emerged from the fracas with nothing more than a mild reprimand from the minister. On a closer examination it is clear that its mildness was more apparent than real. Perrot had been condemned for arresting Bizard since this was a defiance of the king's authority vested in Frontenac, and he had been sent to the Bastille for three weeks to make public reparation for this affront. Frontenac, however, was warned that in future he was not to take action in districts having a local governor without first giving notice to this official. This meant that both Perrot and Frontenac were regarded as having been in the wrong, but Colbert had been obliged to place the onus on Perrot in order not to weaken the royal authority. Moreover, Perrot was now reinstated in his post as governor of Montreal; he was ordered to apologize to Frontenac upon his return to New France, and Frontenac was bluntly told that he was to harbour no resentment against him, but instead was to treat him with all due respect.[72]

For Perrot to be reinstated in his old post was a bitter blow to Frontenac's pride and prestige; it amounted to a moral victory for the governor of Montreal, something that the people in the colony would be quick to appreciate. Frontenac must have felt this far more keenly than Perrot felt his brief sojourn in the Bastille. As for the Abbé Fénelon, he suffered no other punishment than being ordered not to return to Canada, but his chances of ecclesiastical preferment were now very slim indeed.[73] Frontenac was curtly informed that he had no authority whatsoever to bring a criminal action against a member of the clergy or to attempt to force ecclesiastics to testify against one another. In such matters all that he was empowered to do was to place the case in the hands of the bishop, or his grand vicar, or at the very most, send the accused back to France.[74]

At the same time, Colbert took measures to provide checks to Frontenac's authority. He virtually separated the judiciary from the executive, making the Sovereign Council independent of the governor by granting the incumbent councillors royal commissions.[75] He also laid down their order of precedence, Villeray being given the senior post,[76] and ruled that in future all appointments to this body, including the positions of attorney-general and recording clerk, would be made not by the governor and bishop, as in the past, but by the king, which really meant by the minister of marine. And, perhaps most important of all, he appointed an intendant for the colony who was to occupy the third place in the Sovereign Council, after the governor and bishop, but who was to act as president of the Council and perform the same functions and enjoy the same privileges as the first presidents of the French *parlements*.[77] Frontenac's sphere of operations was now restricted to military matters and to seeing to it that all the other officials in the colony, from the intendant down, executed their duties in an honest and efficient fashion.[78]

All things considered Frontenac, during his first three years in office, had not shown himself to great advantage as an administrator. To some extent this can be blamed on the failure of the minister to give any instructions on who was to exercise the functions of the absent intendant, and Frontenac did have some grounds for believing that they devolved on him. The clash with Perrot was basically a fight for control of the fur trade and Perrot received much the same treatment at the hands of Frontenac as he had meted out to those who had opposed him. It was unfortunate for the colony that Frontenac's arbitrary methods obliged Colbert to reinstate Perrot as governor of Montreal. The nature of the historical evidence must also be taken into account in an assessment of Frontenac's role. The contemporary records show Frontenac in a very bad light because they were written by people who had cause to be hostile to him; had they not been highly incensed they would not have written to the minister. Thus, any narrative of this period can hardly fail to read like a Newgate calendar of Frontenac's misdemeanours. It may well be that most of the people in the colony had no cause to complain of his actions; but the man accused of assault can hardly be exonerated on the grounds that there were, after all, a great many people whom he did not harm. Although extenuating circumstances could be pleaded to excuse, in some degree, if not to justify Frontenac's conduct, in the final analysis the main responsibility for the trouble in the colony during these years has to be attributed very largely to Frontenac's egoistic and tempestuous character.

CHAPTER FOUR

FRONTENAC AND THE CLERGY

FRONTENAC'S relations with the clergy can be properly understood only when they are viewed against the background of the relations between church and state in France. In the latter half of the seventeenth century a confused but bitter struggle was in progress between the members of the Gallican movement and the ultramontanists. In practice Louis XIV was almost as much the head of the church in France as Henry VIII had earlier made himself in England. He claimed jurisdiction in questions of appointments to senior ecclesiastical posts, and to some extent in doctrinal matters; yet the link with Rome was real and it proved inordinately difficult to devise a clear-cut separation of spiritual and temporal powers. Between 1663 and 1682 there were continual conflicts arising from the claims of the Gallicans to the supremacy of the Council of prelates in matters of faith and the counter-claims of the pope to infallibility in such matters. Louis XIV vacillated between these two forces. He could not allow the supreme claims of the Gallican church, since this would have created a power in the land perhaps strong enough to challenge his own. Yet to deny the claims of the Gallicans to the supremacy of the Council logically implied papal infallibility, since there had to be some authority to render final judgement in questions of morality and religion. This led to turmoil and friction, with Louis XIV supporting first one, then the other, but never wholeheartedly supporting either. The French clergy thus had two masters, the king and the pope, both demanding their obedience; the separation of powers between church and state was not only ill-defined but in contest. This made the king and his ministers very sensitive and suspicious; the slightest manifestation of independence by the clergy appeared to them to be an attempt to challenge the authority of the state. It was this climate of opinion that was transplanted to New France by officials of both church and crown.

Another factor, of particular significance to Canada, was the vehemently anti-clerical attitude of the minister of marine. Colbert regarded the clergy as little more than parasites; he was struggling to increase the economic strength of the kingdom by every means at his disposal and he bitterly resented the continued existence of the hordes of clergy who, it was estimated, consumed one quarter of the country's wealth [1] yet contributed little or nothing of a tangible nature. He betrayed his thoughts on this question in a memoir discussing the causes of the great wealth of England and the Netherlands as compared to France, wherein he remarked: "There are no monks in Holland or in England." His schemes for the strengthening of the French economy demanded an increase in the population to provide a greater labour force and a larger market for the country's produce; here was another reason for his detestation of the clergy—they were celibate. He regarded this condition as active disloyalty, if not subversion, and stated that the clerics "not only shirk the labour which would aid the common good, but also deprive the public of all the children whom they could produce to serve useful and necessary functions." [2]

In New France it was the Society of Jesus that was the most suspect in Colbert's eyes and Frontenac's official instructions stated that if the Jesuits "wished to carry the ecclesiastical authority farther than it should extend, it is necessary that he should give them gently to understand the line of conduct which they must observe, and in case they do not mend their ways he will adroitly oppose their schemes without its producing any rupture or bias, and advise His Majesty of all that occurs in order that he may impose the proper remedy." [3] These written instructions were accompanied by a verbal briefing by the minister himself. [4]

No one can subject Frontenac's dispatches to a critical examination without becoming aware that he was frequently more concerned with giving the minister not a true account of events or conditions, but with telling him what he thought the minister would like to hear. Frontenac's long apprenticeship at the Court had made him very skilled in this. Since Colbert had stated that he would like to hear that the Jesuits were being kept in their place, Frontenac was quick to assure him that they were; but in order to do this he had first to demonstrate that they had overstepped the mark or were attempting to do so. Thus, in his first dispatch, after he had been in the colony only a matter of weeks, he stated that the priests of the Quebec seminary and the grand vicar were completely under the control of the Society of Jesus, and even the head of the Recollets was under their sway. He also accused the Jesuits of engaging in the fur trade, claiming that their missions in the Indian villages had for their aim more the conversion of beaver than the conversion of savage souls. To curb these activities, and to let the Jesuits feel the weight of his authority, he obliged them to obtain a passport from him before proceeding out of the colony, either to their missions in the west or across to France.[5]

At the end of his first year as governor, Frontenac had several things to complain of regarding the clergy. One of the most serious was his claim that the Jesuits were attempting to institute a form of Inquisition in the colony "a thousand times worse than that of Italy or Spain." According to his account, the curiosity of the priests in the confessional-box knew no bounds. He claimed that they had paid spies in every district reporting on all that went on; and what was worse, whenever they uncovered evidence that someone's morals were lax, they reported their findings to the husband or parents concerned. Frontenac stated that upon learning of this he had remonstrated with the clergy to cease the practice, but to no avail, and therefore he had warned that anyone carrying such tales without furnishing solid proof would be punished severely as a calumniator. Two days after he had delivered this warning, he wrote, a case arose which showed the need for his taking quick action. A husband had been informed that his wife was unfaithful to him, and he had threatened to kill her. The wife went to see Frontenac who promptly had the informer brought before him; she confessed that although she had only her own suspicions to go on, a Jesuit had told her to inform the husband. Frontenac states that he threatened the woman with imprisonment, made her retract her accusations before a notary, then smoothed over the trouble that had divided the man from his wife. This, he claimed, had made others think twice before causing similar mischief.[6]

Undoubtedly the seventeenth-century Canadian clergy were puritanical. During Frontenac's second administration, at the request of the intendant, the superior of the Sulpicians in Paris several times ordered the members of the Montreal seminary to adopt a less bigoted attitude towards their parishioners.[7] However, their severity was perhaps partly caused by the conditions with which they found themselves faced. With so many men spending a year at a time or even longer in the west, it is not surprising that some of their wives became involved in scandals, or that husbands arrived home to find additions to their families which were difficult to account for. Frontenac himself stated that moral turpitude was widespread in the colony. In 1672 he asked the minister to send out some marriageable girls because the bachelors "were responsible for no end of licentiousness in the homes of their neighbours, and particularly was this so in the more remote settlements where the women were quite content to have several husbands, whereas many of the men had difficulty in finding wives." [8]

If the situation was as bad as Frontenac proclaimed it to be, then it would not be surprising if the clergy took active steps to rectify it and they may well have gone farther than a man accustomed to the lax atmosphere of the Court considered justified. It must also be remembered that at this time the clergy were in very short supply. Many settlements did not have a resident *curé* but had to depend on itinerant priests sent out from Quebec by the bishop. In fact, in 1683 the intendant de Meulles declared that at least three-quarters of the *habitants* did not hear mass more than four times a year. [9] It is noteworthy, however, that Frontenac made no mention of the sad state of the people's morals when accusing the Jesuits of having instituted an Inquisition. Nor did he ever refer to this situation again.

One criticism that Frontenac had of the Jesuits was their attitude towards Colbert's so-called "Frenchification" policy. The best definition of this policy is that given by Colbert himself in a dispatch to Jean Talon:

> Always endeavour by every possible means to encourage the clergy . . . to bring up in their communities as many Indian children as possible, so that being educated in the maxims of our religion and in our customs they, along with the settlers, may evolve into a single nation and so strengthen the colony. [10]

Two years later Frontenac was ordered to do everything possible to increase the population, and one means suggested by Colbert was to induce the Indians to live among the Canadians and to adopt French manners and customs. [11]

This policy affords an excellent example of the difficulties attendant upon governing Canada by remote bureaucratic control. Colbert can perhaps be excused for imagining that such a policy could achieve any success, but there can be little excuse for Frontenac's persistently encouraging him in this mistaken idea. Years before Colbert took over the direction of Canadian affairs, the clergy had expended a great deal of time and energy in an attempt to weld French and Indians into a single civilized Christian society. In 1636 Father Le Jeune had established a seminary for Indian children at Notre Dame des Anges. Seven years later the project had to be abandoned; the pupils had either run away, refusing to be cooped up in the classroom and subjected to discipline, or else they had sickened and died. In 1668 Bishop Laval had tried to found an Indian seminary, with no better success than Father Le Jeune; by 1673 his six Huron children had all escaped. The Sulpicians at Montreal had a similar experience and the Recollets too had earlier had to admit defeat. The Ursulines were the only ones who could claim any success at all; by 1668 they had managed to train and educate seven or eight girls who subsequently married Canadians, but this was all they had to show for thirty years' work.[12]

Colbert was convinced that the reason for the dismal failure of his policy was not that it was completely unrealistic, but that the clergy, or more specifically, the Jesuits, were opposed to it. He instructed Frontenac to do everything possible to make them change their views in this matter.[13] Frontenac was very quick to agree with Colbert that it was really the Jesuits who were to blame, and he opposed allowing their missionaries to found new missions in the distant Indian villages, on the grounds that it would be better to assimilate the Indians at the missions already established than to allow the Jesuits to spread out into regions where the main attraction was beaver pelts rather than the saving of savage souls.[14]

When he founded his post at Cataracoui in 1673 he requested the Iroquois to give him nine of their children, and he assured them that he would not treat these children as hostages as previous governors had done. Instead, they would be taught the French language, manners and customs, and when they returned to their villages other children should be sent in their place so that eventually the entire Iroquois confederacy would be assimilated.[15] This part of Frontenac's speech may have been very pleasing to Colbert, to whom a copy was of course sent, but it is very doubtful if it had the same effect on the Iroquois. In his reply, the Iroquois spokesman very adroitly made their compliance with this request dependent upon the French giving them aid in their war with the

55

Andastes.[16] The following year the Iroquois came to Montreal and presented him with eight of their children, four boys and four girls. If the Iroquois demanded a *quid pro quo* in the shape of military aid against the Andastes, Frontenac makes no mention of it; but it seems rather unlikely that they would have made what was for them a tremendous sacrifice, considering the great store they set by their children, without expecting something in return. If the Iroquois did request military assistance from Frontenac, regardless of whatever he may have promised them, they did not receive it. This may be one reason why the western Iroquois suddenly became so bitter towards the French the following year, after they had finally succeeded in crushing the Andastes.

When informing the minister that the Iroquois had presented him with these eight children, Frontenac was loud in his own praise, pointing out that no other governor had ever enjoyed such success and that the Jesuits had been astounded.[17] It is difficult to see why the Jesuits should have been so surprised; their missionaries in the Iroquois cantons had been keeping Frontenac informed of the deliberations that were taking place on the matter and they had done all they could to persuade the Iroquois to give Frontenac the children he had requested.[18] In fact, these missionaries probably deserve a good deal of the credit for the Iroquois' compliance with Frontenac's request. Frontenac, however, went on to inform the minister that the children were now his hostages and as such constituted a guarantee that the Iroquois would remain at peace with the French.[19]

Frontenac's dispatches for the years 1675 to 1678 inclusive have not survived, and consequently there is no evidence as to how well Frontenac succeeded in "Frenchifying" these children. With the boys he probably had no greater success than had the intendant Duchesneau, who adopted three Indian boys with the intention of bringing them up along with his own sons. No sooner had he outfitted them with clothes than they disappeared. Somewhat disconcerted by this, but still determined to do all he could to follow the minister's wishes, he decided to try again with two more boys, but he was far from sanguine of success. "If I allowed them every freedom I would be able to hold them," he wrote, "but my intention is to accustom them gradually to our ways in my home, and the slightest constraint rebuffs them."[20]

The Jesuits and Sulpicians had learned to their cost that when the Indians lived in close contact with the French, each race quickly acquired the worst habits of the other. The Indians became depraved by liquor and committed the most horrible crimes while under its influence; the French, more particularly the youths, acquired the Indians' irresponsible attitude, refusing to take orders from either the civil authorities or their own parents, and, what was worse in the eyes of the church, making the most of the Indian girls' lack of inhibitions. Consequently, the members of these orders adopted the policy of keeping the Indians under their charge well away from the French settlements. The Sulpicians had a large number of Iroquois and Algonquins at their mission on Mount Royal, over a mile from the town proper. The Jesuits had founded a similar mission near Quebec for the Hurons who had fled before the Iroquois in 1649, and several years later they founded a mission on the south shore of the St. Lawrence opposite Montreal for the members of the Mohawk nation who had been converted to Christianity. As a result of the ending of the Iroquois attacks in 1665, many *habitants* took up land near this Mohawk mission. The Jesuits, seeing their efforts to convert their charges being undone by this contact with Christians, obtained from the intendant a concession of land some five miles up river at Sault de la Prairie—known today as the Lachine rapids—but Frontenac refused to confirm the grant and put every obstacle in the way of the mission. According to the Jesuits, he resorted to threats of imprisonment and other menaces, and allowed a tavern to be established near the Indian villages.[21] Frontenac maintained that the Jesuits were merely trying to get hold of good land in a remote area so that no one could see what they were up to.[22] In 1677, in a dispatch which unfortunately is not extant, he explained in some detail why he was so opposed to this particular mission.[23] Colbert, however, was not very impressed by Frontenac's arguments, for in 1680 the king granted the Jesuits the lands at the Sault under the conditions they had requested.[24] Whereas Frontenac had declared that the Indians must be induced to live among the French and not in separate villages, Colbert now declared that such villages could not help but be most advantageous to the colony, and Frontenac was ordered to do everything possible to encourage them.

In 1685 Denonville told Colbert's son, the Marquis de Seignelay, who had succeeded as minister of marine upon his father's death in 1684, that Colbert's "Frenchification" policy had been a complete failure from the beginning; but the mission villages at Sillery, Lorette, Sault de la Prairie and the Mountain were, he claimed, a distinct success.[25] The governor of New York, Colonel Dongan, fully endorsed Denonville's views on this point and was greatly perturbed by it. In 1687 he reported that the Jesuits had converted many of the Iroquois and had induced six to seven hundred of them to remove to New France, "and more like to doe, to the Great Prejudice of this Government if not prevented."[26] The measure of success achieved by the Jesuits and Sulpicians with their Indian missions can, to some extent, be gauged by the fact that these Indians remained loyal to the French throughout the Iroquois war, resisting all the blandishments of their own people and the government of New York to return to their old villages in the Iroquois cantons, or to new ones on land offered them by the governor of New York.

All in all, Frontenac's relations with the Jesuits can be summed up as frustrated hostility. His claims that they were engaging in the fur trade were never supported by any evidence whatsoever. But at the same time it is easy to see how suspicion could arise; the Jesuit missions were always located in the Indian settlements and the missionaries quickly established good relations with the Indians. The French fur traders were quick to take advantage of this and to establish trade centres near the Jesuit missions. Thus the Jesuits inadvertently served the interests of the fur traders, their missions gave them every facility for making a fortune in furs, and Frontenac refused to believe that they were not availing themselves of these opportunities.*

The really amazing thing is that, although Frontenac quarrelled with almost everyone in a position of authority in the colony, he never had any open disputes with the Jesuits. The main reason for this seems to have been that these men, who must have been of a high level of intelligence, adroit, and with polished manners, otherwise they would not have been members of the Society of Jesus, refused to be drawn into conflict with him. Following his bitter

* Even modern scholars are not immune from condemning the seventeenth-century Jesuits on nothing more substantial than the fact that they had the opportunity to make illicit profits and therefore can be assumed to have done so. See C. W. Alvord, *The Illinois Country 1673–1818*, p. 69: "There can be no doubt that the religious order drew a profit from the partnership [with the fur traders], since the Jesuits have always proved themselves thrifty and shrewd in the handling of their property."

struggle with Perrot and the Sulpicians, he informed Colbert: "It is only the Jesuits who have not appeared in any way in all this, despite the fact that they probably have had as much to do with it as the others. But they are more adroit at concealing their designs."[27]

By contrast, Frontenac's relations with the bishop and the members of the seminary at Quebec were always strained. Bishop Laval had crossed to France in 1671 to obtain financial aid from his family for the annates he had to pay as Bishop of Petrea. Until his return in 1675, the grand vicar Abbé Bernières defended the authority of the bishop against what the clergy regarded as the encroachments of the governor. Frontenac had not been in the colony very long before there was trouble over the deference he demanded should be paid his own person and the members of the Sovereign Council when they attended mass on the four high feast days. A dispute over such an issue may seem rather trivial today, but in the closely stratified society of the seventeenth century such things were of great significance to the people concerned. At Versailles it made all the difference in the world whether a lady was seated on a chair with arms, one without, or on a stool; duels were fought and men died to decide who should pass through a doorway first. Thus Frontenac was not being puerile when he demanded that he should make his entry into the church at the head of the Sovereign Councillors, escorted by the members of his household, and preceded by the Sovereign Council's bailiff, with the churchwardens following somewhere in the rear. He also demanded that the Sovereign Council take precedence over the churchwardens in receiving the honours of the incense at mass. The grand vicar objected to this and maintained that the churchwardens had always had the privilege of following directly behind the clergy. Frontenac therefore requested Colbert to order the grand vicar to comply with his wishes in this matter, claiming that it was an attempt on the part of the clergy to raise their authority above that of the Crown.[28] Colbert was quick to uphold Frontenac's demand.[29]

Thus encouraged, Frontenac pressed his advantage and now demanded that the same deference be paid him and the Sovereign Council every Sunday. But by this time Bishop Laval had returned to Quebec and he would have none of it, and this time neither would Colbert. In the king's name, Colbert stated that Frontenac was demanding honours not accorded to provincial governors in France and that he could not be upheld in such pretensions.[30] Frontenac, however, continued to press his demands on the clergy and in 1679 he received a stinging rebuke from the Court.[31]

Another vexing problem, of far greater consequence to the colony than church protocol, was that of resident curés in the country parishes. Each parish wanted to have its own priest and the king was anxious to bring this about. Three things stood in the way: there were not enough priests to go around, and consequently the bishop was forced to keep his priests moving from parish to parish. Even if he had had enough priests to allow each parish to have its resident *curé*, in the majority of the districts there were too few *habitants* and they were too poor to support a *curé*. Lastly, Bishop Laval was not at all eager to see the priests established in parishes, since this would have made them much more independent of his control; he was very reluctant to relinquish his power to move the priests around as he saw fit,[32] as was also his successor, Bishop St. Vallier.[33] This vexing question of resident priests continued to cause friction between bishop and royal officials after Frontenac had been recalled [34] and it was still far from settled when he returned in 1689. Down to the end of the century, the intendant Champigny struggled to find a satisfactory solution that would please everyone, but with small success. This was, however, one contentious issue between crown and clergy in which Frontenac was involved only to a very limited degree and, if anything, he appears to have exercised a moderating influence.

In 1677, two years after Bishop Laval returned to Quebec, Colbert instructed Duchesneau that since the bishop "pretends to an authority a little too independent of the royal authority, and since for that reason it would perhaps be as well if he did not take part in the deliberations of the [Sovereign] Council, you must examine carefully every means and avail yourself of every opportunity to cause him, of his own free will, not to desire to attend any more. But in this you must conduct yourself with great restraint and reserve, and take very good care that no one whomsoever discovers what I write to you on this subject." [35]

Although Frontenac and Laval never quarrelled openly—the bishop was a man of stern character and a very powerful personality, not at all the sort of man whom even Frontenac cared to challenge directly—their acrimonious comments in their letters to their respective correspondents make it quite plain how they felt towards each other. Relations between them were soon so strained that third parties began scurrying for cover lest they get hurt in the expected conflict. In 1679 the Abbé Tronson instructed Dollier de Casson that whenever he had to act upon orders of the bishop in any controversial matter, he had first to get the latter's orders in writing; and should it be thought likely that the orders in question would cause trouble, then de Casson was to send them to Abbé Tronson so that he could produce them at the Court and so justify the conduct of the Sulpicians at Montreal.[36]

Frontenac was not satisfied to report only the difficulties that arose as a matter of course; he went out of his way to create them. Thus it was in 1681, when the Seminary proposed having mass celebrated in the king's magazine in Lower Town to save the people resident there the fatigue of climbing the hill in bad weather. Frontenac gave no indication that he was opposed to the idea, then suddenly posted a sentry at the magazine to prevent the priest entering, and made a great outcry that the clergy were flouting the royal authority. Laval's friends at the Court did their best to make the minister understand that no move would have been made towards celebrating mass in the storehouse had it been suspected that Frontenac would be opposed to it. But the minister was not impressed by their explanations; Frontenac had convinced him that it was another attempt by the clergy to usurp the royal authority, one which only his vigilance had foiled.[37]

The major source of friction between Frontenac and Laval was the sale of brandy to the Indians. The bishop, the secular clergy, the Jesuits and the Sulpicians were all adamantly opposed to this. Frontenac and his followers were strongly in favour of letting the Indians have all the brandy they wanted, and here the governor had the active support of Colbert. The opposition of the clergy stemmed from the terrible effects that liquor had on the Indians. The reason for this was not that liquor had different physiological effects on Indians than on white men, but that the Indians lacked the moral and social inhibitions that act as a restraining influence on Europeans. The Indians drank brandy in order to become intoxicated; by means of liquor they were transported into a strange new world of experience, utterly unlike anything they had ever known before. It was to them what drugs are to some people today, and its consequences were frequently as disastrous. Once they had had a taste of raw liquor they would do anything to get more until they were incapable of swallowing, and while intoxicated they committed the most heinous crimes.

Nor were these crimes the whole story. When they became besotted the Indians were unable to hunt or defend themselves against their enemies; and after giving them a few drinks, unscrupulous traders could get their entire winter's catch of furs for a jug or two of brandy. When the Indian awoke from his debauch he found himself stripped to the buff, even his blanket and musket gone, and nothing to show for his winter's trapping or trading with distant tribes but a splitting headache and a sour stomach. Indian families, who were now dependent to a large extent on European-manufactured goods, were sometimes reduced to the last stages of misery and starvation as a result of such incidents. A further danger was that liquor reduced the Indian's resistance to disease. In 1701, when the crucial peace between the Iroquois and the French and their allies was being negotiated at Montreal, Callières forbade the sale of liquor to the Indians, fearing a general massacre if any group of them were to become drunk, and also because influenza was rife among some of the delegates. As he explained to the minister, to have allowed them to have brandy while they had this inflammation of the lungs would have been fatal.[38]

Nor was Callières the only layman who saw good reason why the sale of liquor to the Indians should be banned, or at least rigidly controlled. Other royal officials who shared this view were Denonville, Champigny, Duchesneau, Vaudreuil, Meneval, the governor of Acadia, and Pierre Boucher, one-time governor of Trois Rivières. Pierre Boucher stated:

All the Indians who reside near the Europeans become drunkards and that does a lot of harm to our Indians, for, of those who were very good Christians, many have relapsed. The Jesuit fathers have done what they could to prevent this evil. The Indians drink only to get drunk, and when they have begun they will give everything they own for a bottle of brandy in order to drink to oblivion.[39]

One of the most famous of the *coureurs de bois*, Greysolon du Lhut, stated that he had spent ten years among the western tribes, and during that time he had never seen brandy traded to the Indians "that great disorders did not occur which went so far as to see a father killing his son, and the son throwing his mother on the fire, and that . . . generally speaking, it is impossible to trade brandy in the bush and at the foreign missions without running the risk of these calamaties." [40] Another man with a good deal of experience among the western nations, Louis Jolliet, the famous explorer, maintained that anyone caught taking brandy into Indian country should be punished by death,[41] and Jacques Le Ber, one of the most active and wealthy merchant fur-traders in New France, shared Jolliet's views.[42] Jolliet's uncle, Charles Aubert de la Chesnaye, whose opinions were listened to with respect by the minister, was strongly opposed to the brandy trade, and in 1677 he informed Bellinzany, Colbert's assistant, of his views.[43]

One account gives an all too graphic picture of the effect brandy had on the Indians:

> The village or the cabin in which the savages drink brandy is an image of hell: fire flies in all directions; blows with hatchets and knives make the blood flow on all sides; and all the place resounds with frightful yells and cries. They bite off each other's noses, and tear away their ears; wherever their teeth are fixed, they carry away the morsel. The father and the mother throw their babes upon the hot coals or into the boiling kettles. They commit a thousand abominations—the mother with her sons, the father with his daughters, the brothers with their sisters. They roll about on the cinders and coals, and in blood. In this frightful condition they fall asleep among one another; the fumes of the brandy pass away, and the next morning they awake disfigured, dejected and bewildered at the disorder in which they find themselves.[44]

Although this sort of thing did not always occur when the Indians got hold of brandy in large quantities, it occurred frequently enough to make those who witnessed such a scene, if they had any conscience at all, violently opposed to the unrestricted trading of brandy.

The story was the same in New York. In 1687 Peter Schuyler, a magistrate of Albany, informed Governor Dongan: "We find that the selling of strong liquor to the Indians is a great hindrance to all designs they take in hand, [they] stay a drinking continually at Shinectady, If your Excellency would be pleased to prohibit itt for two or three months would do very well."[45] And Dongan was glad to oblige, ordering that those found guilty of supplying liquor to the Indians would be heavily fined or whipped by the public executioner if they had not the amount of the fine. A few years later this order was repeated by Dongan's successor, Governor Fletcher.[46] Even the English and Dutch interlopers who evaded the Albany laws and traded in the Indian villages, and who were generally regarded as scum, were appalled by the effects their liquor had on the Indians; so much so that they used to lace their rum with laudanum so that the savages would be rendered unconscious before they could do too much harm in their drunken frenzies.[47]

The Indians themselves, in the rare instances where their views on the subject are recorded, made it plain that they regarded liquor as a curse inflicted on them by the white man. In 1693, chiefs of four of the Iroquois nations petitioned Governor Fletcher at Albany : "Wee desire your Excellency will be pleased to prohibite the selling of rum whilst the warr is soe hott, since our soldiers cannot be kept within bounds when they are drunk."[48] The following year the Onondagas told the Albany authorities: "Wee desire you will discharg' the selling of rumm to any of our Nations. Let our Indians have powder and lead instead of rumm."[49] And again in 1698 the Mohawks sent a message to the Albany commissioners, saying "that the people of Schenectady had of late brought Rum to their Castles and bot with it their corn whereby they were in Danger of Starving." They expressed the "desire this may be forbid and that they may have leave to break the Cegs when any rum is brot there." The Albany record continues: "They were answered that care should be taken to prevent any Rum being brought to them, and that they should bring the Rum Traders to Albany."[50]

The tribes allied to the French were of the same opinion. Anything they might have said on this subject to Frontenac was suppressed in his dispatches to the Court; but at the great peace conference of 1701, in the final assembly before the delegates returned to their respective lands, an Ottawa chief rose and, speaking for all the Indian nations, replied to Callières's farewell address. In his speech he said: "you told us that brandy would do us harm; we have drunk none here and are taking none back with us; we ask you to give us an escort to prevent anyone giving it to us as we pass through the settled areas, and in case there are any French fugitives at Michilimackinac who have brought brandy with them to trade with us, we ask you that we be allowed to pillage them."[51]

In the face of all this evidence one might well ask how there could be any controversy over the sale of brandy to the Indians. The answer is a mixture of economic exigencies, human greed, and —some claimed—political expediency. There was one group that refused to countenance any evidence which ran counter to their own interests. This group had powerful adherents; numbered among it were Colbert, de Lagny, Frontenac, Talon, La Salle and a number of traders, pedlars and *coureurs de bois* whom la Chesnaye stigmatized as *canaille*.[52]

For Colbert's attitude there was some excuse; he had no first-hand knowledge of the problem and had to rely on the conflicting testimony of others. His main aim in life was to bolster the French economy; viniculture was a major industry and the problem of marketing the products of the French vineyards appears to have been almost as acute in the seventeenth century as it is today.[53] Consequently, when Colbert knew that brandy could be exchanged for furs at a large profit, he was extremely loath to curtail this market. In the case of Frontenac, Talon, and the members of the fur-trading fraternity, their motives in denouncing all restrictions on the brandy traffic were clearly mercenary. One jug of brandy could bring as much as 100 *livres* weight of furs, and the usual rate was 50 *livres* weight per jug,[54] whereas at the western posts a blanket was worth approximately 4 *livres* weight of beaver.[55] This meant that more furs could be obtained with a few kegs of brandy than with whole canoe-loads of more durable merchandise.

Prior to 1665 the sale of liquor to the Indians had been forbidden by the governor and the Council but the order had been evaded continually. When Courcelles and Talon arrived to administer the colony the restriction was renewed. In 1668, after Talon had begun to take an active part in the fur trade, he had the Sovereign Council lift the restriction and allow the free sale of liquor to the Indians on condition only that they were not allowed to get drunk.[56] The clergy were immediately up in arms; the bishop declared the matter a reserved case and those known to be engaging in the traffic were refused absolution.[57]

This, then, was the way matters stood when Frontenac arrived in the colony. He immediately claimed that it was another example of the clergy usurping the royal authority. He maintained that they had grossly exaggerated the seriousness of the problem, except in the case where someone gave the Indians brandy "in order to get them drunk and so obtain their furs at lower prices." But, he went on, there was no greater harm in the French selling liquor to the Indians than in their selling it to the Dutch or English, who got drunk just as easily as any Indian.[58] This, of course, was exactly what Colbert wanted to hear. Frontenac, however, did issue an edict forbidding the *habitants* of Trois Rivières, Batiscan, and Champlain and surrounding districts to trade liquor to the Indians for their firearms, blankets, parkas, etc., on pain of a 50-*livres* fine; the Indians, for their part, were to be put in gaol and fined one moose hide.[59]

The clergy were far from satisfied with such petty restrictions and the bishop persisted in refusing absolution to brandy pedlars. The intendant shared their views and he informed Colbert that nothing less than a total ban on the sale of liquor to the Indians was needed.[60] Colbert then solicited the views of Talon, who disagreed with Duchesneau.[61] The minister next informed the intendant that he would have to provide statistics as to the number of murders, assassinations, fires and other excesses caused by brandy. Apparently quite sure that Duchesneau could not provide such figures, Colbert added that if the situation were as bad as the bishop claimed, the king would certainly ban the sale of liquor to the Indians, but, since creditable witnesses declared that the situation was not as the bishop stated, the king would not stop a profitable trade merely to curb the excesses of a few. He argued further that brandy was a stimulus to trade: it attracted Indians to deal with the French and kept them from going to the English and Dutch heretics. This last would have meant not only a loss of trade to the French but also a loss to the true faith. In consequence, Duchesneau was ordered to support Frontenac in the latter's attempts to curb Laval's usurpation of the civil authority.[62]

The argument that the Indians would go to the English and Dutch traders if the French refused to supply them with brandy was frequently advanced by Frontenac's coterie, but it will not bear too close an examination. In the first place, the tribes trading with the French could not go to Albany, as the Iroquois would never have allowed them to pass through their lands to deal at first hand with the Albany traders. Nor did the French allies ever show any great desire to trade through the agency of the Iroquois, except, on occasion, to bring the French to heel. For the same reasons there was but slight danger of the French allies imbibing Protestant heresy with English rum. Moreover, the danger of this last must have been slight indeed, otherwise the Jesuits would have manifested alarm. The Chevalier de Vaudreuil, several years later, had something to say on this point; in 1701 he informed the minister: "it has been claimed that if the Indians did not get brandy from us they would go to the English. I can assure you that even if a few drunkards did go to them, twice as many others would come to us." [63]

In 1678 the king decided to settle the matter once and for all; he ordered that an assembly be convoked of the twenty leading *habitants* engaged in the fur trade, who were to give their views on the brandy question to enable him to decide what action should be taken.[64] But leaving nothing to chance, or the free expression of opinion, the minister sent a memoir to brief the members of this assembly as to what conclusions he expected them to arrive at. He began it by summing up very briefly the main arguments of the opponents of the brandy trade. He then went on, in much greater detail, to give the arguments of those who advocated the unrestricted sale of liquor to the Indians. He commenced by stating that it was unheard of for a bishop to interfere with trade and that if abuses arose, it was for the civil authorities to punish those responsible; and he went on to state that so far as Canada was concerned, the interdict would be very dangerous, because to declare something a sin in Canada which was not regarded as a sin anywhere else in Christendom would cause the people to defy the regulations, orders and injunctions of the church in other matters. He maintained that although there were examples of the abuses cited, they were not prevalent enough to warrant the bishop's interdict and moreover, those Indians committing the abuses had not been converted to Christianity. Thirdly, he claimed that brandy was needed to attract the Indians to the French settlements where they could be taught the elements of Christianity; and finally, if the Indians did not get liquor from the French they would go to the English, which would mean the loss of the fur trade and a loss to the true faith.[65]

With a briefing such as this, and Frontenac deciding who would compose the assembly, the outcome should have been a foregone conclusion. It is noteworthy that such men as La Chesnaye and Charles le Moyne were not selected. La Chesnaye declared, perhaps out of pique at being omitted, that those who had been selected were all men having an interest in the brandy trade and that Frontenac had manipulated them "as a man first in authority could easily do."[66] La Chesnaye, however, appears to have overestimated Frontenac's persuasive powers, since five of the twenty men declared themselves strongly opposed to the brandy traffic on religious, moral and economic grounds.[67]

The following year the king, disregarding Colbert's pronounced views, issued an edict which forbade all his subjects, French and Indian alike, to transport liquor to the Indian villages or to give the Indians visiting the French settlements enough to make them drunk.[68] Once the edict had been registered and promulgated by the Sovereign Council, the bishop withdrew the interdict in accordance with the king's orders.[69] On the face of it this seemed to be an equitable piece of legislation; but the clergy knew only too well that so long as men such as Frontenac were responsible for enforcing it, there was small chance of its being effective. In any event, Frontenac could not have curbed entirely the abuses which the edict was intended to guard against, but he certainly could have done much more than he did. Throughout Frontenac's second administration, whenever the intendant Champigny attempted to enforce the edict he was balked by the governor; and when the *habitants* saw Frontenac openly conniving at its evasion, there was little hope of their abiding by it.

In the battle over brandy the Sulpicians had remained in the background, although they were just as much opposed to the abuses as were the Jesuits.[70] The main reason for this was that they had been strictly ordered by the Abbé Tronson, their superior in Paris, to avoid taking part in all such controversies.[71] Upon his first arrival in the colony Frontenac had been on excellent terms with the members of the seminary at Montreal and he had informed Colbert that their superior, Dollier de Casson, appeared to have the best of intentions.[72] Then, as a result of the Fénelon fracas, Frontenac's attitude towards the Messieurs de St. Sulpice underwent a violent change. In his attempts to have Fénelon condemned by the Sovereign Council on charges of sedition and rebellion for his support of Perrot, Frontenac became embroiled with all the members of the Montreal seminary, a member of the Quebec seminary, and the vicar-general. He first attempted to trick the Sieur Francheville of the Quebec seminary and the Sieur Rémy of the

Sulpicians into giving evidence against Fénelon by assuring them that their statements would not be used against the accused.[73] When they discovered that he fully intended to use anything they said against Fénelon, they refused to testify, pleading benefit of clergy.[74] Frontenac then tried to gain his point by having the Sovereign Council levy fines against them,[75] but this was as stupid an action as it was ineffectual; those fined merely declined to pay and the Sovereign Council could do nothing about it, since it was only the Sulpicians who had the privilege of owning private property and their holdings were all in France where the writ of the Quebec Council did not run.[76] At the height of the dispute Frontenac tried to prevent the vicar-general from occupying the bishop's place at the Sovereign Council during the latter's absence, but the Abbé Bernières politely and firmly refused to give way.[77]

Try as he might, Frontenac found himself frustrated at every turn in this battle; when he ordered the Sieur Rémy arrested, this ecclesiastic submitted, then quoted chapter and verse of the statutes to show that the arrest had been effected in an illegal manner.[78] Frontenac had expected to enforce his will by intimidation; when this failed he was enraged and vented his spleen on innocent bystanders. He had two youths arrested for no other reason than their having acted as canoe men for a Sulpician, the Abbé d'Urfé, on a trip from Montreal to Quebec. As a result, the Sulpicians were unable to get anyone to do anything for them, since to do so was to incur the wrath of the governor. When the Abbé d'Urfé called on Frontenac to protest against the calumnies of the governor's secretary, Frontenac flew into a rage and virtually threw the Abbé out of the room. Later, when d'Urfé was making arrangements to cross over to France, Frontenac forbade him to take his valet who, the Abbé claimed, was most necessary to him since he was always deathly ill at sea. Frontenac even placed guards on the ship to make sure that the valet did not steal on board surreptitiously. The Abbé informed Colbert that everyone in the colony "who did not blindly support the governor's interests" could expect similar treatment.[79]

In antagonizing the Abbé d'Urfé Frontenac had blundered badly, for shortly afterwards Colbert's son was married to the Abbé's cousin and Colbert pointedly informed Frontenac that in future he would do well to be especially considerate of the Sulpicians in general and the Abbé d'Urfé in particular.[80] Moreover, when the dispatches of 1674 from Canada had all been read and those persons sent to the Court by Frontenac or who had made the trip of their own volition had been heard, it was clear to the king and Colbert that Frontenac had gravely abused his authority. The clergy's claims of immunity from the civil courts, unless ordered to stand trial by their bishop, were upheld and it was ordered that the vicar-general be allowed to take his rightful place in the Sovereign Council. Frontenac was curtly ordered to cease obliging the clergy to obtain his permission before leaving the confines of their particular districts; he had to cease tampering with their mail and, in general, cease his tyrannizing over them.[81]

For their part in the dispute, the Messieurs de St. Sulpice were taken severely to task by the Abbé Tronson. They were ordered to preserve a strict neutrality in such affairs in future and, no matter what happened, to show respect and submission to Frontenac, since all complaints against them made by the governor would be listened to at the Court.[82] Despite the fact that Frontenac chose to disregard Colbert's orders and continued to insist on the clergy's obtaining passports from him before leaving the confines of the colony, the Sulpicians did their best to remain on good terms with him, and in 1676, upon his return from Cataracoui, they invited him to dine at the seminary. This cordiality is all the more striking since the Sulpicians were at that time engaging in practices which, if Frontenac had been aware of them, would have given him an excellent opportunity to pay off a few old scores. In 1677 the Abbé Tronson discovered that some members of the order in Montreal had been sending furs to Paris under assumed names to be sold for their personal accounts. He immediately forbade the practice, emphasizing that it was a matter of the utmost urgency. At the same time he ordered that their servants were to cease trading in furs for the profit of the seminary; he was very disturbed at the necessity for this since it meant a considerable loss of revenue and, although he was able to send funds to make up the loss that year, he doubted if the order could support the added expense for very long.[83] This may well be the reason why, a short time later, the Sulpicians abandoned their mission at the Bay of Quinté on Lake Ontario. Three weeks after Tronson wrote this letter, Colbert sent instructions to Duchesneau ordering him to see to it that the servants of the clergy took no part whatsoever in the fur trade.[84] Whether or not it was Frontenac who had informed the minister of this activity is not known, but there is no evidence that there was any trouble between him and the Sulpicians in this connection.

Two years later, in 1679, the Abbé Tronson, who was well versed in the ways of the Court, saw a means to gain the goodwill of Frontenac and at the same time obtain redress of grievance against Perrot, who was making life most unpleasant for the Sulpicians and many others in Montreal.[85] Upon his return to Canada after his brief sojourn in the Bastille, Perrot had made his peace with Frontenac and the two of them had entered into an uneasy alliance in their fur-trading ventures.[86] By this time Frontenac's credit at Court was definitely on the decline, the minister was becoming more than irked by his excesses, and in his constant accusations against all who opposed him he had been detected in so many exaggerations that they were no longer accepted at face value.[87] When Perrot subsequently returned to France he quickly sensed which way the wind was blowing and he began scheming to obtain the appointment as governor of the colony should Frontenac be recalled. Unfortunately for the success of this scheme, he was foolish enough to talk about it and word of this reached the Abbé Tronson's ears. He promptly informed the members of the Order in Montreal, "here is a means to divide these two." [88]

Whereas before, Mme de Frontenac had supported Perrot at Court against the charges laid by the Sulpicians, she ceased to do so upon learning of Perrot's treachery. The Abbé Tronson quickly allied himself with Mme de Frontenac and the two of them began scheming together to bring about the discomfiture of Perrot. She now lent her support to the Sulpicians' complaints of Perrot's conduct and in return the abbé assured her that he would do nothing without first consulting her. "She is convinced," he wrote, "of the service that I have rendered her with M. Colbert, to whom I have made no complaints at all of M. de Frontenac. She will not fail to inform him of everything that has happened and to speak highly of the attitude that I have maintained towards her, as to which she shows herself well satisfied, and with reason, for, despite the fact that I had excellent opportunities to act otherwise in the private audiences which M. Colbert very graciously accorded me, I have made no attempt to say anything which could do the slightest harm to the peace which you have effected with the governor."[89]

The Abbé Tronson scrupulously kept his side of the bargain. In April, 1681, he informed Dollier de Casson, "There is great dissatisfaction here with M. de Frontenac, but I indicated that for our part we had every reason to be satisfied with him." [90] Thus, Frontenac's relations with the Sulpicians were quite good, with the single exception of the Fénelon case; but after that the Sulpicians had had to walk very warily indeed. The lack of conflict between them and the governor during the ensuing seven years was perhaps due more to the restraining influence of the Abbé Tronson on the Sulpicians and Mme de Frontenac on her husband than to any great affinity between the principals.

The one religious group with which Frontenac was always on excellent terms was the Recollet order. In 1670 four friars had arrived at Quebec and in 1673 Colbert requested their provincial to send out two more "of the most vigorous." He hoped to have a few sent out each year "in order, by this means, to balance the too great authority which the Jesuits have acquired in that country." [91] Two years later five Recollets arrived at Quebec, and the following year, one. Frontenac was well pleased to follow Colbert's suggestion of using the friars as a foil for the Jesuits. In 1673 he did his best to prevent the Jesuits sending one of their missionaries to Acadia, hoping to keep this field vacant until a Recollet could be sent; he finally had to give way, but he allowed the Jesuit, Father Perron, to go only for the winter. [92] He made sure that it was a Recollet who was sent as chaplain to Fort Frontenac, and others were sent to La Salle's posts in the Illinois country. One reason why Frontenac was anxious to have Recollets at these posts was that they made no difficulties over the trading of brandy to the Indians, for if they had, they would very quickly have lost favour with both Frontenac and Colbert.

With the Recollets enjoying Frontenac's favour, it is not surprising that the bishop and the Jesuits regarded them with a jaundiced eye. Despite the fact that in the more remote settlements the *habitants* rarely heard mass and many of them died without the comfort of the last rites, the bishop still refused to allow the friars to leave the confines of Quebec. [93] In 1681 they obtained a grant of land in Upper Town from the king to build a hostel and began building a chapel along with it. The bishop objected to this, partly because it would be practically on the door-step of his palace and very close to the Jesuits, but mainly because he considered another chapel in Upper Town quite unnecessary, and this particular one a positive eyesore.[94] But the Recollets refused to heed the bishop's orders and they received the full support of Frontenac, who had been appointed apostolic general syndic of the order in Canada.[95] Consequently, when Frontenac was recalled the following year they found themselves in serious difficulties. La Barre and de Meulles, the newly appointed governor and intendant, investigated the dispute, came to the conclusion that the bishop was in the right, and so informed the minister.[96] Yet the Recollets still refused to submit: they defied the bishop, the governor and the intendant. It was only after the governor had read to them the minister's explicit orders that they were to obey their bishop that they finally gave way; but even then they did so grudgingly and with a very bad grace.[97] With the recall of Frontenac they should have realized that they would have to tread softly in future, but this, apparently, was something that did not come easily to them, probably from lack of practice.

Frontenac's relations with the clergy were dominated very largely by the attitude of the king and his ministers towards the church and the clergy in France. The Society of Jesus was the *bête noire* of the minister; therefore Frontenac's dispatches were filled with accusations of their nefarious activities, most of which were patently false and none of which he was able to substantiate. With the Sulpicians he at first was on good terms, then clashed with them over Fénelon's role in the Perrot dispute, but when he was pointedly informed that Colbert was favourably disposed to the members of this order, he quickly ceased to be antagonistic. Since the Recollets enjoyed the protection of the minister from the outset, Frontenac gave them his fullest support. It may be that he would have done so anyway, but there is room for doubt on this point. His relations with the bishop and the members of the Quebec seminary were rarely, if ever, good. These clerics were highly suspect by the Court; the king and the minister of marine were convinced that they wished to reduce the royal authority in the colony, and Frontenac did everything he could to foster this belief.

The attitude of the Court had not, however, made it inevitable that there should be conflicts between the governor and the clergy; the Marquis de Denonville later demonstrated that it was quite possible for a governor to be on good terms with the clergy with no discernible lessening of the royal authority and without the minister's seeing anything reprehensible therein. In fact, Frontenac's successor, le Febvre de la Barre, was instructed by the king personally that he desired the governor and the clergy to mind their own affairs without interfering with or criticizing each other.[98] Louis XIV had had quite enough of the continual bickering and quarrelling in the colony. In his dealings with the clergy, Frontenac had employed his considerable talents as a courtier with great adroitness, but in the end it availed him nothing. The clergy in France, although suspect, were not without influence at the Court; by acting as he did Frontenac ensured that they would do everything in their power to discredit him. Despite the fact that the religious orders quarrelled constantly among themselves, they were, with the exception of the Recollets, united in their hostility to Frontenac; and as events were to show, there was a limit to the number of enemies a man in his position could make.

CHAPTER FIVE

THE FUR TRADE

THROUGHOUT the French regime, furs were to Canada what gold and silver were to the Spanish colonies of Mexico and Peru. The reasons for this are not hard to find. The St. Lawrence, Ottawa and Great Lakes waterway provided the French with easy access to the heart of the continent, whereas the English and Dutch to the south were hemmed in by the Alleghany mountains. Their only gateway through this mountain barrier was the Hudson and Mohawk river system, and the Iroquois effectively barred their access to the north-west by this route. Moreover, it was the tribes north of the St. Lawrence, the Huron and Algonquin nations with whom the French traded, who were able to procure the best grades of fur, since the animals in the northern regions had heavier pelts. The geographic advantages enjoyed by the French in the fur trade would, however, have meant nothing had there not been such a ready market for furs in Europe. In the seventeenth century broad-brimmed beaver felt hats, which cost from twenty to thirty *livres*,[1] were worn by all men who could afford them—and doubtless by many who could not. Consequently, down almost to the end of the century, when styles changed, beaver pelts were the furs most in demand for the European market; and the pelts that commanded the highest prices were those that had been worn or slept in by the Indians and hence were known as *castor gras*, or greasy beaver. The grease and sweat on the Indians' bodies and the smoke in their lodges made the pelts supple and loosened the long, coarse guard-hairs which then were easily removed, leaving only the soft under-fur used for the finer quality of felt.

Here again the French were in an advantageous position; the northern tribes used fur robes as protection against the elements to a far greater extent than did the tribes to the south. Since the beaver is very prolific and more easily trapped than most animals, the Indians used this fur more than any other for their robes and so produced the coveted *castor gras* in large quantities. Thus, every-thing combined to make beaver the mainstay of the Canadian fur trade. For moose hides, too, there was always a large market, leather being far more in demand then than it is today; the army consumed large quantities and so did the civilian saddlery trade. The furs of other animals—otter, mink, marten, weasel—were used by the luxury trade and in goodly quantities for trimming the official robes of clerics and lawyers. These last furs, always referred to as *menus pelleteries*, were sold on the free market without restriction; very rarely is any mention even made of them in the contemporary accounts until the turn of the century when, owing to the collapse of the beaver market, the Canadian traders began requesting the Indians to bring in these furs rather than beaver.[2] From this it can only be assumed that throughout the latter half of the seventeenth century the market for *menus pelleteries* was stable and the prices probably lower than for beaver. Since Canada was the only French possession able to supply these commodities, they enjoyed a protected market at home and the surplus beaver was exported to Holland, whence much of it, mainly of a type known as *Moscovie* or *veule*, was transhipped to Russia. And from there, curiously enough, some of this beaver was shipped back again to western Europe, the reason being that Russian furriers had developed a process to remove the soft under-wool used by the hat makers, leaving only the long glossy guard hairs.[3] After being treated in this fashion, beaver pelts made handsome fur coats.

When, in 1675, Oudiette and his associates—usually known as the Company of the Farm—obtained the monopoly on the purchase of all beaver pelts and moose hides, along with the entire fur trade at Tadoussac, for an annual fee of 350,000 *livres*,[4] the ministry of marine at the same time fixed the prices which the Company had to pay for beaver in Canada. At first the price was set at 4 *livres* 10 *sols*, regardless of quality, but the Company soon found that it was getting far too much of the poorer grades, and a scale of prices was therefore adopted : 5 *livres* 10 *sols* for *gras*, 4 *livres* 10 *sols* for *Moscovie* or *veule*, and 3 *livres* 10 *sols* for *sec* or dry beaver, that is, beaver that had not been worn by the Indians and was not well cured. When the Canadian traders brought their beaver in to the Company's office at Quebec, the furs were sorted as to quality, then weighed in bundles of twenty, thirty or up to a hundred. To make sure that the Company agent gave honest value, the merchants had the right to appoint one of their own clerks at their own expense to check the weighing and grading. The agent then deducted one quarter of the value of the furs as the Company's *quart*, or commission, and paid the balance, not in cash, but in bills of exchange negotiable for fifty per cent of their face value two months from the date of issue, and the balance four months later. It is fair to assume that many of the *habitants* would not be in a position to wait this long for their money and would therefore sell their furs at a discount to the wealthier merchants, who would thus reap an extra profit. In addition, all beaver and moose hides had to be brought in to the Company's office before October 20 in order that they could be baled and loaded on board the ships before the close of navigation.[5]

The fact that the prices for beaver were guaranteed, regardless of quantity, acted as a decided stimulus to the trade. In the 1670's the need to limit the quantity was not apparent; by the time it did become so it was too late. For it was not enough merely to regulate prices to the producer; lasting stability demanded that the amount produced be no more than the market could absorb, and this proved to be beyond control. It was not only unfeasible to regulate the amount of beaver produced in Canada, but it also proved impossible to maintain the market in France because it was at the mercy of such vagaries as fashions in men's hats—a narrower brim, for example, could play havoc with the market—and the use of cheaper hat-making materials such as rabbit fur, sheep wool and llama fur from Peru reduced the amount of beaver required. Eventually it began to look as though the economy of the colony would be crushed beneath an avalanche of beaver as the amount exported to France on to a shrinking market increased by leaps and bounds, until the minister, at his wits' end, began seriously to contemplate abandoning the colony entirely.[6] It was beaver that paid the administrative costs of New France, and even allowed the French government to make a sizeable profit for some twenty years through its lease to the Company of the Farm, beaver that furnished the wealth of the colonial middle class, paid for the imports of European goods, provided the capital for other economic activities such as lumbering and fishing, and provided the livelihood of a very large segment of the Canadian population; yet it was all based on very shaky foundations.

There is no evidence that Colbert was aware of all the dangers inherent in this situation, but he did see very clearly that New France would be far stronger were its economy to be diversified and the fur trade kept under control. To him the main dangers latent in the fur trade were its tendency to weaken the military security of the colony and to starve other economic activity out of existence by absorbing most of the colony's very limited supplies of capital, labour and commercial talent. In 1666, when Talon was advocating the establishment of posts in the west, Colbert informed him that it would be far better to concentrate French activities within an area which they could hope to hold securely than to grasp too great an expanse in the interior and one day be forced to abandon part of it with the consequent loss of prestige for France.[7] And a few years later, when the fur trade suffered a temporary decline, he was not at all perturbed; rather the reverse, in fact. He informed Talon that such things were to be expected periodically and that if "Canada found itself deprived of this trade, the settlers would be obliged to engage in fishing, prospecting and manufacturing, which would yield them far greater benefits."[8] To keep the settlers concentrated in the central colony and engaged in these more worthwhile activities, Colbert insisted that they must be prevented at all costs from going to the distant Indian villages to obtain furs; instead, the Indians had to be given every encouragement to bring their furs down to the colony. This was the keystone of his policies for New France; he fully realized that if the tendency of the fur trade to shift out of the colony proper into the west were not checked, then his plans for the colony's economic development would be undermined.

Frontenac's responsibilities were, then, quite simple; in fact, deceptively so. All he had to do was make the *coureurs de bois* abandon their colourful but economically baneful way of life and have them engage in, for them, less remunerative and more humdrum occupations which would ultimately be of far greater benefit to the colony. He had also, of course, to ward off external threats to the French hold on the western fur trade; Colbert did not want to see the fur trade strangled, he merely wanted to keep it under control. And finally, Frontenac had to abstain from taking any part in the fur trade for his private profit and to see to it that neither his servants nor any members of his staff engaged in the trade on either his or their own account; he and the members of his household had to be above reproach in this respect.[9]

Frontenac always vehemently maintained that he was doing everything in his power to implement Colbert's policies. But he had not been in the colony long before letters began to reach the

Ministry of Marine declaring that he was not only engaging in the fur trade for the profit of himself and his associates, but was striving to obtain a monopoly over a large part of it. In his dispatches to the minister Frontenac denied the accusations and retaliated by accusing his accusers of the same crimes. Only some of the evidence submitted to the minister against Frontenac has survived—much of it was given orally—but what remains is convincing enough.

Within a year of his arrival in the colony Frontenac founded his post at Cataracoui, a post excellently located for trade with the Iroquois confederacy and as a base for trading expeditions to the tribes farther west. A more opportune time could not have been chosen for this enterprise. The Iroquois were at war with the Andastes and the Mohicans, hence they were in no position to oppose this encroachment on their hunting grounds. They had been resolved, in any event, to trade at Montreal rather than Albany, for the Anglo-French war with the Netherlands had caused a serious shortage of goods in New York with a consequent rise in prices.[10] Moreover, Fort Frontenac was no sooner built than the Dutch recaptured New York and retained it until the following year. This upheaval made it impossible for the Albany traders, who had a jealously guarded monopoly on the fur trade in New York province,[11] to compete with Frontenac and his associates and it enabled the latter to consolidate their trade relations with the Iroquois without interference.

When Colbert was informed of the construction of the fort he showed a marked lack of enthusiasm,[12] despite the fact that Frontenac had assured him that the post, in conjunction with a barque he intended to have built, would give the French control of the entire lake and that everyone was agreed it was "the biggest thing that could be done for the advancement of religion, for the security of the colony and the increase of trade." He also maintained that it would be easy, by dint of a little labour at two or three places along the river, to enable flat boats and canoes to travel from Montreal to the fort "with far greater ease than one ascends the Rhône."[13] Colbert was not convinced; the building of this distant post was completely contrary to his wishes and he regarded it as a distinct threat to his policies. He informed Frontenac that he was not to make long trips up the St. Lawrence in future but to devote his time to concentrating the *habitants* in villages where they would be better able to defend themselves from attack, instead of allowing them to become scattered about in wilderness outposts.[14] Frontenac countered by claiming that his fort and his great address in dealing with the Iroquois delegates were the only things that had prevented the Five Nations from launching an attack on the colony.[15] This last extravagant claim will not bear a close examination; at that particular time the Iroquois, far from constituting a threat to the colony, were themselves being hard pressed by the Andastes and were pleading with the French for military aid.

Once built, the maintenance of the fort apparently proved to be too expensive a proposition for Frontenac's own purse. With the exception of the supplies that he took from the king's stores and some other material obtained from Talon's agents, the cost of the initial expedition and the supply convoys sent up later the same year he paid for with his own funds and his personal credit, the whole amounting to over 15,000 *livres*.[16] Moreover, Colbert would never for one moment have tolerated the private ownership of such a post by the governor of the colony. Upon his return to Montreal from Lake Ontario Frontenac made an arrangement with two Montreal merchants, Le Ber, who was one of the richest men in the colony, and Bazire, who was the agent of the *Compagnie de l'Occident*, whereby they were to take over the post and operate it at their own expense.[17] Just what personal benefits, if any, Frontenac expected to derive from this arrangement is not known. He certainly regarded it as merely a temporary expedient, for a few months or weeks after it was made La Salle left for France to plead at the Court, with Frontenac's full backing, for the concession of Fort Frontenac and the surrounding lands, which he duly received.[18] It is hardly likely that Le Ber and Bazire would have gone to the trouble and expense of taking over the post had they known of Frontenac's arrangement with La Salle. This may explain why in 1674 Le Ber was a strong supporter of Frontenac, particularly during the Perrot fracas, but later he was one of the governor's most bitter opponents and rivals in the fur trade.

By the terms of the concession which La Salle received from the king, he was required to maintain a garrison of twenty men for two years at Fort Frontenac, to clear the land, to build a church within ten years, and to maintain a chaplain at the post in the meantime. In other words, it was regarded as a seigneury held under normal seigneurial tenure and La Salle received no monopoly rights on the fur trade in the area whatsoever, it being specifically stated that all *habitants* settling at the post had the right to trade with the Indians.[19] Since La Salle had no intention of introducing settlers, this stipulation was a dead letter. La Salle also agreed to repay Frontenac the amounts that the governor had expended on the fort, but this obligation was never completely discharged and as La Salle's creditor Frontenac had a vested interest in his ventures. Throughout his first administration Frontenac did everything he could to advance La Salle's interests, and during his second administration his ties with La Salle's lieutenants and commercial heirs, Henri Tonty and the Sieur de la Forest, were every bit as close; in fact, Frontenac has to be regarded as virtually their partner in the fur trade.

On the strength of La Salle's concession Frontenac and his associates were able to monopolize the French share of the Lake Ontario fur trade. That Frontenac personally engaged in this trade for his own account is vouched for by none other than La Salle who, in one of his lengthy memoirs, off-handedly states that for several consecutive years Frontenac went up to Cataracoui with forty canoes to trade with the Iroquois.[20] The people of Montreal had clearly foreseen this development; they had instantly recognized that Fort Frontenac would be a means to forestall them. They had protested against it vigorously, but to no avail; Perrot's imprisonment had shown them, as it had been intended to do, that opposition to Frontenac's schemes was dangerous. Fortunately for Montreal, the Lake Ontario trade was only a small part of the total French trade, the bulk of which was with the Ottawas farther west. The ones who were threatened the most severely by Fort Frontenac were not the merchants of Montreal but those of Albany.

Once La Salle had his barque and brigantine constructed at Fort Frontenac it was very easy for his men to transport trade goods to the Iroquois villages, and by taking the goods to the cabin doors of their customers they were able to offset the much lower prices of similar goods at Albany. The Senecas, for example, who were the most numerous and most westerly of the Iroquois nations, were saved a journey of well over two hundred miles by La Salle's men. The Albany merchants never made any real attempt to counter this threat; they were content to wait for the Iroquois to come to them with their furs rather than to take trade goods to the Iroquois villages, and they had enacted strict laws to prevent interlopers forestalling them.[21] What perhaps inhibited them more than legal barriers was the problem of communications; it was far more difficult and costly for them to transport goods by pack-horse over forest trails than for La Salle's men to transport them down Lake Ontario by sail. Another reason may have been that the Albany merchants had no need to go far afield for furs since large quantities were smuggled down to them by the French.[22]

Colbert made only two exceptions to his policy of concentrating French activities in the St. Lawrence valley. The first was that possession could be taken of distant lands if there was the danger of some other nation occupying them and so threatening French trade, though Colbert saw little danger of this occurring in the visible future; the second contingency was the possible discovery of some new route from Quebec to a southern sea where an ice-free, year-round port could be established. This, Colbert considered, would be of tremendous value to the colony because, as he put it, "the worst thing about Canada is the entrance to the river which, being so far north, allows ships to enter only during four, five or six months of the year."[23] In August, 1674, just three months after Colbert wrote this dispatch, Louis Jolliet returned to Quebec from his voyage down the Mississippi to within a few days' journey of the Gulf of Mexico.[24] Here seemed to be the route that Colbert desired; moreover, it passed through a vast area peopled by tribes having an abundance of furs. But the minister had no intention of allowing this discovery to undermine his schemes for colonial development, and when Jolliet petitioned the king to be allowed to establish a settlement in the Illinois country, he was curtly refused on the grounds that the population in the colony proper would have to be greatly increased before there could be any thought of settling these distant lands.[25]

Frontenac and La Salle, however, evolved a scheme to gain, through the influence of their friends at the Court and by skilfully disguising their real aims, what had been denied to Jolliet.[26] In 1676, apparently without informing the minister, who would have been most unlikely to approve, Frontenac went to Niagara to speed the construction of a new post.[27] The following year La Salle crossed to France and succeeded in obtaining the king's permission to engage in exploration to locate the mouth of the Mississippi and to build forts wherever necessary on the same conditions as applied to his concession at Fort Frontenac: that the undertaking be accomplished within five years, that he do no trading whatsoever with the Ottawas or any of the other tribes who traded their furs at Montreal, and that the undertaking be executed entirely at his own and his associates' expense. To help defray the costs, he was granted a monopoly of the trade in buffalo hides.[28]

The granting of this concession marked a turning point in the history of New France. It doomed any chance of success that Colbert's plans for the colony might have had. Colbert granted the concession to La Salle—under the king's name—because it appeared to be one way to discover the desired southern sea route to Canada and at the same time perhaps to locate supplies of valuable minerals at no expense to the crown. In 1678 La Salle returned from France and in December he was at Fort Frontenac accompanied by the Sicilian soldier of fortune, Henri Tonty. The following November they built the first of their posts, at the mouth of the St. Joseph River, and a few months later Fort Crèvecoeur was built on the Illinois, to be followed soon after by Fort Prudhomme on the Mississippi below the Ohio. From these bases they were able to monopolize the trade of the Illinois and Miamis tribes who previously had traded with the Ottawa middlemen. Not satisfied with this, La Salle and his men soon began trading in the Ottawa country where the better-quality furs were to be obtained. La Salle also began issuing his personal licences permitting the recipients to send canoes to trade in the south-west.[29]

Three years after La Salle had received his concession Colbert became rather irked by the paucity of results and by the frequent complaints that reached him of the activities of this "explorer." Writing over the king's signature he informed Frontenac that La Salle had to stop his practice of issuing his personal permits to trade with the Indians in the west and, he added, "so far I have seen little success attend the enterprises of the Sieur de la Salle in the discovery of the western part of Canada."[30] Frontenac was quick to defend his associate; he informed the minister that despite incredible hardships and disasters, La Salle was now ready to continue his explorations and would descend the Mississippi to the sea the following spring. As for La Salle's issuing of trading permits, Frontenac did not deny it but tried to minimize the fact, stating that La Salle had issued not more than three or four to persons who had aided him in one way or another in his explorations and that these permits were valid to trade only within the confines of La Salle's concession.[31]

It might be asked why, since La Salle had been granted the monopoly only of buffalo hides, anyone would see any need to obtain a permit from him before trading in that area. The answer is that Frontenac and his associates chose to regard the buffalo hide monopoly as covering trade in all furs in the Illinois country. Whenever Frontenac issued permits to anyone to travel into the west, he inserted a clause barring the recipient from all trade in the area of La Salle's concession.[32] Any *coureurs de bois* found in the region south of the Great Lakes without the permission of Frontenac and La Salle had their trade goods confiscated.[33] To Colbert, the royal permission granted to La Salle to engage in the fur trade at bases in the west had been a means to an end, namely, exploration of the Mississippi route to the sea. But to La Salle and Frontenac, exploration was not the end but the means to engross the lion's share of the western fur trade.

One of the consequences of the creation of these western posts, first on Lake Ontario, then in the Mississippi valley, was to shift the centre of the fur trade away from Montreal to these and other focal points in the west. This would have been the tendency in any event, but Frontenac and La Salle—with the unwitting assistance of Colbert—accelerated it. In order to compete with Frontenac's associates on something like even terms, the Montreal fur traders were now obliged to hire *coureurs de bois* to take trade goods to the Indian villages; had they not done so, La Salle and his men would have had first pick of all the furs in the west. And even if La Salle's men were not in a position to do this, the fear that they were would have caused the Montreal traders to take such action.

This made it well nigh impossible for Frontenac to curb the growing numbers of the *coureurs de bois*, even had he been willing to make a determined effort to do so. Before leaving for Canada in 1672, Frontenac had been instructed to publish an edict forbidding the settlers from hunting or trading outside the confines of the colony without his written permission, countersigned by the intendant.[34] A few weeks after his arrival he promulgated an edict forbidding the sale of trade goods to *coureurs de bois* or the purchasing of furs from them on pain of confiscation of goods and a fine of 150 *livres* or more; anyone caught trading outside the colony without a permit was to be flogged, and sent to the galleys for a second offence.[35] This Draconic law had no appreciable effect, and the following year Frontenac stated that the *coureurs de bois* were increasing in numbers all the time. He blamed the people of Montreal for this, claiming, with good cause, that they were in league with the outlaws and that the officials, instead of aiding him in arresting the miscreants, were the first to give them warning. He also laid part of the blame at the doors of the governors of New York and Albany, stating that they gave refuge to these French renegades in the hope of making use of them in the event of future hostilities between England and France.[36] In 1674 twelve *coureurs de bois* were arrested and brought to Montreal while Frontenac was there. He had one of them put to death out of hand, *pour encourager les autres*, and he boasted that as a result of this and his arrest of the governor of Montreal, all but five of the *coureurs de bois* at large had returned to the colony and promised to mend their ways.[37]

Reports soon began to reach Colbert that Frontenac himself was in league with certain of the leading *coureurs de bois* and was carrying on a lucrative trade, through their agency, for his own account. In 1675 he was ordered to put a stop to this practice.[38] That same year the intendant Jacques Duchesneau arrived in the colony to take up his duties; within a very short time he and the governor were engaged in bitter disputes. Some of their most violent quarrels centred about the fur trade, and the intendant sent very detailed accounts of Frontenac's illicit trading activities to the minister. Colbert could not admit to Duchesneau that he gave these charges credence; to have done so would have reduced the governor's prestige, and since the governor represented the person of Louis XIV, this would have cast a shadow on the king's absolute authority. But the minister was in no doubt as to the truth of the matter and he sent repeated warnings to Frontenac to cease.[39]

In 1678 a new edict forbidding trading outside the confines of the colony was issued by the king and this time it was sent for promulgation not to Frontenac, but to Duchesneau. In this edict it was baldly stated that the prohibition on such trading, contained in the edict of 1676, was being evaded by the issue of too many hunting permits. Henceforward, no one was to be allowed to go more than one league beyond the limits of cleared land. Since it was Frontenac who issued these hunting permits, the king's edict clearly implied that he was responsible for the infractions of the earlier one. At the same time, over the king's signature, Colbert informed Frontenac that although he was certain that no nobleman occupying a post such as that in which Frontenac had been placed would ever engage in trade either directly or indirectly, he still felt it necessary to forbid the practice absolutely. Frontenac had to be so circumspect in this connection that not even a breath of suspicion could exist in the minds of the *habitants*.[40]

One means whereby Colbert hoped to prevent the exodus of the fittest men in the colony to trade up country was the establishment of public markets, to be held three or four times a year in the most convenient centres, so that when the Indians came to the settlements with their furs all the *habitants* would have an opportunity to engage in the barter on equal terms. In ordering that these fairs and markets be established, Colbert concluded by saying that this was one of the most important things to be carried out for the good of the colony.[41] These fairs were held at Montreal, on the common between the river and the town, whenever the Indians came down from the west. The actual fairground was separated from the town by a stream spanned by a bridge. Nearby, the Indians made their encampment but no trading was supposed to take place there. The *habitants* had to obtain a licence before being allowed to trade, but, that done, they could set up their stalls to display their wares just as in the public squares of any European town on a market day.

For the citizens of Montreal this was the most important event of the year. Sometimes as many as four to five hundred Indians at a time came down and *habitants* from as far away as Quebec travelled up to Montreal to share in the trade or just to see the sights.[42] A great feast for the Indians was usually given by the governor in the courtyard of the hospital. The sisters of the Hôtel Dieu thoughtfully preserved the recipe for the main dish. Some six large cauldrons were partly filled with water, to which was added corn, large fat dogs and cats, bears, beaver and any other wild animals available, first lightly grilled over hot embers to remove the hair and fur—it was not customary with the Indians to draw the smaller animals before cooking them. This mixture was allowed to simmer for half a day, grapes and raisins were then added for seasoning and the resulting *ragoût* boiled for another two hours. When it was deemed ready, the chiefs were served first, eating out of wooden bowls, and the rest then helped themselves.[43] Once everything had been consumed they all belched as loudly as they could to show their appreciation to their hosts.

Throughout the duration of the fair, the town's tavern-keepers

86

must have done a roaring trade—the intendants frequently complained that every second house in Montreal appeared to be a tavern—and the task of maintaining order must have been by no means easy. Certainly the scene was a very colourful one as the half-naked, bronzed nomads of the forest rubbed shoulders with the subjects of Louis XIV, the one group barely emerging from the age of wood and stone, the other a product of one of Europe's most civilized epochs, and both equally proud.

If, however, Duchesneau is to be believed, these fairs did little to serve the purpose intended by Colbert. According to his account, as soon as the Ottawas arrived at Montreal Frontenac appointed guards, ostensibly to protect the Indians. In actual practice they used their authority to extort furs from their wards, and to add to the injury, the Indians were obliged to pay for the privilege of having these so-called guards. Then, before any trading was allowed to take place, Frontenac had to be given his "presents" of several packets of beaver pelts; if other furs were offered, they were rejected by the governor, who declared "that such would not open his ears." Duchesneau also claimed that Frontenac, through his agents, purchased a goodly portion of the furs brought down by the Ottawas and permitted non-resident merchants from France to carry on an extensive commerce by similar means, despite the fact that they had been forbidden by the Sovereign Council to trade at the fair. Thus, Duchesneau concluded, when the furs traded or extorted by Frontenac's followers, plus those obtained by the French merchants, were deducted from the total brought down by the Ottawas, very little was left for the *habitants*.[44]

The Sulpicians, too, submitted a memorial to the minister complaining of much the same abuses at Montreal as Duchesneau had described and in greater detail,[45] but as a result of an understanding between their superior in Paris and Mme de Frontenac, they confined their complaints strictly to the crimes of Perrot, making no mention of Frontenac's complicity. The following year, 1681, the disorders at the fair diminished considerably, but only because very few of the Ottawas came down to Montreal, owing to the serious threat of war with the Iroquois and to rumours, spread by the *coureurs de bois*, that smallpox was rife in the colony.[46] This marked the virtual end of the Montreal fur fairs; from then on the bulk of the trade was transacted up country by the *coureurs de bois*, and Duchesneau bitterly remarked, ". . . what is most deplorable is that almost all the furs fall into three or four hands." [47]

Duchesneau claimed that it was impossible to curb the activities of the *coureurs de bois* as long as Frontenac was in league with certain of them, notably two named La Taupine and Du Lhut, the latter being the brother-in-law of the Sieur de Louvigny, a lieutenant in Frontenac's guards. In 1678 Duchesneau learned that La Taupine had gone up country with two companions. The following year he returned alone with a canoe-load of beaver, his two companions having remained in the Ottawa country with Du Lhut. When Duchesneau heard of this he had La Taupine arrested and brought in for interrogation prior to being sent before the courts for trial. But when the accused produced a permit, signed by Frontenac, authorizing him to make the trip to the Ottawa country, Duchesneau had to release him. No sooner had this been done than the town-major of Quebec arrived with a squad of soldiers and written orders from Frontenac to free La Taupine, by force if necessary, should the intendant have imprisoned him. [48]

In his version of this incident Frontenac claimed that La Taupine had persuaded the Ottawas to come down to Montreal to trade, to the great satisfaction of the *habitants*, and for performing this public service Duchesneau had thrown him into gaol. This, Frontenac stated, was merely another example of the petty things that Duchesneau was constantly doing to create suspicions of his conduct in the minister's mind, but he was sure that the minister would never believe all these calumnies. And in a letter to the king he protested his complete innocence of ever having engaged in the fur trade. [49] Duchesneau maintained otherwise. He reported to the minister that the king's orders forbidding trading outside the colony were completely without effect. This was not for lack of effort on his own part, he added; he had published edicts against the *coureurs de bois*, against the merchants who supplied them, against those who gave them asylum when they returned to the colony, and even against those who knew of such activities and failed to report the matter to the local judge; yet it had all been in vain, because some of the leading families in the colony were engaged in these illegal activities and could count on the active support of the governor who sold, through them, the furs that he obtained by various means. "There is," he wrote, "practically a state of general disobedience in this country; it is estimated that the number of those in the bush is nearly five or six hundred, not counting those who go off every day" [50]

Frontenac stated that the agents of the Company of the Farm had asked him not to enforce the edicts against the *coureurs de bois* too severely lest they go over to the English of New York and take their furs to Albany. That this was a distinct danger was vouched for by Duchesneau, who reported that one or two of the leading outlaws had already turned renegade and were scheming to draw all the *coureurs de bois* into the service of the Albany merchants and with them the entire trade of the Ottawas.[51] Frontenac suggested that the best remedy for the situation would be to do as he had done in 1674, that is, hang one of the outlaws as a warning to the others. He asked that a royal edict be issued reincorporating the death penalty, and that the edict of 1672, embodying stiff penalties against those who supplied the outlaws and purchased their furs, be renewed. He also suggested posting squads of men at the river passages to arrest the *coureurs de bois* as they came and went. Then, in the same dispatch, he declared that harsh measures might well drive these men into the Albany camp, and therefore he advised the minister that it would not be wise to impose anything stronger than an edict against those equipping and giving refuge to the renegades, with corporal punishment for a second offence.[52] The rather startling inconsistency in Frontenac's recommendations reflects very clearly the dilemma that the government was in.

By this time Colbert was convinced that Duchesneau's accusations, placing all the blame for the activities of the *coureurs de bois* on Frontenac's shoulders, were true, since they were amply substantiated by reports from other quarters. He told Frontenac bluntly: "it is clear to me that this fault stems from you alone because you protect those who follow this calling," and, he added, "I see that all too often you turn the execution of my orders against the purpose for which I give them." [53] Frontenac riposted to these charges by levelling similar accusations at the intendant, maintaining that Duchesneau and his secretary, Denis Riverin, and the Sieur Provost, the town-major of Quebec, were in partnership with La Chesnaye, Le Moyne and Le Ber, the three leading merchants in the colony. He claimed that the *coureurs de bois* were employed by this group, who supplied them with trade goods and received the furs they brought back from up country. He also accused Duchesneau of smuggling vast quantities of trade goods into the colony, intimidating the agents of the Company of the Farm to prevent their taking an inventory of the goods, and refusing to take any action when he was informed that canoes belonging to his associates were leaving for the west.[54]

There can be no doubt that La Chesnaye, Le Ber and Le Moyne employed *coureurs de bois* to trade for them in the Ottawa country —they could hardly have remained in business for so long had they not—but it was now too late for such countercharges to do Frontenac any good. In his dispatches to the Court, his virulent attacks on all who in any way opposed him had been found to contain so many exaggerations and distortions that his criticisms of anyone or anything were heavily discounted by the minister and his officials. Writing in his own hand, something he very rarely did to a provincial governor, Colbert informed Frontenac: "... the public evidence being always against you, and the documents which are sent here being far more convincing, His Majesty cannot forbear to give greater credence to this evidence than to the evidence which you have produced against the other persons." [55] In conclusion Colbert warned Frontenac that the disorders in the colony had reached such a point, the only remedy appeared to be to recall him, since, far from attempting to curb these disorders, it was clear to His Majesty that Frontenac was largely responsible for them. Yet Frontenac continued to proclaim his complete innocence and the complaints against him continued to reach the Court.

In 1681, with what amounted to a gesture of despair, Colbert decided on a radical change of policy. He now issued two royal edicts, the first of which granted a general amnesty to the outlaws, provided they returned immediately to the colony. Those contravening this edict were to be given the lash and branded with a red-hot iron, and for a second offence were to be sent to the galleys for life. The second edict initiated the system of official *congés* which permitted the bearer to go up country in a canoe manned by three men to trade in the Indian villages. Not more than twenty-five of these *congés* were to be granted, free of charge, in any one year by the governor; they all had to be countersigned by the intendant and it was clearly laid down that no one was to receive a *congé* two years in succession.[56] There was nothing to stop the recipient of a *congé* from selling it to the highest bidder if he wished, or hiring others to go up country and trade for him; thus it was not only the able-bodied men who could benefit from them, and it was not long before these *congés* were being sold, quite legally, for ten to eleven hundred *livres*.[57] It was hoped that the general amnesty, coupled with these licences, would cause the *coureurs de bois* to return to the colony and be content to remain there until it came their turn either to receive a *congé* or to be hired by someone who had. By this means, instead of some six hundred of the fittest men being continually out of the colony, only seventy-five would be away at a time and the remainder would be available for work on the land and in the fishing and lumbering industries.

Frontenac stated with great assurance that these measures would quickly put an end to the trouble.[58] Events were to prove otherwise. The news that an amnesty was to be issued conveniently leaked out before the king's edict was registered by the Sovereign Council; in the interim some hundred and eighty men in sixty canoes made a rapid departure for the west. As Duchesneau morosely remarked, once these men had completed their trading up country they would be able to return to the colony with their furs, avail themselves of the amnesty and be in a state of grace so far as the law was concerned.[59]

The effects of the new decrees were reflected by the amounts of beaver pelts received by the Company of the Farm. In 1679, over 68,000 *livres* of beaver were received; in 1680, 69,000 *livres*; then in 1681, after rumours of a forthcoming amnesty had become widespread, the receipts jumped to 82,900 *livres*. The following year they were 90,353 *livres*, and in 1683 they reached 95,489 *livres*.[60] By 1687 the first ominous rumblings of a crisis in the fur trade began to be heard; in that year the Company of the Farm complained that the market in France was glutted with beaver.[61]

However, one of the most notable of the *coureurs de bois*, Greysolon du Lhut—a man who was patently well educated and who possessed both courage and vision in no small measure—maintained that he and some others of the *coureurs de bois* were rendering outstanding service both to the crown and to the people of New France but were receiving precious little thanks for it. He claimed to have mediated between warring tribes and to have settled amicably other disputes that might have led to war; and these tribal wars, he pointed out, interfered with the fur trade by preventing the Ottawas obtaining furs from the belligerent nations to take down to Montreal. But he also stated that in 1678 two *coureurs de bois* named Brochet and Talon, at the head of a band of Ottawas, had pillaged members of two northern tribes of their furs. As a result of this, one hundred and twenty canoes from these tribes had gone to the English posts in Hudson Bay to trade and would have continued to trade there had not another party of *coureurs de bois* gone to their villages, placated them, and restored French credit.[62] Men such as Du Lhut enjoyed tremendous prestige and wielded great influence in the councils of the various Indian nations of the west; and this, plus the fact that they took their trade goods to the Indian villages, spoke their language, and understood their mores and mentalities, were very important factors in the competition with the Hudson's Bay Company traders, who offered cheaper and better goods than anything the French had, but who remained in their posts and waited for the Indians to come to them.[63] Thus it appears that the *coureurs de bois* were not the unmitigated liability that Colbert imagined them to be.

By 1673 the presence of the English in Hudson Bay was worrying others in the colony besides Du Lhut. In May of that year Father Nouvel, a Jesuit missionary stationed at Sault Ste Marie, wrote to Frontenac informing him that Groseilliers and the English traders, by their great liberality, had already induced a large number of the Indians from the Lake Superior area to trade with them, rather than with the French. Some of these Indians, upon their return, had reported that two English ships had landed in the Bay, put about two hundred men ashore, and in four days had built a fort armed with cannon.[64] In a rather feeble attempt to counter this development Frontenac dispatched to the Bay a Jesuit, Father Albanel, who was very anxious to found a mission among the Indians of the area. It was hoped that Father Albanel, who had considerable influence among these Indians, would be able to persuade them to stay away from the English heretics and instead do their trading either at Tadoussac or with the Ottawa middlemen. Albanel was also instructed by Frontenac to try to persuade Groseilliers, should he encounter him, to return to the French service.[65] Before Father Albanel left, Frontenac gave him a letter of introduction to Charles Bayly, the Hudson's Bay Company's governor overseas, who the previous year had established the post on Moose River which had drawn off the Lake Superior Indians. In this letter Frontenac wrote:

I am delighted to have an opportunity as favourable as that afforded by the Reverend Father Albanel, to assure you of the good relations that I am resolved to maintain with you, and which I have no doubt whatsoever you will reciprocate, knowing the great unity and understanding which exists between our two monarchs. I implore you to assist the reverend father in every way you can, and be assured that I will do the same if ever any member of your company comes to this country, as I could not have a greater pleasure than to find an opportunity to demonstrate to you the extent to which I am, sir, your very humble, very obedient servant.[66]

It would be unkind to the intrepid Father to say that Frontenac was sending a boy to do a man's job, but that is really what it amounted to. Father Albanel arrived at Charles Fort in August, 1674. Despite his glowing letter of introduction he received a frosty welcome. Governor Bayly happened to be a militant Quaker who had seen the inside of a French prison on one occasion for expressing his views too forcibly on the subject of "idol priests." [67] Consequently, Father Albanel was sent to England a prisoner on the first company ship that put into the Bay. So ended this attempt to enlist the hosts of heaven against the Hudson's Bay Company.

Frontenac's seeming lack of concern over the presence of the English in the Bay was not shared by other officials in the colony. In 1681 Duchesneau pointed out that the English posts were a serious threat to the French hold on the western fur trade. He wrote:

[The English] are still in Hudson Bay to the north and do a great deal of harm to our fur trade; the Farmers are suffering by the reduction of their trade at Tadoussac and the entire country suffers because they attract the Ottawa nations, and for the one and the other design they have two forts in the Bay, the first on the side towards Tadoussac and the other at cape Henriette Marie on the side towards the Assiniboines.

The only way to prevent them succeeding in what is harmful to us in this respect would be to drive them out by armed force, since the Bay belongs to us; or at least if it is not desirable to go to this extremity, to construct forts on the rivers that flow into the lakes in order to hold the Indians there.[68]

Colbert was not insensitive to these dangers. In 1679, when Radisson and Groseilliers, dissatisfied with the treatment they had received from the Hudson's Bay Company, decided to try their luck once more with their fellow countrymen, Colbert gave them a pardon for their past misdeeds and sent them to Quebec to concert with one of the leading merchants in the colony, the Sieur de la Chesnaye, on the measures to be taken against the Hudson's Bay Company.[69] Frontenac, far from encouraging them, put every obstacle in their path, so much so that they had to disguise their real objective. Radisson requested the governor's permission to take one of La Chesnaye's boats and establish trading posts down the lower St. Lawrence and up the Labrador coast. But Frontenac refused to allow this without the minister's specific sanction, on the grounds that such posts might attract Indians who normally traded at the post of the Company of the Farm at Tadoussac, and also, that Radisson might establish posts in Hudson Bay itself where "they would encounter the English which would perhaps cause strife and wrangling."[70]

These were strange sentiments indeed, coming from a governor of New France, but Radisson and Groseilliers were never ones to be deterred by the orders of a governor at Quebec. Radisson obtained Frontenac's permission to go to England via Boston to see his wife, whom he had left in that country, and from there to France to discuss the Hudson Bay project with Colbert. That is what he told Frontenac he intended to do; but once clear of Quebec on La Chesnaye's boat, he and Groseilliers proceeded to Acadia, where they wintered. Then in July, 1682, they moved on to the Bay where they captured two ships, one an interloper from Boston, the other that of John Bridgar, the newly appointed Hudson's Bay Company governor. After establishing a post of their own, by means of guile they captured and destroyed an English fort; then, leaving eight men as garrison of their own post, they returned to Quebec on one of their captured ships carrying a cargo of a "couple of thousand weight of beaver."[71] By these means the French managed to give the English company some stiff opposition and at the same time they obtained a toe-hold on the upper Bay.

Fifteen years later, in 1697, when the peace of Ryswick ended the War of the League of Augsburg, the vexing question of the Hudson Bay posts had to be referred to a committee for final settlement. In 1699 the committee was still haggling and in March of that year the English commissioners presented a lengthy memorial stating their claims to the posts. One of the main points upon which they based the validity of their claims was the letter from Frontenac to Governor Bayly, written twenty-six years earlier. The English memorial succinctly stated :

In the year 1670 the Company incorporated sent out one Charles Bayly as Governor of their Factorys and Settlements in the Bay with whom M. Frontenac then Governor of Canada by letter of the 8th of October 1673 entertained a good Correspondence not in the least complaining in Several years of any pretended injury done to the French by the Said Companie's settling a Trade and building of Forts at the Bottom of the Bay.[72]

The consequences of Frontenac's letter, like the housemaid's indiscretion, had not been immediately apparent, but Louis XIV and the French plenipotentiaries must have regarded it with a very jaundiced eye.

Frontenac's apparent indifference to the presence of the English posts at Canada's back door might perhaps be ascribed to a failure to appreciate the magnitude of the threat; but another possible explanation lies in the fact that it was his fur-trade rivals, men whom he regarded as personal enemies, who were anxious to take action in the Bay. He and his associates were not greatly concerned with the northern fur trade, as their main field of activities lay in the area south of the Great Lakes. It was La Chesnaye, Le Ber, Le Moyne and their associates, trading in the Ottawa country, who were directly threatened by the Hudson's Bay Company posts. Moreover, Frontenac may have been aware that the Jesuits had provided La Chesnaye with capital on occasion and had advanced funds to Radisson for the projected enterprise in the Bay.[73] At this time, Frontenac was accusing these enemies of his of inciting the Iroquois to attack the French and their allies in order to cause him embarrassment and hinder La Salle's enterprises in the west, which would have been nothing less than high treason. If he really believed these most serious charges to be true it may well be that he did not look askance at the English threat in the Bay, since it endangered those who he believed were threatening him. This explanation is, however, based on the thinnest of circumstantial evidence.

To the south of the colony too, the English seemed to present a grave threat to Canada's economic security. In the 1670's this threat manifested itself mainly in the smuggling of furs to Albany. Although at this time the actual danger was more apparent than real, yet to Colbert and those of his officials who did not take their responsibilities lightly this smuggling was a very vexing problem. The main reason for its prevalence was the simple fact that beaver sold at Albany for some three times the price paid by the Company of the Farm at Quebec and the Albany merchants paid in hard cash, not in post-dated bills of exchange.[74] Moreover, they would accept furs at any time; merchants with beaver left on their hands after the October 20 deadline for its receipt by the Company's agent would be seriously tempted to send them down to Albany rather than to wait eight months and more for their money, and run the risk of the furs being damaged by moths and rodents in the meantime.

Frontenac stated that it was almost impossible to prevent this smuggling, as the Mission Iroquois were the principal agents and he dared not take effective measures to stop them lest they break with the French and return to the villages of the Five Nations. He also placed part of the blame on Duchesneau and the Sovereign Council, claiming that they allowed confessed smugglers brought before them for trial to go scot free. In an attempt to curb the smuggling, Frontenac permitted the agent of the Company of the Farm to establish a post at Chambly, on the Richelieu River, with a corps of guards.[75] But Duchesneau maintained that Frontenac had been careful to see that the stable was empty before locking the door. He pointed out that it had been on September 12 that the agent had submitted his request for the establishment of this garrison, but that Frontenac had refused to allow it until October 24, after the canoes intended for Albany had got well away. In addition, Duchesneau stated that, although he could offer no proof, it was common knowledge that Frontenac and four of his associates had recently sent 60,000 *livres* worth of furs to the English colonies.[76] After Frontenac's recall the Company of the Farm complained that he had carried on a thriving trade with the merchants of Albany and New York from Cataracoui.[77] This post was certainly well located for this purpose, as there was only a short voyage from it to the mouth of the Oswego River which, when followed to its source, left only a short portage to the Mohawk River leading directly to Albany. This route could be used only as long as the Iroquois were not hostile and this may help explain why Frontenac was so loath to take strong action to curb their growing aggressiveness in the west.

However, despite the fact that this smuggling was completely contrary to French government policy, the colony—if not the mother country—derived considerable benefits from it. The higher prices obtained by trading with the English colonies meant greater prosperity for the Quebec and Montreal merchants and some of them—La Chesnaye being one who is reputed to have engaged in the contraband trade [78]—employed a good deal of their profits in such worthwhile enterprises as fishing and lumbering.[79] Moreover, because the quality of much of the English merchandise was so vastly superior to that of the French, it would have been much more difficult for the Canadian merchants to compete with the Iroquois middlemen and the Hudson's Bay Company traders if they had not been able to obtain English cloth and other goods from some source. A further advantage was that the sale of furs to the English colonials brought sorely needed hard cash into the colony, and metal coin was always in very short supply in New France, so much so that until the intendant de Meulles inaugurated his famous card-money in 1685, beaver skins were in common use as a medium of exchange. To some extent, the contraband trade between New France and New York and Boston was similar in cause and effect to that carried on by the Spanish American colonies with the English and Dutch interlopers. Neither royal edicts nor the best efforts of the most conscientious officials could hope to stop the smuggling completely; the only thing that could have done this was an ability on the part of the French to produce manufactured goods of as fine a quality and as low a price as the English.

Colbert's attempts to regulate the fur trade and to base the colony's economy on more stable forms of enterprise were, from a long-range point of view, very sound. But, with the benefit of hindsight, it is obvious that they were doomed to failure. In 1681 Duchesneau informed Colbert that it was useless to think of basing the Canadian economy on anything but furs,[80] and a few years later the Marquis de Denonville told the minister that the beaver trade had been the ruination of the colony.[81] As Frontenac had pointed out, any really determined attempt to prevent the Canadians trading up country would have driven some of them to turn renegade and take their furs to Albany. Moreover, had there been no Canadians trading in the Ottawa country there would have been nothing to stop the northern Indians taking their furs to the Hudson's Bay Company posts. Frontenac was too much the courtier to try to convince Colbert that his policies were unrealistic; instead, he claimed that he was doing his best to implement them, when all the time he was himself actively circumventing them and thereby encouraging others to do the same.

There can be no doubt that Frontenac took every advantage of his position to profit from the fur trade but, unfortunately, there is no evidence to indicate the amount of his profits. It was widely believed, however, that Perrot cleared 40,000 *livres* in 1680; conclusive proof was given the minister that he sent letters of exchange to Paris for over 20,000 *livres* in 1682, and it was reported that he sold 100,000 *livres* worth of beaver in Niort in 1683.[82] It can only be guessed that Frontenac made at least as much as, if not a great deal more than this, since Perrot made these profits with Frontenac's connivance. It is known that Frontenac corresponded with a merchant of Boston named Sergeant and with a certain Mr. Carbonell, a banker in London.[83] This correspondence may have been perfectly legitimate, or it may have been the means he used to bank his fur-trade gains undetected.

But when all that has been said, the fact still remains that had he not availed himself of his opportunities in the fur trade, he would have been a most exceptional governor. His salary was barely adequate for even a frugal man, let alone someone of his extravagant tastes, with an equally extravagant wife to maintain at the Court. Of all the royal officials in New France, very few were not accused of having abused their authority to mend, maintain or add to their private fortunes. Yet if the moral climate of the age did not absolutely condemn such conduct, the minister most certainly did; and, judging by the complaints which the minister received concerning Frontenac's malfeasance, so did many people in New France. However, the most serious consequence of Frontenac's activities in the fur trade was the division of the colony into two hostile factions, the Frontenac-La Salle group and the Montreal traders; this at a time when external threats to the colony, from the English in the north and the Iroquois in the south, made unity most essential.

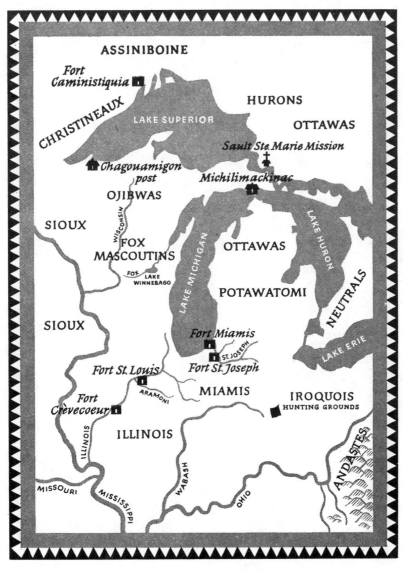

The Seventeenth-century Empire in the West

CHAPTER SIX

THE STRUGGLE FOR THE WEST

THROUGHOUT this period the Iroquois exerted an influence on events in North America out of all proportion to their numbers. Their five cantons stretched in a band from Lake Champlain to Niagara, forming a buffer state between New France and New York. This central position gave them great military and economic advantages; by way of Lake Champlain and the Richelieu River they could strike at the heart of New France and, flanking as they did the St. Lawrence River and Lake Ontario, they could prevent the French using this route to the west. They could also easily reach the main fur-trade route of the French, the Ottawa River and Lake Nipissing waterway to Georgian Bay, by means of the river and lake network between the Ottawa and Lake Ontario.

Owing to their proximity to the northern settlements of New York, the Iroquois were well supplied with English trade goods, which were considerably cheaper and in many respects of better quality than the same commodities offered by the French at Montreal. When once they had exhausted the furs in their own territories south of the St. Lawrence and Lake Ontario, they were forced to begin trapping on the north side of this waterway and to become middlemen, bartering English goods for the furs of the northern and western tribes. For the first half-century after the founding of New France the Iroquois had fought to bar the French from trading with these tribes, and for the same reason it was one of the cornerstones of Iroquois policy to prevent the English gaining direct access to these remote nations. Fortunately for the Iroquois, the Albany merchants showed no particular desire to forestall them, being satisfied to let the Iroquois—and the French smugglers—bring the furs to them rather than to undertake the hardships and perils of seeking to obtain the furs at first hand. Only towards the end of the century did this problem emerge, when aggressive governors of New York, men such as Dongan, determined to challenge the hold of the French on the west. But even then the Iroquois prevented the English from establishing a base on the shores of

Lake Ontario until well on in the eighteenth century. This was the paradox of French-Iroquois relations; by reason of their geographic position and their calculated ferocity the Five Nations were the greatest single threat to the military and economic security of New France, yet at the same time they were the only thing that prevented the English from crippling the French fur trade. Had the Ottawa tribes been able to obtain English goods at first hand, it is more than likely that very few furs would have reached Montreal.

It is unfortunate that our knowledge of the Iroquois and the role they played in the history of North America depends entirely on the written records of the French, the Dutch and the English. Had they themselves left records, our understanding of much that happened during this period would be immeasurably greater. But from the accounts that we have, a reasonably clear picture of the Iroquois character emerges. They were certainly every bit as intelligent as the Europeans with whom they had dealings, and in many instances their leaders were far more shrewd. According to European concepts they were capable of acts of the basest treachery; they constantly amazed the European settlers by their incredible fortitude, and disgusted them by their cruelty. But these traits of treachery, extreme fortitude and equally extreme cruelty they shared with the other Indian nations. The Iroquois were constantly at war with their neighbours and. although far fewer in numbers than the tribes they warred against, they were well able to hold their own. One seventeenth-century observer states that, to compensate for their numerical inferiority, they were the first tribe to practise cannibalism and to inflict fiendish tortures on their prisoners, hoping to terrify their foes into submission.[1] It was this extreme cruelty of the Indians, Iroquois and Algonquin alike, that made them treacherous—by European standards. Every Indian knew from childhood what treatment he would receive were he to be taken prisoner by the enemies of his nation and all his life he schooled himself to endure intense physical pain without flinching, so that were he to be captured he would die like a warrior. It is impossible to understand the conduct of the Indians in their relations with each other and with Europeans without visualizing what it meant for them to be captured. There are numerous accounts of the treatment meted out to prisoners and they all tell the same story.[2]

Once captured, the prisoner was marched by day and tied down at night and left to feed the mosquitoes while his captors slept. Upon arrival at his captors' village, he was made to run the gauntlet and beaten by everyone capable of wielding a club until he reached the cabin prepared for him. Once there he was periodically subjected to such relatively minor unpleasantnesses as having his finger-nails chewed off, his mangled finger-ends placed in the bowl of a pipe and burned along with the tobacco, and blazing brands applied to the more tender parts of his body. This could last for a day or two while a council of the senior men and war chiefs deliberated on his fate. According to the accounts of men who had witnessed such a scene, no more vivid representation of hell could be imagined: the cabin filled with near-naked savages, their bronze skins and cruel obsidian eyes reflecting the flames of the council fire; smoke swirling about in the draughts beneath the roof; the prisoner listening impassively as his fate was being decided. At this council the women could play a decisive role; if one of them who had lost a husband, brother or son in war decided that she liked the looks of the prisoner, she could demand him to replace the man she had lost and this, although it did not happen often, was never denied. In such a case the victim was freed, his wounds dressed, and a few days later a great feast was given at which he was adopted into the tribe. From this time on he was treated as a member of the nation and frequently these adoptees would then join war parties against their former people. But usually the council condemned the prisoner to death in revenge for the death of their own men.

Once this had been settled, the victim was first treated as an honoured guest, brought food and drink and told to eat well as he had a long journey to undertake. Meanwhile the youths and women of the village made everything ready for the spectacle; a stake was planted to which the victim would be tethered, the fires lit and the irons heated. This done, a warrior entered the victim's cabin and told him to have courage, he was about to be burned. The victim was expected to thank his informant for the news and indicate that he was ready. He was then brought out and tethered to the stake by a short rope. And now, with the whole village as spectators, he began his death-chant, recounting all the great deeds he had done during his lifetime, how he had burned his own prisoners, and exhorting his tormentors not to spare him but to give him a warrior's death. While he sang, burning brands were applied all over his body and a necklace of red-hot axe-heads was draped over his shoulders to rest on his back and chest and left there until they had grown cold, whereupon they were reheated and replaced. Pieces of his flesh were sliced off, grilled on the fire and eaten in front of him with a great show of relish. He was asked if he were hungry and was expected to say yes, then to eat a proffered piece of his own flesh and to exclaim that he found it good. He was asked if he were thirsty and when he replied yes, the women poured kettles of boiling water over him. This went on for hours, sometimes days, the poor wretch being tied down to stakes in a cabin at night, until not a part of his body was left unburned. And throughout he had to suffer without complaint or so much as a whimper. Often the victim flung taunts at the jeering spectators, indicating parts of his body that had been overlooked and telling them to watch how a warrior died so that they would know how to act when they were captured by his nation and their turn came. Finally, as the end drew near, the scorched scalp would be wrenched off and red-hot cinders poured on the raw skull. Then, finally, the *coup de grâce* was given and what remained of the charred body would sometimes be cut into quarters and thrown into the cooking pot to be eaten, at other times tossed to the dogs, depending on the degree of fortitude the victim had displayed.

It was this hideous treatment of prisoners that was the main factor governing their mode of warfare, making them such treacherous adversaries by European standards. They had little fear of sudden death, but none of them desired to meet their end *au petit feu*; consequently they took every precaution not to be captured. When they attacked, it was always by surprise, preferably by waiting in ambush. They shrank from pressing an attack unless they had great superiority of numbers and if their first attack failed they took to their heels. If they were caught unawares by a superior force and could not flee, they fought with the utmost ferocity, much preferring to die in combat than to be taken alive. They showed no pity whatsoever for their foes, but they asked none for themselves. The Iroquois, particularly, embodied these traits and were the most hated and feared of all the forest tribes. Because of this, and their extreme stoicism, they were a very proud people. When they failed to attain their ends either by duplicity or by war, they accepted their fate without a murmur. This, at times, invests them with an air of nobility which the seventeenth-century

French, themselves not a squeamish people, were quick to appreciate.

The chief military weakness of the Iroquois was, again, the result of certain traits inherent in the Indian character: their individualism and their total lack of discipline. These made it difficult for them to take concerted action or to make a sustained effort. They were like a ship without a rudder, manned by a quarrelsome crew, able to maintain a steady course only as long as the wind remained constant and some common danger forced the crew to co-operate. The Five Nations possessed these defects to a lesser degree than did the Algonquin tribes, largely as a result of their geographic position, which gave them common economic and military problems. Thus, the Iroquois generally offered a united front on the important issues, whereas their Indian foes were divided and, as often as not, warring amongst themselves. But at the same time, the geographic position of the Iroquois was their Achilles' heel. They were not nomadic tribes as were the Algonquin nations to the north; they lived in permanant villages and to a large extent were dependent on agriculture for their food supply. On almost all sides of them were hostile tribes, and thus they were very vulnerable to a concerted attack by their enemies, for they could not flee any great distance to re-establish their villages and cornfields, as could the northern and western tribes. Consequently, they had to disrupt any coalition of hostile forces that was formed against them by means of military pressure or skilful diplomacy and then to attack their enemies one at a time. In this sort of power politics they became extremely adroit, for had they not they would quickly have been destroyed.

It was vital to New France that the Iroquois should be kept docile, either by force or by diplomacy backed up by force, and that the Algonquin tribes be retained as allies and commercial partners. This task was the major responsibility of the governor, and Courcelles had eminently displayed his abilities in this respect. When Frontenac arrived in the colony there had been peace with the Iroquois for some eight years, French prestige among the Indian tribes had never been higher, and the people of New France no longer went in daily peril of being cut down by marauding Iroquois. But the peace and security of the colony rested on one vital factor over which the French had no control: the war between the Five

Nations and the Andastes,* a war fought for access to the furs of the Mississippi valley. As long as that war continued the Five Nations had to remain at peace with the French. It was a situation that could change at any time, one that required constant vigilance on the part of the governor of New France.

Frontenac's first contact with the Iroquois took place in the spring of 1673 when he founded his trading post at the mouth of the Cataracoui River. The idea of building such a post on Lake Ontario did not originate with Frontenac; Talon had proposed just such a move several years before. He had suggested constructing two forts, one on each side of the lake, and maintaining a sailing barque to cruise along the shores. His motives for desiring these posts and the barque were mainly commercial. He held that the Iroquois garnered over a million *livres* of beaver on the north side of the lake, on lands claimed by the king of France, and that by means of these posts most of this lucrative trade could be diverted from Albany, the accruing profits to be used to defray the administrative costs of the colony. He also claimed that these posts would prevent the English and Dutch of New York from penetrating to the St. Lawrence, and by barring them from the river and the lakes that fed it the French could make them "abandon any ideas they might have of sharing this vast and beautiful country with His Majesty." [3] Actually, this particular argument merely showed that Talon either did not understand the role played by the Five Nations, or that if he did, he did not want the minister to understand it; for it was the Iroquois, rather than any isolated forts that the French might build, who kept the English away from this region. Colbert was not at all enthusiastic towards Talon's proposal. He declined to furnish the hundred regular troops that Talon asked for to man the forts and the barque or the 15,000 *livres* to defray the initial costs. He told the intendant to discuss the project with Courcelles and assist him in carrying it out if the governor was in agreement as to its merits. [4] Since relations between Talon and Courcelles were very strained at this time, and Talon was never one to accept a subordinate role, it is perhaps not surprising that nothing was done about the project.

When Frontenac arrived in the colony he did not wait to discuss ways and means with Colbert. As soon as the ice went out of the

* The Andastes were an Iroquois tribe but, like the Hurons, were not members of the Five Nations. They dwelt on the frontiers of Virginia and Pennsylvania.

river he sent La Salle with instructions to the Jesuit missionaries in the Iroquois cantons, telling them to invite the chiefs of the Five Nations to meet him at the Bay of Quinté the following July.[5] Despite the hostility of the people of Montreal, *habitants* and merchants alike, towards the enterprise, Frontenac's expedition, comprising four hundred men in one hundred and twenty canoes and two flat-boats, negotiated the rapids of the St. Lawrence without incident and arrived at Lake Ontario in mid-July, 1673. Some members of his entourage advised him to build his fort on the south side of the lake at La Famine, but he decided against this as being too close to the Iroquois villages for comfort and likely to arouse the antagonism of the English. Instead, he selected a site in a small bay at the mouth of the Cataracoui River, excellently located for trade with the Iroquois confederacy and useful as a base for trading with the tribes farther west.

When the Iroquois, some four or five hundred men, women and children, arrived at Cataracoui, they were considerably impressed by the size of the French force and the pomp and circumstance with which Frontenac invested all the proceedings. Such things as the gleaming metal breastplates of his guards and the bright red and blue paint of the two flat-boats with their small cannon particularly captured their fancy. While Frontenac was employing his courtier's charm by inviting the Iroquois chiefs to dine at his table, handing out presents to their squaws, and making a fuss over their children, the *habitants* were kept busy erecting a log stockade on the site he had selected. Within five days the work was well advanced and an assembly was convened at which Frontenac addressed the Iroquois, accompanying his speech with lavish presents. Since the Iroquois understood not a word of French it can hardly be said that they were swayed by the power of his oratory, but he was fortunate in having as his interpreter the Sieur le Moyne, who spoke the Iroquois tongue fluently and not only had a thorough understanding of their mentality but also was held by them in very high esteem.[6]

According to the account of this assembly which he sent to the minister, Frontenac appealed first of all to the Iroquois to become Christians and to hearken to the advice given them by the Jesuits to remain at peace with the French and with the Indian nations whom the king had placed under his protection. He stated flatly that he was the master of peace and war, pointing out that having negotiated the rapids with such a large force, he could quite easily do so again and descend on their villages should they not obey his commands. He then went on to exhort them to come to this new post in future to do their trading, promising that it would be well stocked with merchandise at the lowest prices that he could contrive. Finally, he requested them to give him nine of their children, not, as the governors had done in the past, to retain them as hostages, but in order to teach them the French language, manners and customs. He even offered to have them taught a useful trade, but if he expected this last to be any inducement to the Iroquois he had much to learn of the Indian character.[7]

When the Iroquois orators replied to Frontenac, he was quite taken aback by their astuteness and he later remarked to the miniter: "You assuredly would have been surprised, my lord, to see the eloquence, the shrewdness and the finesse with which all their deputies addressed me, and were I not afraid of seeming ridiculous I would tell you that in some manner they reminded me of the Venetian Senate."[8] In fact, the evidence indicates that the Iroquois were by no means as impressed by Frontenac's mixture of threats and promises as he gave the minister to believe. In his dispatch to Colbert he omitted to mention some of the pointed questions that they put to him. They thanked him for exhorting them to turn Christian and agreed to see what could be done about it; they also promised to protect the Jesuits in their villages from the insults of their young men. They professed to be delighted with the prospect of obtaining trade goods so close at hand, but they wanted more specific information on prices. As for giving him some of their children, they promised to discuss the matter among themselves when they returned home. Frontenac's reference to them as his children and his demand that they remain at peace with their neighbours they very shrewdly parried by pointing out that the Andastes were their only enemy, and that it would be shameful of him to allow this tribe to crush his "children."[9]

Frontenac was now forced to qualify some of his earlier statements. He told the Iroquois that he could say nothing about the price of trade goods, since he did not know what the cost of transporting them to the post would be. The appeal for aid against the Andastes he tried to side-step by stating that they could rest assured he would not allow his "children" to perish or be oppressed, but that it was too late in the season for him to organize a campaign that year. He assured them that, when they came to Quebec to inform him of their intentions regarding the children he had asked them to leave in his care, he would discuss the meaures to be taken against the Andastes.[10] This means of extricating himself from an awkward situation into which the Iroquois had neatly manoeuvred him was rather maladroit, as he thereby implicitly obligated himself to give the Iroquois military assistance against the Andastes, assistance which he was in no position to furnish even if he had been foolish enough to contemplate such a move.

Almost every year Frontenac went up to the new post with a dozen and more canoes to trade with the Iroquois, and as long as their war with the Andastes continued they gave every appearance of being subservient to his commands. This appears to have convinced Frontenac that he had great personal influence over them, but events were to indicate that it was not so much a case of Frontenac's having kept the Iroquois docile, but of the Iroquois' having been anxious to appear so. Frontenac, because of the profits to be made in trade with the Iroquois, had a vested interest in maintaining good relations with them, and the Iroquois were equally anxious to remain on good terms with the French while they had the Andastes to deal with. The Iroquois, however, were in a somewhat more advantageous position here, for whenever they chose they could cease to trade at Fort Frontenac and take their furs to Albany. In purely trade relations, then, Frontenac was more dependent on the Iroquois than they were on him; but in the political field, the Iroquois were dependent on the neutrality of the French only as long as their war with the Andastes lasted.

Then, in 1676, the whole basis of the peaceful relations between the French and the Iroquois was shattered. In May of that year the Andastes suffered heavy losses in a surprise attack, not by the Iroquois, but by over two hundred Virginia frontiersmen led by Nathaniel Bacon.[11] The Andastes immediately sued for peace with the Five Nations, quit their lands, and were assimilated by their old enemies.[12] They then began to ravage the Virginia frontier settlements.[13] And at about the same time that the western Iroquois received this great adjunct to their military strength, the eastern Iroquois also were freed from the intermittent attacks of the Mohicans. For some reason that is not clear this Algonquin tribe made its peace with the Iroquois, deserted the French alliance and allied itself with Albany.[14]

With this sudden and unheralded turn in their fortunes, the attitude of the Iroquois towards the French underwent a marked change. Whereas a few years earlier the Jesuit missionaries had commented on how well disposed towards the French were the Senecas and Cayugas,[15] these tribes now became extremely hostile, threatening war to both the French and their allies, and the Jesuits in their midst began receiving the worst of treatment, never knowing from one moment to the next when they would be seized, tortured and burned over a slow fire.[16] The defeat of the Andastes and the defection of the Mohicans had shifted the balance of power to the detriment of the French, who now had to be prepared to counter any Iroquois move. It was precisely at this point, with the Iroquois at the peak of their strength and determined to renew their old struggle to wrest control of the western fur trade from the French and their allies, that La Salle, with Frontenac's full support, began encroaching on lands claimed or coveted by the Iroquois. The expansionist aims of both the French and the Iroquois confederacy now made a clash inevitable.

In 1676 Frontenac and La Salle built their post at Niagara as a base for advances farther into the west. Two years later the Senecas invaded the Illinois country, but were repulsed. The following year La Salle began building his posts in the Illinois country. In two giant leaps the French had advanced their commercial empire to the heart of the continent, thereby outflanking the Iroquois. They now claimed suzerainty over the Illinois' and Miamis' lands, and in so doing they bound themselves to give military aid to these tribes. And all this took place without the minister in Paris knowing the full extent of the French commitments or what was actually going on under the guise of "western exploration." La Salle's new fur-trade base was situated nearly a thousand miles from the main base at Montreal, the communications between the two being flanked throughout most of their length by the Iroquois, who regarded the French action as tantamount to a declaration of war.

Yet, despite the reports reaching Frontenac from the Jesuits in the western missions, the Recollets at Fort Frontenac, and the Sulpicians at Quinté that the Iroquois were preparing to strike back,[17] there is no evidence that he appreciated how dangerous the situation really was. In 1676 he informed the minister that he had met the Iroquois at Cataracoui, had persuaded them that they had nothing to fear from the new French bases in the west, and had reduced them to complete subservience to French interests. Louis XIV congratulated him on this but at the same time warned him not to rely so much on his own persuasive powers that he neglected to place the *habitants* on such a footing that they could repel any attacks that the Iroquois might launch.[18] The following year Frontenac claimed that he had renewed and confirmed the peace treaty with the Senecas and Cayugas [19] and was again congratulated by the king, who ordered him to make sure that nothing transpired that might threaten French security in the lands under his sovereignty.[20] In 1678 Frontenac assured Colbert that all the Indian tribes, even the most remote, were subservient to his will.[21] The following year he informed the minister that Governor Andros of New York had convened an assembly of the Five Nations in order to stir up trouble for the French, but, as these tribes had contracted smallpox at Albany, they now thought more of mourning their dead than of making war; as a result of this he anticipated that they would be more inclined to trade with the French in future.[22] There was, apparently, no indication in any of his dispatches to the Court of there being any serious threat to French interests in the west.

Then the long-pending storm finally broke. In September, 1680, an Iroquois army six to seven hundred strong again invaded the Illinois country. Upon receiving word of the approach of the enemy the Illinois sent their women and children some fifteen miles away for security and made ready for battle. Their chiefs were anything but sanguine of the outcome; many of their young men were away and they had only bows and arrows, whereas the Iroquois were armed with muskets. When the two forces were less than a mile apart the Illinois chiefs prevailed upon Henri Tonty to ask the Iroquois to discuss peace terms. Tonty agreed to undertake this embassy. As he approached within musket range he was met by a scattered volley from the Iroquois host but continued on unscathed until he was among them, whereupon an Onondaga warrior plunged a knife into his chest. When the others saw him to be a "Frenchman" they separated him from his assailant and brought him before their chiefs. During the ensuing parley a warrior stood behind Tonty, knife in hand, lifting Tonty's hair off the back of his neck while the blood seeped from his flesh wound. The Iroquois were not a little disconcerted to find that there were Frenchmen in the midst of their enemies and to learn that Frontenac had taken the Illinois under his protection. They agreed to discuss peace terms with the Illinois and sent Tonty back with their answer. But this was merely their usual tactic of temporizing and playing on their enemies' nerves until they had gained an initial advantage and were better able to launch an assault. During this uneasy armistice, Tonty and his companions slipped away and after enduring great hardships finally reached Michilimackinac in the Ottawa country the following spring. There they learned that the Iroquois had subsequently destroyed the Illinois village.[23] According to accounts which later reached Quebec, a Recollet friar had been killed and several hundred Illinois, mostly women and children, taken prisoner. Shortly afterwards a Miamis village was also attacked, and a number of prisoners taken.[24]

When Frontenac informed the Court of these disasters he assured the king that if the Senecas and Onondagas did not offer him satisfaction for their attacks on the French allies, he would order them to meet him at Cataracoui the following summer to account to him for their actions. At the same time he claimed that it was not so much the Iroquois who were at fault but "certain people, and perhaps the English as well," whose strategems had incited the Iroquois to attack the Illinois in order to hinder the explorations of La Salle. He then went on to state that five or six hundred regular troops would quickly reduce the Iroquois to their former obedience and, he added, "it would be necessary only to let the Iroquois see them, have them appear on their lakes, and without any further acts of hostility it would ensure peace for ten years."[25]

Then, just as he was about to seal this dispatch, worse news arrived. A Seneca chief had been captured by a group of Illinois in the Ottawa country. They had taken their prisoner to a Kiskakon village at Michilimackinac, and there a dispute had arisen over a young Illinois girl who had escaped from the Iroquois and who the Seneca claimed had been his slave. Some of the Kiskakons foolishly began taunting the Illinois on this score, whereupon one of them, in savage fury, snatched up a knife and slew the Seneca chief. The Kiskakons, fearing the dire consequences this would have when news of it reached the Iroquois cantons, became panic-stricken. Without taking any action against the Illinois who had committed the act, as their primitive law required, they abandoned their village and fled to the north.[26]

Such an incident was sufficient excuse for the Iroquois to extend the war to all four Ottawa nations.* Immediately upon hearing of it Frontenac sent one of his officers, the Sieur de la Marque, with a canoe-load of trade goods to the Senecas, hoping by means of these gifts to assuage their wrath and prevail upon them to regard the murder of their chief as a private quarrel. La Marque was instructed to request the Senecas to wait until Frontenac had conferred with them the following summer at Cataracoui before taking any action that might lead to open war. In the meantime, Frontenac assured them that he would oblige the Ottawas to make "every reparation that they could hope for." [27] But this attempt at appeasement had little effect. The Iroquois arrogantly replied that, although they would be willing to confer with Frontenac in the spring, he must come to a conference site of their choosing, the mouth of the Onondaga River on the south side of Lake Ontario. [28]

The seriousness of the situation was now quite apparent to everyone in the colony. As the intendant Duchesneau put it: "There can be no doubt and everyone is in agreement that if the Iroquois are allowed to continue unchecked they will subdue the Illinois and in a short time they will make themselves the master of all the Ottawa nations, and take the [fur] trade to the English, therefore it is an absolute necessity that we should either restore their friendship or destroy them." [29] The responsibility for taking some action to meet the Iroquois threat rested squarely on Frontenac's shoulders, yet all he did was to procrastinate. In March, 1682, he convened a council composed of himself, the intendant, the town-major of Quebec, and the Jesuit fathers Beschefer, Dablon and Frémin. His stated purpose in calling this council was "to examine together the most proper expedients to avert the war which there was reason to believe the Iroquois wished to continue against the Illinois—against whom they had already had much success—and in which the Ottawas and other Indian nations under His Majesty's protection would find themselves involved, which could incur another war in the heart of the country unless steps were taken to prevent it." [30] It is rather curious that he should have called on these five men in particular, since he regarded them all as inimically disposed towards himself. What his motive was can only be guessed at, and it must be borne in mind that, as it is Frontenac's

---

* The four Ottawa nations were the Kiskakons, the Ottawas du Sable, the Sinago and the Nassauakuetoun (or Ottawas de la Fourche). The Kiskakons were the most numerous.

account of what these men stated that has come down to us, we do not know how accurately it reflects what they actually stated.

He asked the members of this council to write down their opinions on the following questions: where the conference with the Iroquois should be held; what preparations should be made in order to hold the conference; their estimate as to how many Iroquois were likely to be hunting in the vicinity of Fort Frontenac at the time—this in order to determine how large an escort would be needed; how the funds could be raised to pay for the escort and the food supplies and presents for the Iroquois delegates. In his reply, Father Beschefer, speaking for Fathers Dablon and Frémin as well as himself, stated that Frontenac should confer with the Iroquois at Fort Frontenac, rather than on their territory, which would involve a loss of face, and that this conference should be held by June 15, before the Iroquois warriors were back from their hunting and able to form war parties. He gave it as his opinion that there would not be many Iroquois in the vicinity at that time, and therefore Frontenac should not take a larger escort than usual, merely fifty or sixty men in twelve to fifteen canoes, lest the Iroquois deputies become alarmed and fear a trap. He added that the Iroquois were too intent on crushing the Illinois to think of attacking the French, one enemy at a time having always been the key to Iroquois policy. He recommended that the presents be liberal and given not only to the elder chiefs but also to the young warriors to deter them from continuing a war which they were pursuing with such vigour and the sure prospect of success.

Provost, the town-major, stated that Frontenac should send his representatives, in case he did not feel inclined to go himself, to confer with the Iroquois at Fort Frontenac; that they should be given the presents which had been promised them earlier; and that the conference should take place at the beginning of June, the date on which they had been requested to come to Fort Frontenac. From the evidence that Frontenac had shown them, Provost declared that he did not think there would be enough Iroquois in the vicinity of the fort at this time to warrant taking a large escort, which might well do more harm than good. As to the furnishing of supplies for the conference, this, he felt, was a problem for the governor and the intendant to solve between them.

Duchesneau, naturally enough, in his recommendations was chiefly concerned with the problems of finance and supply. In order to keep the expense to a minimum he suggested that the conference should be held at Montreal, and if that were not practicable, at Fort Frontenac. He too stated that the conference should be held in early June in order to delay the Iroquois sending war parties against the Ottawas. The cost of the conference would, he pointed out, have to be met by drawing on the agent of the Company of the Farm, but this loan could be defrayed by handing over to the agent all presents in the shape of furs or wampum made by the allied tribes in recognition of French services in averting a war.

It is worthy of note that, according to Frontenac's account, all of these men advised a meeting with the Iroquois in order to appease them. Yet a few months later these same men, and others in the colony, advised Frontenac's successor to take a very strong stand—military action, in fact—on the grounds that any other action would be suicidal.[31]

Frontenac, in giving his own views on these questions, disagreed with the opinions of the others on the essential point. He not only declined to meet the Iroquois on their side of the lake as they had requested, he also declined to meet them at Fort Frontenac. His reasons for this were that he could not go to the fort without a much larger escort than usual "for the security and dignity of his position" because there were large numbers of Iroquois hunting in the vicinity. Also, to take a large party would necessitate drawing on the agent of the Company of the Farm for funds and he had express orders from the king not to do this; in addition to which, a large expedition would alarm the Iroquois and cause them to suspect his intentions. All that he felt it wise to do was to invite the Iroquois to send two or three deputies from each canton to Montreal in June. To justify his not going to Cataracoui to meet them as he had earlier informed them he would, he suggested using the pretext that important affairs or some sort of "indisposition" made it impossible for him to leave the colony at that particular time. To make it clear that he was most anxious to confer with them and reach a peaceful settlement, he suggested that the Iroquois be assured that, to facilitate their journey, food supplies would be made available to them at Fort Frontenac or at any other point en route they might care to indicate. He held that a conference in mid-June would be useless and would necessitate another in the autumn, since by the earlier date he would not have learned what satisfaction the Kiskakons intended to make the Senecas for the murder of their chief. Their decision in this matter could not be known until they came down to Montreal in July or August, by which time he hoped to have received an answer from the minister as to what action to take and possibly he would have received the troops and supplies that he had requested.[32]

If, however, it was useless for Frontenac to confer with the Iroquois at Fort Frontenac for the reasons given, it was equally useless to have the Iroquois ambassadors come down to Montreal at that time. This would have necessitated their remaining in Montreal from June until August. He could hardly have expected these arrogant Iroquois chiefs to cool their heels in Montreal for two months awaiting his pleasure. In fact, Frontenac rejected the advice of the members of the council; not only did he refuse to go to Fort Frontenac as they had stated he should, but he also did not even adhere to his own stated views on the action that should be taken, for it later became apparent that he had not requested the Iroquois to confer with him at Montreal. Under the circumstances, Frontenac's reasons for refusing to go to Fort Frontenac were very weak and it is difficult to escape the conclusion that either he was afraid he would not be able to obtain any sort of satisfaction from the Iroquois and would then be forced to take stronger action, from which he shrank, or else he feared for his own personal safety. That the latter might well have been the case is indicated by his statement that he dared not go to the fort without a larger escort than usual; and three months later, in June, he wrote to the Sieur de la Forest, the commandant of the fort, informing him that he had been told by the Mission Iroquois, who had heard it from the Nipissings, who had been told by the members of an Iroquois hunting party, that the latter tribe were planning to attack him when he went to Cataracoui.[33] His placing any degree of credence in such rumours, particularly third-hand Indian rumours, indicates that Frontenac was far more nervous on this score than a French officer had any right to be.

At the end of July Duchesneau made a final appeal to Frontenac to do something before it was too late. The situation in the west, from all reports, was deteriorating day by day and he pointed out that the longer Frontenac delayed taking some sort of action, the more ineffectual became any action that he could take. He had received word from France that no aid was to be expected from that quarter, and in view of the defenceless state of the colony he regarded it as imperative that Frontenac should confer with the Iroquois in August, otherwise they would be led to believe that the French had abandoned the Illinois to their fate. If an attempt to mediate in the quarrel between the Senecas and Ottawas were not made, he warned, no one could foresee the consequences of such an omission better than Frontenac. He therefore suggested that, since Frontenac feared for his personal safety, he should cross Lake Ontario to the Iroquois side on La Salle's barque, accompanied by the brigantine, both manned by resolute crews, and invite the Iroquois chiefs to confer with him on board.[34]

Frontenac declined to follow Duchesneau's suggestion, pointing out, rightly enough, that to confer with the Iroquois on their side of the lake would show too great a deference to their arrogant demands and so lower his prestige. In any case, he added, such a meeting was impossible to arrange because the barque in question had been badly damaged. A short time earlier the Iroquois of the north shore of Lake Ontario had plundered the canoes of a group of *coureurs de bois* from Fort Frontenac. La Forest had then gone to the Seneca canton in the barque to complain of this but had received no satisfaction whatsoever. Instead, the Senecas had plundered the barque of its supplies, severely damaged its rigging and given the crew a bad beating. La Forest and his men had been lucky to escape with nothing worse.[35] But Frontenac assured Duchesneau that he intended to confer with the Iroquois as soon as he had heard what the Kiskakons had to say.[36] A short time later a band of Iroquois forced their way into Fort Frontenac and took by force a large quantity of merchandise.[37] It was all too clear that in the face of French inaction the arrogance of the Iroquois was increasing by leaps and bounds.

In mid-August, the Kiskakons, accompanied by delegations from the Miamis and Huron tribes, arrived at Montreal. The Kiskakons opened the ensuing council by pleading that they should not be abandoned to the wrath of the Iroquois and requesting Frontenac to intercede on their behalf with the Senecas. Frontenac replied that he had asked the Iroquois to meet him at Fort Frontenac in order to settle the dispute. A Miamis chief then spoke and complained in bitter terms that on four separate occasions the Iroquois had attacked his tribe and carried off prisoners. To this Frontenac could only reply that he would "reproach the Iroquois." When the council met the following day the Hurons asked for aid against the

Iroquois, not only for themselves but also for the Miamis, with whom they had an alliance. The Kiskakons then informed Frontenac that to make amends to the Senecas for the murder of their chief they would give the Senecas one of their children, a boy of eight or nine years, plus a sash of wampum and a beaver robe, saying that they saw no reason why they should give more, since it was not they but the Illinois who had committed the murder. Frontenac rejected this peace offering as inadequate; he ordered them to reconsider and return in three days with their answer. They returned, not in three days but the following day, and flatly declared that their initial offer was as far as they were prepared to go, pointing out that the Iroquois had never made any amends to the Miamis after killing a great many of their people. A Miamis chief then rose and declared vehemently that his nation would not meekly suffer the Iroquois attacks any longer; he and his warriors intended to retaliate in kind. He demanded that Frontenac should ask him to do no other. In reply, Frontenac pleaded with them not to carry things to extremes before he had discussed matters with the Iroquois. The following day, August 20, the council held a final meeting. The allied delegates persisted in stating their determination to defend themselves and to seek vengeance for the losses they had suffered. To this Frontenac replied that he could not permit them to attack the Iroquois, but only to act in self-defence; on no account were they to carry the war into the Iroquois country. He later stated that at the allies' request he gave them plans for forts which they desired to build in their own countries for their protection. As they were about to leave on their return journey he obliged them to promise that they would not attack any Iroquois they might encounter en route.[38]

From the point of view of the allies, this conference could hardly be called a success. They had received no promise of aid and very little comfort of any kind. French prestige undoubtedly suffered accordingly. Frontenac now had no excuse for not going immediately to Cataracoui to confer with the Iroquois as he had obligated himself to do. Yet he made no move in this direction whatsoever. Instead he turned his attention to the colony's defences, which even at this late date were non-existent. During the past years concessions had been granted and the *habitants* allowed to settle anywhere they pleased, as though no possibility existed of their ever being attacked. Most of the seigneuries had frontages of some seven to ten miles; a few of them contained thirty or forty *habitants* but for the most part twelve to fifteen, and as low as five or six was the rule. The only stronghold in the whole of New France was the fort at Quebec, which was in a very poor state of repair. At Trois Rivières there was a wooden palisade of sorts, but Montreal lacked even this. From Rivière-du-Loup-en-Haut to the western tip of the island of Montreal, the colony could have been devastated at any time by the Iroquois.[39]

In the royal instructions that Frontenac had received before being sent out to Canada it had been clearly stated: "The Sieur de Frontenac must have a particular care to undertake the training of the *habitants* in order, not only to maintain them in a state ready to repulse the ravages that the Iroquois could inflict on them, but also to be able to attack the Iroquois whenever required by His Majesty's service and to ensure the security of the colony."[40] This order was repeated every year. In 1673 and again in 1674 Frontenac had informed the minister that he had appointed militia captains in all the districts and was seeing to it that the militia were drilled in the manual of arms.[41] In 1675 a supply of arms and ammunition had been ordered sent to Canada by the king to be held in reserve for emergencies,[42] yet in 1683 Seignelay and Louis XIV were astounded to learn that most of the *habitants* possessed no arms of any sort and new supplies had to be rushed from France.[43]

With the defences of the colony in this state it is small wonder that the Iroquois saw little to fear from the French. At the same time, their own strength was growing and their aggressiveness with it. In 1681 they had taken a large number of Illinois prisoners and killed and eaten as many more. The nation of Chats from the borders of Virginia, numbering some six hundred men, women and children, had surrendered voluntarily to the Iroquois for fear that they might suffer a fate similar to the Illinois. The skull of the chief killed by the Illinois at Michilimackinac had been brought back to their canton by the Senecas, who vowed that they would wreak their vengeance on the Kiskakons. They had recently obtained a large supply of arms and ammunition from Albany and were making plans for another campaign against both the Illinois and the Miamis.[44]

While all this was happening, Father Lamberville, the Jesuit missionary with the Onondagas, was struggling desperately to divert the war from the Miamis and prevent it spreading to the

French settlements. At great personal risk he managed to save one Miamis prisoner from the fire, hoping that when Frontenac came to the general assembly of the Five Nations that he had so frequently promised to hold, the Iroquois would agree to present this prisoner to the governor and so enable him to effect an honourable peace between the Iroquois and the Miamis.[45] But Frontenac made no move towards convening this conference. Instead, in September, he began a tour of the island of Montreal to mark the sites where forts should be built.[46] He had not gone far when the Sieur de la Forest arrived from Fort Frontenac with a deputy from the Onondagas. This chief, Tegannissorens, stated that in response to Frontenac's request, brought to them the previous autumn by the Sieur de la Marque, that the Iroquois should confer with him at the fort in the spring, he had gone to Cataracoui along with delegates from the other four nations. Not having found Frontenac there, he had come on alone, being assured by La Forest that he would find the governor at Montreal. Frontenac replied that it was not in the spring but at the end of August that he had asked them to send their ambassadors to the fort. Tegannissorens, who was a very skilful diplomat, did not press the point as to the difference in dates, nor, apparently, did he point out that it was now nearly mid-September, yet Frontenac still had made no move to go to the fort to meet with the Iroquois representatives. Instead, on behalf of the Five Nations for whom he was empowered to speak, he requested Frontenac to go in his barque to Ochuguen at the mouth of the Onondaga River to confer with their chiefs. He declared that the Iroquois had no desire to wage war with the Ottawas, Hurons or Miamis, and asked Frontenac not to believe all the rumours to the effect that they were about to march against the Illinois.

In reply Frontenac stated that he was unable to go to Ochuguen that year to confer with them. He declared that he was delighted to hear the Iroquois were so peaceably inclined but he also asked why they would not agree to end their war with the Illinois, and he pointed out what the consequences might be were they to continue with it. What answer if any Tegannissorens made to this is not recorded. Although Frontenac already knew that he had been recalled to France he asked the Iroquois not to take any action before he had discussed the whole issue with them the following spring. Then, after presenting Tegannissorens with a complete outfit of clothing well-encrusted with gold braid and lace, a musket, powder and ball, and a dress for his daughter, Frontenac sent him on his way.[47]

If Frontenac actually believed Tegannissorens's protestations of the Iroquois' peaceful intentions, he was the only responsible person in the colony who did. Everyone else was convinced that this embassy was merely a rather obvious gambit in the Iroquois policy, which was to drive the French out of the western fur trade by crushing their allies one by one, just as they had previously conquered the Hurons, the Andastes, the Mohicans and other tribes. This ambitious plan depended for its success on one thing—preventing any intervention by the French, for it was only the French who could unite the intended victims and organize a concerted attack on the Iroquois villages. Thus they would do everything in their power to keep the French inactive, and make all manner of promises; then, when the western allies of the French were crushed and there was no longer any great danger of a concerted attack on the Iroquois villages, they would launch their entire strength against the French settlements. The first step in this plan had already gone into effect; the Illinois and Miamis were under attack and had already suffered heavy losses. Once these tribes were crushed it would be the turn of the Ottawas; if the Iroquois succeeded in seizing hold of Michilimackinac they would then be able to dominate the Great Lakes, and the French hold on the western fur trade would be destroyed. This was the consensus of opinion in the colony.[48]

When Tegannissorens arrived back at Onondaga, Father Lamberville wrote to Frontenac to inform him of the state of affairs there. He declared that had Frontenac been willing to meet the Iroquois at Lake Ontario, even at that late date, his mission would not have been in vain. For the Illinois there was no hope, he claimed, and, the Miamis being in their path, the Iroquois would fall on them too. But Frontenac could have persuaded them to spare the Miamis "who now regarded themselves as lost for lack of a word from the French governor." All that Tegannissorens had recounted on his return had been well received by the Onondagas, Father Lamberville stated; but although this chief was not ill-disposed towards the French, neither he nor any other of the western Iroquois feared them and they were all prepared to strike at the colony at the first provocation. From his unenviable position in the enemy camp he described the existing situation in uncompromising terms: "Several times they have insulted the French without being called to account, and this has led them to believe that the French are afraid of them. They gain every year from our losses; they crush our allies and make Iroquois of them; they do not hesitate to say that, after adding to their own ranks from those we have abandoned, and strengthened by those who would have been able to aid us in waging war against them, they will descend *en masse* on Canada and overwhelm it in a single campaign." [49]

Frontenac's successor, Le Febvre de la Barre, after conferring with the leading men in the colony on the situation shortly after his arrival, stated: "I have found this colony on the verge of being forced into war by the Iroquois and in a condition to succumb." [50] The whole Great Lakes area smouldered with war and preparations for war. No river was safe, every portage was a potential ambush, and every village wondered how long it would be before the enemy would strike. The Iroquois were pillaging French canoes wherever they encountered them; they were already at war with the Illinois and the Miamis; the danger was great that the Ottawas would either be crushed in turn or would secede from the French alliance and join forces with the Iroquois against the French. Had this last happened the colony's economy would have been ruined, and, in the defenceless state in which Frontenac left New France, a concerted attack by even the Iroquois alone would have wrought havoc.

Frontenac, however, upon his return to France gave a very different picture of conditions in Canada. He assured the minister that when he left the colony the Iroquois "wished always to live on good terms and in friendship, not only with the French but also with all the Ottawas, Kiskakons, Hurons and others." In support of this claim he submitted a memorial to the minister, the main theme of which was that the Iroquois really meant no harm but had been subverted into hostility by his personal enemies. He implied that the Iroquois were being directed in all their actions by a group whom he denoted by the vague impersonal French pronoun *on*. He never identified this group except as the personal enemies of himself and La Salle, meaning, of course, that they were his fur-trade rivals and the Jesuits. He stated that although he had clearly informed the Iroquois that he would confer with them at the end of August at Fort Frontenac, after having had an opportunity to discuss the situation with the Ottawas, *on* had given them to believe that the conference was to take place in the spring. *On* had also incited them to demand that he should meet them on their side of the lake in the hope that he would refuse this request, thereby causing the Iroquois to show their resentment at his refusal by attacking the French or the Ottawas, or at least the Illinois. He then explained why he had refused to meet the Iroquois there. Some of his reasons, such as the heavy expense that this would entail since he would need a large escort for the security and dignity of his person, are debatable, but on the whole his refusal to meet them on their territory was justified. In the meantime, he stated, he had begun sending arms and ammunition to Montreal in order to show all concerned that the colony was prepared to defend itself. Frontenac also stated that he went himself to Montreal to get the harvest brought in and to let it be seen that he still intended to go to Fort Frontenac with a larger escort than usual. Just how he assisted with the harvest is not clear and the statement about his intending to go to Fort Frontenac is even more dubious.

He next claimed that his personal enemies were so determined to bring about hostilities between the French and the Five Nations that they had caused a party of Iroquois to pillage the French canoes and La Salle's barque on Lake Ontario. *On* had also incited two Iroquois to declare in their nation's council that they would attack not only the Illinois but also the French, even La Salle if they encountered him, adding several insults against Frontenac for good measure; "those who were inciting them" hoped thereby to drive him to attack the Iroquois. But, said Frontenac, he refused to swallow the bait, judging that it was only a ruse, that the insults had been uttered by Iroquois who had been bribed by his enemies, "and that they had pillaged the merchandise of the men at [Fort Frontenac] and railed against the Sieur de la Salle only because of the protection given him in his explorations by M. de Frontenac." Therefore he had resolved to do nothing more than to continue his defence preparations against an Iroquois attack "although he in fact did not believe that they had all the evil designs that were being trumpeted forth, because for the past ten years they had always shown their good will and been very compliant." He overlooked the fact that this last was contradicted by a statement he had made in 1681: "the Indians are becoming hostile despite everything that I say to hold them in check; the journeys that I make nearly every year to Fort Frontenac no longer impress them as they did in the beginning." [51]

He next stated that in order to give the Iroquois something to think about, he had made no secret of the renewed protection he had accorded the Ottawas—he failed to mention the Miamis here —and the permission he had granted them to build forts and to defend themselves against attacks. But according to his earlier account this "protection" had consisted of nothing more than his ordering them not to attack the Iroquois under any circumstances, but only to defend themselves if attacked. It is difficult to see how the Ottawas could feel protected in any way, or the Iroquois deterred, by this. As for the permission to build forts, it is equally difficult to see why the Ottawas would require his permission before building them; in fact, it is very doubtful if they ever made such a request, and they certainly did not build any forts. The idea of cooping themselves up in a fort was completely alien to the Indians' concept of warfare; for defence they relied on the speed of their legs and the cover of the forest; for attack they relied on ambush and sneak raids, guerilla, not siege warfare. The minister and his advisers, however, could not be expected to know this.

Finally, Frontenac made the bold assertion that the Iroquois had sent their ambassador, Tegannissorens, to assure him that the Five Nations wished to remain on good terms not only with the French, but also with the Ottawas, Hurons, "and others." The two words "and others" were perhaps intended to obscure the fact that the Iroquois were at that time already at war with the Illinois and Miamis. On the basis of this Iroquois embassy, Frontenac maintained that he had been justified in rejecting Duchesneau's pleas that he go to Lake Ontario to confer with the Five Nations and in continuing instead the policy that he had pursued all along, whereas "someone held in less esteem by the Indians and lacking his knowledge of their ways and the intrigues in the colony, might well have incurred much useless expense and undertaken measures which would have been prejudicial to the colony." [52] This reference to his having prevented needless expense was a very neat touch, well calculated to appeal to the king and the minister; he was to use the self-same argument in very similar circumstances during his second administration.

This memoir contains not merely distortions and dangerous half-truths, but obvious contradictions. It must be remembered, however, that when the crisis had to be faced, Frontenac was in a rather wretched position, albeit one very largely of his own creation. He had made powerful enemies, and being unscrupulous himself, he very likely regarded them as being equally so. For the past few years his foes at Quebec had been goading him unmercifully, giving him no rest. His influence in Court circles was waning as complaints about his conduct poured in from all sides, and for the past year or two the clergy in the colony—and perhaps the laity as well—had been informed by their correspondents in France that he was soon to be recalled.[53] It would be astonishing if rumours of this had not been circulated throughout the colony, emboldening his enemies and dismaying Frontenac himself and the members of his own faction.

And to add to it all, after he had successfully excluded his rivals from Lake Ontario and the Ohio Valley, the trade of the first area had been shattered and that of the second seriously threatened by the sudden hostility of the Iroquois. If his enemies did not openly gloat over his discomfiture on this account, he probably felt that they were doing so privately, and he may well have convinced himself that they were responsible for it. This might explain why he was so negligent of the Ottawas, with whom his enemies traded. There is no evidence whatsoever to justify Frontenac's accusations that it was these men who had incited the Iroquois. Certainly, Father Lamberville was strongly opposed to war and the Montreal fur traders could have been in no doubts as to what would happen to their commerce with the Ottawas were the war to spread. What these men wanted was to curb the Iroquois before it was too late and a full-scale war with all its horrors fell on the colony. Unfortunately, Frontenac could not bring himself to accept advice from this quarter and his procrastination merely emboldened the Iroquois and caused the situation in the west to worsen rapidly. Furthermore, he may have feared that were he to take a strong stand against the Iroquois, it would put an end to any lingering hopes he might have had of regaining their trade, which had proved so profitable to him in the past. Then came the crowning blow of all, word from France of his summary dismissal from office. The times must have seemed sorely out of joint to Frontenac.

If this analysis in some measure explains why Frontenac behaved as he did, it still does not permit of a condonation of his conduct. The question still remains: to what extent was Frontenac responsible for the perilous state of French interests in North America at the time of his recall? The underlying cause of the trouble was the determination of the Iroquois to gain control of the western fur trade. A more immediate cause was the upsetting of the balance of power in favour of the Iroquois, resulting from their defeat of the Andastes and the defection of the Mohicans. Clearly, Frontenac was in no way responsible for these circumstances. But the price of peace and security was constant vigilance, and once the Iroquois had succeeded in crushing the Andastes it was inevitable that they would renew their old struggle to wrest control of the western fur trade from the French. This situation having arisen, it was the governor's responsibility to cope with it, and this demanded three things: bold countermeasures to prevent the Iroquois gaining the initiative, the strengthening of the French alliance with the tribes hostile to the Iroquois, and the strengthening of the defences of the central colony.

It should have been apparent to Frontenac, as it certainly was to others in the colony, that the only thing the Iroquois respected was strength; any attempt to appease them they interpreted as weakness, which merely served to encourage their aggressiveness. Had Frontenac, following the Seneca attack on the Illinois and Miamis and the wounding of Tonty, called the Iroquois to account—as he had assured the minister he would—he might have retained the initiative. If he had gone to Fort Frontenac to confer with the Five Nations—as he had so frequently declared he intended to do—and there made it plain that the Illinois, Miamis, Hurons and Ottawas were under the protection of the French crown and any attack on them would be regarded as an act of war against the French, the prospect of possible concerted attacks from all these nations and the French might well have made the Iroquois consider very carefully before stripping their own villages of their warriors for an attack on the Illinois. They would probably have been too nervous about the safety of their own women and children to undertake a distant campaign.

The main source of strength to the French, both economic and military, was their alliance with the nations hostile to the Iroquois. Without this alliance New France would have been doomed; it was essential that it be maintained and strengthened at all costs. Yet instead of encouraging the allies to resist the Iroquois and promising them every assistance, he virtually abandoned them to their fate. Instead of strengthening the alliance, he gravely weakened it.

In addition to taking measures to retain the initiative and trying to prevent the continuance of hostilities, Frontenac should also have taken swift action to strengthen the defences of the colony. When the minister was finally brought to realize the seriousness of the threat to French interests in North America he sent some two thousand regular troops to Canada.* Had Frontenac, instead of obscuring the seriousness of the situation, appealed for such reinforcements and warned the minister what would happen were they not immediately dispatched, then the responsibility for the consequences would have lain at the minister's door, not at Frontenac's. There was no possibility whatsoever of such a force being sent when Frontenac failed to make the urgency of the situation clear to the minister. Moreover, he made no move towards strengthening the colony's defences until just before his departure, and at that late hour he could do no more than indicate some of the more exposed places where forts should have been built. It remained for his successor to build them.

Only one thing could have deterred the Iroquois from attempting to drive the French out of the west: their being convinced that the attempt would be disastrous for them. Frontenac made no real effort to convince them of this; instead he procrastinated and made feeble attempts to appease them. Nothing could have been better calculated to incite the Iroquois to war than such a policy. It is by no means certain that Frontenac, with the best will in the world, could have deterred the Iroquois and retained the initiative, but he has to be condemned for making no real effort to do so. Procrastination and appeasement may sometimes prove to be the best policy to pursue; this was clearly not one of those times.

In the final analysis it looks very much as though Frontenac, fearing that he was to be recalled, wanted only to delay the onset of full-scale hostilities between the Iroquois and the French until he was safely out of the colony, when he could claim, with some hope of being believed, that it was not he but his successor who was responsible for whatever ensued. And this is exactly what he did claim upon his return to France. In his memoir to the minister he

---

* Approximately three hundred and fifty troops were sent to La Barre, five hundred were sent with Denonville, plus an unknown number of indentured farm labourers, eight hundred were sent with Vaudreuil, and three hundred were sent in 1688.

presented a very distorted picture of the situation in the colony, trying to make it appear that he had left New France secure and in no danger from the Iroquois. Then, after the war had begun in earnest, he declared that he had kept the colony at peace during the ten years of his first administration and that his successors had plunged recklessly into a needless war.[54] That Frontenac had to resort to such devices to account for his actions is in itself a condemnation of his stewardship.

CHAPTER SEVEN

FRONTENAC AND THE SOVEREIGN COUNCIL
1675–1682

WITH the arrival of the dispatches from the Court in the autumn of 1675, Frontenac had found himself deprived of a good deal of authority. He could no longer remove or appoint members of the Sovereign Council at will and this court, now sovereign in fact as well as name, soon demonstrated that it had no intention of allowing the governor to dictate to it, as had been his custom in the past. From Frontenac's viewpoint this was bad enough; but what was to prove far worse was the appointment of an intendant who had complete charge of justice, civil administration and finance. Colbert warned Frontenac that he must moderate his attitude and show more tolerance towards the failings of others. He was now reduced to acting in a purely supervisory capacity in civil affairs; he had to allow the intendant, the Sovereign Council and the subordinate officials to perform their functions without interference, and whenever necessary he had to lend them the support of his authority. Only if these officials acted in such a manner that the well-being of the colony and the king's service were endangered could Frontenac intervene.[1] In the eyes of Colbert, the fact that the governor was still supreme in military matters and could exercise the royal authority to ensure the good government of the colony was as much power as any provincial governor required. A governor with any talent for leadership should, he felt, be quite happy to let the subordinate officials exercise their functions without interference.

Jacques Duchesneau, the newly appointed intendant, had had some fourteen years' experience in the royal service, at least nine of them as *Trésorier de France* at Tours;[2] he early showed that he intended to act as *intendant de justice, police et finances* in fact as well as in name. Consequently, before the year was out Frontenac was complaining to Colbert of his reduced authority and charging that it had been brought about by the malicious slanders of his enemies.[3] Over the king's signature Colbert curtly replied that "it is my intention that you should confine yourself to the limits of the authority given you."[4] But, as Colbert should have realized by this time, it was very difficult to convince Frontenac of anything not to his liking. The minister, however, showed exemplary patience, and in the face of increasing bickering between Frontenac and the Sovereign Council over petty matters, he gave the governor more explicit instructions: "It is easy for those in command of the forces and the people to allow themselves to be easily flattered and persuaded that they must oversee everything and be kept informed of all the affairs of justice, administration and finance. His Majesty directs me to tell you that he desires that you should regard this as the main point to which you must give your constant application, as it is impossible for the king's service to be effective unless there is complete accord between the two persons who have to act, exercise his authority and work for the good of the people and the development of the colony."[5]

Frontenac, however, had not the slightest inclination towards acting in union with the intendant, nor, it must be added, did Duchesneau make it particularly easy for him to do so. Frontenac availed himself of every opportunity to make things difficult for Duchesneau. An example of this occurred in the granting of land concessions. In 1676 the minister, in the name of the king, ordered that in future all such concessions had to be made conjointly by the governor and the intendant and bear both their signatures.[6] Frontenac refused to obey this order, claiming that it was beneath his dignity for his signature to be accompanied by that of the intendant on these documents which would be open to the gaze of the public. He insisted that two documents be drawn up, one to be signed by him, the other by Duchesneau, who agreed to this arrangement only in order to avoid arguments.[7] Taking it for granted that the governor was sending copies to the minister of the title-deeds bearing his signature, Duchesneau dispatched copies of those he had signed to the Court. Frontenac then omitted to send copies of some of these concessions and at the same time complained to Colbert that Duchesneau, without consulting him, was granting concessions of land by virtue of his own authority alone. When the minister investigated he found copies of title-deeds signed by Duchesneau and no corresponding documents bearing Frontenac's signature. Colbert immediately sent a blistering letter to the intendant.

I again learn from the letters of M. de Frontenac that you have taken it upon yourself to grant concessions on your sole authority, despite the fact that according to the dispatches of May 20th, 1676, which you acknowledged by your letter dated September 9th, you were only given the authority to grant concessions jointly with M. de Frontenac. I confess that I cannot understand how it is possible that a man such as you should act contrary to the wishes of the king, as clearly explained by his letters patent, which you have received. And since in this matter you have committed a reprehensible error, His Majesty desires that you should revoke and declare null and void all the concessions granted by you and grant them anew on the advice of M. de Frontenac and jointly with him. In addition His Majesty desires that you make no further grants except under the conditions expressly laid down in his letters patent; that you have them registered by the Sovereign Council, where they can be reviewed, and that you send me the decree of registration.[8]

Frontenac's enjoyment of Duchesneau's discomfiture was short-lived; the intendant, to establish his innocence, had only to explain what had transpired. Moreover, he was able to show that Frontenac had himself granted concessions without referring them to him for duplication. He informed the minister that he had rectified this by granting the requisite deeds in all but one instance, that of a concession granted to Noel l'Anglois, because, as he put it, "once a good carpenter, he has become a loafer; he believed himself to be a gentleman because he had a seigneury and it will result only in his family becoming a charge on the colony."[9] This single exception served to prove to the minister that Frontenac had made grants, and one such to a dubious character, without the intendant's participation. When this dispatch reached the Court the minister saw clearly that he had blamed the wrong man. Frontenac was immediately informed in the king's dispatch that in future, and without his creating any further difficulties, all concessions were to bear both his and the intendant's signatures.[10]

With Frontenac engaging in such tactics to discredit the intendant, it is not surprising that relations were strained between them. At the same time, although far more sinned against than sinning, Duchesneau did not adopt a very conciliatory attitude in his relations with the governor. Knowing what manner of man he had to deal with, and knowing also, as he must have done, how great was Frontenac's influence in Court circles, he should have realized that no matter how much he might have right on his side, this alone would count for very little in any conflict he might have with Frontenac. There can be little doubt that Duchesneau was honest and conscientious, but he allowed himself the luxury of being outraged by Frontenac's malversations and abuse of his authority. Had he been able to conceal his personal feelings and in his reports to the minister show a more detached view, his accounts of Frontenac's depredations would have carried more weight and he would have spared himself such reprimands as the following from the minister: "I must say that the tone of all your letters clearly shows your disinclination to pay the respect which you owe to M. de Frontenac, and although it appears from the letters of M. de Frontenac that his conduct leaves something to be desired, there is assuredly in yours, and in all that you say and write, far more to be censured than in that of M. de Frontenac." [11]

It was also very easy for Frontenac to damn Duchesneau in the minister's eyes by labelling him a tool of the Jesuits, particularly when the intendant supported the claims of the clergy in the brandy dispute.[12] And while Frontenac was continually depicting himself as fighting valiantly to protect the royal authority against encroachments by the clergy, Duchesneau was naïve enough to inform Colbert that although he realized it would mean his being regarded as unduly under their influence, he had to state truthfully that the clergy were claiming nothing not their due or that was not accorded them in France.[13]

Duchesneau was by no means the only official who came into conflict with the governor. Frontenac always considered that since he represented the king, his word was law, and Colbert never succeeded in disabusing him of this notion. Anyone in the colony who dared to cross him, no matter how much he might consider that he had the law on his side, quickly learned that it was dangerous to oppose Frontenac's private interests. In 1678 the Sieur Migeon, bailiff of Montreal, informed the Sovereign Council of the activities of certain *coureurs de bois* and arrested one of them. Perrot immediately arrested Migeon. When the Sovereign Council decided to investigate the matter, Frontenac forbade them to take any action whatsoever, declaring that Perrot had acted on his orders. He then ordered Migeon to ask Perrot's pardon, imprisoned him for two months, and set him free only after he had paid a two-hundred-*livre* fine.[14] At the same time he sent his guards to release a soldier who had been sentenced by the bailiff to five years' labour service for killing an Indian woman, then took the convicted man into his own service and put him to work doing repairs on the Château St. Louis.[15] When the Sovereign Council protested at this high-handed disregard for due process of law, Frontenac blustered and stormed at them, charging that their protests verged on sedition.[16]

The Abbé Tronson complained personally to the minister in strong terms of the part Perrot had played in this affair.* Since the governor of Montreal was in Paris at the time the complaint was made, Colbert severely reprimanded him in public and informed him that if he did not mend his ways upon his return to Canada, he would be dismissed from his post.[17] Colbert followed this up by instructing Frontenac that in future he was not to levy any fines nor arrest anyone on his own authority, nor order the local governors to arrest anyone, except for the crimes of sedition or intelligence with an enemy of France, "something which is hardly likely ever to occur," he added. Any infraction of this edict, Colbert warned, would result in the governor responsible for it answering to the king for his conduct.[18] This order appears to have done little to reassure the officers of justice at Montreal, for the following year the seigneurs' attorney tendered his resignation to avoid having to act in cases in which Frontenac and Perrot had an interest.[19]

That it was distinctly dangerous for an officer of the law to try to render impartial justice in any such case is evidenced by the fate of the Sieur Peuvret, chief clerk of the Sovereign Council. He declared that the governor had frequently threatened that it would go harshly with him if he failed to report on all that occurred at meetings of the Council which the governor did not attend. Peuvret complied with this demand only because he was sure that Frontenac meant what he said. One evening in February, 1679, after a meeting of the Sovereign Council, Peuvret was anxious to return to his home which was some distance removed from the town, but decided that he had best report to Frontenac first, for he knew that if he did not Frontenac would send his guards to bring him back.

* The Sulpicians were the seigneurs of the island of Montreal and as such had the right to nominate the governor and the officers of justice in their seigneury, subject to royal approval.

The governor was at dinner when Peuvret appeared, but he interrupted his meal and retired to his private office, followed by his secretary and Peuvret. Frontenac first of all demanded to know if anything further had been done in his case against the wife of Ignace Bonhomme, who was accused of having insulted the governor and who claimed in her defence that the governor's guards had ill-treated her.[20] Peuvret replied that four witnesses had been heard and two remained still to be heard. Frontenac thereupon demanded to see the record of the hearing, but Peuvret declined to oblige on the grounds that it would be out of order and a grave dereliction on his part to show Frontenac the depositions of witnesses in a case in which he was an interested party.

At this Frontenac lost his temper completely and called Peuvret a low-born, ill-bred rogue. He declared that he was above the law and "not to be confused with other persons who had lawsuits; that anything which concerned himself also concerned His Majesty." He would teach Peuvret and everyone else their duty, and how they were to behave towards him. This violent outburst caused Peuvret to let Frontenac have the record of the hearing. Upon reading it the governor was even more irritated. Peuvret tried to tell him that it was all perfectly regular and that in any event, all he did was to write down what he was told. But Frontenac was now beyond reason. He continued to heap insults on the clerk's head. By this time Peuvret had had all that he could stand. He declared it was outrageous that he should be so treated for having carried out his duties to the best of his abilities. Had he known that he would be treated like this, he stated heatedly, he would never have brought the record in the first place, and what was more, he would be glad to resign his position, which he had held since the first foundation of the Sovereign Council. This infuriated Frontenac all the more. He threatened that when Peuvret was no longer clerk he would still be obliged to come at his bidding, if only for his amusement. Reiterating that he would teach Peuvret and everyone else their duty, he began once again to abuse this sorely tried official. Peuvret declared that this was too much and turned to leave. Frontenac then caught him by the coat and called for his guards. When Louvigny, the captain of his guards, appeared, Frontenac ordered him to put the clerk in the cells, and there he remained for a few days.[21]

Two months later Peuvrot declared in a written statement that

Frontenac had continually threatened him with the harshest treatment and had sworn to ruin him completely if he failed to insert in the records of the Council whatever Frontenac ordered. Since the governor had already imprisoned him once, he knew only too well that Frontenac meant what he said and would have no compunction in doing it again. This, Peuvret explained, would ruin him, as he was a widower with five children to look after and only his salary and a small section of land to support them on. Moreover, he had been given a licence by the king to build a sawmill which would be ready to start operations in the spring; were he to be imprisoned there was no one he could leave in charge of the enterprise. He had, he claimed, already invested three thousand *livres* in it, mostly borrowed capital. Thus, if Frontenac ordered him to insert anything in the Council records contrary to the king's *déclaration* of 1675, or to the orders of the Council, he had no alternative but to do so. He wished it to be understood that he would have done this only to protect his family and to prevent his own and his creditors' financial ruin.[22]

Although Frontenac had thus succeeded in disciplining the clerk of the Sovereign Council for seditious tendencies, he had less success against the attorney-general and certain of the councillors. In 1675, when the Sovereign Council had been reorganized by the king, it had been laid down that the intendant was to occupy the third place, after the governor and bishop, and "as president of the said Council, to ask for the opinions, collect the voices and deliver the judgements, and in addition have the same functions and possess the same privileges as do the first presidents of our courts." [23] Nowhere in this *déclaration* did it say that Frontenac was to be accorded the title of chief and president, and it was certainly stated specifically enough that he was not to act as such.

What is most important but far from obvious in this document is the significance of the terms used. "Collect the voices" meant something more than merely counting the votes of the Council when they rendered a verdict; in fact, it would seem that no vote was taken. Instead, each member would express his views and when all had been heard the president would render a verdict in accordance with what he took to be the general or majority opinion. This meant that the intendant, who was empowered to act as president, had far more real power than if he had merely called for a vote and counted the ayes and nays; it meant, in effect, that the verdicts and decisions of the Sovereign Council were those of the intendant acting on the advice of the other members.[24]

Since most of the members of the Council had had no legal training and had no other basis for judgement than their own common sense and a knowledge of the people and conditions in the colony, which might at times be vitiated by their private interests, such a system had much to recommend it. Moreover, the French government at this time was determined to maintain a tight control over the affairs of the realm through the agency of its royal officials, particularly the intendants. It can readily be seen, then, how a governor of Frontenac's temperament would resent the intendant's exercising such power, for it offered this official endless opportunities to slight the governor; and Duchesneau's character being what it was, it is more than likely that he availed himself of his opportunities. This would make Frontenac's conduct in the Sovereign Council more intelligible. It would also explain the stubborn refusal of the intendant and the Council to accede to Frontenac's subsequent demands.

At a meeting of the Sovereign Council in 1676, and again in March, 1678, when the intendant left the chamber temporarily, Frontenac made an attempt to collect the voices, but desisted when some members of the Council voiced their protests.[25] During this time Frontenac's feeling of frustration at being relegated to the role of a mere figure-head in the Sovereign Council grew until he could hardly contain himself. And each time he gave vent to his feelings the intendant and the members of the Council were quick to confute him with arguments based on precedents and royal edicts. On one occasion the intendant told him bluntly that his position was that of an honorary councillor, and his only prerogative was to be accorded titular precedence.[26] Although this last was quite correct, Frontenac could not be reconciled to it, still less to having it pointed out to him in this fashion.

By the winter of 1678–79 he could stomach it no longer; he suddenly claimed the right to preside over the meetings of the Sovereign Council in the absence of the intendant. He also claimed a conclusive voice in their deliberations and that he be styled chief and president on the records and public notices of the Council.[27] He based these claims on the fact that in the king's dispatches he was referred to as chief and president of the Council.[28] It was quite true that in the dispatch of May 12, 1678, he was referred to as such, but the context was rather ironical. It stated: "You must allow the officers duly appointed to render justice to my subjects, complete freedom to perform their duties, and at the same time you must, as chief and president of my Sovereign Council, support its officials in rendering justice swiftly and fairly in accordance with my edicts and the customs that they observe." [29] Moreover, this was not the first time that Frontenac had been given these titles; they occur in the king's dispatch of 1676 and also in that of the previous year, dated April 22, [30] the last having been written nearly two months previous to the king's proclamation reorganizing the Sovereign Council. Thus it must have been perfectly clear to Frontenac that the secretary who had drafted the dispatch had merely employed an old recurring phrase; but for lack of anything more valid, Frontenac seized on this flimsy excuse in an attempt to regain the mastery over the Council which he had held prior to 1675.

Duchesneau refused to entertain for an instant the governor's claims and the attorney-general was quick to notice that Frontenac had been styled chief and president in the king's dispatch of April, 1675. From that he drew the obvious conclusion that it was merely a clerical lapse. He therefore decided that the king had made no change in the proclamation of 1675 and he considered that he had no alternative but to demand that its terms be upheld. However, in an attempt to avoid a struggle with the governor, he suggested that the Sovereign Council should request Frontenac and Duchesneau to leave the matter in abeyance until a decision could be obtained from the king, and in the meantime the governor and intendant would be referred to simply as *monsieur le gouverneur* and *monsieur l'intendant*, with the intendant continuing to exercise the same functions as he had done previously. Both the members of the Sovereign Council and the intendant were agreeable to this and two councillors were delegated to propose this compromise to the governor. When they broached it to him he was infuriated, gave vent to threats and imprecations, declared that he had no intention of waiting eighteen months for the king's pleasure, and then ordered the Council to assemble the next day. At this meeting he accused the members of failing in their duty; he exhorted them to reflect on the seriousness of their actions and not to oblige him to use his personal authority. After making this threat, he and the intendant retired from the chamber, whereupon

135

the Council, refusing to be intimidated, decided to request the governor to accept their suggestion and to abandon all thought of using his authority to make them disobey the king's orders.[31]

Frontenac angrily rejected this decree and at the next meeting of the Council he ordered that henceforth he had to be treated as chief and president. He ordered the clerk of the court, in the king's name, to accord him these titles in his minute book and in the registers of the Council's proceedings. He further demanded the right to veto any resolutions of the Council that were not to his liking and that the attorney-general draw up all motions in accordance with his views; in effect, he demanded absolute obedience to his personal wishes, failing which he declared it to be his duty to discipline the members of the Council.[32] According to the intendant's account, Frontenac had several times stated that he had written to the Court to have the *déclaration* of 1675 repealed, and at the same time he had maintained that he should by rights have the same functions in the Sovereign Council as the Duc d'Orléans had in the king's councils, or that the chancellor had in the *Parlement*. Duchesneau also claimed that Frontenac had boasted that he had reason to believe the king would grant him the same prerogatives as had the princes of the blood in the royal councils.[33] That there was more than a little substance to Duchesneau's accusations on these scores is vouched for by Frontenac's attempts to explain them away, for in doing so he virtually admitted that he did entertain such notions.[34] He also claimed that in any legal proceedings in which he himself was a party, the attorney-general and the Sovereign Council had to treat the case as one in which the king's interests were at stake. When they repeatedly refused to acquiesce in these demands he became violent, pounding the table —on one occasion he overturned it—threatening and abusing them in the strongest language, and shaking his fist in their faces.[35] But the Sovereign Council still refused to submit. They rested their case on the *déclaration* of 1675, and the attorney-general later declared that he would have been guilty of disobedience to the king's orders had he sanctioned Frontenac's attempts to suborn authority delegated by the king to the intendant and the Sovereign Council.[36]

In the meantime, the routine business of the Council was being held up. When the councillors suggested that the issue be left in abeyance until the cases before the Council had been dealt with, Frontenac refused to hear of it; the Council had first to submit to his demands, and this, with equal stubbornness, the members refused to do. Late in April, at the Council's weekly meeting, when Frontenac ordered the clerk of the court to inscribe in the minutes the rank and intitulation he demanded, the intendant protested as usual and as usual to no avail, then rose from his place, saying: "Let us go, gentlemen, there is nothing we can do here as long as monsieur the governor employs force and allows us no freedom of discussion. Let us go and draw up a statement of what has just taken place." At this Frontenac told Duchesneau that he could leave if he wished, but he ordered the councillors to remain in their places in the king's name. Duchesneau, seeing that the councillors were making no move to follow him, returned to his chair. And there they all sat, glowering, not saying a word, until the usual hour for adjournment.[37]

Spring became summer and the impasse seemed no nearer solution. Then, at the end of June, Frontenac gave the Council a week in which to reflect on what was required of them in order not to be treated as guilty of disobedience; but still they remained adamant. Frontenac then declared that it was a matter requiring action by the king. On July 4 the attorney-general and two of the councillors, Villeray and Tilly, received written orders from the governor to leave Quebec. D'Auteuil, the attorney-general, was ordered to retire to his house at Sillery, five miles outside the town; Villeray was sent to the house of a Sieur Berthelot, fifteen miles away, and Tilly to that of the Sieur de St. Denis, five miles away. All three men were ordered to remain at these places until the ships were ready to sail in the autumn, whereupon they were to embark for France and account to the king for their actions.[38] The three officials had to comply with the order; had they not done so there was no telling what Frontenac might have done. Moreover, to have refused would have left them open to the charge of disobedience and sedition, if not open rebellion. Frontenac next tried to get the remaining members of the Council to deal with the outstanding cases and business, which by this time must have constituted a formidable back-log, but the councillors, taking their cue from the vicar-general, refused. They declared that the membership of the Council was not complete and they could not regard themselves as constituting the Sovereign Council. Frontenac stormed that he would inform His Majesty of their stubborn disobedience, but this had no effect.[39]

The exiling of these senior officials to points a few miles outside the town was far harsher treatment than might at first appear, in the attorney-general's case at least. For d'Auteuil was an old man, suffering from a serious lung ailment and he was now removed from medical care. A friend of his protested to the governor, stating that d'Auteuil's death would be on his head were the attorney-general not allowed to return to Quebec. This person also stated that both Tilly and Villeray would be financially ruined if they were not allowed to return to their seigneuries to attend to the harvest. But all that Frontenac would agree to was that the members of the Sovereign Council could meet at d'Auteuil's residence to confer with the attorney-general on the action they should take to put an end to the impasse.[40]

At this meeting it was decided that they would consent to Frontenac's being accorded the rank, titles and functions he demanded, but only after a protest had been submitted by the attorney-general in order to avoid their being held responsible by the king for contravening the *déclaration* of 1675. Frontenac rejected this out of hand, then left for Montreal.[41] When he returned two and a half months later, he found the Council still, as he put it, "of the opinion to make no distinction whatsoever between a governor whom the king had established chief and president of their company, and any other particular individual."[42]

But the summer was advancing; the ships would soon be leaving with the dispatches to the Court and the letters of all concerned to their friends in high places, giving full accounts of all that had transpired. Moreover, the dispatches that Frontenac had received from the minister earlier that summer had been none too reassuring. He had been severely reprimanded for the trouble he had caused over church honours and he had been curtly informed that he and the local governors would answer to the king if they continued to levy fines or imprison people arbitrarily.[43] Consequently, Frontenac suddenly decided that it would be wise to moderate his attitude until after the last ships had sailed and communications with the Court had been severed for another year. When two of the councillors now approached him and requested that he hold his demands in abeyance until the king could give his decision, and that in the meantime the exiled councillors and the Sieur d'Auteuil be allowed to return to Quebec and take their places at the Sovereign Council, he consented on condition that the dispute should not be mentioned by anyone at the meetings of the Council. This was agreed to and the intendant undertook to see to it that the councillors abided by the condition.[44]

Frontenac now attempted to achieve by means of a subterfuge what he had failed to achieve by force. The night before the Council meeting, the clerk went to see Duchesneau and informed him that he had been sent for by Frontenac earlier that evening and that the governor had ordered him to inscribe on the Council's register for the following day's proceedings the rank, style and title that Frontenac had earlier demanded. He had also ordered Peuvret to do this in such a way that the members of the Council would not be aware of what was taking place.[45]

When the Council convened the next morning, October 16, Duchesneau calmly requested Peuvret to begin the register. Frontenac immediately demanded that they first read the orders received from the Court, but Duchesneau insisted that it was customary to begin by opening the register. In what must have been a tense silence, Peuvret began writing. After a few moments the intendant asked him to read what he had written. Peuvret hesitated, then replied that he had not quite finished. Duchesneau persisted and told him to read what he had so far written. Peuvret then rose and read out: "The Council assembled, at which were Monsieur the governor, chief and president of the said Council, Monsieur de Bernières, grand-vicar of Monsieur the bishop of Quebec, Monsieur the intendant, performing the functions of president in accordance with the king's Proclamation."[46] Duchesneau turned to Frontenac, reminded him of the agreement he had made not to make any mention of the causes of the contestation between himself and the Council and pointed out that if he insisted on the rank, style and title being so recorded, it meant that the dispute was beginning all over again. Frontenac tried to dismiss the incident as of no significance and demanded that they proceed with the reading of the orders from the Court. D'Auteuil then rose and stated that he would consent to Frontenac's being given these titles and prerogatives, but only after he as attorney-general had submitted an official protest which was to be read and registered by the Sovereign Council. Frontenac would not agree to this but he accepted instead a proposal that no ranks or titles be inscribed on the register and that the proceedings of each meeting be recorded under the heading "the Council assembled" and nothing more. The intendant was agreeable to this and the understanding was put in writing and approved by Frontenac.[47] Nine days later Frontenac stated that he wanted to add something to the agreed intitulation, but the Council, suspecting that this was a mere ruse to reopen the issue once the ships had sailed, refused, and agreed only to take cognizance of any new proposals he might care to make.[48]

And there the matter rested when the ships sailed for France. The Council was proceeding with business as usual, despite the absence of the Sieur de Villeray who had been sent to the Court to account for his crimes in opposing the governor's will. The Sieurs d'Auteuil and Tilly, whom Frontenac had earlier ordered to cross over to France, were excused the voyage; Tilly, who five years earlier during the Perrot dispute had given way out of cowardice, was excused because he had informed Frontenac privately that he disapproved of the attorney-general's attitude and did not want to be associated with it;[49] d'Auteuil was excused because of his ill-health, which Frontenac was pleased to scoff at, labelling it "the pretext of the continuance of his infirmity, real or imagined, that the attorney-general has adopted to exempt him from it."[50] D'Auteuil himself stated his only regret was that his health would not permit him to make the voyage and give an account of all that had transpired between the Sovereign Council and the governor.[51] Frontenac, in giving his version of events to the minister, claimed that Duchesneau was responsible for all the trouble and that he feared he would have been held at fault had he allowed himself to be deprived of his rank as chief and president of the Council, which the king "has always done me the honour to grant me."[52] He also expressed great surprise that Villeray, far from appearing perturbed at the prospect of explaining his actions to the king, seemed on the contrary to be confident of obtaining the king's support for his conduct.[53]

It is difficult to say whether Frontenac was really sure of receiving the king's approval of his actions, or whether he was dissembling. To have behaved as he had done should indicate that he was convinced of his own rectitude. Certainly if he had had any doubts at all of the reaction at the Court, the last thing one would have expected him to do was to send Villeray to France to give his version of events. On the other hand, Frontenac never looked very far ahead in any of his actions; he always seized on temporary expedients to solve immediate problems, regardless of the fact that these expedients, by delaying trouble, compounded it. Thus, when the last ships sailed for France he knew that no matter what the attitude of Louis XIV and Colbert might be, no one in New France, including himself, would hear of it for another nine or ten months. He may have felt that there would be time enough to worry about consequences when the ships from France were sighted rounding the Island of Orleans the following summer.

Twelve days after the ships had sailed, the Sieur d'Auteuil died at the Hôtel Dieu. His son and Duchesneau both claimed that Frontenac had hastened his end.[54] The rough treatment he had received at the governor's hands was anything but conducive to the well-being of an elderly invalid. An appointment to the vacant post of attorney-general now had to be made and Duchesneau, who had foreseen this eventuality some two years earlier, had taken the precaution of obtaining letters of reversion from the minister.[55] When the Council met, everyone was in agreement that d'Auteuil's son should be given the post. No choice could have been better calculated to arouse Frontenac's ire; but, nothing daunted, Duchesneau requested the governor's approval of the appointment. Frontenac, of course, refused, maintaining that the blank commission Duchesneau intended to use was out of date, that the intendant had no instructions from the king as to the appointment, and that d'Auteuil, being only twenty-one, was too young for the post. Over Frontenac's protests the Council ruled that the intendant should appoint whomsoever he thought fit. Duchesneau filled out the blank commission in d'Auteuil's name and despite Frontenac's protests, it was registered by the Council, d'Auteuil being accepted as acting attorney-general with the stipulation that he should obtain letters of dispensation from the king on account of his youth.[56]

Had it not been that d'Auteuil was the only man in the colony with the qualifications and training required for the post, it would appear that Duchesneau and the Sovereign Council had selected him purely to defy Frontenac; and there can be little doubt that this factor did enter into it. But d'Auteuil had graduated in law from the University of Paris, and he had been admitted to the bar of the *Parlement de Paris*; moreover, upon his return to Canada he had worked under his father's tutelage for two years, gaining experience ready to succeed to his father's post.[57]

Surprisingly enough, the winter of 1679–80 was a very tranquil one so far as the Sovereign Council was concerned. Frontenac rarely attended the meetings, and the register is headed simply "The Council assembled." [58] When the ships from France finally arrived in October, 1680, it must have been an anxious moment for all concerned while the seals on the official dispatches were being broken, followed by the most intense chagrin for Frontenac, triumph and gloating for the Sovereign Council, and satisfaction blended with misgivings for Duchesneau.

The king's dispatch to Frontenac began :

M. le comte de Frontenac, I was astounded to learn of all the new disputes and new divisions that have occurred in my province of New France . . . all the more so since I gave you clearly and firmly to understand, both in your instructions and in all the letters that I have written you in the past years, that your one main purpose must be to maintain unity and tranquillity among all my subjects living in that country. But that which astonishes me even more is that in nearly all the strife that you have originated, there is very little justification for all that you have laid claim to. My edicts, decrees and proclamations have made my wishes so clear to you that I have all the more reason to be astonished that you, who must always see to it that no one whomsoever evades their execution, you have advanced claims that are completely contrary to them. [59]

Having condemned Frontenac's conduct in general, the king then made it plain that in his struggle with the Sovereign Council the governor had been in the wrong on all counts. His demand that he be given the title and prerogatives of chief and president was declared completely contrary to the *déclaration* of 1675. And, the king added, "I am all the more surprised at that claim since I am assured that it is only you alone in the whole of my kingdom who, being honoured with the title of governor and lieutenant-general in a country, has wanted to be named chief and president of a council such as that of Canada." This clearly implied that Frontenac had demeaned both himself and the royal authority by his pretentions. He was ordered to cease, once and for all, from advancing such preposterous claims, and the king spelled this out in words of one syllable, stating that Frontenac had no authority to retain in his possession the register of the Council, or to collect the voices of the Councillors at their meetings, or to deliver the judgements;

these functions, the king stated, belonged to the intendant. Frontenac's exiling of the attorney-general and the two councillors "for such a flimsy reason" was most displeasing to the king and, Louis XIV added, had it not been for the definite assurances given him by Frontenac's friends that he would act with more moderation in the future and avoid all such acts, he would have recalled him at once.

Colbert, too, had a few things to say. Writing in his own hand, he informed Frontenac that his exiling of d'Auteuil and the councillors was unpardonable and it was only the hope that he would radically alter his conduct in future that had spared him from having heavy damages deducted from his salary. Colbert further informed Frontenac that the king had examined the evidence himself very carefully and as a result was convinced that Frontenac was responsible for all the trouble in the colony. But, in spite of this, Louis had decided to allow him to remain at his post for another year in the hopes that he would mend his ways, although, he bluntly added, the king saw little hope of this occurring: "His Majesty sees clearly that you are quite incapable of adopting the spirit of concord and tolerance that is needed to obviate all the dissension which occurs in that country." [60] And officials at the Court now began receiving soliciting letters from men anxious to obtain the post of governor of New France. It had not taken long for word to circulate that Frontenac was soon to be recalled. [61]

Duchesneau, for his part, was informed that he had to alter his attitude or else expect to have his career in the royal service abruptly terminated. The king informed him that Frontenac's attempts to usurp the intendant's functions in the Sovereign Council did not justify his conduct; all that he was permitted to do in such circumstances was to lodge a protest with the governor, stating his reasons for doing so, warn him that he was obliged to inform the king of what was occurring, and show the governor a copy of his dispatch containing this report. That done, if Frontenac still refused to modify his stand, then Duchesneau was to submit and carry out the governor's orders. On no account was an intendant to resist a governor who represented the authority and person of the king; the king reserved to himself the right of judging and remedying affairs of this nature. [62] Colbert, in his dispatch, informed Duchesneau that if he could not stop antagonizing Frontenac he would do better to return to France and retire to his home at Tours. [63]

Unfortunately for Duchesneau, he did not possess sufficient strength of character to follow these instructions. While it is true that a weaker man might well have allowed himself to be intimidated by Frontenac, it still did not require a great deal of courage for a man in his position to stand up to the governor. But it did require a great deal of self-control and strength of character to rise above Frontenac's continual provocations. Had he been able to treat the governor's abuses with detachment he would have gained the moral ascendancy, and his restraining influence on Frontenac would have been far greater. Duchesneau knew full well what was required of him by the minister, but it was beyond his capacities, and he virtually admitted as much to Colbert in his dispatch of November, 1679, when he stated with considerable feeling: "I believed that I could not neglect to tell you the exact truth of what was going on in this country and thereby expose myself to whatever the consequences might be, in order to obtain for it the well-being that it expects from your patronage. If I had considered only my personal interest and had disregarded and abandoned that of the colony, I would have behaved differently and would have put myself in a position upon my first arrival here to retire to France and live at ease with my family." [64]

As to the Sovereign Council, it had scored a decisive victory over the governor. Its members had resisted his attempts to reduce them to subservience and they had been upheld by the king and the minister. With the reinstatement of his old foe, Villeray, Frontenac's humiliation was complete. Consequently, they would have been less than human had they not gloated while registering two decrees. The first was a decree of the Council of State, declaring in precise terms that in all the Sovereign Council's records and promulgations, Frontenac was to be accorded the title of governor and lieutenant-general, nothing more, Duchesneau was to be accorded the title of intendant and perform the functions of a president of the superior courts, and no one was to be accorded any title or function other than those contained in his commission. [65] The second decree was issued by the Sovereign Council itself, appointing d'Auteuil to the position of attorney-general—previously he had been only acting in that capacity. Shortly before his death the elder d'Auteuil had written to the minister, pleading that his son should be allowed to succeed to his position. [66] The king having granted this request and furnished the requisite letters patent, the latter were now duly registered by the Sovereign Council and d'Auteuil officially installed.[67]

Frontenac's reaction to this reversal of his fortunes was to proclaim his complete innocence of all error or wrong-doing. Writing to his friend the Maréchal de Bellefonds, he complained bitterly that he was a much-abused man, long-suffering and possessed of infinite patience in the face of the most insufferable provocations. In a surly mood he declared: "I will have nothing more to do with the intendant, the bishop, or the Jesuits." [68]

It would appear that he really believed himself to be completely blameless and Duchesneau seems to have spoken the truth when he wrote in 1679: "The spectacle of all the officers of the Council uniting to prevent any damage being done to the king's Proclamation caused monsieur the governor to launch into strange fits of passion against them; even going so far as to call them seditious rebels. He has tried to make their common accord appear to be a cabal, and this is the term he has always used in an attempt to discredit all that has been done for the good of the country and to render suspect the most honest persons." [69] Thus, with Frontenac in an unchastened mood and undoubtedly vengeful, and with the Sovereign Council flexing its new-found muscles despite Frontenac's declaration that he would have no further disputes with his old foes, trouble there was bound to be; nor was it long in coming.

Villeray and d'Auteuil, the latter at last feeling secure in his position, now treated Frontenac with studied politeness but scant courtesy. Every time he inveighed against them for their attitude towards him, he received curt answers tinged with sarcasm. Not content to parry Frontenac's invective, they carried the war to his territory by undertaking strong measures against the *coureurs de bois*. On December 10 a Montreal merchant named Bouthier appeared before the Sovereign Council to demand the protection of the court against the governor of Montreal, who had personally attacked him, seized a quantity of his furs and driven him out of the town at sword-point, solely because Perrot suspected Bouthier of having made disparaging remarks about his activities in the fur trade.[70] From all accounts the situation in Montreal was deplorable. Despite the severe reprimand that Perrot had received from Colbert, upon his return to Montreal, instead of mending his ways, he had attempted to prevent anyone lodging further complaints against him by terrorizing the populace. In this he received considerable assistance from Boisseau, an agent of the Company of the Farm who enjoyed Frontenac's protection. When the Sieur Migeon, bailiff of Montreal, arrested certain *coureurs de bois* in Perrot's employ, Perrot promptly arrested him and Boisseau seized all the furs he could find in Migeon's house. Not satisfied with that, Perrot quartered a sergeant and two men in the bailiff's house for twelve days, where they did considerable damage to the furnishings, and this in spite of the fact that Madame Migeon was in labour at the time. As a result of such treatment, Migeon resigned his post.[71]

One of the bailiff's guards had been imprisoned twice by Perrot for interfering with illicit brandy-peddling by Perrot's men, and two of his sergeants had been wounded for the same cause. Others in the town complained of being assaulted by Perrot's adherents and of receiving nothing but threats of worse treatment when they demanded satisfaction from the governor. One of Perrot's more outspoken critics awoke one morning to find all the fruit trees in his orchard cut down. And when the Ottawas came to Montreal Perrot stationed his guards to prevent all but his own and Frontenac's supporters from trading with them. On one occasion he was reported to have traded the clothes off his back to an Indian who then paraded around the town dressed as the governor, while Perrot boasted that he had made a profit of thirty *pistoles* on the exchange. It was estimated that in 1680 alone he had made some 40,000 *livres* profit out of the fur trade [72] and two years later the Abbé Tronson, informing Dollier de Casson that Perrot had sent letters of exchange to Paris for over 20,000 *livres*, then remarked: "Judge if after that anyone will question the trade that he carries on; I told M. Seignelay and I held the proof in my hand." [73]

In view of all this, and knowing full well that Perrot enjoyed Frontenac's protection, the Sovereign Council determined to take matters into their own hands. On October 13, 1680, they decided to send one of their own members, the Sieur de la Martinière, to Montreal to investigate matters and to take whatever action he deemed necessary. In the three weeks that he spent on the island, Martinière certainly made his presence felt. He arrested *coureurs de bois* and seized contraband goods right and left.[74] Since he was closely associated in the fur trade with La Chesnaye, *Le Ber* and le Moyne, it is more than likely that it was not their *voyageurs* but those of La Salle whom he prosecuted so assiduously. Be that as it may, Frontenac was very disturbed, and the following spring, when the Council proposed sending Martinière and d'Auteuil to Montreal to renew the drive against the *coureurs de bois*, he vigorously opposed any such move. To justify his stand he declared that the king had had two ends in view in forbidding trade with the Indians outside the confines of the colony : to maintain law and order and to protect the revenues of the Farm. He then argued that sending Martinière and d'Auteuil on commission to arrest the *coureurs de bois* would defeat the ends desired by the king, because the amount of all fines levied on the *coureurs de bois*—the usual fine being two thousand *livres*[75]—should go to the Farm, and since the commissioners' expenses would have to be deducted from the amounts received in fines, their expenses would thus reduce these sums. Peculiar though this logic may seem, it was no whit more so than that contained in his second argument, wherein he claimed that the people of Montreal were very disturbed by rumours of sterner measures being taken against the *coureurs de bois* and those who supplied them, and he believed that if these measures were actually taken there might be serious disturbances. And since it was his responsibility as governor to preserve good order in the colony, he could not permit of anything that would tend to upset it.[76]

Needless to say, it did not take Duchesneau long to tear these arguments to shreds.[77] The Council rejected Frontenac's remonstrance, thereby infuriating him, and sent the two commissioners off to the head of the colony. According to Duchesneau, they suffered a great deal of abuse and harsh treatment at the hands of Frontenac's followers[78] and Frontenac himself put every obstacle in their way.[79] At the end of June, Martinière and d'Auteuil returned to Quebec, and the following month the results of their investigations were placed before the Council. Both Perrot and Boisseau were charged with various crimes and Frontenac regarded this attempt by the Council to try his followers as an attack on his authority. The Council accused Frontenac of impeding justice, claiming that he was delaying the hearing of the charges laid against these two officials to prevent their cases being heard before the ships sailed for France, and so prevent the findings of the court being sent to the king until the following year. They also accused Frontenac and Boisseau of intimidating witnesses to prevent their giving evidence, thereby rendering the Council helpless to protect the people against these abuses. At one point they requested Frontenac to absent himself from the hearings because of "the protection that he accords to the said Boisseau in everything."[80] Finally, the Council defied the governor and sent the entire proceedings to the king to prevent Frontenac using his arbitrary authority to quash the charges.[81]

That year, the dispatches from the Court arrived in August and they should have made it very apparent to Frontenac that the patience of both Louis XIV and the minister was all but exhausted. The King's dispatch stated:

> I admonish you to banish from your mind all the difficulties that you have created so far in the execution of my orders; to behave with good-natured moderation towards all the *habitants*; to strip yourself of all the personal animosities which up till now have been almost the sole incentive of all your actions; nothing being more inconsistent with the duty which you have to discharge for me in the position that you hold. . . . I see clearly that everything gives way to your private enmities, and that that which concerns my service and the execution of my orders is rarely the sole motive of your actions.[82]

And in the final sentence of this dispatch Frontenac was informed that unless the king learned that his orders were achieving better results than they had in the past, there would be no alternative but to recall him.

In his reply Frontenac once again protested his complete innocence of all wrong-doing. He declared: "Your Majesty will plainly see that I have never had to endure more than when I have been made to appear violent and as a man who would disturb the officers of justice in the duties of their office." He accused Duchesneau of having deliberately goaded and provoked him with slanderous accusations and calumnies. He claimed that the trouble all stemmed from the fact that M. Duchesneau had found a way to "gain complete control over the proceedings of the Sovereign Council."[83]

Finally, Frontenac took a step which made his recall inevitable. During the preceding twelve months the attorney-general had balked him at every turn in the Sovereign Council and this had so infuriated Frontenac that he now ordered d'Auteuil to cross over to France to account to the minister for his insolent and captious behaviour. To justify this rash action he used the excuse that at the time of his appointment, d'Auteuil had not been of the required age. In 1680, when he issued the letters patent to d'Auteuil permitting him to succeed to the position, the minister had been aware of d'Auteuil's age; at least, he had been informed of it by d'Auteuil's father.[84] Frontenac, however, left no doubts in the minister's mind of the real reasons for his action: "That which determined me," he explained, "is the way that he has induced the Council to persist in their affronts against me at every meeting held since the adjournment."[85]

Frontenac also claimed that the Sovereign Council had so far forgotten its obligations that, in spite of the authority vested by the king in a governor-general, it wished to make him submit to its jurisdiction.[86] There was a certain element of truth in this statement, for the Sovereign Council had sought, if not to try Frontenac, at least to make him a party to a trial whereat he would have had to justify his actions to the Council. This issue arose out of a violent personal conflict between Frontenac and Duchesneau. The trouble began one day in March, 1681, when Duchesneau's sixteen-year-old son, accompanied by his father's valet, Vaultier, was accosted on the street by Frontenac's follower, Boisseau. According to young Duchesneau, Boisseau called him foul names and threatened to thrash both him and his father at the first opportunity.[87] Young Duchesneau and Vaultier retorted with a few well-chosen insults reflecting on Boisseau's parentage and probity. Boisseau reported the incident to Frontenac who demanded an immediate explanation from Duchesneau. The intendant then sent his son and Vaultier, accompanied by the boy's preceptor and a secretary, to Frontenac, but instead of tendering their apologies to the governor for insulting a member of his following, young Duchesneau demanded that Boisseau apologize to him. At this Frontenac lost his temper, rushed at the lad, began belabouring him with his cane, and nearly tore the sleeve off his coat. Only the intervention of the governor's secretaries spared the intendant's son from worse damage. Young Duchesneau and those with him managed to escape from the room, but on the way out of the château Vaultier was set upon by Boisseau and some of Frontenac's servants. When they reached home, Duchesneau, fearing that the governor in his fury would order his son taken by force, barricaded his house and armed his servants. Later, Frontenac sent an officer to the intendant, demanding that his son and servant be sent to the château. Duchesneau refused on the grounds that they had been too severely mal-treated the first time. Meanwhile Bishop Laval, having heard that Frontenac intended to take the lad and the servant by force, went to Frontenac with his vicar-general and another ecclesiastic, to offer his services to settle the affair before things got completely out of control. Frontenac told Laval that he intended to make the intendant submit, by force if necessary, but he finally agreed to hold his hand until nine o'clock the next morning. The bishop then hurried over to see the intendant, who still refused to send his son and Vaultier to Frontenac. He gave Laval a written statement of his reasons for this which Laval took to the governor. Frontenac rejected this account as false but he agreed that Laval should return and try to induce the intendant to let him, accompanied by certain of his ecclesiastics, bring the intendant's son to the château and remain with him in Frontenac's presence while he was being in-terrogated by the governor. Duchesneau agreed to this, stating that he would do whatever was needed to settle the matter, except to allow his son to be taken by force. As to the servant, Vaultier, Duchesneau demanded guarantees that he would not be physically maltreated in any way or summarily imprisoned, and he offered to have him committed to trial on whatever charges Frontenac wished to prefer.

Upon being reapproached, Frontenac accepted the intendant's proposals respecting his son, but demanded that Vaultier be handed over to him unconditionally. At this, Duchesneau himself com-mitted Vaultier to gaol, to forestall the governor. Laval then man-aged to persuade Frontenac that the cases of Vaultier and young Duchesneau were not necessarily dependent one upon the other, hence the latter case could be settled immediately, while Frontenac reserved the right to take whatever measures he saw fit in that of Vaultier. Three days later Frontenac changed his mind. He now went to the bishop and demanded that the intendant should hand over his servant unconditionally before there could be any settle-ment respecting his son. Laval reminded Frontenac that he had given his word to allow young Duchesneau to appear before him in the presence of the bishop. At this Frontenac stamped out, re-peatedly shouting that he had revoked his word.

A few hours later Frontenac sent an officer to the bishop's palace, where Duchesneau's son was staying in order to be ready to accom-pany the bishop to the château at a moment's notice, with orders to fetch the boy. Bishop Laval could do no other than accede to this direct command. The lad was led away by the officer and, upon his arrival at the château, Frontenac had him placed under lock and key and kept there for a month. Vaultier too was forcibly removed from the prison by Frontenac's guards and immured in a cell in the château where he was allowed to see no one.[88] Their imprisonment in this fashion was completely contrary to the king's edict of 1679, which forbade a governor to imprison anyone arbitrarily for anything less than sedition or intelligence with an enemy of the state. At the next meeting of the Sovereign Council Frontenac was asked to show cause for Vaultier's being retained prisoner without being brought to trial, to which the governor could only make the rather empty threat that he would report their insolence to the king. After much heated wrangling, and over Frontenac's angry protests, the Council voted to send the records of this case to the Court.[89]

Frontenac subsequently denied ever having struck Duchesneau's son and he declared that the boy had been guilty of gross impudence towards Boisseau who, incidentally, was at this time awaiting trial by the Sovereign Council on other charges and was later dismissed from his post and shipped back to France on Colbert's orders. Frontenac also claimed that he had been insulted by young Duchesneau when he tried to question him. Mme Frontenac, in a memoir which she submitted to the minister in defence of her husband, also denied that he had laid a finger on the boy, but, she added, he indubitably had merited a sound thrashing for his insolence, and the fact that he had not received it was sufficient to prove that her husband was the most moderate of men.[90] As to the intendant's barricading his house and arming his servants, this, they both claimed, was nothing short of armed rebellion.[91]

The day following the Council's disposal of the Vaultier case, Frontenac carried things to an extreme that must have made even Mme de Frontenac despair when she learned of it. In one of his impassioned outbursts he arrested an elderly member of the Sovereign Council, the 63-year-old Sieur Damours, and held him a prisoner for six weeks. The previous April, Damours had obtained a passport from the governor permitting him to send a canoe to his concession at Matane and to send a barque to the same destination once the river was free of ice. That Frontenac should require anyone to obtain his passport for trips such as this was in itself contrary to the explicit instructions of the minister. Upon the return of his barque on August 12, Damours went down to the wharf to superintend its unloading and was arrested by one of the governor's guards. He was conducted to the château and brought before Frontenac who demanded to know why he had sent his barque to Matane without obtaining a passport. Damours explained that he had obtained a passport the previous April covering the canoe and the barque. Frontenac declared that this passport had been for the canoe only. Damours, with mock civility, begged the governor's pardon, and then stated that he had been under the impression that the original passport was for both. Moreover, he added, the barque had gone only to his concession at Matane and he had been led to believe that the king had sanctioned that "we could go without hindrance to the lands that he had granted us." This apposite but insolent reply caused Frontenac to lose control of his temper. He immediately sent for his guards. When they rushed in he stormed at Damours, shouting that the councillor would learn in prison what the king's intentions were and could remain there until he did. With that Damours was marched off to the cells.[92]

The following Saturday, when the Sovereign Council met, there was a very tense feeling in the air. Just as the meeting was about to begin, Mme Damours entered the chamber and without a word placed a sealed envelope on the table. The Council immediately turned to deal with this missive, knowing full well what it contained, but Frontenac interrupted, declaring that this procedure was out of order and insisting that they continue with routine business. The Council overruled him and proceeded to read Damours's letter, in which he requested that he be informed of the charges against him and that he be brought to trial in the normal manner. Duchesneau then requested the governor to make his intentions known to the Council. Frontenac brusquely refused, claiming that it was no affair of the Council's and that Damours would have to answer to the king for his insolence. The Council refused to heed this, and, despite Frontenac's furious remonstrances, they proceeded with the trial of their fellow-councillor. This meant, as in the Vaultier case, that Frontenac was treated as a party to the suit, and, judging by the manner in which d'Auteuil conducted the hearings, the governor rather than Damours was the one on trial. Finally, over Frontenac's continued protests, the Council decided to send their deliberations on the case to the king.[93] Much though it must have cost him, Frontenac was now forced tacitly to admit that this time he had gone too far. He dared not send Damours to France; Duchesneau and the Sovereign Council had very neatly out-manoeuvred him by committing his prisoner to trial on Frontenac's own charges, which were clearly *ultra vires*. He had no alternative but to release Damours, who reappeared at the meetings of the Sovereign Council in October.[94]

When the account of all these happenings reached the Court, accompanied by Duchesneau's secretary, Denis Riverin, and the attorney-general, all the influence in the world could not have saved Frontenac. Mme de Frontenac and her friends, including the Comte d'Estrades, M. de Monars and others as influential, used their best efforts with the king's councillors in his support, but to no avail. Seignelay studied the evidence and interrogated Riverin and d'Auteuil personally, and Louis XIV demanded that he be informed of all that had transpired.[95] Despite their previous awareness of Frontenac's ungovernable temper they must have been shocked to learn of his violence against a boy in his teens and an elderly man, the one the son of a very senior royal official, the other a member of the Sovereign Council—not to mention his arbitrary imprisonment of another of the king's subjects, the lowly valet, Vaultier. They must also have asked themselves what effects these actions would be likely to have on the Canadian people. The sight of the governor's guards and the archers of the town-major marching through the town from the Château St. Louis to the intendant's house, then to the bishop's palace, to arrest persons of such consequence, and the intendant barricading his house and arming his servants with pikes and swords ready to stand off the governor's guards, must have caused a considerable stir among the populace.

In March, 1682, the Abbé Tronson wrote: "There will be changes made in Canada this year. They are convinced that the good of the country demands it."[96] Louis XIV and Seignelay decided finally that the only way to restore tranquillity in the colony was to dismiss Frontenac. And at the same time it was determined, with some reluctance, to recall Duchesneau as well, since to have left him in his post while recalling Frontenac would have cast a shadow on the royal authority vested in the governor-general; and also, it would have been regarded as a personal slight by Frontenac's powerful friends at the Court.[97] On May 9 the letters recalling both

Frontenac and Duchesneau were issued.[98] Six months later they were both on their way back to France. So ended Frontenac's first regime, the most turbulent in the entire history of the colony.

In 1680, Colbert, writing over the king's signature, had reiterated to Frontenac in great detail exactly what his duties were. The most important, he wrote, was to ensure the military preparedness of the colony; the *habitants* had to be given military training and the defences of the colony maintained to prevent any aggression on the part of the Iroquois and enable the settlers to live in peace and security. Once that condition was assured the governor had to do everything possible to guarantee the social and economic welfare of the people. Colbert wrote:

> Your sole aim must be to develop and strengthen this colony and to attract new settlers by the protection and good treatment which you afford to those already there. It is plain that the conduct which you have pursued up to now is very far removed from these principles, particularly in your hounding of the leading citizens and in forcing many others through personal dissatisfaction to return to France. Above all, meditate well on the fact that in order to achieve these aims you must have neither partiality nor prejudice towards anyone; you must give every liberty to all the merchants and to all the ships which carry on any commerce there; encourage continually all the *habitants* to engage in the cultivation of the land, trade, manufacturing, fishing and anything else that could be of profit to them; and, to keep them at work in the settlements, stop them roaming about in the woods in the hope of profits which tends towards the utter ruination of the colony and the small amount of commerce that it can engage in. In these few words consists the gist and the end of what must be your entire efforts and of all that you can do to make your services pleasing to me.[99]

How well had Frontenac carried out these instructions? Colbert himself gave the answer when, in 1680, he stated that New France "runs the risk of being completely destroyed unless you alter both your conduct and your principles." He then went on to say:

All the corporate bodies and nearly all the private individuals who return to this country complain of clear-cut cases of ill treatment meted out to them in a manner quite contrary to the spirit of moderation which you should exercise in the maintenance of peace and good order among the people, all as enjoined in my orders and dispatches. My revenue collectors complain that trade is being lost and destroyed by the *coureurs de bois*, that they receive no protection and that you permit neither the departure of the ships at times when they could leave, nor freedom of navigation on the rivers without your permits and passports. The bishop and his clergy, the Jesuit fathers and the Sovereign Council, and, in one word, all the public bodies and private persons, they all complain.[100]

Even Francis Parkman, a staunch advocate for Frontenac and the historian who has done more than any other to create the generally accepted estimate of him, had difficulty in defending Frontenac's sorry record in civil affairs. Parkman asserts that there was not "much doubt that many of his worst outbreaks were the work of his enemies, who knew his foible, and studied to exasperate him." [101] There is enough truth in this statement to make it misleading. Certainly, Frontenac's enemies gave him no rest, because he gave them none. He would still have had some enemies even if he had not been possessed of his "foible"—no one in his position could avoid it—but they alone would not have set the colony by the ears. Parkman has done little more here than to confuse, all too neatly, cause and effect.

The only aspects of Frontenac's conduct that the king and the minister did not condemn were his care for the military security of the colony and his relations with the Iroquois and the tribes allied to the French. The reason for their silence on this, the most important aspect of Frontenac's government, was that they were not aware of the true nature of the situation. Had they been, this alone would undoubtedly have resulted in Frontenac's instant dismissal from office, as it did that of his successor three years later. Yet it is here that the Frontenac myth flourishes most vigorously. He is forgiven his sorry record in civil affairs because, as an eminent modern scholar puts it : "Whatever his faults . . . he was the perfect frontier governor . . . and perhaps his greatest claim to fame was his astute handling of the Indian situation." And Parkman claimed that when Frontenac was recalled "he left behind him an impression, very general among the people, that, if danger threatened the colony, Count Frontenac was the man for the hour." [100] But the people of New France—as distinct from a handful of officials and clergy—have, unfortunately, left no record of their impressions, and what evidence there is indicates very clearly that the opposite impression to that imagined by Parkman was the prevalent one throughout the colony.

CHAPTER EIGHT

LA BARRE'S ABORTIVE WAR

THE man who succeeded Frontenac as governor of New France was Le Febvre de la Barre. He was a member of the *noblesse de robe*, a lawyer rather than a soldier, and in the course of his sixty years he had held several important civil posts under the crown. Son of a former mayor of Paris, he had been appointed an officer of the judiciary (*maître des requêtes*) in 1646, and later served as intendant in Paris during the Fronde, then successively as intendant of Grenobles, Moulins and Auvergne, before being appointed governor of Cayenne in French Guiana.[1] In 1666, when he was placed in command of an expedition being sent to the West Indies to defend them against the English, Colbert de Terron, the intendant at Rochefort, warned the minister that La Barre was the wrong man for the job, having no stomach for war. His subsequent actions in the Caribbean area gave Colbert de Terron no cause to revise his opinion.[2]

For the post of intendant, the Court had selected the Sieur Bégon, who was reputed to be a man of outstanding qualities, but at the last moment it was decided to send him to the West Indies instead. In his place, his brother-in-law, Jacques de Meulles, a relative of Colbert's by marriage, was chosen.* [3] Before they left for New France, both de Meulles and La Barre were instructed that one of their most important tasks would be to restore order and good government in the colony and to avoid at all costs the quarrels that had done so much damage during the previous administration. To make doubly sure that there would be no repetition of these disturbances, Louis XIV went to the trouble of instructing La Barre

* At this time, May, 1682, Jean Talon was trying very hard to get back to Canada. He was striving to obtain an appointment to establish a hostel for the poor and aged at Quebec. When Seignelay failed to approve of the scheme, Talon offered to go to Quebec at his own expense to found this *Hôpital Général*, asking only that he be given royal protection. Observers at the Court were perplexed by this and deduced that Talon expected that de Meulles would not remain long in Canada and that if he, Talon, were on the spot he would have a good chance of succeeding to the intendancy.

personally on the manner in which he was to conduct the government of the colony.[4]

During the first few months after their arrival at Quebec, relations between La Barre and de Meulles appear to have been amicable enough. They had their hands full trying to get the members of the Sovereign Council to forget the passionate divisions of the previous government and to turn their attention to the administration of civil affairs and the dispensing of justice.[5] Before he had been in the colony a year, however, La Barre began to show a marked tendency to act in a very autocratic manner and to usurp functions that clearly belonged to the office of intendant. He even went so far as to claim the title of head of the Sovereign Council, but the minister rapidly disabused him of this notion.[6] And de Meulles, who was a born intriguer but not a very clever one, appears to have believed that he could discredit La Barre sufficiently in the eyes of the minister to have him stripped of most of his authority and himself allowed to act as governor in all but name. He went about this in so flagrant a manner that Seignelay, upon reading de Meulles's dispatches, exclaimed that the man must be out of his mind even to suggest such things, and he seriously questioned the wisdom of allowing de Meulles to remain any longer in his post. A blistering letter from Seignelay sufficed, however, to bring de Meulles to his senses, and, on the surface at least, the discord was smoothed over sufficiently to allow the civil administration of the colony to function effectively.[7]

Such problems as these faded into insignificance when contrasted with the major task confronting La Barre, that of retaining the western fur trade in the face of attacks by the Iroquois on the French allies on the one hand and the keen competition of the English posts in Hudson Bay on the other. The under-secretary who had drawn up La Barre's official instructions had made it all seem very simple. Of the threat from Hudson Bay, this official appeared to be unaware; as to the Iroquois threat, La Barre was required to reduce these tribes to obedience and prevent them attacking both the Illinois and the other allies who supplied the furs, and the Canadians who brought these furs down to Montreal from the west. All this could be done, it was suggested, by taking a body of five to six hundred Canadians to the borders of the Iroquois country and this would suffice to frighten them into submission. But he was to attack them only as a last resort, and only if he were absolutely certain that he could bring such a campaign to a speedy and completely satisfactory conclusion.[8]

Shortly after his arrival at Quebec La Barre called together all the leading men in the colony to obtain their opinions, and after discussing the matter with them he realized that it was impossible to reconcile his instructions with the existing situation. These men were unanimous in declaring that the Iroquois, incited by the English, were determined to break the French hold on the western fur trade and were following a deliberate policy of keeping the French inactive by alternate threats and peaceful gestures while they conquered the French allies one by one. As a good example of this shrewd policy, they cited the peace envoy sent by the Onondagas the previous month to confer with Frontenac. De Meulles informed the minister that this had succeeded in duping Frontenac and restraining the French from taking any action while the Senecas pressed their attacks against the Illinois. They were all agreed that the only way to curb the Iroquois was by the threat of force, and if that did not suffice, by the use of it.[9] La Barre immediately sent an urgent appeal to the king, asking for two or three hundred regular troops to guard the colony and garrison Fort Frontenac, and a hundred and fifty indentured labourers to work on the land while the militia were under arms. With the aid of these reinforcements he proposed to march an army of twelve hundred men to the Iroquois country, spend the winter in their cantons, and from this base send out raiding parties of Canadians and allied Indians to track down the Iroquois and destroy them piecemeal.

As for the threat presented to the fur trade by the English posts in Hudson Bay, La Barre was quick to appreciate its seriousness. According to reports reaching him from the west, the Hudson's Bay Company men were going up one of the rivers in the direction of Lake Superior and were inducing the Indian tribes of the area, by means of their cheaper merchandise, to trade at their posts rather than at Montreal. In an attempt to curb this threat he issued permits for trading with these particular tribes and sent orders to du Lhut to use all his influence to deter them from going down to the Bay. He also persuaded several of the leading merchants in the colony to join with La Chesnaye and his associates in the formation of a Canadian Hudson's Bay Company for the prime purpose of contesting the hold that the English company had already gained in the Bay.[10]

The following spring, when the Iroquois refused to come to Montreal to confer with the governor, answering instead that he could come to them if he desired a conference, La Barre and de Meulles were confirmed in their view that a full-scale campaign would have to be undertaken. They now sent a ship to France post-haste and as secretly as possible to inform the minister of their plans and to request reinforcements. This time they asked for six hundred regular troops, one thousand muskets, and as many swords. In the meantime, they stated, they intended to use the Iroquois' own tactics by temporizing and keeping their plans for the campaign as dark as possible.[11] Hardly had this ship left Quebec with these dispatches than La Barre received word that his hopes of receiving reinforcements from France were very slim indeed. A private letter dated March 8 informed him that Frontenac had given the minister definite assurance that he had negotiated a peace settlement with the Iroquois before leaving the colony. Since Frontenac could claim ten years' experience as governor and La Barre only a few weeks', the king and Seignelay were more inclined to give credence to Frontenac's appraisal of the situation than to La Barre's.[12]

This placed La Barre in an extremely difficult position. The Iroquois were now sending strong war parties to attack not only the Miamis but also the Ottawas. From these latter tribes the French derived two-thirds of their furs. But all that La Barre could do was quietly to reinforce the western posts and somehow try to avert an open clash with the Iroquois. He intended to follow this course of action, he informed the minister, "in order to give you the time needed to obtain from the king definite decisions on the matter."[13] Accordingly, he sent the Sieur le Moyne to the Onondagas to try to persuade the Five Nations to confer with him at Montreal later that summer. At the same time he sent an officer of his guards, the Chevalier de Baugy, with men and munitions to take over the command of Fort St. Louis from Henri Tonty. To Michilimackinac he sent thirty men commanded by Morel de la Durantaye, a retired officer of the regular army, where they joined forces with du Lhut and his men just in time to deter a Cayuga war party from attacking the Ottawas. At the request of La Salle he sent a sergeant of his guards with a body of men to Fort Frontenac to prevent the Iroquois' pillaging the supplies at this post and to strengthen its dilapidated defences.[14] Le Moyne, not without considerable difficulty, persuaded the Five Nations to confer with La Barre at Montreal. When their chiefs arrived, La Barre opened the conference by giving the Senecas liberal presents to expunge their rancour over the death of their chief in the Illinois camp two years earlier; but he obtained no satisfaction when he demanded to know why they were attacking the Illinois. Tegannissorens, the Onondaga spokesman, is reputed to have answered defiantly, "They deserve to die; they have shed our blood." [15] La Barre did not press this point further. But the Iroquois delegates did agree to have their general council approve La Barre's demand that the Ottawas and Hurons be left in peace, and to return the following spring to ratify this treaty.[16]

La Barre was well enough satisfied with the results of the conference; he had prevented the war spreading for the time being, thereby gaining a breathing spell, and during this respite he hoped to receive definite instructions from Versailles. If, as he and de Meulles urged, the minister agreed to their waging a campaign against the Iroquois, then troops and the necessary munitions and supplies would have to be sent out early in the following year. But if the minister decided against war, then all that could be done would be to try to appease the Iroquois with sizable presents when they returned to Montreal in the spring. Should this prove to be the case, La Barre requested permission to return to France in the autumn for a few months to explain to the minister the true state of affairs in the colony; for, as he bluntly stated in a separate dispatch to Colbert: "The situation in this country is not understood either by you or by my lord the marquis; it has been depicted to you in a fashion far removed from the truth." [17]

And while La Barre, from a distance of three thousand miles, was striving to make the minister understand the urgency of the situation, Seignelay himself was too concerned with other questions to pay much attention to Canadian affairs. On May 26 the king left Paris for a two months' sojourn in the provinces; on the 28th, when Seignelay followed him, the dispatches for Canada were still to be drafted. These matters had perforce to be cursorily dealt with by the minister in his coach as it lurched over the pot-holed roads of northern France.[18] Under such circumstances it would not be surprising if Seignelay relied more on his recollections of the verbal assurances given him by Frontenac than on a close examination of La Barre's and de Meulles's lengthy dispatches.

In November, just before the last ships of the year sailed from the colony, a frigate finally arrived at Quebec bearing the long-overdue orders and instructions from the Court. When La Barre read them he must have despaired, for they made it all too plain that Seignelay had failed completely to comprehend the realities of the situation in Canada. The king's dispatch began with a series of platitudes to the effect that nothing could be worse for the colony than war. La Barre was instructed to pacify the Iroquois by diplomatic means. To tone down their insolent attitude two hundred troops with their officers, one thousand muskets and the same number of swords were being sent, along with the other supplies requested by the governor and intendant and 20,000 *livres* in specie. This last was to be used only if war was absolutely necessary, in which case the Iroquois were to be crushed quickly, forced to come to terms and prevented from interfering with the fur trade.[19] The king and the minister appeared to be completely ignorant of the fact that the Iroquois were already at war with the French allies; they required La Barre to avert a war that had already started.

The following year, in May, an ambassador from the Senecas arrived at Quebec to assure La Barre that his nation had no desire to do anything that might disturb their peaceful relations with the French. La Barre was very sceptical of the sincerity of this embassy, and he remarked that "past experience indicates that they have never discussed or treated for peace except when they wished to perpetrate a great deception and launch a surprise attack."[20] His suspicions were confirmed somewhat sooner than he had expected. Shortly after the arrival of the Seneca chief four *coureurs de bois* reached Quebec from the west. The previous March they and their eleven companions had been pursued and captured by a large Iroquois war party near Fort St. Louis in the Illinois country. Their seven canoes and all their merchandise, valued at over 15,000 *livres*, had been seized. After keeping them captive for nine days, the Senecas had turned them loose in the wilderness without food or canoes and with only two broken muskets, threatening to kill them if they were found in the vicinity of Fort St. Louis again. These men managed to make their way to an Outagamis village, and while they were there a messenger arrived from the Chevalier de

Baugy at Fort St. Louis with letters for Durantaye at Michilimackinac appealing for aid, and for Governor La Barre to inform him
that the Senecas were attacking the fort. De Baugy, with twenty-
four French and twenty-two allied Indians, had managed to beat
off the initial assault but at the time of writing they were dangerously short of food and ammunition. Some of the *coureurs de bois*
then headed for Michilimackinac to bring assistance to the be-
leaguered garrison; the remaining four went on to Quebec as fast
as they could. De Baugy managed to drive the Senecas off after six
days of siege, inflicting heavy casualties, but the issue was still in
doubt when La Barre received word of the assault. The governor's
first action was to seize the Seneca chief who was still conferring
with him and throw him into prison.[21]

Francis Parkman has advanced the theory, based on the testimony of Gédéon de Catalogne and La Salle, that La Barre embarked
on his subsequent campaign against the Iroquois to protect his
own fur-trading ventures. He goes on to claim that La Barre was
goaded into this rash action because, after he had granted the
Iroquois his permission to pillage any French canoes they encountered not bearing his passport, they had pillaged instead canoes that
not only did have his passport but in which he also had a financial
interest.[22] Several of La Barre's contemporaries stated that he was
taking a very active part in the fur trade,[23] despite explicit orders
from the king forbidding such activities.[24] De Meulles sent a lengthy
report to Seignelay accusing the governor of having entered into
partnership with Frontenac's old rivals, Le Ber, Le Moyne, and
La Chesnaye, and of having taken over La Salle's fur-trade organization, lock, stock and barrel.[25] It was quite true that La Barre removed La Salle's men from their control of the posts in the Illinois
country, replacing them with his own appointees, but he did have
some justification for this. La Salle's concession had been for a
period of five years only and this time-limit had expired; moreover,
the minister had made it plain that he was extremely dissatisfied
with the paucity of results shown by La Salle in his explorations.[26]
But as de Baugy, whom La Barre placed in command at Fort St.
Louis, wrote in a letter to his brother, the prospect of quick profits
in furs rather than the king's service was his main incentive,[27] just
as it had been La Salle's and Tonty's. De Meulles also accused the
governor of smuggling furs down to Albany, and Lahontan, for
what his statement is worth, substantiates the charge.[28] The in-

tendant's accusation that La Barre was issuing licences wholesale was echoed by the agent of the Company of the Farm, who complained that in 1683 over one hundred and twenty such permits had been issued instead of twenty-five.[29] La Barre did not expect to remain in the colony more than five years;[30] he apparently intended to make as much as he could out of the fur trade while he had the chance.

But the assertions that La Barre gave the Iroquois his permission to pillage La Salle's canoes are very dubious. The original author of this accusation was La Salle who, for sheer mendacity, had few equals. Gédéon de Catalogne repeated the charge, stating that La Chesnaye persuaded La Barre to instruct the Iroquois to pillage any canoes not carrying his passport,[31] but this account was written thirty years after the event and is demonstrably not too reliable. Another source of the accusation was Colonel Dongan, governor of New York. In a letter to the Marquis de Denonville dated September 9, 1687, in which he was seeking to justify the hostile actions of the Iroquois, and written over three years after the events described, he related that the Senecas had informed him they had pillaged the French canoes on orders from La Barre.[32] It may be that Dongan was confused by the fact that all governors of New France were referred to as Onontio by the Iroquois; in using the title in this instance they may have meant Frontenac, and Dongan, or his interpreter, understood them to mean the then governor, La Barre.

La Barre at the time vigorously denied the charge made by La Salle and he informed the king:

That which occurred at Montreal in August of last year . . . was so public and so authentic . . . that the entire country is witness that I have never spoken of declaring the said Sieur de la Salle an enemy of the country, nor invited the Iroquois to consider him as such. They made strong complaints about him to me and I told them that when the time granted him for his explorations expired, the king wished to see him in France; that I was sending out [to the west] a gentleman appointed by myself and I gave them a sash of wampum to make them cease causing the French, no matter who, any more trouble, and by this present revoking the instructions that had been given them by my predecessor, the Comte de Frontenac, to pillage all the French who were not the bearers of his seal.[33]

The Abbé Belmont confirms La Barre's statement; in describing this conference held with the Iroquois in Montreal in 1683, he states: "The right to pillage the French trading without permission was taken from them by a gift of five sashes [of wampum]."[34] Frontenac had had an obvious motive for giving the Iroquois his permission to pillage any canoes not bearing his passport. He had traded with them personally at Cataracoui every year until they became hostile, and La Salle's canoes and barques had to skirt Iroquois territory to reach his posts in the Illinois country. Moreover, he had used his authority to exclude, quite illegally, all but La Salle's men from the trade of the Illinois country. To protect himself and his associates from unwelcome competition in this area, and in the trade with the Five Nations, he may have enlisted the aid of the latter tribes before they turned openly hostile. Finally, although de Meulles accused La Barre of disregarding all the king's edicts concerning the fur trade and sent the minister very detailed accounts of the governor's activities in this field, he never made any mention of La Barre's having granted the Iroquois the right to pillage French canoes. If there had been the slightest trace of evidence to cause the intendant to suspect La Barre of such an act, then he would have been only too quick to inform the minister. Thus the burden of the evidence indicates, if anything, that it was more likely to have been Frontenac than La Barre who gave the Iroquois this dangerous privilege.

In any event, Parkman's argument, that La Barre undertook his campaign against the Iroquois because they had pillaged canoes in which he had an interest, is immaterial. The French had to send trade goods, arms and munitions to the posts in the Illinois country or else abandon the Illinois and Miamis to their fate. It did not matter who owned the canoes going to the Illinois country, or how many passports they had, they were still French canoes and the western Iroquois were determined to stop them.

When the news of the Iroquois attack on Fort St. Louis and the pillaging of the French canoes reached the colony, La Barre was urged from all sides to launch a full-scale attack on the Iroquois. The colony's merchants had over 100,000 écus worth of trade goods at the Ottawa posts; they feared that if the Five Nations were not curbed quickly the war would spread to this area.[35] The commanders of the western posts and the Jesuit missionaries with the French allies all claimed that there was no other course but to carry the war to the Iroquois country.[36] And in the colony itself the war fever reached an intense pitch.[37] Thus, far from rushing headlong into war, as Parkman maintains, La Barre was virtually pushed into it.

But, as La Barre later commented ruefully, the French, despite their fervour, were quite unprepared for any such war. They had no true conception of the real strength of the foe, nor of the type of warfare they would have to wage; and in the event of Iroquois reprisals, the colony's defences were non-existent. There had been no attacks on the colony for the past eighteen years, and during the previous Iroquois wars the Cayugas and the Senecas, who at that time numbered some sixteen hundred men, had been neutral. Nor had the French previously been faced with the problem of defending posts in the Illinois and Ottawa countries and maintaining to them lines of communication over a thousand miles long. As for the troops and supplies sent from France in 1683, these had proved to be pitifully inadequate. Instead of the five or six hundred regular soldiers requested by La Barre and de Meulles, they had been sent one hundred and fifty raw recruits of the Troupes de la Marine, only one hundred and twenty of whom were physically fit for the rigours of a campaign. To make matters worse, the intendant at Rochefort had omitted to send any clothing or food supplies with these men; he had also neglected to send the funds for their pay and maintenance. Of the thousand muskets that had been promised, seven hundred and forty had to be sent back as completely useless; instead of four small brass cannon, heavy iron ones had been sent that could not be transported by canoe; and of the thousand swords, six hundred were found to be broken on arrival. La Barre and de Meulles had immediately dispatched an urgent appeal for more effective aid, this time demanding seven or eight hundred trained troops and the necessary arms and supplies. It was, La Barre emphasized, of the utmost importance that these reinforcements should arrive that same year, for if he were defeated in his projected campaign, the colony would be at the mercy of the Iroquois. He closed this dispatch with the desperate plea: "Therefore have the kindness, my lord, to let us know promptly the wishes of His Majesty in order that, should we not receive succour, he will see fit to grant me leave to withdraw by the last ships, as I cannot bring myself to see this country perish under me and my government."[38]

When word of this reached France, La Salle, who was at Rochefort at the time, declared that there was no truth whatsoever in these alarmist reports and that he intended to tell M. de Seignelay so. But Machault Rougemont, the official to whom he told all this, informed M. de Villermont that he did not believe any reliance should be placed on anything La Salle said.[39] Whether or not Seignelay was more credulous than Rougemont is not known, but certainly if La Salle did so speak to the minister it could not have helped the situation, and it may be one of the reasons why Seignelay was still so reluctant to believe that the Iroquois threat need be taken seriously.

In the meantime, La Barre was making hasty preparations for a campaign. He sent an officer and eighty men with a supply convoy to Fort Frontenac. The militia was called out and orders were sent to Durantaye and du Lhut to bring as many coureurs de bois and allied Indians as they could to Lake Ontario to link up with the main force.[40] But as Colbert de Terron had remarked some years earlier, La Barre had no real stomach for war. Now that he was brought face to face with the fact that in the space of a few weeks he would be leading an army against a savage enemy, his nerve failed him. He began searching for some means, any means, to avoid the issue. By July 16 the troops and militia, numbering nearly eight hundred men, had been mustered at Montreal.[41] They wasted ten days there while La Barre entered into correspondence with the governors of New York and Massachusetts, informing them of his plans to invade the Iroquois cantons; he even gave Governor Dongan of New York an approximate date, August 20, when he expected to launch his attack and requested that the Iroquois be given no succour by the English.[42] Rumours now began to fly about the colony that La Barre had no intention of attacking the Iroquois but intended instead to arrange some sort of peace settlement. When the intendant heard of this he pleaded with La Barre to press the war to a vigorous conclusion and warned him that not to do so would have disastrous results both for New France and, once the king learned of it, for La Barre himself.[43] He also wrote to the minister, stating that he was convinced La Barre had no intention of attacking the Iroquois. He stated, "I can find no disposition whatsoever in the mind of M. le Général to wage war with the Iroquois; I believe that he will content himself with going by canoe to Cataracoui . . . and then have the Senecas come in order to treat for peace with them and so trick the people, the intendant, and if one dare say it, His Majesty." [44] His prognostications proved to be so correct that one is led to suspect him of composing this part of his dispatch after the event and not before.

Be that as it may, La Barre and his small army, accompanied by nearly four hundred Mission Iroquois and allied Indians, were by this time slowly portaging their way up the St. Lawrence. By the first of August they had gone no farther than Lake St. Francis, where La Barre received letters from Father Lamberville of the Onondaga mission, pleading with him not to take any precipitate action. Father Lamberville claimed that the Onondagas were anxious to treat for an honourable peace and had persuaded the other tribes to let them negotiate for all; they requested La Barre to send the Sieur le Moyne with the French terms as soon as possible and they promised him safe conduct. If this offer were not accepted and La Barre attacked any one of the Five Nations, Lamberville warned that the French would find themselves at war with them all. This, he sombrely predicted, could result only in the destruction of New France, as the Iroquois would not stand and fight, but would harass the French army from ambush, then melt away into the forest to return and strike again. He pointed out that the French troops were unskilled at this type of warfare; they would be worn down and destroyed piecemeal while the French settlements went up in flames. The Iroquois braves, he continued, were loudly boasting that if the French had the temerity to invade their country, it would be an excellent opportunity to discover whether or not it was true their flesh had a salty flavour. [45]

This was all that La Barre needed. He now rushed on ahead of his forces to Fort Frontenac and sent word to Lamberville that if the Iroquois were willing to give him satisfaction he would be perfectly agreeable to accept the mediation of the Onondagas rather than to resort to war. When de Meulles, who was at Montreal expediting the dispatch of supply convoys to the army, heard of La Barre's intentions he sent a letter couched in the strongest terms, urging the governor to dismiss any thought of treating with the Iroquois. He maintained that they would make him all manner of promises in order to deter him from launching an attack, but would regard the French with contempt were this policy to succeed, and they would thereby be encouraged to disregard their promises and intensify their aggressiveness. "There must be absolutely no peace with the Iroquois," he wrote, "no matter how advantageous some may make such an eventuality appear; you must understand that if we do not destroy them they will destroy us." [46]

When the Sieur le Moyne, who had been with the rear-guard of the army in command of the Mission Iroquois, reached the fort, La Barre sent him to Onondaga, at the request of the Iroquois, to discuss the preliminaries of a peace settlement. With him, La Barre sent the Seneca chief who had come to Montreal as ambassador and had there been made prisoner. That La Barre should have brought this chief with him on the campaign lends substance to de Meulles's claims that the governor had had no intention, from the moment the expedition was organized, to do other than discuss peace terms with the Five Nations.

For the next two weeks La Barre impatiently waited for the Sieur le Moyne to return from Onondaga with the Iroquois ambassadors. Meanwhile, his forces were encamped in the low-lying ground near the fort, doing nothing but consume their meagre rations and grow more sullen at the turn events were taking. Before long, food began to run short and a dread form of influenza* started to spread among the troops. La Barre sent five hundred of the Troupes de la Marine and militia, along with two hundred Mission Indians, to La Famine on the south side of the lake, where it was hoped they would be able to eke out their supplies with fish and game and also escape the contagion. When word finally arrived that the Onondagas would meet him at La Famine to discuss peace terms La Barre crossed the lake, only to find that the forces there were laid low with the dread disease. [47]

On September 3 the deputies of the Onondaga, Oneida and Cayuga cantons arrived at La Famine, accompanied by the Sieur le Moyne, who was so ill he was barely able to walk. They were quick to appreciate the desperate condition of the French forces. Two days later the conference began. La Barre, who had himself contracted the fever and was at death's door, was attended by such of his officers as were well enough to stand. Hotreouati, an Onondaga chief, spoke for the Five Nations. He began by offering the

* The epidemic was the tertian ague, the deadly form of influenza that swept through Europe in 1918–19.

French a potion to cleanse their blood of the poisonous air they had breathed en route from Montreal, indicating that the Iroquois were fully aware of the desperate plight of the French forces despite their attempts to conceal it. Secure in the knowledge that the French were virtually at his mercy, that not one of them would leave the shores of Lake Ontario alive were he to give the word to his warriors, he contemptuously dictated the Iroquois terms for peace and La Barre meekly accepted them. He warned La Barre that he feared for the safety of the French troops on the lands of the Iroquois, therefore the governor would be well advised to send them back to Quebec where they could sleep in safety. In future the French would have to come to La Famine when they wished to confer with the Iroquois; Montreal, he sardonically added, was too far away and at Fort Frontenac there were so many grasshoppers it was impossible to sleep at night. The quarrel between the French and the Senecas he declared to be ended : the pillaging of the French canoes was not sufficient justification for war since no blood had been spilled, and as recompense he promised La Barre a thousand beaver pelts. He gave his word that the Miamis would not be harmed by the Iroquois in future, but the Illinois they were determined to exterminate or perish in the attempt. To this La Barre could reply only that the Iroquois must see to it that in warring with the Illinois they did not harm any French *voyageurs* they encountered en route to that country or in the vicinity of Fort St. Louis; but Hotreouati vouchsafed nothing on this point.[48]

The morning after the treaty was concluded, La Barre returned to Fort Frontenac with his wretched forces. From there he sent a barque to Niagara where it intercepted Durantaye at the head of a force of seven hundred men, one hundred and fifty of them *coureurs de bois*, the rest allied Indians, and gave them orders to return to Michilimackinac.[49] Durantaye had had to exercise all his powers of persuasion to get the Ottawas to join him in the projected war. When they learned that the campaign had been abandoned without a blow being struck, what little faith they had left in the French as an ally was considerably diminished.[50] La Barre himself left his dispirited army to make their slow way back to Montreal while he went on ahead by canoe, taking with him the Sieur le Moyne, who was extremely ill. His own condition was such that his officers did not expect to see him alive again,[51] and, if de Meulles is to be believed, most of them were so incensed by his conduct they would have preferred it so. As it was, many of the men died before reaching Montreal and more succumbed after their return.

Meanwhile, in France, the king and the minister, upon receiving word that La Barre intended to launch a campaign against the Iroquois, had reluctantly acquiesced. Orders had then been issued for three hundred Troupes de la Marine to be sent to New France, but only two hundred were actually sent and they added little to the military strength of the colony; they had been issued with muskets that de Meulles described as little better than children's toys, and, as with the troops sent the previous year, no funds for their pay nor food supplies for their maintenance had accompanied them.[52] That the minister was far from convinced of the necessity for a campaign against the Iroquois is made quite clear in the king's dispatch to La Barre. After telling him of all the unpleasant consequences that such a war would entail for the colony, he instructed the governor that although by continuing the war he might be able to destroy the Iroquois completely and thereby add to the glory of the king's armies, he had, if it was at all possible, to make peace. By restoring tranquillity to the king's subjects in this fashion, the dispatch continued, he would be in a position to strengthen the colony by the means indicated in all the king's previous letters.[53]

These belated instructions reached La Barre upon his return to Quebec. He could fairly claim to have obeyed them to the letter. But when the king and Seignelay learned the terms of the treaty made with the Iroquois, and what these terms implied, they immediately recognized them for what they were, a humiliating defeat. At a time when Louis XIV was making France the most feared nation in Europe, a savage of the American forest had dictated terms to one of this proud monarch's governors. The king and his minister now, and for the first time, took cognizance of the fact that the Iroquois were at war with the Illinois, who were under French protection. The next ships to Canada brought La Barre's recall. The king informed de Meulles: "I have no cause to be satisfied with the treaty made between the Sieur de la Barre and the Iroquois; his abandoning of the Illinois has displeased me greatly and it is this which has determined me to recall him."[54]

In fairness to La Barre it must be stated that he had shown an awareness of the nature of the threat to the military and economic security of New France, both in the north and the south, and he had made an attempt to remove these threats. That the newly formed Canadian Company of the North enjoyed little success in competing with the English in Hudson Bay was no fault of La Barre's. This failure can be attributed largely to the treachery of Radisson, who once again had defected to the English, led their ships to the French post at the mouth of the Nelson River, and seized 60,000 *livres* of beaver pelts. This loss was a crippling blow to the Canadian merchants who had invested over 120,000 *livres* in the enterprise.[55] And even though La Barre failed dismally against the Iroquois, largely through his own inadequacies but partly as a result of circumstances, he at least made no attempt to exculpate himself afterwards by giving a false picture of the situation. In his report to the minister concerning his abortive campaign and the treaty that he had arranged with the Iroquois, La Barre gave a strictly factual account of the proceedings, concealing nothing. As a result, Louis XIV and the minister were finally forced to face the bleak facts of the situation and to take active measures to cope with it. There can, however, be no mistaking that the decision to recall La Barre was a sound one; he had demonstrated his incompetence beyond all doubt. Moreover, the state of his health alone made his recall essential; a year after his return from Lake Ontario he still had not recovered from the effects of the influenza; he was subject to periodic paroxysms that racked his ageing frame and paralysed his speech muscles. When he did embark for France in the summer of 1685 it was not thought likely that he would survive the crossing.[56]

The minister and Louis XIV were themselves partly to blame for the now perilous condition of French interests in North America. It was they who had accepted Frontenac's reports at face value and it was they who had given such impossible instructions to La Barre, requiring him to make peace with the Iroquois on French terms at a time when these powerful tribes were determined to drive the French out of the west and were already at war with the French allies, and then reluctantly agreeing to a campaign against the Iroquois without supplying the means needed to bring such a campaign to the speedy and definite conclusion they demanded. That La Barre failed ingloriously is clear; but others contributed to his failure in no small measure.

CHAPTER NINE

DENONVILLE'S LIMITED WAR

To succeed La Barre, Seignelay chose the Marquis de Denonville, a brigadier and colonel of the Queen's Dragoons, who was regarded as one of the best officers in the kingdom.[1] Denonville was a very different type of man from either Frontenac or La Barre; the only thing he had in common with the former was his thirty years of active military service. That he was an excellent regimental commander is evidenced by his meticulous attention to detail and his care for the good discipline and welfare of his troops. He was possessed of a high moral character and a very stern sense of duty; moreover, he had the exceptional quality of being honest, even with himself. Although not sanctimonious or bigoted, he was deeply religious, and he can perhaps best be described as that rare type in the France of Louis XIV's day, a puritan soldier. Yet there was something wanting. He clearly lacked warmth of character, and in all his writings there is nothing to suggest that he was possessed of anything akin to a sense of humour. With all his virtues— or perhaps because of them—the impression remains that an evening spent in his company would have been very tedious, whereas, by way of contrast, an evening spent with Frontenac would have been most diverting. The problems facing the governor of New France in 1685, however, were not such as could be solved by charm alone, and the lack of it did not detract in any way from Denonville's ability to grapple with them.

His chief task was clearly stated in his official instructions:

The principal aim which he must have is to establish tranquillity for the colony by means of a firm and solid peace, but in order that this peace should be a lasting one, it is necessary that the pride of the Iroquois be humbled, and the Illinois and other allies abandoned by the Sieur de la Barre sustained; he must begin with a firm and vigorous policy and make the Iroquois understand that they will have everything to fear if they do not submit to the conditions that he desires to impose on them.[2]

173

The king left the problem of accomplishing this, either by peaceful means or by waging a campaign against the Senecas, entirely to Denonville's discretion, and he gave orders for five hundred Troupes de la Marine to be raised and sent to the colony. Denonville, after selling his regiment for 20,000 *écus* to a nephew of Mme de Maintenon,[3] supervised the recruiting of these men himself, and thus they were of a much higher calibre than the troops sent out to Canada in 1683 and 1684. Several of his senior non-commissioned officers were half-pay officers who had resigned their commissions and volunteered to serve under him in that capacity, with the understanding that they would be granted commissions as soon as vacancies occurred.[4]

On the first of August Denonville, accompanied by his wife and daughters, arrived at Quebec. Although he had obtained all the information he could on conditions in Canada before leaving France and was better informed than the minister on this score,[5] he was still rather staggered by the immensity of the task facing him. Not only were there no places of security for the *habitants* in the event of an attack, but the remnants of the seven companies of the Troupes de la Marine already in the colony were badly disorganized; only a third of them had muskets and even these few weapons were virtually worthless.[6] There was not a single magazine or storehouse at Quebec where powder and arms could be kept in any degree of security, and the king's stores were in a shocking state of confusion. The intendant, Denonville soon discovered, had been trafficking in these goods for his private profit. He very quickly put a stop to this practice by having three locks put on the door, one of the keys being retained by himself and the other two by the intendant and the commissary.[7] Without waiting for the minister's permission he had a powder magazine built at Quebec and set the troops to work building a palisade around Montreal; by the time the king's dispatch arrived ordering him not to proceed with this last project owing to the expense, the palisade was almost completed.[8] He gave the intendant the opportunity to mend his ways, but when de Meulles showed no inclination to do so, he reported his malversations to Seignelay who immediately had him recalled.[9]

In the Sovereign Council there was no friction at all between the governor and the other members. Both Denonville and the newly appointed bishop, St. Vallier, requested that they might be excused from giving their opinions at the Council meetings, on the grounds that they had too many other things to attend to. Seignelay, however, after being briefed by an under-secretary on the manner in which the Sovereign Council functioned, decided that this would establish a bad precedent and ordered that the governor was to give his opinion whenever he attended the meetings.[10]

The flagrant abuses in the fur trade caused Denonville not a little concern. For military reasons alone he was opposed to the founding of more fur-trading posts in the far west. As he saw it, the condition of New France was such that it would have to concentrate its entire resources merely to defend the settlements from attack, let alone maintain a chain of posts over a thousand miles from the main supply base, which was itself in a very vulnerable state.[11] Upon hearing of the debauched lives being led by many of the *coureurs de bois* in the Indian villages, he toyed with the idea of rescinding all *congés*, but he finally decided to defer this issue, lest the Iroquois interpret such a decision as meaning that the French were preparing for a campaign against them—which was in fact the case. He therefore satisfied himself with enforcing much stricter regulations governing the conduct of *congé* holders. During Frontenac's and La Barre's administrations the *congés* had always been issued to their particular favourites, who had come to regard these permits as their personal prerogative, granted them by the king to the exclusion of everyone else in the colony. Denonville quickly disabused them of this notion by granting only twenty-five *congés* and all of them to the poorer families who had been excluded from such favours in the past.[12] In thus putting the king's orders into effect, Denonville made enemies of some of the most influential families in the colony.

Although he saw very clearly that there was an urgent need for reforms in the colony's internal administration, Denonville's immediate task was to deal with the external threat to the colony's security. It was clear to him that New France was caught in a giant pincers: in the north the English were once more the masters of Hudson Bay, thanks to the treachery of Radisson, and their posts again threatened to deprive the Canadians of the northern fur trade; to the south the English of New York were supporting the Iroquois in their attempts to drive the French out of the west.[13] The fate of the colony was reduced to a question of time; it required time to make the colony secure against attack, yet if the French did not humble the Iroquois quickly, the allies in the west would be either crushed one by one or else forced into an economic and military alliance with the Five Nations and the English. With every month that went by, this danger increased.

Within a month of his arrival in the colony Denonville began making active preparations to cope with these threats. From the outset he was ably seconded by the Chevalier Hector de Callières, who had been sent out in 1684 to replace Perrot as governor of Montreal. The Chevalier, who was a brother of François de Callières, the noted diplomat and one of Louis XIV's four private secretaries, was to play a leading role in the history of New France during the next two decades. Although only thirty-six years old when he arrived in New France, he had already had twenty years of active military service with the Régiment de Navarre and was a very competent officer, but too much of a martinet for the liking of some.[14] He also had a rather irascible temperament which was not improved by frequent attacks of gout. The following year, 1686, Denonville's task was made considerably lighter by the arrival of Jean Bochart de Champigny, who succeeded de Meulles as intendant. Although this post was the first royal appointment that Champigny had held,[15] he proved to be one of the ablest intendants that New France ever had. Like Denonville, Champigny was deeply religious, but, as he was to show on several occasions, he had no hesitation in opposing the wishes of the clergy when they conflicted with crown policy. He was a man of exceptionally strong character and a member of one of the oldest and wealthiest families of the *noblesse de robe*. He was possessed of a very caustic tongue and did not hesitate to employ biting sarcasm, even in his dispatches to the minister, but of humour there is no discernible trace in his writings. This is perhaps not to be wondered at, since official dispatches are not very apt vehicles for wit. He had, however, the very annoying habit of appearing always to be in the right in any controversy and, in general, of being a pillar of rectitude. One reason for his receiving the appointment was that he and Denonville were old friends; thus it was hoped that the bitter divisions of the past would be obviated. In this the minister was not disappointed, much to the surprise of the people of New France.[16]

Denonville had been quick to see that the English of New York were a greater, if less immediate, threat to Canada than were the Iroquois, and he suggested that the menace of both the Five Nations and the English colonies could best be removed by Louis XIV's purchasing the province of New York from James II.[17] But the likelihood of this occurring was slight. Meanwhile, the recently formed Canadian Company of the North was determined to recoup its losses by driving the English out of Hudson Bay.[18] In 1685 the king had granted them the right to establish posts in the area for this express purpose.[19] The following year Louis XIV and James II appointed commissioners to settle once and for all the conflicts arising from their territorial claims in North America. In the meantime their respective subjects were strictly enjoined to commit no acts of hostility whatsoever.[20] But before these orders were received at Quebec Denonville had decided to give the Canadian company active military support. In the spring of 1686 he sent a party of one hundred men, thirty French and seventy Canadians, overland from Montreal to James Bay. The expedition was commanded by a regular French officer, the Chevalier de Troyes, and the Canadians were led by Pierre d'Iberville and two of his brothers, Jacques de Sainte Hélène and Paul de Maricourt. At the end of their long journey through the wilderness, without a doubt one of the worst journeys in the world, the French and Canadians rather exceeded their instructions and took by force the three English posts at the foot of the Bay—not to mention 50,000 prime beaver pelts.[21] Despite the anguished outcries of the Hudson's Bay Company directors and the protests of the English government, the French refused to give up the posts and they still held them when war broke out in 1689.

The economic and military threat of New York and the Iroquois, however, was not so easily dealt with. Colonel Thomas Dongan, the aggressive Irish Catholic governor of New York, and the Albany merchants were doing everything in their power to seduce the Ottawa tribes away from the French alliance and Dongan was encouraging French *coureurs de bois*, with some success, to settle at Albany and take service with the local merchants.[22] Dongan maintained that all territory south of the Great Lakes clearly belonged to the English Crown and that the fur trade north of these lakes must be open to the English traders as well as to the French.[23] In 1686 a party of Albany fur traders, guided by Canadian renegades and convoyed part way by the Senecas, made their way to Michilimackinac where they offered their goods at prices far lower than those charged by the French. Worse still, the Ottawas, as a result of the weakness displayed by Frontenac and

177

La Barre, had displayed considerable hostility towards the French.[24] The quality and cheapness of the English trade goods had been a sore temptation to these middlemen to forget their ancient hatred of the Iroquois and enter into a commercial alliance with the Five Nations and the Albany men. The prospect of immunity from attacks by their old foes, particularly when the French had so conspicuously failed to give them military support, was a further strong inducement. Consequently, it was only with great difficulty that Durantaye and Father Enjalran at Michilimackinac prevented this alliance from being consummated. They finally persuaded the leading chiefs of the Ottawa and Huron nations to go down to Montreal in the depths of winter to confer with Denonville, and he succeeded in holding them, for the time being at least, to the French alliance.[25]

Dongan planned to send another and larger party to Michilimackinac the following year and he persuaded the Senecas to return several Huron and Ottawa prisoners whom they had recently captured, in order to cement the alliance. He also entertained plans for building a fort at Niagara to keep the Albany–Michilimackinac route open and sever French communications with the Illinois and Mississippi areas.[26] Denonville was kept fully informed of Dongan's designs by the Jesuit missionaries in the Iroquois cantons and by an agent whom he had sent down to New York to report on the English movements.[27] He was by this time quite convinced that the only way to save the colony was to attack the Iroquois the following year. As he informed Seignelay, they were pillaging any French canoes they encountered and were harassing the allies on all sides until these tribes were on the point of deserting the French.

Yet, despite the obvious necessity to wage war, Denonville was fully aware of the terrible risks it would incur and he warned the minister that with the colony's defences in such a dissipated state, a war would be an extremely risky undertaking; he wrote that "only the troops that you send us and the forts that we shall have to build can guarantee our security." [28] He was also very much aware of the formidable problems involved in any such war, and with startling prescience he stated:

> . . . their remoteness from the colony is great, as also is the problem, owing to the rapids, of getting at them swiftly with

the necessary supplies. Apart from that, it is still not certain that we can contact their forces in going to them, for, when they discover themselves to be weaker than us they will flee into the forests. I hope that this will not be a matter merely of burning their villages and destroying their crops, but it is by no means certain that they will stand and die in order to prevent this happening. A war with them could easily last for several years. Keeping to the woods as they do, they can burn our settlements at will unless God renders them blind to their own power. There, my lord, is the harm that can occur in warring with them; and even when we have ruined the village of the Senecas, this is all that could be done during one campaign because the other villages are so far removed that it is impossible to go to the nearest of them the same year; hence this village could sustain itself and recoup its forces that same year with the aid of the others, who could unite with them to wage war against us.[29]

What was actually needed to hold the west against the Iroquois and the English, he stated, was a force sufficiently strong to attack both flanks of the Five Nations at once; one army to attack the Mohawks and Oneidas on the eastern flank and at the same time frighten the English at Albany into quiescence, the remainder of the troops to join forces with the Ottawas and Illinois at Lake Ontario and attack the Senecas. The two armies would then drive the Iroquois in on the centre, ravaging all their villages and making it impossible for any of them to succour the others. That done, a fort would have to be built and garrisoned at Niagara to replace the post abandoned by La Salle's men, and armed barques maintained on lakes Ontario and Erie to safeguard the communications with the Illinois and serve as a base for raids on the western Iroquois, should they somehow recoup their losses and renew their aggression. But Denonville felt that the forces at his disposition were quite inadequate for this task. He considered that he had barely enough men to attack the Senecas alone, and he dared not wait for reinforcements from France which he had no surety he would receive.[30]

Denonville could see no alternative but to grasp the nettle firmly and strike at the Iroquois as hard as possible, for not to have done so would have meant losing the west by default. With the colony in its defenceless state, he had to keep his plans as secret as possible, lest the Iroquois should forestall him and attack the French settlements first. The Onondagas, who were rather perturbed when they learned that more troops had arrived in the colony, proposed a conference at Fort Frontenac to settle the most recent disputes between themselves and the French, and Denonville quickly agreed to the meeting. His aim was to lull them into a false sense of security, a trick that the Iroquois themselves had used on several occasions in the past and were to use again. When Father Lamberville came to Quebec from Onondaga to arrange for this conference, Denonville, knowing this Jesuit's desire for peace at almost any price, did not divulge his plans for the campaign. Had he done so, Lamberville very likely would have refused to return and be a party to tricking the Iroquois; having laboured so long and earnestly to convert them to Christianity, he had a vested interest in these tribes, and his failure to return might well have caused the Iroquois to suspect Denonville's intentions.[31]

In the meantime, preparations for the campaign went on apace. Supplies were sent to Fort Frontenac and the garrison at Chambly was strengthened. Boards were cut to size for flat-boats, then stored away out of sight, ready to be assembled at the final moment.[32] Orders were issued for the construction of forts and stockades in each seigneury, and at Denonville's behest the Sovereign Council ordered that every man in the colony over the age of fourteen had to provide himself with arms.[33] Very explicit instructions were sent to the commanders of the up-country posts. Tonty and La Forest were ordered to march with as many of the Illinois as they could muster to the southern flank of the Senecas and there wait until the main army had invaded the Seneca country. Denonville fully expected that the Senecas would flee at his approach, but with the Illinois waiting on this flank they might be forced to stand and fight. Durantaye was ordered to remain at the Toronto portage and du Lhut at Detroit to intercept the Albany traders should they venture once more to Michilimackinac. At these posts Durantaye and du Lhut were to assemble as many allied Indians and *coureurs de bois* as they could, then join forces at Niagara and await further orders. Nicholas Perrot and another *coureur de bois*, Boisguillot, were ordered to muster as many men as they could at Michilimackinac. Every precaution was taken to ensure that there would be adequate supplies at all these western bases and the Jesuit missionaries were pressed into service as liaison-officers, passing on Denonville's orders to the post commanders.[34]

On June 10 the troops and militia were mustered at Montreal. In all there were 832 Troupes de la Marine and 930 Canadian militia; another hundred Canadians were employed in transporting supplies.[35] While the final preparations were being made, the ships from France docked at Quebec with eight hundred regular troops on board, after a record crossing of only thirty-three days. The Chevalier de Vaudreuil, newly appointed commander of the Troupes de la Marine, had arrived a few days earlier; although in a weakened condition after the voyage, when he learned that a campaign was under way he insisted on rushing on to Montreal to take part in it, without even waiting for his baggage to be disembarked.[36] Had these reinforcements arrived the previous year attacks could have been launched on both flanks of the Iroquois cantons simultaneously, but it was too late for this now. The new troops were distributed among the settlements to guard against surprise attacks. On June 13 the army left Montreal and the following day it was joined by four hundred Mission Indians who had spent the previous night in their war dances and gorging themselves with a feast of dog-flesh. These warriors certainly added colour to the army; most of them were naked except for animal tails behind them and antlers on their heads. Their faces and bodies were painted in black-and-red bars with white or black flashes and their bodies coloured with crude drawings of animals, while their nostrils and ears were pierced with metal rings and spikes—all calculated to raise their own morale and strike fear into the hearts of their adversaries.[37] For the next two weeks the men toiled up the St. Lawrence, portaging their arms and supplies around the seemingly endless rapids, then returning to drag the flat-boats up the surging current, often up to their armpits in the river, constantly in danger of being swept off their feet and smashed against the rocks. Three hundred of the men were disabled by leg injuries in this fashion. Accompanying the army was the intendant. When the Cedars Rapids were reached he went on ahead with fifteen canoes loaded with food supplies in order to have everything prepared for the victualling of the forces the moment they arrived.

Ahead of the main force Denonville sent scouting parties who seized several Iroquois who were lurking along the river, among these being Oréaoué, one of the leading Cayuga war chiefs who had been a thorn in the side of the French for many years.[38] And at Fort Frontenac Champigny, either on his own initiative or more probably on Denonville's orders, had a group of so-called neutral Iroquois seized near the fort. Another larger group he invited into the fort for a feast; once inside the stockade they were made prisoners.[39] The reason advanced for Champigny's using this strata-gem was that he did not have enough men to take them by force.[40] Actually, these Iroquois were members of the Cayuga nation who had moved to the north side of the lake to be out of reach of the Andastes during their late war.[41] They had recently attacked and pillaged French canoes on the lake; many of their young men had already joined war parties against the French allies and it was expected that the rest of them would do so before long unless they were checked. To have allowed them to remain there would have endangered Denonville's lines of communication. There was also the distinct possibility that during the campaign in progress some of the French would be captured by the Iroquois, in which case Denonville hoped to be able to save them from the torture fires by using his own prisoners as hostages.[42] The French were embarking on a war against heavy odds and against a cruel, relentless foe; Denonville was obliged to use every possible means to weaken the enemy, and for sound strategic reasons he could not permit these Iroquois to remain on the north side of the lake.

The method employed by Champigny in taking the one group captive was most certainly a dubious one and the whole episode has been criticized bitterly by latter-day historians who, judging the issue by the moral values of their own day and confusing the different groups of prisoners and the means used to capture them, have succeeded in generating a good deal of heat but very little light. It is worthy of note that none of Denonville's contemporaries, in commenting on the matter, saw anything amiss in it, except Father Lamberville, the Abbé Belmont and Frontenac. The two clerics had a vested ecclesiastical interest in these Iroquois, and Frontenac, although he adopted a self-righteous attitude towards Denonville's actions and tried to blame the entire war on this incident in an attempt to disparage Denonville, was himself not above attempting to do much the same thing on one occasion. In any moral judgement on this issue it must be borne in mind that the Iroquois themselves frequently used such methods and that Denon-ville and his officers were the products of a harsh school, that of active service under Louvois. Seventeenth-century warfare in Europe was just about as brutal and savage as that waged by the Iroquois and every bit as destructive of civilized values.

On the first of July Denonville arrived at Cataracoui with the main forces. He was very relieved to find that Father Lamberville was already there. Believing that Denonville had come merely to confer with the Iroquois, Lamberville had persuaded two of the leading Onondagas to accompany him. These men, the son and a brother of a chief who had always been well disposed towards the French, were released and sent back to their villages.[43] One of the main reasons why Denonville had told Lamberville that he would confer with the Iroquois at Cataracoui had been to effect this missionary's safe removal from Onondaga without the Iroquois' suspecting what was afoot until the army was safely past the rapids on the St. Lawrence, where it would have been fatally easy for the Iroquois to wait in ambush and inflict heavy casualties.[44] The day after Denonville's arrival at the fort another party of "neutral" Iroquois was taken by force, bringing the total number to some fifty men and one hundred and fifty women and children.[45]

That same day La Forest arrived from Fort St. Louis in the Illinois country. He reported that Tonty, Durantaye and du Lhut had assembled at Niagara with one hundred and eighty *coureurs de bois* and four hundred allied Indians. What was even more important, the dangerous English threat to the French trade with the Ottawas and Hurons had been nipped in the bud. Durantaye had captured a party of thirty Albany traders on Lake Huron and another such party led by French renegades had been captured at Detroit. These renegades were later given a summary trial and executed.[46] The Albany men were sent back to Quebec and lodged in gaol as a reprisal for the English retaining prisoner the Canadians they had captured in Hudson Bay.[47]

On the fourth of July the army crossed to the south side of the lake, then skirted the shore to keep the Iroquois guessing which canton the French intended to attack and so prevent them from consolidating their forces. On the tenth, just as the army reached the disembarkation point, the Niagara forces appeared out of the morning mist. This juncture, timely to the very minute, was a tribute to the intense care with which Denonville had made his plans. Unfortunately, Tonty had been unable to persuade the Illinois to march to the southern flank of the Senecas; rumours of an Iroquois assault on their own villages had kept them immobile. This seriously diminished the prospects of a crippling blow being inflicted on the enemy, but there was nothing that could be done about it. A day was spent in building a stockade to protect the boats, canoes and food supplies for the return journey. Four hundred men had to be left to garrison this redoubt, for had the Iroquois managed to destroy the boats and supplies, very few of the French would have seen Montreal again.

For two days the motley army marched through the forest towards the Seneca villages. The men were loaded down with their arms, equipment and thirteen days' rations, burdens made all the heavier by the suffocating heat and the clouds of black flies and mosquitoes. In the van, under the command of Callières, were the allied Indians and the *coureurs de bois* led by Durantaye, Tonty and du Lhut. Between them and their objective were three defiles. The first two were negotiated without trouble. Then, near the end of the day's march, as the weary advance guard neared the last defile, the Senecas struck from ambush. Their ragged volley did little damage. At the first shot the Canadians and their Indian allies took cover, then returned the fire. The sudden rattle of musketry and the shrill war cries of the Senecas caused momentary panic among the Troupes de la Marine in the rear. Denonville and Vaudreuil quickly rallied them and brought them up at the double to aid the forward battalion. The enemy immediately turned and fled. They had mistaken the advance forces for the main army. In their panic they threw away their muskets and blankets. Twenty-seven of them lay lifeless on the ground and blood-stained tracks indicated that many more had been wounded. It was later learned that about a hundred in all had received mortal wounds. The French losses were six killed and eleven wounded; the allies lost five of their warriors.

At the end of this brief skirmish the French, too worn out by the heat and their lengthy march to pursue the Senecas, camped where they were. The allied Indians, whose main function was to have been to follow the fleeing enemy and cut down as many as possible, found more engaging things to do. With no further thought for the quick they turned their attention to the dead, butchering the still-warm bodies of the fallen Iroquois and hacking them into quarters for the cooking pot.

The following day the army continued on to the first of the

Seneca villages. It was completely deserted, and marks of the haste with which it had been abandoned were quite apparent. The huts, the caches of dried food and the corn standing in the adjacent fields were now systematically destroyed. For nine days the army, like locusts, moved from village to village, destroying everything that could possibly keep a primitive people from starvation. Owing to the distance and the difficult terrain, it was not possible to go on to attack the Cayuga villages. Sickness had begun to spread among both the French and the allies; some of the latter slipped away without a word and Denonville had a hard time preventing the remainder from departing before the work was finished. Returning to the boats, the sick and wounded were sent back to Fort Frontenac while the rest of the army continued along the south shore of the lake to Niagara, where a log fort was quickly built. This was intended to forestall any attempt by the English to build a fort at that strategic spot, and also to act as a base for allied Indian war parties who Denonville hoped would now be emboldened sufficiently to harass the Senecas in their own country should they return to restore their villages. Leaving a garrison of one hundred men under the Sieur de Troyes at the new fort, Denonville and the army returned to Fort Frontenac, then down river to Montreal, arriving there on August 13.[48]

In this campaign Denonville had accomplished little more than he had expected and not as much as he had hoped. However, as the French now realized, it was no mean feat to march an army into the country of the most distant and powerful of the Iroquois nations. The significance of this was not lost on the Iroquois, the French allies or the English at Albany. Although Denonville had not succeeded in crushing the Senecas, he had prevented the Iroquois and the English from breaking the French hold on the western fur trade. And that alone was no small accomplishment.

CHAPTER TEN

THE IROQUOIS' TOTAL WAR

UPON his return to Quebec, one of Denonville's first acts was to ship thirty-six of the fifty-eight-odd male Iroquois prisoners to France where they were sent to Marseille to serve in the galleys.[1] He had been ordered, as had La Barre before him, to take as many Iroquois prisoners as he could for this specific purpose.[2] The minister assured Denonville that these Iroquois "would lack for nothing" and ordered him to send as many more as he could capture during the course of the war.[3] The French navy was always in dire need of rowers for the galleys; the supply of able-bodied criminals, Huguenots, Senegalese and Turkish slaves was never adequate, and, contrary to popular opinion, these men were not badly treated according to the lights of the time. They were a valuable property, hard to replace, and of little use unless kept healthy. To be sent to the galleys was regarded as no worse than being impressed into the army.[4] On the minister's specific orders these Iroquois prisoners received religious instruction and extra rations. He also ordered that they should not be chained nor shaved;[5] in these respects they were much better treated than were the Huguenots and criminals, and in comparison with the manner in which the Iroquois dealt with their own prisoners, they were treated like pampered guests.

For political reasons Denonville would have preferred not to send his Iroquois prisoners to France, and he advised the minister, "since we may be able to arrange a general peace settlement sometime in the future, I believe that it would be very useful for the colony if you were to keep them in a place where they can be recalled if need be."[6] But in complying with the minister's orders he showed—quite apart from humanitarian considerations —very poor judgement. As he had indicated, the chief value of these prisoners was as hostages or bargaining counters in future negotiations with the Iroquois, and to send them to France meant that they probably would not be available to him when needed. There was also the serious risk that they would not survive the ocean crossings, let alone a sojourn on the benches of a galley where

186

they would be exposed to all manner of European diseases to which they had little resistance. But to Denonville all orders had to be obeyed and he wrote to the minister : "In sending these prisoners as I have done, it was my belief that I had blindly to obey His Majesty's orders." [7]

When this task had been seen to, Denonville, whose health had suffered from the exertions and anxiety of the past few months, took fresh stock of the military situation and found it none too reassuring. The Senecas had been dealt a hard blow, but their fighting strength had been reduced very little. Denonville's task was not merely to defeat the Iroquois, but to crush them quickly and prevent them ravaging the French settlements. He and Callières were in agreement that two armies were needed to finish the war satisfactorily, yet without adequate forces there was little doubt that it would drag on indefinitely. He wrote to the minister asking for another eight hundred trained men and a hundred and fifty recruits. In the meantime he began making plans for another campaign and for small raiding parties to harass the Iroquois. But what weighed most heavily on his mind was the defenceless condition of the colony. The Iroquois had already begun attacking the outlying settlements, cutting down men working in the fields, burning barns and homes. A supply convoy sent to Forts Frontenac and Niagara had been ambushed on its return journey; eight men had been killed and one taken prisoner. Denonville stated that it needed only a hundred determined Iroquois to lay waste all the settlements above Trois Rivières. That they had not already done so he could only attribute to the fact that God had made them blind.[8] To add to the colony's troubles, the king's ships had brought measles and smallpox to Quebec, causing a great many deaths among the *habitants* and decimating the Mission Indians. Among the victims were the wives and children of the Iroquois taken prisoner during the Seneca campaign; they had been placed among the Mission Indians and nearly all of them died of the epidemic shortly after their arrival.[9]

Until such time as the colony could be made secure by a crushing assault on the Iroquois, the best that could be done was to build forts in each seigneury, where the *habitants* could take cover in the event of attack. Denonville and Champigny entertained the ambitious idea of having the *habitants* build their homes around these forts in compact villages, as did the settlers in the frontier sections of the English colonies. Several years before, Colbert had ordered that the land was to be settled in this fashion, but no attempt had been made to put the plan into effect. And without strong compulsion from the authorities there was no possibility of the *habitants* themselves doing so; they all wanted land with river frontage and plenty of elbow-room between themselves and their neighbours. The governor and intendant did eventually succeed in getting forts built in the more exposed areas,[10] but try as they might, they could not get the *habitants* to take adequate precautions for their own safety. In all the defence measures the chief obstacle was the apathy and stubbornness of the *habitants*. In words that were all too prophetic, Denonville remarked that perhaps after a few of them had been killed the others would come to realize the urgency of the situation.[11]

In 1688 disease again took an extremely heavy toll in the colony; some fourteen hundred of the troops and *habitants* succumbed. This, out of a total population of about eleven thousand, represented a terrible catastrophe.[12] To make matters worse, small parties of Iroquois continued to raid the outlying settlements.[13] The previous November a large force of Iroquois had laid siege to Fort Frontenac, burning the crops, killing the cattle, keeping the garrison prisoners and coming dangerously close to burning down all the buildings with showers of flaming arrows. During the winter one hundred of the garrison died of disease, and at Niagara eighty-nine of the garrison there fell victims to scurvy; they too had been kept cooped up in the fort, unable to go out to hunt for fear of being cut down.[14] Denonville now came to realize that these forts on the borders of the enemy country were worse than useless in time of war; they were nothing but prisons at best and tombs at worst for their garrisons, who were unable to harm or hinder the enemy in any way. In addition, it required an army at immense cost to convoy supplies to them in safety.[15]

In the face of this increasing enemy pressure Denonville revised his estimate of the forces required to crush the Iroquois in a single campaign; he now declared that it would need three separate armies, invading their cantons simultaneously on both flanks and the centre. This meant a total force of four thousand men, four to five hundred flat-boats, and supplies on hand sufficient for two years.[16] There was no hope whatsoever of his receiving reinforcements in such numbers, for Europe was once again on the verge of war and the minister had already informed him that only three hundred men could be spared for Canada that year.[17] Seeing no possibility of settling the issue quickly by force of arms, particularly in view of the continued ravages of disease among the French troops and militia, Denonville decided that the only thing to do was to try to arrange a peace settlement with the Iroquois. Both he and Callières were convinced that the colony could not be made secure until the Iroquois had been crushed and that any peace settlement the Iroquois agreed to would merely be used by them to concentrate their forces against the western tribes.[18] The alternative, however, was a long-drawn-out war of attrition and although the French, with their superior resources, could expect eventually to emerge victorious from such a struggle, it could only be after the piecemeal destruction of the settlements from Montreal to below Trois Rivières, for the French defences were proving to be woefully inadequate against the Iroquois guerrilla tactics. But if a peace settlement could be arranged, the colony would at least be spared this for the time being. Meanwhile, in the sincere belief that his detailed dispatches had failed to impress upon the minister the complexity and gravity of the situation,[19] Denonville decided to send Callières to Versailles to try to obtain the forces and decisions needed to crush the Iroquois and curb the aggressive policies of the officials in New York who were claiming vociferously that the Iroquois were British subjects and under the protection of the British Crown, yet at the same time were actively supporting them in their war on the French allies.[20]

Having decided to open peace negotiations, Denonville sent four of the Iroquois prisoners back to their villages to invite their chiefs to confer with him. Governor Dongan of New York did everything in his power to prevent the conference taking place, but Father Lamberville was finally able to persuade the Onondagas, Cayugas and Oneidas to send their chiefs to Montreal.[21] On June 8, 1688, the ambassadors arrived. Denonville sagely began the discussions by inquiring whether it was possible to negotiate a treaty at all, since the governor of New York claimed that they were subject to him and could make no treaties without his being consulted and giving his consent. This pricked the pride of the Iroquois chiefs and their spokesman, Hotreouati, replied heatedly that they acknowledged no one as their master; they had received their lands from the Great Spirit and had never been defeated in war by either the

English or the French.[22] When Denonville insisted that all the French allies be included in the treaty, the Iroquois chiefs were most reluctant to agree, and even while the discussions were taking place a group of warriors in their escorting party ambushed and pillaged three canoes of up-country Indians on their way to Montreal, killing some of them and taking the rest prisoner to the Iroquois villages.[23] Finally, however, it was agreed that a general peace settlement between the Five Nations and the French and all the French allies would be negotiated. The Iroquois ambassadors agreed to induce the Mohawks and Senecas to accept the peace terms and Denonville accepted their demand that when this was done he would abandon the post at Niagara, which he had intended to do in any case. In return he received the right to send supplies and reinforcements to Fort Frontenac without interference from the Iroquois, who even offered to escort a supply convoy to the fort, an offer that was firmly declined. A mutual exchange of prisoners was another stipulation, and Denonville promised to have those Iroquois who had been sent to France brought back and returned to their villages. It was agreed that this treaty would be ratified by all the nations at Montreal the following year. In the meantime a truce was declared and the Iroquois agreed that any acts of hostility committed by the French allies before Denonville was able to inform them of the peace would not prejudice the ratification of the treaty.[24]

To have obtained such terms, under the circumstances, appeared to be a great accomplishment, but with his habitual honesty Denonville informed the minister: "God alone has saved the colony from total ruin this year. I can claim no credit for it. M. de Callières will be able to inform you better than I can write, how much we relied on Father Lamberville and with what dexterity he prevented the storm with which we were threatened from striking us."[25] On the face of it, the colony's economic and military security seemed to be assured without the need for further bloodshed and destruction. But this was more apparent than real; the main issue between the French and the Iroquois, control of the western fur trade, had not been resolved. There could be no hope of the Iroquois' relinquishing their aims here, particularly with Governor Dongan of New York doing everything in his power to urge them on. It was certain that the Iroquois would abide by the terms of the treaty not a day longer than it suited their convenience—in this respect they were no different from more civilized nations—and Denonville, clearly foreseeing this danger, sent the Sieur de la Forest to the Illinois posts with supplies of ammunition and orders to have the allied nations remain on their guard and unite their forces if an attack appeared imminent.[26] In fact, both sides were seeking merely temporary advantages by means of the treaty and Denonville could not for a moment relax his vigilance. He did, however, take advantage of the respite to send a large party of Canadians to Michilimackinac to bring the furs which were stored there down to Montreal. Owing to the Seneca campaign, no furs had been brought down from the Ottawa country for three years and a great many people in the colony were close to financial ruin, even starvation, with their principal source of income cut off.[27]

Then, just two months after the cessation of hostilities, New France was again in jeopardy. A few weeks after returning to their cantons from Montreal, the Oneides, Onondagas and Cayugas sent ambassadors to inform Denonville that the Senecas and Mohawks had agreed to the signing of the peace treaty and to arrange a date for a meeting to ratify it. On their way to Montreal these ambassadors were ambushed near Fort Frontenac by a party of Hurons. Kondiaronk, the Huron chief who was responsible for this action, feared that a peace settlement would serve only to free the Iroquois for an attack on his people. He had no faith whatsoever, and with good reason, in the intentions of the Iroquois to abide by the terms of the proposed treaty. One of the Iroquois ambassadors was killed and another had an arm broken by a musket-ball; the survivors were taken back to the Ottawa country. They bitterly protested to Kondiaron at this act of "treachery" and he cunningly feigned ignorance of the peace negotiations. He declared that Denonville had instructed him to ambush their party and made sure that word of this reached the Iroquois villages. This enraged their warriors and they immediately began preparing to attack the French settlements. Meanwhile, the Iroquois ambassador who had been wounded had managed to escape from his captors and was found by the garrison of Fort Frontenac. When he told them what had happened they managed to convince him that the French had had nothing to do with it. They dressed his wound and sent him to Onondaga with an escort. He arrived just in time to prevent the Iroquois war parties leaving for Canada. He induced the Five Nations to send another embassy to Montreal to arrange for the ratification of the peace treaty, but the delay had allowed Sir Edmund Andros, the newly appointed governor of New England, time to intervene. He sent word to the Iroquois requiring them to confer with him; consequently, the Iroquois chiefs went, not to Montreal, but to Albany.[28]

When Denonville learned of this he had no doubts whatsoever that Andros would do everything in his power to disrupt the peace and restore the state of hostilities between the French and the Iroquois. But for the next twelve months there was nothing that he could do except hope for the best and prepare for the worst. He had requested the minister to send back the prisoners from the galleys and to see to it that they were given the best of treatment.[29] The winter passed uneventfully and Denonville was impatiently awaiting the arrival of the ships from France to prove to the Iroquois that their kinsmen had not all died in chains, as the English claimed.[30] Spring became summer and still the ships did not arrive. Nor was there any word from the Iroquois cantons that they were ready to ratify the peace treaty. No one in Canada knew that there had been a revolution in England and that England was now at war with France. Everything was ominously still.

Many in the colony mistook this uneasy calm for peace; lulled into a false sense of security they became careless. On Denonville's orders, Callières had crossed to France the previous autumn to make clear to the minister the precarious position of the colony and to submit proposals for an attack on New York province. Both Callières and Denonville were convinced that this was the only means by which the Iroquois could be curbed quickly, short of employing a large army at great expense. And New York, they claimed, could be conquered with less than half the force it would take to subdue the Five Nations.[31] With Callières gone, Vaudreuil took over the command at Montreal; unfortunately, he was not the stern disciplinarian that Callières was. There being no sign of the Iroquois, the defence precautions became slack. The *habitants* were now permitted to stay on their isolated homesteads instead of remaining in the security of the forts.[32]

By the Fifth of August there was still no word from France. But early the next morning there was from the Iroquois. During a violent hailstorm fifteen hundred of their warriors crossed Lake St. Louis undetected and then dispersed among the homesteads at Lachine. Instead of being inside the forts, the *habitants* were sleeping in their own isolated homes. At dawn the Iroquois struck. Before the *habitants* had time to realize what was happening many of them were cut down. Women and infants were butchered along with the men, their bodies hideously mutilated. More were taken prisoners, to be dealt with at leisure. As the houses and barns went up in flames, the terror-stricken survivors fled to the forts.

When word of the disaster first reached Montreal, Denonville immediately gave orders that everyone was to take cover in the forts and remain there. Considering the fragmentary, incoherent information he was receiving on the movements of the enemy, who must have appeared to be everywhere at once in overwhelming numbers, this was the only order that he could have given. At the same time he sent Vaudreuil with a detachment of three hundred men to the stricken area. Unfortunately, Vaudreuil, although a brave officer, was not noted for being exceptionally intelligent. He took the command to remain in the forts too literally. On the way his officers learned that the main body of the Iroquois were nearby, three-quarters of them dead drunk—the houses at Lachine were notorious for being overstocked with liquor.[33] One of the senior officers, the Sieur de Subercase, gave the order to fall on the enemy, but Vaudreuil, who was in the rear, countermanded the order, declaring that his instructions were to get everyone inside the forts. Subercase and the other officers protested vigorously, and it was with great indignation and reluctance that they finally obeyed.

When the detachment reached Fort Roland at Lachine, Vaudreuil sent word back to Denonville asking for more men. The governor immediately dispatched some eighty men under the command of the Sieur de Rabeyre. When this detachment was in sight of Fort Roland it was ambushed by the Iroquois but put up a stiff resistance. The officers in the fort demanded permission to lead a sortie against the enemy and catch them between two fires. Vaudreuil refused, claiming that his orders were to remain inside the fort. Only one officer and a handful of men from Rabeyre's party reached safety. Of the remainder, a few were killed and the rest captured, but many of these subsequently managed to escape. Later that day the Iroquois retired to the south shore of Lake St. Louis. When night fell the garrisons of the forts at Lachine could see the faint glimmer of fires on the far shore and knew that the Iroquois would be celebrating their victory by burning some of their prisoners alive. It was later learned that they had roasted and eaten five children. The others were reserved for a like fate in the villages of the Five Nations; many of them, however, were spared and eventually returned to New France.

Although the losses suffered were nowhere near as great as first reports indicated, the sudden ferocity of the attack spread terror everywhere. Only twenty-four of the French were actually killed at Lachine. The most reliable accounts state that some seventy to ninety prisoners were taken, and it has been established that forty-two of them never returned; the rest either escaped or were subsequently freed. Of the seventy-seven houses in the area, fifty-six were destroyed.[34]

For the rest of the summer and autumn the Iroquois sent small parties to cut down the *habitants* in their fields, kill their cattle and burn their crops, their barns and their homes, then fade back into the forest before the French could organize parties to pursue them. In the face of this, Denonville decided that Fort Frontenac would have to be abandoned. Although the fort had proved to be nothing but a military liability, Denonville was reluctant to take such action because it meant a loss of prestige for the French. But the military situation demanded it. The garrison had been kept prisoners by marauding Iroquois, afraid to venture outside the stockade and unable to harm the enemy in any way.[35] The previous year, supplies had been sent to the fort but it had required a few hundred men to convoy them there.[36] With every man needed to defend the settlements it was impossible to send such a force out of the colony again. Moreover, supplies were very scarce, since the ships from France still had not arrived. On September 24 Denonville sent orders to the officer commanding the fort to raze it to the ground, leaving nothing standing lest the English should occupy it, then retire to Montreal with the garrison.[37]

Not all the news was bad, however. Shortly after the attack on Lachine the Canadians whom Denonville had sent up country the previous year had returned with 800,000 *livres* of furs.[38] This was cause for great rejoicing. At about the same time, a scouting party of twenty-eight Canadians under du Lhut and Mantet, sent out by Denonville, encountered two canoes containing twenty-two Iroquois on the Lake of Two Mountains. The Canadians saw the Iroquois first and manoeuvred so that the low-lying sun shone in their enemies' eyes. When the Iroquois did espy the Canadians they immediately made for them, yelling in bloodthirsty anticipation. The Canadians waited. When the canoes were within musket range the Iroquois dropped their paddles and began firing. None of the Canadians were hit. While the Iroquois were trying desperately to reload, the Canadians paddled swiftly up and fired a volley at close range. Eighteen of the Iroquois went to the bottom of the lake; three were taken alive. These last were brought back to Montreal and burned at the stake over a slow fire in the Place Royale by the Mission Indians.[39] And as the townspeople watched the long-drawn-out agonies of their foes, they gained a full realization of what their own people who had been taken prisoner had had to endure, and what they themselves would have to endure should they be so unfortunate as to be captured by the Iroquois.

In mid-October, two months overdue, the ships from France finally arrived. When Denonville and Champigny read the dispatches from Versailles, dated the first of May, the bitter irony of their contents must have made them wince. Louis XIV informed them that "they must study every possible means to negotiate a peace directly with the Iroquois and to maintain the colony in tranquillity until, circumstances being different, His Majesty may more conveniently make decisions which will give him the mastery over the neighbouring lands." Were this to prove impossible, Louis instructed Denonville and Champigny that, with the Iroquois, obviously the best defence was offence; the governor was ordered not to remain on the defensive but to use all his available forces, both troops and militia, to carry the war to the enemy and to give every encouragement and assistance to the Indian allies to do likewise.[40] The ships brought also a dispatch of a later date recalling Denonville, and along with it his successor, Frontenac.

Thus, unfortunately for his later reputation, Denonville had the misfortune to leave the colony immediately after the Iroquois had gained a victory in a war that was to last for another ten years. He was always scrupulously honest in his dispatches to the Court. When he scored a success he did not dwell on it at great length but treated it as only what was expected of him and let it go at that. Nor did he cast blame on anyone else when things went wrong, and he always did his best to ensure that others got the credit they deserved. By failing to extol his own accomplishments and by giving objective, detailed accounts of his failures he provided much of the ammunition used by his detractors of a later age.

Not only has the havoc caused at Lachine been greatly exaggerated, but many historians have placed the entire responsibility for it on Denonville's shoulders. The evidence does not warrant any such harsh and superficial judgement; the contemporary accounts contain no such condemnations, and some exonerate him from all blame. In the final analysis, the persons responsible for the Lachine massacre were the Iroquois. By their customary tactics they had gained a victory over the French. A full-scale war between the French and the Iroquois was inevitable sooner or later. This much had been obvious for the past nine years. The French could not contemplate for a moment the abandonment of the western fur trade, and nothing less could have prevented hostilities with the Iroquois, whose policy it was to keep the French inactive as long as possible by diplomatic means while they crushed the French allies one by one. Until 1688 the New York authorities had tried to restrain them from attacking New France proper, owing to the conference being held between the French and English governments to settle their outstanding differences in America.[41] But at the same time, although Dongan maintained that the Iroquois were British subjects and therefore inviolable from French attack,[42] he gave them every encouragement in their war against the French allies, promising them supplies of arms and food, and sanctuary for their women and children should the French attack their villages.[43]

Then, in the spring and early summer of 1689, the whole situation had changed. While New France was cut off from all news of events in Europe, the English colonies, on the first of March, had learned of the Revolution in England and had been quick to grasp its implications.[44] In April, rumours were circulating that war had been declared between England and France,[45] anticipating by a few weeks the ship that was on its way from England to give notice to the colonial governors that a state of war existed.[46] In June, three merchant ships from Bordeaux and La Rochelle arrived at Quebec, but they brought no dispatches from the Court and apparently no word of the war with England; most likely they had left France before hostilities had begun.[47] Once the Iroquois learned that England and France were at war, nothing could have prevented them launching their full strength against Canada. In their previous wars with the French they had had to fight alone; now they felt they could count on the active military support of their English allies. On August 16, Philips and Van Cortland wrote to Mr. Blathwayt, secretary of the privy council: "The Canton Indian nations above Albariy hearing of war between England and France are gone to fight the inhabitants of Canada." [48] Thus it could be argued that it was not Denonville's sending of the Iroquois prisoners to the galleys, or Kondiaronk's ambushing of the Iroquois ambassadors, that sparked the Lachine massacre, as so many historians would have it, but the seizure of the throne of England by William of Orange.

After the Iroquois assault on the colony and the receipt, in October, of word that England and France were at war, New France at long last knew exactly where it stood. It had to be total war; there could no longer be any hope of safeguarding the colony itself, let alone the western fur trade, short of it. No quick campaign with limited forces would suffice, nor could anything now be achieved by negotiation. The Iroquois had either to be crushed by force or New France would be. Denonville had early recognized this, and he had tried to solve the problem by waging a preventive war with inadequate forces; the attempt had failed as he had feared it would. He had also foreseen clearly what would happen were the Iroquois to launch a sudden attack in force on the colony, and he had done everything possible to guard against it. But when all that has been said the fact still remains that Denonville was in command at the time of the first real assault on the colony, therefore he has to accept the responsibility for the French defeat. This, how-ever, does not justify all the blame for either the outbreak of the war, or the initial French defeat, being heaped on his head. Yet it was as well for New France that he was recalled, for both his health and his self-confidence had been seriously undermined by the events of the past four years. Moreover, he lacked one quality all too essen-tial for a military commander in times of war, namely, good luck.*

* Misfortune was to dog Denonville to the end; his declining years were em-bittered by the disgrace of his son, who, on orders of the king, was cashiered for surrendering his regiment without a fight to George Hamilton, Earl of Orkney, at Blenheim in 1704. See G. M. Trevelyan, *England Under Queen Anne: Blenheim*, 393–4; *Annales de l'Hôtel Dieu de Québec* (ed. A. Jamet, Que., 1939), 235, n. 1.

CHAPTER ELEVEN

FRONTENAC RETURNS

THE reasons for Frontenac's reappointment as governor of New France are very obscure. From what fragmentary evidence there is it appears that his own influence at the Court, and that of his friends, sufficed to obtain the position for him. Immediately after his return to Paris in 1682 he began assiduously to mend his political fences by telling everyone who cared to listen how well he had governed the colony and that the Court was very well pleased with his conduct of affairs in Canada; so much so, in fact, that he fully expected to be given some mark of consideration by the king.[1] He told his story so often and so convincingly that he soon persuaded his friends and acquaintances of its truth. This was not such a difficult task as it might appear. The evidence concerning his actions in New France was buried in the documents that had been read by only a few officials in the Department of Marine and that were already gathering dust. With Frontenac constantly giving his plausible account of events in circles where there was no one to refute him, and with his wife and friends echoing it assiduously, this version was bound to gain some degree of credence. Thus, when complaints began to reach the Court of La Barre's conduct, Frontenac became hopeful of obtaining his reappointment as governor of New France.[2]

That his well-organized campaign was gaining ground was shown when, in August, 1685, he was granted a gratuity of 3,500 *livres* which it was expected would be repeated annually.[3] Although this must have been very gratifying to his ego, particularly when rumour had long since had it that he had received double that amount,[4] it could have been but small financial comfort to a man of his extravagant tastes, accustomed to spending well over ten times as much in a year. In 1676 he had obtained an edict from the Council of State similar to the one granted him in 1672, preventing his creditors seizing any of his properties, movable or immovable, or the revenue therefrom, for a period of two years.[5] When this expired he solicited and was granted its renewal "for such time as it shall please His Majesty." [6] But it is doubtful if the king would have felt inclined to protect him from his creditors after recalling him in disgrace, and it is significant that in 1691 Frontenac lamented the fact that he had consumed his entire estate.[7] By 1688, he must have been in dire need of an appointment of some sort.

In the autumn of that year Callières returned to France to report on the state of affairs in the colony and whilst at Versailles he took the opportunity to solicit the post of governor-general for himself.[8] Denonville does not appear to have made a definite request to be relieved of his command, but he had intimated that his health was broken and that he was no longer fit for the ardours of active campaigning,[9] and it may well be that he had instructed Callières to inform the minister, or perhaps merely to hint, that he would like to return to France. In any event, Callières was to be disappointed. On May 1, 1689, the Abbé Tronson, superior of the Sulpician order in Paris, wrote to Dollier de Casson in Montreal: "The Marquis [sic] de Frontenac has at last obtained, by his perseverance and through the good offices of his friends, his return to Canada." [10] At the same time Denonville was given the sinecure of assistant governor, under the Duc de Beauvilliers, to Louis XIV's grandson, the Duc de Bourgogne.[11]

There is, however, no evidence at all to suggest that Denonville was replaced by Frontenac because Louis XIV or Seignelay regarded the former as incompetent; in their dispatches dated May 1, 1689, they made plain their entire satisfaction with Denonville's conduct of affairs.[12] Despite this, it is frequently alleged or implied that Frontenac was sent back to Canada to save the colony from the consequences of Denonville's supposedly inept policies, as evidenced by the Lachine massacre and the abandonment of Fort Frontenac.[13] It is necessary only to compare the dates on which the above-mentioned events occurred with the date of Frontenac's reappointment as governor to appreciate how wide of the mark this judgement really is. Frontenac received the appointment as governor of New France in April, 1689; [14] the Lachine massacre and the abandonment of Fort Frontenac did not occur until the following August and late September respectively. Frontenac could hardly have been reappointed to retrieve a situation which had not yet occurred and could not have been foreseen.

Important though the changes in the government of Canada may have seemed to the persons directly concerned, and even to the people of Canada, events had occurred in Europe which, by comparison, dwarfed them. Although Callières's and Denonville's suggestions for an assault on New York had aroused interest, the complicated diplomatic manoeuvres which preceded the War of the League of Augsburg kept the attention of the king and his ministers riveted elsewhere. By April, 1689, France was at war with the Empire, Spain and the Dutch Netherlands, the "Glorious Revolution" had placed William of Orange on the throne of England, and James II was in Ireland at the head of some 30,000 troops, fighting to gain control of that troubled country in order to use it as a base to drive William out of England. Louis XIV hoped that the presence of James in Ireland would at least prevent William's dragging England into the anti-French coalition; to further this aim he supplied James with a corps of experienced French officers. Although Louis does not appear to have been too sanguine of James's succeeding in regaining the throne of his three kingdoms, the possibility of its happening could not be ruled out entirely, and it was this factor that dominated the thoughts of the French government on the strategy to be adopted in North America during the early months of 1689.

An attack on New York, such as Denonville and Callières were urging, required that William should retain his hold on England and the colonies declare for him; thus, on the first of May, Seignelay wrote to Denonville, ". . . although his Majesty considers this proposal to be sound, he does not think that it would be convenient to execute it at present." [15] Then England declared war on France.[16] Immediately Louis XIV and Louvois altered their plans. They now decided to remain on the defensive along the French frontiers and to concentrate French military and naval forces against the most dangerous foe, England. The Mediterranean and Atlantic fleets were united and took the offensive against English and Dutch shipping. Seven French battalions, seven thousand men in all, were sent to Ireland to bolster James's nondescript forces and to make up for the absence of the five thousand crack troops of the Irish brigade serving with the French armies on the continent.[17] By the beginning of June, Callières's and Denonville's plan for the conquest of the colony of New York had been accepted, but with serious modifications. On June 7 Frontenac received his instructions as commander of this combined land and sea assault.[18]

The plan of campaign, as amended by Louis XIV, called for two

French warships under the command of the Sieur de la Caffinière to escort the annual supply ships to the mouth of the St. Lawrence. There, Frontenac was to go on to Quebec on one of the merchant ships, sending Callières ahead, by the fastest means possible, to muster a force of nine hundred Troupes de la Marine and six hundred Canadians, and to organize the necessary transport and supplies. Once this task had been accomplished, instructions were to be sent to Caffinière to proceed to a point off Manhattan Island. Meanwhile, leaving Vaudreuil in command in New France, Frontenac and Callières were to take their army to Albany via the Richelieu River and Lake Champlain, capture this town, leave a garrison there, and then proceed down the Hudson to capture New York, being assisted in this by a naval bombardment from Caffinière's ships.*

When this had been accomplished, the principal officers of New York were to be imprisoned along with the wealthier residents, who were to be held for ransom. The artisans and labourers were to be retained to work for their new masters. Any Catholic residents of the colony who swore allegiance to the French crown were to be allowed to remain in possession of their estates; all the other colonists were to be expelled either into Pennsylvania or New England and their goods and chattels seized. All French fugitives, particularly Huguenots, were to be shipped back to France. Once the French forces were firmly in control, Frontenac was to return to Quebec, leaving Callières as governor of the conquered province with a force adequate for its defence against English counter-attacks. It was fully expected that Frontenac would then be able to conclude a firm peace with the Iroquois who would be in no position to reject any terms he might impose on them.[19] Thus, in one bold stroke, a telling blow would have been struck against the English, an important acquisition made which would be of inestimable value when the eventual haggling over peace

---

* Denonville's plan had called for two separate forces: one of eight hundred men from Canada to capture and destroy Albany and lay waste the outlying settlements, then return to Quebec with the prisoners—being prepared to repel Iroquois attacks on the return journey—the other six frigates and twelve hundred men, operating quite independently of Canada, to capture New York from the sea and hold it, then use it as a base to ravage the coast as far as Boston and to keep the Iroquois in check. It was a much more practicable plan than that finally adopted by Louis XIV, and it might well have enjoyed a large measure of success.

terms began—provided the French managed to retain their hold on the conquered province—the Iroquois fangs would have been drawn, and the western fur trade made secure for the French traders.

Had the French officials at Rochefort, the elements, the Iroquois, and the American colonists been willing to co-operate whole-heartedly, then this scheme would have had a fair chance of success. Excellent though it may have seemed on paper, once it was translated into action things began to go wrong. The expedition was scheduled to sail from La Rochelle by June 14 at the latest, but owing to the lack of crews the ships did not leave that naval bottle-neck until July 23.[20] All the way across the Atlantic they were buffeted by strong west winds, which were to be expected at that time of year; consequently they did not reach Cape Breton until September 13. Fog and head winds caused further delay. Frontenac and Callières finally arrived at Quebec on October 12, the merchant vessels two days later. Even had the colony been in a condition to supply the men and materials needed for the expedition, it was now too late in the season and the enterprise had to be abandoned.[21]

When Frontenac learned of the state of affairs at Montreal and also that both Denonville and Champigny were there, he decided to join them at once. He considered, however, that the dignity of his position and person would not allow of his making the journey without a large escort.* He therefore compelled the leading citizens of Quebec and a large detachment of *habitants* to accompany him, and this necessitated having several boats caulked. Heavy rains

* Some historians make it appear that Frontenac received a tumultuous welcome from the people of Quebec upon his arrival, basing the assertion on statements in the oration preached by Father Goyer, Recollet, at Frontenac's funeral nine years later. A more dubious source than a seventeenth-century French funeral oration can hardly be imagined and this one was certainly no exception. Cannon were always fired in salute when the governor arrived at Quebec or Montreal, the clergy had been warned to show no chagrin when Frontenac arrived and the people must have been relieved to see the supply ships from France, which were long overdue. None of the contemporary accounts mention any show of satisfaction being made by anyone at Frontenac's return and it is most significant that Frontenac himself, in his first detailed and lengthy dispatch, is silent on this point. In fact, it looks very much as though no real welcome was accorded at all, and a sullen attitude on the part of the people may well be the reason why Frontenac compelled the *bourgeois* and *habitants* of Quebec to accompany him to Montreal in the rain, to remind them that he was not to be so treated with impunity.

further delayed his departure; thus it was over a week before he was able to get away.[22]

The seven-day boat trip up the St. Lawrence in foul weather perhaps gave Frontenac's impressed escort an opportunity to reflect on what the return of their old governor would mean to them and to New France. During his seven years' enforced sojourn in France he had lost none of his courtier's wiles; he was still as completely without scruples as he had shown himself to be during his first administration, but in his official instructions he had been warned against attempting to pay off old scores, and he had received explicit orders that he was to stay on good terms with everyone.[23] In some respects Frontenac's position was more secure this time; Colbert was dead and the Marquis de Seignelay, his son and successor as minister of marine, was not the man that Colbert had been.* Moreover, within the year Seignelay himself was to die and be succeeded by Frontenac's kinsman, Louis Phélypeaux de Pontchartrain, a conscientious minister of modest talents who vainly pleaded with Louis XIV not to be given the onerous charge of the department of marine because he knew nothing at all about its affairs. When Frontenac later learned that his close relative had been appointed minister of finance and of marine, his personal expectations rose considerably. The position of governor-general of New France, so eagerly pursued a short time earlier, now seemed most unsuitable to a seventy-year-old nobleman of Frontenac's connections and record of service. He immediately wrote to Pontchartrain requesting that he be given a more honourable and tranquil appointment. He felt sure that the minister would not wish to see a member of his own family fall into decrepitude and end his days without means, without dignity and without distinction. But this plea met with no response although it was repeated year after year.[24]

Of greater significance to Frontenac in some ways than Pont-

---

* Seignelay had been placed in charge of Canadian affairs in 1681 and Colbert entertained grave doubts as to his son's capacities. Noting that he did his work with great speed, not sparing himself until it was finished, Colbert remarked that this precipitation prevented Seignelay from reflecting on his decisions. Colbert also commented on Seignelay's facility to grasp things swiftly, saying: "I fear nothing so much as that facility because it leads him to hold a good opinion of himself and to be satisfied with a first acquaintance with things . . . which, being superficial, will never make him a capable man." See Pierre Clément (ed.), *Lettres, instructions et mémoires de Colbert* . . . (Paris, 1861–73), III, part 2, 9–10, 12–13.

chartrain's appointment was to be, was the fact that Jean Baptiste de Lagny, the intendant of commerce, was in charge of Canadian affairs at the Ministry of Marine. De Lagny, a tax farmer and a director of the Levant Company and the Company of the North, was a close personal friend of Frontenac's; the Canadian dispatches passed through his hands, important decisions were referred to him, and he was in a position to bring Frontenac's point of view to the minister's attention and to see to it that any criticism of the governor's actions was given scant consideration.

When the Abbé Tronson learned that Frontenac had been re-appointed he immediately wrote to Dollier de Casson at Montreal, warning him, "Take good care to forewarn everyone so that no one will appear distressed at the return of M. de Frontenac, for it could be reported to him and have evil consequences. It is essential to retain his friendship. As he is supported at the Court his conduct will be upheld there and complaints will not be listened to readily." [25] And M. de Brisacier wrote to the members of the seminary at Quebec warning them, in much the same terms, to watch their step. [26] This time, however, it was the clergy who perhaps of all the groups in the colony had least to fear from Frontenac. During his first administration they had been Colbert's *bête noire* and this had encouraged him to oppose them in everything, almost as a matter of principle. But now things were very different at the Court. Colbert was dead. During the winter of 1683–84 Louis was secretly married to Mme de Maintenon and the moral climate of Versailles underwent a marked change. Piety rather than libertinism now became the order of the day and Primi Visconti remarked that the Court had the air of a seminary. This—and perhaps his advancing years may have had something to do with it too—was to be reflected in Frontenac's attitude towards the Canadian clergy. M. de Brisacier commented that he had begun to think of the next world and was anxious to avoid trouble because he knew that to become embroiled in fresh disputes would be a sure way to earn the king's marked disfavour. [27]

Perhaps the most significant difference of all between his first and second administrations was the fact that this time Frontenac had serving under him three very capable men possessed of strong wills. Champigny, the intendant, a member of a wealthy and influential family, was not afraid to send a stinging rebuke to Pontchartrain himself when he felt that the minister's criticisms were unwarranted[28] and, unlike Duchesneau, he had enough strength of character to ignore many of Frontenac's idiosyncrasies. Callières, the governor of Montreal, was a tough veteran soldier, inclined to be a martinet, and the last person in the colony to stand for any nonsense from anyone, even the governor-general. More significant still, Callières could communicate almost directly with Louis XIV; his brother, François de Callières, the famous diplomat, was one of the king's four private secretaries.* Consequently, the governor of Montreal was a rather dangerous man to cross. Vaudreuil, the commander of the Troupes de la Marine, who had an enviable military reputation to which he added considerable lustre in Canada, was also a man whose opinions were listened to with respect in the Ministry of Marine. Thus, surrounded as he was by three men such as Champigny, Callières and Vaudreuil, and in view of his earlier fall from grace, Frontenac was compelled to be somewhat more circumspect in his actions. And from this, the members of Frontenac's impressed escort could have derived some comfort as they proceeded up-river in the pouring rain.

When he eventually reached Montreal, Frontenac found Denonville and Champigny labouring to bolster the feeble defences of the upper colony against renewed Iroquois attacks. The troops and *habitants* had been, according to Frontenac, reduced to a state of exhaustion by the harassing raids of small Iroquois parties roaming about the island and also by the defence measures taken by Denonville, of which he was scornfully critical. Bad as the situation undoubtedly was, Frontenac, in his first dispatch to the minister, grossly exaggerated the havoc caused by the enemy. Whereas Henri Tonty stated that the losses in killed and captured at Lachine were one hundred and twenty, and the Abbé Belmont that they were nearer ninety,[29] Frontenac claimed that over two hundred men, women and children had been slaughtered out of hand and over one hundred and twenty taken prisoner. As for the recently arrived fur brigade with its 800,000 *livres* of furs, he dismissed it with the dubious comment: "This abundance delights only a few merchants and a small number of individuals who have a share in it, but the colony as a whole is thereby neither richer nor more content."[30]

What disturbed Frontenac far more than the destruction at

* In January, 1701, François de Callières succeeded M. Rose as the king's first secretary, *qui avait la plume*.

Lachine was to learn that Denonville had sent orders to the commandant at Cataracoui to destroy the fort and return to Montreal with the garrison and as much of the post's supplies as could be transported. Frontenac immediately ordered a detachment of three hundred men with eight months' supplies to proceed to the fort in the hope that they would arrive before Denonville's orders had been carried out. He maintained that this fort was all that had prevented the English from taking the western fur trade from the French, that since the Iroquois had demanded its destruction, this alone should have compelled Denonville to maintain it, and that its destruction would have a bad effect on the western allies who now had no safe retreat from the Iroquois.[31] Frontenac's arguments, however, will not bear too close a scrutiny. There is not the slightest trace of evidence that Fort Frontenac ever had barred the English from the western fur trade. It certainly had not prevented Dongan's parties from trading with the Ottawas in 1685, nor had it in any way been responsible for their capture the following year, and it most certainly could not prevent the Iroquois from trading with the western tribes whenever the latter so desired. At the peace negotiations of 1688 the Iroquois had not demanded the destruction of the fort but had agreed to allow Denonville to maintain it; it was the fort at Niagara that had caused them concern. There can be no doubt that its destruction meant a distinct loss of prestige for the French, and this was an important consideration so far as the western allies were concerned, but there also can be no doubt that this factor was far outweighed by other military considerations which dictated the abandonment of the post. Frontenac's claim that its destruction deprived the western allies of their only safe retreat from the Iroquois was quite ridiculous. The western allies had never had any contacts with Fort Frontenac; it lay in the heart of the Iroquois hunting grounds, well off the Ottawa River route used by the French allies, and had never been anything more than a trading post for the Iroquois fur trade and a staging post on the Great Lakes route to the west, a route which could be used with any degree of safety only when the Iroquois were at peace.

Denonville and Champigny strongly protested Frontenac's decision; under the circumstances they regarded it as the height of folly. It was so late in the season that the river and lakes might well have frozen before the convoy could return, and there was the added danger of an ambush by the Iroquois. One of the prisoners taken at Lachine, who had subsequently escaped, reported that the enemy were waiting in strength along the river, ready to attack any convoy that tried to get through to Cataracoui.[32] In any event, Denonville and Champigny knew from experience that the fort was virtually useless in a war with the Iroquois.[33] Champigny stated that "this fort, to speak the truth, is a prison for the confinement of its garrison, it can hinder the comings and goings of the enemy only when they venture within musket range."[34] A few years earlier de Meulles had come to precisely the same conclusion,[35] and Lahontan, for what his opinion is worth, later stated that Denonville had done the only thing possible in ordering the fort destroyed,[36] and Henri Tonty was in agreement with this opinion.[37] In Champigny's eyes, the extreme cost and difficulty of supplying the fort, necessitating convoys of several hundred men each time, alone made its abandonment imperative.[38] With every man needed to defend the Montreal area, the colony did not have sufficient resources in either manpower or supplies to maintain it.

Still, Frontenac refused to listen. Despite the strong disinclination for the enterprise shown by the Canadians who were ordered to man the canoes—an attitude that Frontenac attributed to "the lack of discipline that has been allowed to permeate the *habitants*"—the expedition finally left Lachine on November 6. Before it had gone two leagues it was met by the garrison coming down from Cataracoui. They reported that the fort was destroyed, to the great relief of the members of the supply convoy, who immediately returned to Montreal.[39] Frontenac was infuriated, but for the present there was nothing more he could do.

His next move was to attempt to open peace negotiations with the Iroquois. At Denonville's specific request the minister had ordered that the Iroquois prisoners who had been sent to the galleys at Marseille were to be released and sent back to Canada.[40] This had been done; they returned on the ships that brought Frontenac. In his subsequent dispatches to the Court, and apparently to everyone else, he made it appear that he was chiefly responsible for the release and return of these captives.[41] He also claimed that the war with the Iroquois was due solely to the manner in which these prisoners had been taken and their subsequent treatment, which, he intimated, would never have happened had he been in command.[42] In this last he can be believed, and it is certainly to his credit, but in actual fact the only prisoners taken by treachery had been some of the so-called neutral Iroquois; the ones from the Five Nations cantons had been legitimate prisoners of war, taken by force along the route of the French army. Moreover, war with the Iroquois would have come had Denonville taken no prisoners at all in the 1687 campaign.

Early in November Frontenac sent three of the returned prisoners back to their villages to try to persuade the Iroquois to meet with him the following spring to discuss a general peace settlement.[43] Champigny was very dubious of anything constructive resulting from this embassy; as he saw it, the Iroquois, after their recent victories and with the English giving them their full support, were hardly likely to consent to a peace settlement on terms acceptable to the French. He was of the opinion that the colony must prepare to carry the war to the enemy and he turned his attention to having new flat-boats built, ready for spring.[44] Unfortunately, Champigny's views proved to be all too correct. When the released prisoners spoke in the council of the Five Nations at Onondaga, two delegates sent by the Albany magistrates appealed to the council to spurn Frontenac's embassy. The Iroquois needed no urging; they rejected the peace bid and swore to continue the war against the French.[45] That they meant what they said they made very clear by an attack on the French settlements at La Chesnaye and Ile Jésus, a few miles to the north of Montreal. They burned nearly all the farms right up to the forts and massacred many of the *habitants*.[46] Frontenac blamed the failure of his peace overture on the machinations of certain unnamed individuals in the colony who, either out of sheer folly or for more dubious motives, had entered into secret negotiations with the Iroquois.[47]

Frontenac's next task was to reorganize the Troupes de la Marine, for war and disease had carried off nearly four hundred men in the past three years. He reduced the number of companies from thirty-five to twenty-eight, having a total complement of some fourteen hundred men. This done, he left the defence of the upper colony in the hands of Callières and returned to Quebec. During the next few months he devoted himself to his old pastime, wrangling with the Sovereign Council. This time the point at issue was the protocol to be observed when he attended its meetings. The Council no longer held its sittings in the governor's residence, the Château St. Louis; it now occupied more imposing quarters in the intendant's palace. This last was new since Frontenac's first administration; the building had formerly been Talon's brewery which had proven to be a very unprofitable venture and had been converted, at considerable expense, to include a residence for the intendant and quarters for the Sovereign Council. It also included a gaol. Although Frontenac's commission as governor had been duly registered by the Council upon his arrival, for a long while he did not deign to take his place at its meetings, despite the fact that he had been invited to do so by both the intendant and the attorney-general. Knowing Frontenac of old, the councillors rightly assumed that he expected his initial attendance to be surrounded with the maximum of pomp and circumstance. They therefore delegated the attorney-general to call on him and find out exactly what he wanted. But Frontenac refused to co-operate; he would reply only that the Council knew full well what was expected of it.

Since there was no official procedure laid down by the king for the reception of a governor, the Council now began to comb through its registers to see how governors in the past had been received. This proved to be of little help, since other governors had taken their seats at the Council without any fuss or fanfare. On the 20th of February they delegated four councillors to attend Frontenac and request him to inform them of the manner in which he expected to be received. His reply to this delegation was that he was astounded the Council should have to ask him what to do; it was up to them to suggest how they intended to receive him and he would then be pleased to decide what action to take. The Council thereupon proposed that when Frontenac came he should be escorted to his seat by four councillors. Villeray, the senior councillor, took this proposal to the governor, who rejected it on the grounds that it was not in accordance with the practice employed in the sovereign courts in France. Villeray requested Frontenac to inform the Council how the *Parlement de Paris* had received Louis XIV the first time this monarch had taken his place at a *lit de justice*. Frontenac told him to ask the bishop, but St. Vallier prudently refused to be drawn into the matter and asked to be excused. So once again Villeray trudged through the snow, up the hill to the Château, to inform Frontenac that the Council would send four of its members to escort him across Upper Town, down to the intendant's palace, and then up the stairs to his place at the Council table. And if this did not satisfy him, Villeray asked, would he please tell them what would so that they could get the matter settled once and for all. But Frontenac still had a card or two to play. He now informed Villeray that he would have to know how the Council intended to receive him when he came to subsequent meetings after his first attendance; he also demanded to see the minutes of the Council meeting where the question had been discussed.

By this time Champigny had had all that he could stand. He informed the Council that in his view they had done everything possible to satisfy Frontenac, and until the king answered their request for a ruling on the manner in which a governor should be received, they need do nothing more than had been the practice in the past. And with this he washed his hands of the whole affair, leaving the members of the Council to settle the matter as they saw fit. So, on the 6th of March, the Council again sent Villeray to see Frontenac, this time with the proposal that on the governor's subsequent attendance at the meetings, they would delegate two councillors to attend him in the antechamber and escort him to his place, and that if this did not please him, if he would indicate what more he required they would be pleased to comply. These terms of unconditional surrender Frontenac immediately accepted; to have refused after Champigny had wearied of the game might well have caused the rest of the Council to follow suit, which would have left Frontenac in a rather ridiculous position. He now informed Villeray he was very gratified to learn that the Council had such a high regard for his character and position, and that he could never have permitted them to go beyond the bounds of decorum in the matter of his reception. In any case, he added, he did not expect to make his first appearance at a Council meeting until after Easter.[48]

Now, when Frontenac attended the sittings of the Council—and as Champigny tartly remarked, he rarely missed a meeting—the captain of his guards entered the chamber first to announce the governor's arrival. The presiding officer then had to suspend all business, order the chamber cleared, and delegate two councillors to go to the head of the stairs to receive and escort the governor to his place before business could be resumed.[49] Although Frontenac certainly had a penchant for display and ceremonial, it would appear that the main reason for all this bickering over petty details was his desire to score off the Sovereign Council. Most of its members had been in office during his first administration; they had been witnesses of, and parties to, his recall in disgrace. Lest this should colour their attitude towards him, he had first to humiliate them and so regain the moral ascendancy. To some extent he succeeded in this.

All things considered, Frontenac's actions during the first few months of his second administration must have caused many in the colony to fear that—like the Bourbons of a later age—he had learned nothing and forgotten nothing during his enforced sojourn in France.

CHAPTER TWELVE

MILITARY ORGANIZATION IN NEW FRANCE

THE administrative framework of Canada under the old regime was organized on a permanent military footing. In times of war this authoritarian structure gave New France a considerable advantage over the English colonies to the south, and goes a long way towards explaining how it was that the Canadians were able to hold the vastly greater numbers of the English colonies at bay for so long. Throughout King William's War Frontenac was fortunate in having under him such capable officers as Callières, Vaudreuil and Champigny. Callières had acted as second-in-command under Denonville, and under Frontenac he was responsible for the tactical direction of the French forces. This came about for two main reasons: most of the fighting took place in the Montreal area, and this town was the main base for all offensive operations against the Iroquois and New York; and second, Frontenac was quite willing to allow Callières to exercise this tactical command. Under Callières was Vaudreuil, the officer commanding the Troupes de la Marine, and it was he who led the troops in the field. Although there was little love lost between Callières and Vaudreuil, there is no evidence of any trouble between them sufficient to impair military operations and they both appear to have agreed well enough with Frontenac. This was perhaps due to the fact that he spent most of his time at Quebec and gave them a free hand in the tactical direction of the war, if not in its strategical direction. For this, Frontenac deserves to be commended.

It may seem odd today, but the man who had one of the most responsible military functions of all was a civilian official, the intendant. Although he had little or no direct say in the formulation of military policy, its execution was, to a very large extent, dependent on how well he discharged his responsibilities. He was responsible for paying, feeding and clothing the troops, supplying them with arms and munitions, arranging for their billets and, when necessary, for their hospitalization. He also had to allocate materials and labour for work on the fortifications as well as transport and supplies during campaigns. Since he was allotted only a set sum each year by the minister of marine for war and general administration, the manner in which he utilized these funds had no small bearing on the conduct of military operations.

One of the major problems with which Champigny was faced was the excessively high rate of wear and tear on equipment during campaigns in the Canadian bush. This was something that the minister, comfortably ensconced at Versailles and perhaps thinking in terms of European parade-ground soldiering, never sufficiently appreciated. When the minister criticized the intendant severely for what he considered to be his excessive demands on the military funds, Champigny more than once became exasperated. In 1693 he informed the minister in no uncertain terms and in great detail of the reasons for the high cost of military operations in Canada, adding that these expenditures could not be reduced "unless it were decided to abandon the colony completely and leave it a prey to its enemies." He pointed out that every war party had to be equipped with canoes or snowshoes, arms, ammunition, food and clothing; in addition there were other parties being sent at frequent intervals to Acadia, the Illinois country, Michilimackinac and even beyond. "If all this," he wrote, dipping his pen in acid, "and an infinity of other things could be done without expense in a new country half ruined by war, it would be a most admirable secret which, with all my heart, I wish I had been able to discover in order to satisfy His Majesty and please you." [1] For an intendant to send such a stinging rebuke to the minister required not only some degree of courage but also a deep conviction of the justice of the case.

Although the intendant had these considerable military responsibilities, it was still the governor who decided how best to use the available men and material; as Champigny once reminded the minister, it was "M. de Frontenac who decides what is to be done and afterwards I have only the responsibility of accomplishing it as economically as possible." [2] In all such matters the governor was supposed to confer with the intendant; once a decision to undertake military measures had been reached by the governor, the intendant allocated the necessary supplies and kept the governor informed of the cost.[3] Thus, the intendant of New France performed the military functions which in the modern Canadian army would be carried out by the Service Corps, Pay Corps, Ordnance

Corps and Quartermaster-General's Department. He also had certain responsibilities akin to those of the present-day Department of Veterans' Affairs; he settled retired soldiers on the land, pleaded to the Court for pensions for disabled officers or their widows and orphans, and on occasion he settled the estates and executed the wills of soldiers who died on active service. He had to attend to the prisoners of war and at the close of hostilities he arranged for their return in exchange for French nationals. Finally, the war once over, he acted as something similar to a War Assets Corporation, disposing of surplus war equipment by sale to private persons.

Throughout the war, it was the militia, rather than the regular troops, that did most of the fighting. This militia comprised every able-bodied man in the colony and could be ordered out at a moment's notice by the governor and his subordinates. In each district in the colony a captain was appointed to command the local militia unit and, although he received no pay, his position did carry a great deal of prestige. These *capitaines de milice* were chosen from among the *habitants* and were usually the men to whom the *habitants* would naturally have turned for leadership. They were in many ways the most important group in the colony, much more so in some respects than the seigneurs. Their duties were not only military: they had civil functions as well; in fact, they acted as the intendant's agents in the country districts, communicating his orders to the *habitants* and seeing to it that they were carried out. In some respects they can be likened to the justices of the peace in Tudor England; without them the administration of New France could not have functioned effectively.

Service in the French army was, at that time, regarded as a fate little or no better than being sent to the galleys. Most Frenchmen have always had a natural reluctance to leave their own shores for very long, and the chances of any of the Troupes de la Marine who were sent to Canada ever returning to France were extremely slim. In most cases, their families would never hear of them again. Moreover, the death-rate on troop ships crossing the Atlantic was very high, and for those who did survive there then remained the prospect of campaigning against the Iroquois with all that it implied. Consequently, when the intendant at Rochefort received orders to raise troops for Canada, the able-bodied men in the district quickly made themselves scarce and every precaution had to be taken, once the required number had been rounded up, to prevent them escaping. To this end they were usually placed on the Ile d'Oleron until the ships were ready to sail.[4] It is, then, not surprising that the Troupes de la Marine sent out to Canada in the seventeenth century were rather a poor lot, lacking training, discipline and the physical stamina needed for campaigning in the North American forest. In 1687 Denonville wrote: "I said nothing in my dispatch of the wretched behaviour of the troops on the day of our attack on the Senecas. What can one hope to do, Monseigneur, with such men as these?"[5] Consequently, it was the Canadian militia that was relied on to fight the war and the regular troops were used largely for garrison duty in the forts, as a labour force on the land, for work on the fortifications or as artisans employed in the towns.

There were some Canadians recruited into the Troupes de la Marine, and Frontenac stated that these men were rendering incomparably greater service than the French-born soldiers, who were, he declared, of little use for campaigning in the bush and for river travel until they had had several years' experience.[6] In the closing years of the war Champigny stated that there were fewer than three hundred, or even two hundred, of the troops fit to march on campaigns in the forest, but when travelling by boat or canoe, some seven hundred could possibly be pressed into service. "There is no gainsaying," he added, "that these are very wretched soldiers and that the *habitants* are worth incomparably more in the war, for voyages and for other duties."[7] On campaigns the militia were, however, led by officers of the Troupes de la Marine, both Canadians and French, who performed valiant service under the most exacting conditions and suffered very heavy casualties.

The system of using the troops as a labour force had been inaugurated by the intendant de Meulles. In the spring of 1685 he had found himself faced with a very awkward problem; he had no funds with which to pay the troops. There was also at that particular time a serious shortage of labour owing to sickness and death among the more able-bodied *habitants* who had accompanied La Barre on his abortive campaign against the Iroquois. De Meulles solved both problems by allowing the soldiers to hire themselves out to the *habitants*, and so be ensured of their keep and pay for their labours until funds should arrive from France. The *habitants* were permitted to hire the soldiers but were forbidden to pay them more than ten to twelve *livres* a month; they also had to feed their hired help on feast days and Sundays as well as on work days, and the soldiers were forbidden to wear their uniforms while so employed.[8] A fortnight later de Meulles amended his ordinance to permit soldiers who had a trade to work by the day, and *habitants* who required help only for short periods were allowed to hire soldiers at a daily rate instead of by the month. The soldier-tradesmen were to be paid not more than fifteen *sols* (about seventy-five cents) a day, over and above their keep, and the *habitants* were forbidden to pay them more on pain of a ten *livres* fine.[9] Many of the troops, however, were unable to find work, owing to their advanced age and other disabilities, and once the spring sowing was finished the *habitants* had no further need of extra help. Consequently, de Meulles had to inaugurate his famous card money, which he fondly thought would be merely a temporary expedient, in order to pay the men.[10] From this point on the card money, which was nothing more than decks of playing cards inscribed across the face with values in *livres* and signed by the intendant, was constantly in circulation in the colony. No sooner would it all be called in than the intendant would find himself obliged to issue a new lot. On the whole, the system, despite all its attendant evils, served the colony well and at least enables Canada to lay claim to being the first country in the world to have paper currency.

Once inaugurated, the system of allowing the troops to hire themselves out for wages led to serious abuses. The soldiers, naturally enough, greatly preferred working for wages on the farms or in the towns to serving with their companies, and their officers encouraged the practice, since the men were perfectly willing to forgo their military pay in exchange for their freedom. Not only did it free them from the onerous military discipline but financially they were far better off. At this time, a sergeant was paid 17 *livres* 5 *sols* a month, a corporal 10 *livres* 1 *sol* 1 *denier*, lance-corporals (*anspessade*) 7 *livres* 17 *sols* 7 *deniers*, and the private soldier 6 *livres* 9 *sols* 1 *denier*. From the pay of all the non-commissioned ranks a deduction of 4 *livres* 10 *sols* a month was made for their rations.[11] There were also other deductions for clothing and hospitalization. This meant, when translated into present-day currency, that at the end of the month the sergeants were lucky if they found themselves with approximately $13.00, the corporals $5.50, lance-corporals $3.25, and the private soldiers less than $2.00 that they could call their own; and a jug of brandy cost between $1 and $3 in Montreal, depending on the scarcity of supplies.

Champigny complained vociferously that when the troops were needed for a campaign, too many of them were not available, being scattered about the colony working in civil occupations with their captains' permission.[12] What made it extremely difficult to curb the abuse was the method of paying the troops. There was no elaborate accounting system; every so often a muster parade was held by the intendant or his deputy, heads were counted and checked against the rolls, and the captains received an amount sufficient to pay the number of men in their companies present and accounted for. Thus the captains made very sure that the men were all there for these parades; when Champigny's deputy at Montreal, the Sieur de la Touche, began calling the muster parade without warning, the officers protested and demanded a day's advance notice. The Sieur de la Touche, who was a very conscientious official, declared that this delay was purely "to have enough time to recall the soldiers working for their captains' profit, without which they would not be permitted to work and would always be available in the garrison."[13] In this dispute Frontenac supported the officers.[14] What may well have caused him to support them was the fact that they were so miserably paid. The captains received $90 (90 *livres*) a month, lieutenants and supernumerary captains—that is, captains not attached to a company—$60, ensigns and supernumerary lieutenants $40, and supernumerary ensigns $30 a month.[15] It is easy to see how great would be the temptation to add to their incomes by any means possible, particularly in view of the high cost of living in Canada, and when a situation arose whereby the men were quite willing to forgo their army pay in return for their freedom to work for wages of $1 to $1.50 a day with their keep, it is hardly surprising that both officers and men took advantage of it.

One result of the abuse was that the men who were retained at their posts had to do all the guard-duty and fatigues for their absentee comrades and became completely worn out.[16] Then, too, some of the officers were not content with merely retaining their men's army pay; they also demanded a share of the wages the soldiers received from their civilian employers and refused to release them from their military duties unless they first agreed to this.[17] Champigny eventually despaired of being able to correct these abuses. Had the soldiers themselves been willing to lodge complaints against their officers, then he could have taken action, but this the men refused to do. Champigny informed the minister: "Although I and my deputy ask before the troops on parade if they have any complaints, the soldiers claim to be perfectly content. I know what the trouble is but have no way of correcting it. I even know that were I to obtain fair treatment for them many of them would still hand over their pay in order to avoid being persecuted and be free to go off and work."[18] Eventually the abuses became so flagrant that Bishop St. Vallier—never the most circumspect of men—intervened and ordered the clergy to refuse absolution to any captain known to be withholding his men's pay. This did no one any good. The minister, naturally enough, took the attitude that the bishop was trying to usurp the civil authority, particularly when an officer as notable as Vaudreuil was refused absolution by the curé at Ste Anne's.[19] The bishop was politely but firmly informed that he was not to meddle in things that did not concern him.[20] Frontenac admitted that the bishop might have grounds for stating that some of the officers were withholding their men's pay, but he added that he had received no complaints from the men, which is hardly surprising. He went on to say, however, that he would be careful not to abandon the troops to the greed of their officers and that if the abuse became excessive he would compel them to give the men their due.[21]

What distressed Champigny more than anything else was the fact that when a *habitant* serving in the militia was killed, the colony had lost one its greatest assets. It took seventeen or eighteen years to produce a good *habitant*, who by that time most likely was married and supporting a family, whereas the Troupes de la Marine were not allowed to marry and their losses could conceivably have been replaced by recruits sent from France. As intendant, Champigny was responsible for the social and economic welfare of the colony, and consequently he regarded the Troupes de la Marine as an expendable force and the *habitants* as too valuable to be used for military purposes unless it were absolutely essential. In 1691 he informed the minister :

It is very aggravating for the poor *habitants* of this country to find themselves continually ordered out for the war when the majority of the soldiers are not; they have never yet refused to march, but they, as well as their families, are reduced to such a miserable state, I believe it to be urgent that they be employed in some other manner for fear of disheartening them completely and casting them into the depths of despair. It was apparent to me during my last trip that some of them were very discontented at always being called out while many of the soldiers remained working.[22]

In desperation, Champigny finally proposed that the best way to eradicate the abuses, and at the same time make the Troupes de la Marine a more effective fighting force, would be to discharge them all from the service and let them get married. Since the majority of them were labourers rather than soldiers, it would be better, he suggested, to have them settle down on land of their own and after a few years they would become good *habitants*, fit for active service with the militia. Thus, the colony would, in the long run, benefit from their work on the land and they would at long last be of some use as fighting men in time of war. Furthermore, the king would make a sizeable financial saving since he would be spared the cost of their pay and upkeep. The only persons who would be opposed to such a scheme, Champigny suggested, were the officers who had come to regard their men's pay as a perquisite of their office.[23] Although Champigny was probably being sarcastic when he broached this plan, it still had a good deal to recommend it, considering all the peculiarities of the Canadian military situation.

Apart from criticizing the officers' corps, Champigny did make some military reforms in his own department. Examples of these were the changes he made in the feeding and clothing of the troops. Normally, the men received a subsistence allowance and foraged for themselves, but this proved to be impossible with the price of food as high as it all too frequently was in New France. To overcome this difficulty, Champigny bought up foodstuffs in bulk when the price was low and issued it to the troops, deducting the cost from their pay. This relieved the plight of the men and, or so Champigny claimed, cost the Crown nothing except a small charge for the storage of grain.[24] Until 1687 the captains supplied their men with some articles of clothing such as boots, shirts and stockings and charged for them—this being a generally accepted method for the captains to make a profit for themselves. Champigny quickly put a stop to this on the grounds that the officers were issuing clothing of a very poor quality and that in the outlying posts they did not provide any at all. He purchased a stock of the necessary clothing on the king's account and issued it to the men as required on repayment.[25] Several years later, after he had returned to France, it was reported on good authority that Champigny had made a very good thing out of these arrangements, realizing a private profit of 25,000 *livres* a year, which amounted to slightly more than double his annual salary. It would seem that he imported the supplies for the troops himself under the name of the Sieur Hazeur, a Quebec merchant, and then made it appear that he was purchasing the goods from Hazeur at prices which allowed a small profit for Hazeur and a large hidden one for Champigny.[26] Such an arrangement would have been all too feasible; the surprising thing is, if the story be true, that Frontenac did not get wind of it.

Until 1690 the troops wore a uniform consisting of a pale grey jacket with blue facings and copper buttons, grey breeches and stockings, shirt, cravat and a wide-brimmed hat. The sergeants had red facings and gilded buttons on their grey-white jackets, and red breeches and stockings.[27] Although this turnout could have looked very smart on the parade-ground, the climate and the peculiar character of military operations in Canada made it most impractical; consequently, in 1692, the type of clothing worn by the *coureurs de bois* was adopted for the troops.[28] Thus the Canadian army can perhaps claim to have been the first to have adopted a form of battledress for active service.

Another military problem with which the intendant was faced was the billeting of the troops. There were no barracks in the colony; the officers and men were either quartered in the various forts or else billeted on the *habitants*. In the latter case the *habitants* had to provide straw for mattresses, a cooking pot and the use of the fireplace for the men; for their part the troops had to provide their share of the fire-wood,[29] which must have been no small chore, considering that all cooking was done over an open fireplace or in an outdoor bake-oven and that the same fireplace was the sole means of providing heat during the long winters. This system appears to have worked well enough; there is a singular lack of reference to any difficulties or problems arising from it in the official correspondence. On just one occasion is there mention of certain officers having complained on their turn to France of the primitive conditions under which they had been expected to live in Canada. Upon being questioned by the minister, Frontenac and Champigny replied that these officers had had no just cause for complaint, since most of the people were reduced to sleeping on straw; only the wealthier people had proper beds, and very few of them enjoyed the luxury of sheets.[30]

All the soldiers had a deduction made from their pay to cover the cost of any hospital treatment they might need. When they fell sick or were wounded they were cared for in the hospitals run by the religious orders at Quebec and Montreal. Owing to the inflated prices of food and other goods, the cost of caring for the troops far exceeded the amount they contributed from their pay and a supplementary grant had to be made from the Crown revenues for each hospitalized soldier. Unfortunately, the amount of the Crown grant was never adequate and for a time Frontenac and Champigny paid to the hospital at Montreal—which cared for most of the troops— over a *livre* per man per day out of their own pockets, something they did not let the minister forget when he complained at the size of the grant being made to the hospitals from the Crown revenues.[31]

Although there were undoubtedly many abuses at the lower military levels, it is by no means certain that they impaired the effectiveness of the colony's war effort. The complaints of Champigny have to be regarded with reserve since his purpose in making some of them was, to some extent, to embarrass Frontenac. He roundly condemned certain military abuses during Frontenac's regime, whereas he had pleaded extenuating circumstances to excuse these selfsame abuses under Denonville. Moreover, the abuse that he complained of the most, the continual use of the *habitants* instead of regulars for war parties, was itself an attempt by the senior officers to wage the war more effectively. Against such a foe as the Iroquois it would have been worse than folly to have employed men who were not physically fit, and Champigny himself stated that only two or three hundred of the Troupes de la Marine were fit for guerilla warfare. Thus Frontenac, Callières and Vaudreuil can hardly be blamed for employing the militia rather than regulars, harsh though this was on the *habitants*. And since they could not be used in the actual fighting, it was eminently practical to let the regulars perform useful non-military tasks. If they were well paid for it, so much the better for them : the money remained in the colony and was quickly put back into circulation. If the officers profited, albeit illegally, the men did not object. The practice of defrauding the men of some of their pay was firmly established in the seventeenth-century French army—and in other armies too, for that matter. Louvois, the great military reformer, had failed to stamp out the custom, therefore Frontenac and his subordinates cannot be criticized too severely for having failed to do so.

CHAPTER THIRTEEN

FRONTENAC'S BORDER RAIDS

BY the end of the year 1689 the people of New France considered their plight to be desperate. There seemed to be no way of curbing the continual Iroquois attacks. Small parties of the enemy could easily infiltrate among the settlements unseen. All too often the first warning the *habitants* had of the enemy's presence was to hear musket shots, then to see smoke rising from a neighbour's buildings. Before a force could be mustered to seek out the foe they would have disappeared to strike again in another quarter, leaving only charred ruins and mutilated bodies. Sometimes the bodies were not found and it could be presumed that the victims had been taken alive, to suffer, in all probability, a more hideous death in the Iroquois villages.

But if it was extremely difficult to come to grips with the Iroquois, there was another foe whom the Canadians blamed for much of their agony: the English of New York. It was English muskets, lead and powder with which the Iroquois were armed, English knives and hatchets that were used to scalp and butcher the Canadians, and English officials at Albany who were urging the Iroquois on. Moreover, this foe was not so elusive; they could be made to stand and fight or else be slaughtered. For some time the Canadians and their leaders had been itching to carry the war into New York province and give the English colonials a taste of the horrors of Indian warfare. Champigny remarked that the youth of the colony showed themselves very eager for an attack on the English [1] and there must have been a good deal of talk in Montreal, even before Frontenac's return, of a prospective mid-winter assault on Albany. Word of this quickly reached the English; most likely the Mission Iroquois of the Sault spoke of it to their friends and relatives in the Mohawk villages, who would be quick to pass it on to the traders and officials at Albany. As early as October, 1689, Edward Randolph was writing from Boston to the Bishop of London: "I have certain intelligence that the French mean to attack Albany in January, when the lakes and rivers are all frozen. I doubt not that they will take it unless orders arrive from England to prevent them." [2] Forewarned, however, was not forearmed in this instance. New York and New England were in a state of virtual anarchy as, taking advantage of the overthrow of James II in England, disaffected elements in the northern colonies imprisoned the king's officials and set up revolutionary juntas. In New York Jacob Leisler seized power, but in Albany control was retained by the authorities loyal to Sir Edmund Andros who were now as much concerned with this immediate threat as with the more remote, if more deadly, one offered by the French.[3] Frontenac, however, was not aware of this state of affairs when he gave his orders for three war parties to ravage the English border settlements; at least there is no evidence to indicate that he was.

In January these parties were mustered, one at Montreal, another at Trois Rivières and the third at Quebec. The Montreal party, led by Nicolas d'Ailleboust de Mantet and two of the Le Moyne brothers, Ste Hélène and Iberville, was made up of two hundred and ten men, one hundred and fourteen Canadians and the rest allied Indians, most of these last being from the two Iroquois missions at Montreal. Their objective was the small town of Schenectady. For several days they marched through the deep snows of the forest, dragging their supplies and equipment on toboggans. Arriving within sight of the town shortly before midnight, they found no sentinels posted and one of the gates in the stockade not closed. The inhabitants had become so divided by the bitter struggle between the Leisler and Andros factions that they had refused to take orders from anyone, even for their own protection.[4] While the disputing residents slept soundly, the Canadians and their Indians slipped inside the walls and posted themselves in groups of six or seven by each house. Then, as it had been at Lachine, so it was at Schenectady. A shrill war cry shattered the cold silence of the night. Doors were smashed open and the slaughter began. Men, women and children were hacked down as they struggled terrified out of their beds. Few had any chance to offer resistance. Those who did manage to hold off the attackers momentarily had their houses set ablaze and either died in the flames or were slaughtered as they tried to break out. Some sixty persons were killed, and the Mayor of Albany later wrote: "The Cruelties Committed at said Place no Penn can write nor Tongue Expresse; ye women big with child ripped up and ye children alive thrown into ye flames, and their heads dashed in pieces against the Doors and windows." [5]

Once the brief resistance had been quelled, the victors rested on their arms. Fifty to sixty old men, women and children had somehow survived the first fury of the attack and they had their lives spared. The Canadians had lost only one of their own men killed and one Indian ally. In one of the houses thirty Mohawks were found, but they were not harmed. Frontenac, convinced as he was that he could persuade the Iroquois to come to terms, had given specific instructions that any Iroquois encountered were to be spared.[6] Across the river from the town itself was a small fort in which Captain Sander, a town magistrate, with a few men stood ready to fight. The French officers informed him that it was contained in their orders that they were not to harm so much as a chicken of his because he and his wife had saved several French prisoners from the Mohawk fires in the past. He persuaded them to spare the homes of some few others in the town, but the remainder of those still standing were put to the torch. At noon, leaving little but grey mounds of ashes and the blackened pillars of stone fireplaces in the surrounding whiteness to mark where Schenectady had once stood, the Canadians and their allies set off on the long march home. They took with them fifty horses loaded with plunder and twenty-seven of the prisoners, men and boys, who were fit for such a journey. The rest were set free, to make their way to Albany as best they could, many of them arriving there with frozen limbs.

During the return journey to Montreal the men failed to remain in a group. Sixty leagues from Schenectady the Indian allies went off to hunt; one evening ten stragglers failed to catch up with the main body; then forty of the Canadians decided to push on ahead, leaving only fifty to sixty men in the main party, and soon seven of these fell behind. By this time the main force was almost within sight of Montreal. The need for precautions appeared to have passed. But the thirty Mohawks who had been spared at Schenectady had hastened to their villages and raised a war party of eighty warriors to pursue the French. They caught up with the stragglers close to Montreal, capturing nineteen of then.[7]

On January 28 the war party led by the Sieur Hertel, consisting of twenty-five Canadians and twenty-five Indians, left Trois Rivières. On March 27 it reached the English settlement of Salmon Falls, near Portsmouth on the Maine coast. The story was the same as at Schenectady. No watch was being kept in the three small stockaded forts. Hertel divided his men into three parties. At dawn they attacked simultaneously. The settlers, caught in their beds, had little chance to resist. Some thirty-four people of both sexes and all ages were killed and fifty-four, mostly women and children, were taken prisoner. Then the scattered farms in the district were put to the torch and the horses and cattle all slaughtered. When a scout brought word that a body of militia was hurrying to the scene from Portsmouth, Hertel called his men together and began his retreat. Encumbered by their prisoners, they were overtaken by the enemy at a river, swollen by the spring flood. On the far side Hertel's men made a stand. They killed and wounded several of their pursuers, held them off till nightfall, then slipped away.[8]

A few days later they linked up with the third war party, led by the Sieur de Portneuf. Hertel sent all but thirty-six of his men back to Quebec with some few of the prisoners; the rest of these hapless captives had to be handed over to the Indian allies. The French, however, did later ransom several of them from the Indians and treated them with every kindness once they reached Quebec. Frontenac and Mme de Champigny, the wife of the intendant, particularly distinguished themselves in this connection.[9] Portneuf, with fifty Canadians and sixty Abenakis from the St. François de Sales mission, had left Quebec on January 28. Later they had been joined by two other groups of Abenakis before Hertel's party met them. The combined force, numbering some four to five hundred men, made its way slowly towards its objective. On May 25 they were discovered by the garrison of Fort Loyal on Casco Bay. Thirty men from the fort sallied out to attack what they thought were a few marauding Indians. They were cut to pieces before they realized their mistake. Only four men escaped back to the fort.

This skirmish gave the alarm to the whole area. The settlers immediately took cover in four small blockhouses and under cover of darkness they managed to gain the shelter of the main fort. Although Portneuf had received strict orders from Frontenac not to attack any strong points but only to destroy the isolated settlements,[10] he now laid siege to the fort, digging trenches up to its very walls. When the defenders saw crude mines being set, they surrendered. Sixty-six men with a number of women and children were made prisoners. All the cannon in the fort were spiked, the munitions and the fort itself destroyed. For two leagues around, the abandoned homes were burned. Three to four hundred people in the surrounding area fled in terror to the safety of Portsmouth. Their grim work done, the French made their way back to Quebec, arriving there on June 23.[11] They brought back with them four or five prisoners, including the commander of Fort Loyal, Sylvanus Davis, who complained bitterly that the French had broken the terms of surrender by not giving their captives safe conduct to the nearest English town as had been agreed upon, but instead had turned most of them over to the Indians who had killed several, in particular the wounded. He did, however, give the French credit for having treated him well enough during the journey and at Quebec, where he was brought before Frontenac. "He treated me civilly," Davis remarked, adding that Frontenac had informed him that the governor and people of New York were really to blame for the French attacks on New England, since it was they who had unleashed the Iroquois against New France. Davis answered that New York, and not Boston, must answer for this; whereat Frontenac commented that they were, after all, one nation. "True," replied Davis, "but two distinct governments." [12]

Frontenac claimed that these raids would force the English on to the defensive and deter them from joining with the Iroquois to attack New France from several quarters.[13] In fact, they had the very opposite effect. It was these raids that caused the northern English colonies to unite—something that always took a great deal of doing—and to organize their combined forces for a full-scale assault by land and sea on New France. He also claimed that their success had had considerable effect on the morale of the people of New France and the Indian allies. There can be no doubt that they raised the morale of the Canadians; after a steady diet of casualties and destruction, the knowledge that losses had at last been inflicted on an enemy must have raised their spirits. But Frontenac's assertion that it would have the same effect on the Indian allies is not quite so tenable. It would on the Abenakis, the Mission Iroquois of Montreal and the Acadian Indians who had taken part in the raids; to this extent his claims was justified. But the effect on the up-country tribes was rather dubious. To them, the real foe was the Iroquois; the English had never done them any harm.

The most trenchant criticism of Frontenac's strategy, however, was that delivered by the intendant, and since military strategy was not his *métier* he may well merely have been voicing the views

227

of the subordinate commanders, probably those of Vaudreuil, with whom he was always on good terms. Champigny maintained that the French forces should have been combined into a single striking force and an assault made, not on three small settlements at widely scattered points, but on Albany. He stated that with an additional hundred men the force that had razed Schenectady could have destroyed Albany, and he wrote: "If this blow had been struck against Albany we would have seen the Iroquois greatly humbled, because it is from there that they obtain all the succour they need, being out of reach of Manhattan and Boston, particularly during the winter." [14] And at least one of the officers with the war party had strongly favoured attacking Albany rather than Schenectady, but Frontenac's orders had been specific that the latter town was to be attacked.* In 1682 La Barre had informed the minister that if he had to attack the Iroquois he would also be obliged to attack Albany, since it was from there that the Iroquois obtained their arms and supplies.[15] A few years later both Denonville and Callières had strongly advocated destroying this town as being the most effective way of curbing the Iroquois.[16]

Champigny's arguments are also substantiated by the governor of New York who, in pleading with the governors of the other provinces for aid in defence of the northern frontier, stated, without too much exaggeration:

I need not relate unto you of how great import the preservacon of this place is, being the only bulwark and safeguard of all Their

* In his letter of November 17, 1690, to Mme Frontenac, in which he gives a detailed and glowing account of the border raids, Monseignat, Frontenac's secretary, states that the leaders of the Schenectady party intended to attack Albany but that they were not specifically ordered to do so, only to undertake what they considered could be accomplished with success and with little risk. He also states that when the party was close to both Albany and Schenectady the officers were persuaded by their Indian allies that their force was not large enough to attack the former. This places the responsibility for the choice of objective on the Indian allies or the officers commanding the party; but a member of the raiding party who was captured by the Mohawks and taken to Albany for questioning declared: "When they were within some miles of Shinnechtady ye officers had a consultation about falling upon Albanie, one monsr. De Tallie who had been formerly here [Albany] did Presse hard to Attaque it; Butt because there orders was Expressly for Shinnechtady ye DeSign on alb⁹ was put by." The other information given by this prisoner, which can be verified from other sources, is strictly accurate. See *The Livingston Indian Records 1666–1723*, p. 160.

Majesty's plantacons on the main of America, and if, for want of strength, the French should assault and gain Albany how farr your Government and all the English Colonys on both sides of us would be endangered, you can easily judge. For we have nothing but that place that keeps our Indians steady to us, and the loss of that must be the loss of them, and the loss of them must be the loss of all the King's interest on this continent.[17]

And the Massachusetts officials were of the same mind. "Albany is the dam, which, should it through neglect be broken we dread to think of the inundation of calamities," wrote the Council to the Governor of Connecticut.[18] It was at Albany that the Iroquois held their councils with the English; when the Governor of Virginia and William Penn wished to confer with the Five Nations they had to go to Albany to do it.[19] By virtue of its charter Albany had a monopoly on the fur trade with the Iroquois and all tribes "to the Eastward Northward and Westward."[20] This monopoly the merchants of Albany guarded jealously and as a result no love was lost between them and the people of the other provinces and even the other towns in New York. When Virginia and Pennsylvania wished to purchase the Susquehanna lands conquered by the Iroquois, these tribes refused to consider it and placed the lands in question under the suzerainty of New York to prevent the colonies to the south occupying the territory. Virginia and Maryland regarded this transaction with deep suspicion[21] and at least one Crown official in New England regarded the Dutch of New York as no better neighbours than the French.[22] Throughout the previous ten years it had been the merchants and officials of Albany who had spurred the Iroquois on in their attempts to wrest the western fur trade from the French; it had been men from Albany who had invaded the Ottawa country in 1686 and 1687 and come dangerously close to seducing these tribes from the French alliance. Under these circumstances, had Frontenac concentrated his forces against Albany, not only would the Iroquois supply base have been destroyed, but the eastern cantons of the Five Nations would have had to look more to their own security than to sending large war parties to ravage the French settlements, and the New England colonies would most likely not have been so eager to attack Canada.

CHAPTER FOURTEEN

THE AMERICAN ASSAULT ON CANADA

FOLLOWING his border raids, Frontenac again tried to enter into negotiations with the Iroquois. He appears to have been convinced that they were little more than rebellious children whom he could restore to a proper sense of their filial duties by cajolery and threats.[1] Despite the failure of his earlier embassy, in the spring of 1690 he sent one of his officers, the Chevalier Dau, accompanied by an interpreter and two canoe men, to the Iroquois cantons.[2] When the Chevalier and his companions arrived in the Iroquois country they received a warm reception: his interpreter and the canoe men were burned to death over a slow fire and the Chevalier himself narrowly missed the same fate; he was made to run the gauntlet and then turned over to the English to languish in prison for two years until he escaped and eventually returned to Quebec.[3]

At this time the Iroquois were at the crest of their power. During the winter one of the Ottawa tribes had made peace with the Senecas and in February three of their chiefs had gone to the council of the Five Nations at Onondaga to ratify this treaty in the presence of representatives from Albany. They had agreed to use their best efforts to induce the other Ottawa tribes to break with the French and enter the Iroquois alliance.[4] Word of this first reached Frontenac from Michilimackinac; Durantaye, the commandant at this post, sent two Canadians in the depth of winter to warn the governor that all the Ottawa tribes were on the verge of making a separate peace with the Iroquois and turning on the French.[5] Frontenac maintained that this had come about as a consequence of the abandonment of Fort Frontenac,[6] but the allies themselves made it plain that the main reason for their defection was their mistrust of Frontenac's appeasement policy towards the Five Nations. To them it seemed the height of folly to release Iroquois captives or spare any of these tribesmen who fell into French hands at a time when the Iroquois were killing the French at every opportunity, and burning and eating their captives. The Ottawas were convinced that a peace between the French and the Iroquois would merely free the latter to concentrate their attacks on the western tribes, and consequently they had decided to turn the tables by making a separate peace, leaving the French rather than themselves to bear the full brunt of the Iroquois war.[7]

As soon as the rivers were free of ice Frontenac sent a detachment of one hundred and forty-three men, convoyed part way by thirty more, to Michilimackinac with liberal presents for the Ottawas in an attempt to prevent their deserting the French alliance. The command of this party was given to the Sieur de Louvigny, who had been an officer in Frontenac's guards during his first administration and subsequently had become a merchant fur trader in Montreal. Louvigny was also commissioned to take over the command of Michilimackinac from Morel de Durantaye, who was recalled to Montreal. When the detachment was some seventy-five miles from Montreal, the advance party ran into an Iroquois ambush and eight Canadians were killed. At this some of the officers were all for turning back, but Louvigny led sixty of the men in a counterattack. They caught the enemy unawares, exulting over their success. When the French poured a sudden volley into the Iroquois at close quarters, then charged down on them, they broke and fled in panic. Of their thirteen canoes only four were launched and got away, carrying a good many wounded. All told, some thirty Iroquois were killed and four taken prisoner, two men and two women.[8]

Frontenac, in his dispatch to the minister, stated that Louvigny and his party arrived at Michilimackinac just as the Ottawa ambassadors were about to leave for Onondaga to return their Iroquois prisoners and ratify the peace treaty. He also claimed, with his habitual rodomontade, that it was only the news that their "*ancien père*" had returned to Canada that caused them to abandon this peace embassy and to go down to Montreal to confer with him instead.[9] Other accounts state that the French had great difficulty in dissuading the Ottawas from proceeding to Onondaga, but finally induced them to assist in the torturing of one of the Iroquois captured en route. When the victim showed himself unable to bear the torments of his captors, he was taunted as a craven, unworthy to die a warrior's death, then quickly dispatched and boiled and eaten. This effectively put an end to the Ottawas' peace negotiations with the Five Nations for the time being, and they at last agreed to go down to Montreal.[10]

In mid-August the garrison of the fort at the western tip of the island of Montreal saw the far side of the Lake of Two Mountains covered with canoes, paddling directly for the narrows at Ste Anne's. The cannon of the fort were fired to sound the alarm. Then, as the canoes approached, to everyone's great relief they were seen to hold not Iroquois, but members of all the up-country nations. There were over five hundred of them, their canoes laden with 300,000 *livres'* worth of furs. In telling the minister of their arrival, Frontenac stated that "the joy of all the *habitants* and merchants at this event, which was so unexpected, is almost beyond belief." [11] This is in marked contrast to his comments the previous year when, just before his return to the colony, an even larger shipment of furs was brought down to Montreal. On that occasion he had stated sourly that only a few merchants and others stood to gain from it; the colony as a whole gained nothing and saw no cause to rejoice. [12]

When the allies met Frontenac in a general council, their spokesmen questioned him closely on his policy towards the Iroquois. Ouanabouchie, a Nipissing chief who had accompanied the French in the raid on Schenectady, pointed out that the Mohawks who had been found in the town and spared on Frontenac's orders had later pursued the French and captured several of them at the very gates of Montreal. Subsequently, when he and his men returned to Michilimackinac, Frontenac had ordered them not to attack any Iroquois they encountered en route unless the Iroquois attacked first, and as a result they had suffered some casualties. In view of all this, they could only conclude that Frontenac wanted to make peace with the Iroquois. He demanded to know exactly what Frontenac's policies were. Le Baron, a Huron chief, spoke next, and he exhorted Frontenac to press the war against the Iroquois as well as the English. When the Mission Iroquois demanded to know why the Ottawas had been negotiating for peace with the Five Nations, an Ottawa chief replied that since the French had themselves been negotiating for peace with the enemy, they had had to look to their own interests and try to prevent the full weight of the Iroquois attacks from falling on them alone. [13] In the face of this criticism Frontenac was forced to disavow his appeasement policy. He now promised that he would press the war against the Five Nations until they sued for peace, and that when this occurred he would undertake no negotiations without the allies' participation. He exhorted them to harass the enemy unceasingly and promised that his forces would do the same until the time was ripe to attack the Iroquois in their villages. The allies appeared to be satisfied with this change in French policy, and the next few days were taken up by feasting and the trading of their furs.[14]

While this activity was still in progress a scout reported that a large army of English and Iroquois had assembled at Lake Champlain. The report was confirmed by an officer of the Chambly garrison who had been out reconnoitring in the area. Frontenac immediately mustered the troops, some of the militia and the Mission Iroquois to repulse the impending attack; the up-country tribesmen were invited to join the expedition. Twelve hundred strong, Frontenac and his motley army crossed the river to Prairie-de-la-Magdelaine and camped there for three days. Scouts were sent out, but they could find no trace of the enemy. Frontenac then marched the army back again. Two days later, on September 4, smoke was seen rising from burning homes at La Fourche on the south shore, half a mile from where Frontenac's forces had encamped. The *habitants* of the area and the troops from the nearby fort had been in the fields gathering the harvest and had neglected to carry their arms. The officer commanding the garrison at the fort had not bothered to keep sentries posted or have a corps of men ready for emergencies; consequently, the enemy had an easy time of it. Twenty-one men and four women were killed or captured; the houses, barns and crops in the area were all burned. In his dispatch to the minister Frontenac made much of the fact that he had persuaded the Indian allies to accompany his forces to La Prairie, but he neglected to mention the subsequent enemy attack. At the same time the Iroquois raided several other isolated settlements, killing some twenty-eight *habitants* and soldiers, including two officers.[15]

At the time no one realized how close to disaster the colony had actually stood. The raid on La Fourche had been carried out by a party of twenty-nine Albany militia, led by Captain John Schuyler, and a hundred and twenty Iroquois.[16] They had formed part of a much larger force raised to march on Montreal while another expedition, raised at Boston, went by sea to attack Quebec. This dual assault was a direct consequence of Frontenac's raids on the English settlements the previous winter. *Delenda est Nova Francia* had been the theme of the deliberations in the English colonial assemblies following these raids.[17] The plan of campaign drawn up by the provincial commissioners at New York had called for eight hundred and fifty-five militia from New York, Maryland and New England to join with a large force from the Five Nations. But when these men assembled at Albany they proved to be far fewer in numbers than had been agreed upon. As the force made its way up Wood Creek towards Lake Champlain, dissension broke out among the militia commanders; provisions and canoes were lacking and some of the men came down with smallpox. When the western Iroquois heard of this last they refused to come near and the bulk of the militia turned back, whereupon Leisler imprisoned their commander, Major-General Winthrop, and his officers.[18] John Schuyler managed to salvage something from the confusion, but since his raid was not in sufficient strength and did not coincide with the maritime assault on Quebec, it was possible for Frontenac to concentrate his forces against each threat in turn.

On October 8 the Sieur Provost, town-major of Quebec, received word from the Abenakis of Acadia that a Boston fleet was on its way up the St. Lawrence. He immediately sent a small boat down river to reconnoitre and a canoe to Montreal to warn Frontenac. He then called in the *habitants* from the surrounding countryside and set them to work digging trenches and strengthening the log palisade that had been built at the rear of the town the previous winter.[19] The people, some of whom were panic-stricken, removed themselves hastily from their homes along the river-bank and, taking only what they could carry, found quarters wherever they could in Upper Town. The sisters of the Hôtel Dieu hastily dug a trench in their garden to bury their silver and altar vessels, and made ready to quit the town and go to Lorette.[20]

Frontenac, when he received the news of the impending attack, was just about to leave Montreal for Quebec. He and the intendant immediately set off by canoe in all haste. This was a situation that required no deep insight nor strategic planning; during his earlier military career Frontenac had taken part in numerous sieges of towns on both the offensive and the defensive side. The rules for this type of military operation were well established and Frontenac must have known them by heart. The difference this time, however, was that the besieging force came by water, and this dictated the tactics that had to be employed by both sides.

Upon receiving word the day after he left Montreal that the enemy fleet was off Tadoussac, Frontenac acted swiftly. He sent orders to Callières telling him to bring all the troops and militia available, leaving only a skeleton force at Montreal. At Trois Rivières he paused just long enough to order every man to Quebec. When he arrived there himself four days after leaving Montreal and accompanied by two to three hundred men, he found the defences prepared and the cannon sited. His arrival with these reinforcements, and the news that every available man in the colony was on his way to help defend the town, raised the spirits of the people greatly. To maintain their morale he ordered the sisters of the Hôtel Dieu to remain where they were, lest their leaving should alarm the rest of the populace.[21] He had, in fact, arrived not a moment too soon, for three days later the Boston fleet, commanded by Sir William Phips, was in sight of the town. In all it numbered thirty-four sail: four large ships, four somewhat smaller, the rest ketches, barques and brigantines.[22] Had the land attack on Montreal not foundered and the marine assault on Quebec been so long delayed, both before and during the voyage, nothing could have saved New France. Just the week before the Boston fleet appeared there had not been more than one hundred and fifty men left in Quebec all told; most of them had gone to Montreal when word was received that the up-country tribes had come to trade their furs. Quebec could then have been taken without a shot being fired, and the French afterwards admitted it.[23]

Shortly before ten o'clock the next morning, October 17, a pinnace flying a white flag put off from the admiral's ship carrying an envoy, Major Thomas Savage. When the pinnace reached shore, the major was blindfolded and conducted by the steepest possible path to the Château St. Louis where Frontenac awaited him with the intendant and the senior officers. It was in scenes such as this that Frontenac excelled; no one knew better than he how to invest the proceedings with a sense of drama, smacking of the Court of Versailles, or perhaps of the theatre. When his blindfold was removed, Major Savage found himself in "a stately Hall full of brave Martiall men" [24] dressed as though for a royal levée in gold and silver lace, ribands and plumed hats, their hair powdered and curled, their expressions anything but those of men who feared what events might bring.[25] Visibly impressed, the major handed Frontenac an ultimatum couched in phrases as severe as the four puritan preachers who were attached to Phips's council of war could make it. This document began: "The warrs between the two crownes of England and France doth not only sufficiently warrant;

But the destruction made by ye french, and Indians, under your command and Encouragement upon the persons and Estates, of their Majesties subjects of New England, without provocation on their part, hath put them under the necessity of this Expedition for their own Security and satisfaction." It then went on to demand the immediate surrender of the colony's forts, stores and military establishment. Frontenac was required to accede to this demand within the hour, failing which Phips declared that Quebec would be taken by force of arms.[26]

While the French officers were hurriedly translating this ultimatum, Major Savage, having recovered his composure, coolly drew a watch from his pocket, handed it to Frontenac, and announced that he must have a reply by eleven o'clock, no later. Frontenac answered that he would not keep the admiral waiting quite so long, and, indicating his officers, he inquired of Major Savage if he really believed that these gentlemen would consent to their governor's accepting such harsh terms. The major then asked if Frontenac would be good enough to put his reply in writing, whereat Frontenac made his justly famous rejoinder : "I have no reply to make to your general other than from the mouths of my cannon and muskets. He must learn that it is not in this fashion that one summons a man such as I. Let him do the best he can on his side as I will do on mine."[27] With that, Major Savage was re-blindfolded and conducted back to his pinnace.

Frontenac's proud challenge was not at all what the New England men had expected, and when they learned, later in the day, that almost the entire military strength of the colony was waiting to oppose them, they realized full well that their plans had gone awry. Their chances of success were also greatly reduced by the lateness of the season. In April a ship had been sent to England to plead for aid in the projected assault on Quebec and the expedition had delayed sailing in the hopes of obtaining help from the mother country. When no reply was received by the 9th of August, Phips's fleet had set sail, made over-confident by the ease with which Port Royal in Acadia had been captured earlier in the year.[28] But it was now October, and if they were going to take Quebec they had to do it quickly. There was no possibility of a protracted siege. Frontenac had only to stave them off for two or three weeks at the very most, when they would be forced to retire or run the risk of being trapped in the Gulf by the freeze-up and destroyed by the elements.

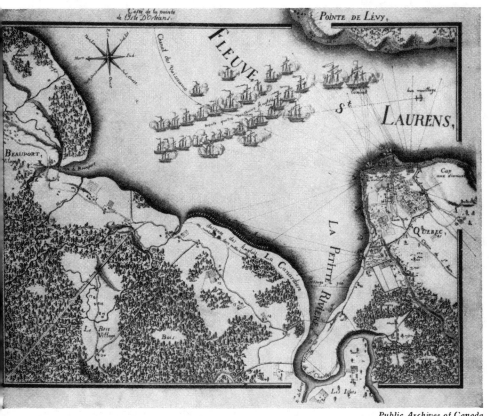

Phips' Assault on Quebec

By the time that Major Savage had returned to the flagship with Frontenac's answer, the tide had been missed and no attempt was made to land troops that day. In the evening Callières reached Quebec from Montreal with an additional five or six hundred men. The next day an attempt was made to land on the Beauport flats. Owing to rough weather only one boat reached the shore and the men had a rough time of it, being assailed from the cover of the brush by the *habitants* of Beauport before the incoming tide enabled them to get away. The following day Major John Walley, who commanded the land forces, got twelve to thirteen hundred men ashore at La Canardière on the Beauport flats, just across the St. Charles River from Quebec. This river could be forded at low tide at two points, one near the river's mouth, the other a little higher up, and the plan was for the smaller boats in the Boston fleet to transport the army's field guns and supplies to the Quebec side of the St. Charles and lay down a barrage of cannon fire to cover the crossing of the army. Meanwhile, some of the larger ships were to go up the St. Lawrence to a point opposite the town. When the signal was given that the main army was across the St. Charles and had begun its assault on the hill leading to Upper Town, these ships were to land two hundred men on the St. Lawrence flank beneath the French guns and they were to attempt to storm their way up the cliff into Upper Town. The other warships were to go above Quebec in the hope of drawing off some of the defending forces to repulse a possible landing in that quarter.[29]

Frontenac made no attempt to oppose the landing, for two reasons. Until the enemy boats actually put in to shore he could not be sure where they would land; and secondly, he could not have got his troops across the St. Charles to attack the enemy in any case, because their forces landed at high tide, when the fords across this river were flooded with over seventeen feet of water.[30] Once the landing had been effected, however, Frontenac still pursued a waiting policy. He declined to send his main forces across the St. Charles to engage the enemy when the tide dropped because, as he later explained, by so doing he would have had that river at his rear, making his retreat hazardous. He also maintained that the terrain on the Beauport flats was swampy and covered with brush, highly unsuitable for the deployment of regular troops. In order to take Quebec from where they were the enemy had to cross the St. Charles; Frontenac therefore decided that it would be better to hold his main forces on the Quebec side of this river and attack the enemy as they attempted the crossing at one or both of the two fords, meanwhile allowing small parties of Canadians to harass them from cover, Indian-style.[31]

The moment the New England men moved to higher ground after their landing they came under fire from the Canadians. This galling fire continued as they marched towards the river fords. Later that day, instead of coming into the mouth of the St. Charles to cover the army's crossing and bring supplies, the Boston ships sailed upstream opposite the town and began cannonading it. Apart from frightening the poor nuns at the Hôtel Dieu almost out of their wits, they did little damage. Instead they suffered considerably from the return fire and consumed large quantities of powder at a time when their land forces had only what was in their powder horns. When the army camped for the night a deserter from the Troupes de la Marine was brought in. The information he furnished as to the strength and disposition of the French forces made the hopelessness of the situation quite apparent to Major Walley and his officers. Next morning things looked no better. The men had had nothing but two ship's biscuits each to eat since landing, and the rum supply had now run out. The night had been bitterly cold and being without dry clothes or blankets they had suffered acutely. Still expecting that the fleet would bring supplies and provide covering fire while the army at least made an attempt to ford the St. Charles, Major Walley moved his forces closer to the town. Meanwhile, Phips's four larger ships began cannonading the town again at first light. They were soon forced to break off this artillery duel when they received several hits at the water-line and suffered damage to their spars. Phips's mainmast was hit and nearly brought down. At this he cut his cable and retired from the action. Two of the other ships continued a desultory fire; then they too broke off the engagement. At five o'clock in the evening they moved upstream and attempted a landing above Cape Diamond but were beaten off after suffering some casualties. The main army, in the meantime, remained inactive, unable to attempt a crossing of the St. Charles without naval support. Walley expected the ships to bring him supplies on the evening tide, but they did not come. His men were now falling sick with the dread smallpox at an alarming rate. The Canadians continued to harass them and just across the St. Charles the main French forces were drawn up, waiting. At a council of war it was decided that nothing remained but to return to the ships, rest the men, and then if circumstances permitted, attempt a frontal assault on the town.

The next morning the ice on the pools was thick enough to bear a man, a grim reminder that time was running out. The Canadians continued their attacks, keeping up a constant fire, falling back when detachments were sent against them, and inflicting four casualties, only one of which proved fatal. At one point the Canadians came under fire from the New Englanders' cannon, and although none of them were hit it probably had a deterrent effect. Late that night Major Walley made an attempt to get his forces back to the ships. After midnight the regiments silently withdrew to a mustering point near the beach, drawing back their guns. Before daylight the boats began to row ashore, but too many of the men crowded down onto the beach, all anxious to be among the first off. Walley immediately saw that utter confusion would result and that it would be impossible to get them all away before daylight. He thereupon abandoned the attempt and ordered the boats to return to the ships. However, the operation, although abortive, had been accomplished without the French becoming aware of what was going on.

The following day, October 21, the story was the same. Frontenac held his main forces on the right bank of the St. Charles, waiting expectantly for them to attempt a crossing and keeping a wary eye on the movements of the enemy ships. Some detachments of volunteers crossed the river to harass the enemy and Major Walley sent several companies to clear them out of the swamps and thickets near his main forces. He ordered them to maintain a brisk fire until dark and force the Canadians to keep their distance. When the light began to fade the sick were sent off, for, as Walley commented, "two or three boats might goe off well enough unsuspected." That done, he informed the officers and the master gunner that the army would re-embark after dark at high tide, half a regiment at a time. When the boats put in to shore, despite the best efforts of the officers all semblance of order and discipline rapidly disappeared. The men crowded down to the beach and struggled to climb into the boats as soon as they approached. The sailors were obliged to beat many of them back and to thrust some overboard to prevent the boats being swamped. But somehow they were all taken off. They left behind five of their six cannon, a quantity of ammunition and a drum.[32]

It has been argued that Frontenac, in allowing the New England forces to withdraw unmolested in this fashion, neglected a magnificent opportunity to inflict a crushing blow on the enemy.[33] But there was a very sound reason why Frontenac did not interfere with their embarkation. It was impossible for him to do so, even had he been warned in time that it had begun, because the St. Charles River stood between his main forces and the embarking enemy. Since the tide was in, the two fords across this river were flooded with over seventeen feet of water. Moreover, the night was pitch-black and pouring with rain,[34] and whatever else his forces were trained for, they were not trained for large-scale night manoeuvres, nor would their muskets have functioned with damp powder.

Later in the day the Americans held a council of war on the flagship; there was some discussion of attempting a landing beneath the French guns at Lower Town, but there was little doubt in anyone's mind that the troops were not up to it. The question was finally settled when a storm arose, scattering the ships from their moorings and reminding the mariners that time was running very short. On October 25 the fleet raised sail and slipped downstream out of sight of Quebec. The next day the prisoners taken by Phips on his way up the St. Lawrence were exchanged for those taken by the Canadians during the border raids, and after threatening to come back the following year with a stronger force, the Massachusetts men set course for home.

During the return voyage the Boston fleet ran into violent storms. Phips himself did not reach Boston until late in November. Some of his ships were blown as far afield as the West Indies; one ship was wrecked on Anticosti Island and two or three others were lost at sea. Accounts differ widely on the casualties suffered by the New England forces. Phips stated that they had not lost more than thirty men. Apparently he was taking into account only the casualties suffered at Quebec from enemy action. Frontenac claimed that the enemy had suffered over five hundred casualties. As to their own losses, the French were much more conservative; Champigny stated that they had had seven men killed and eleven or twelve wounded, Father Couvert that they had had six men killed and twenty wounded, and Frontenac does not mention the

French losses at all. Although Phips's figures of only thirty fatal casualties suffered in action may well have been correct, the failure of the expedition proved to be a crippling blow to New England. Governor Sloughter wrote:

> The whole country from Pemaquid to Delaware is extreamely hurt by the late ill managed and fruitless expedition to Canada, which hath contracted £40,000 debt and about 1000 men lost by sickness and shipwrack and no blow struck for want of courage and conduct in the Officers, as is universally said and believed.[35]

Yet Frontenac could hardly claim to have won anything resembling a brilliant victory, for no battle had been fought. Phips's forces had been defeated by the elements and their own inadequacies, rather than by force of arms. It was not so much the guerilla tactics of the Canadians or Frontenac's superior generalship that had forced the enemy to abandon the field but rather smallpox, lack of supplies, the inclement weather, the lateness of the season, the failure of the naval forces to give adequate support to the militia, and most of all the failure of the land assault on Montreal to materialize in sufficient strength and at the right time. If a battle had been fought the odds would have been decidedly in favour of the French, and Frontenac has been criticized for not bringing his forces across the St. Charles River and engaging the enemy on the Beauport flats. Had he done so, it is alleged, he could have driven them into the river.[36]

With the benefit of hindsight it is quite apparent that Frontenac missed an excellent opportunity to destroy the enemy completely. If he had possessed the information available to the modern scholar, there would be little excuse for his not having done so. But the French took no prisoners who could have divulged the enemy's plans and Frontenac had no way of knowing the full extent of the conditions prevailing among the enemy: the lack of liaison between the ships and the land forces, the ravages of smallpox in the ranks, their shortage of food and ammunition, their low morale and worse discipline. To take Quebec from La Canardière the enemy had to ford the St. Charles, and Frontenac could only assume that they intended to make the attempt; therefore, as he pointed out, the best place to engage them was on the Quebec side of this river. The cannon he had sited on the fords could have wrought havoc on them as they waded across, the Canadians on the Beauport side could have harassed their flank and rear, and the Troupes de la Marine could have attacked those who did reach the other side and have hurled them back into the river before they had time to re-organize their ranks.

Moreover, there was another strategic factor that Frontenac had to bear in mind: the enemy ships gave their forces one great advantage over the French—mobility. Frontenac had no way of knowing that the entire enemy force was on the Beauport flats; there might, for all he knew, be another force on the ships—as in fact there was, but they were men too sick to move. Were he to have crossed the St. Charles at low tide with his main forces to engage the enemy, their ships might have effected a landing at Lower Town or farther up-stream where Wolfe's men were to land one day. And once his troops became engaged, as he pointed out, it would have been extremely difficult for them to get back to Quebec. Low tide occurred only in mid-afternoon and in the hours of darkness before dawn; with the tide rising behind them at the fords at over two feet an hour the French, once they were across, would have had only three to four hours at the most before being cut off from Quebec for nine hours.* Frontenac was nervous about the defences at the rear of Quebec; he had sited a battery of eight guns on the heights that dominated Upper Town and some smaller pieces lower down the slope close by the palisade.[37] When Phips made a determined attempt to put a party of men ashore in the Anse aux Mères, they were beaten off, indicating that Frontenac was aware of the danger of an attack being launched on that flank.[38] We know now that Phips intended to land only two hundred men beneath the guns of Lower Town, but Frontenac, having no way of knowing what size force he might be intending to land on that flank, had to be prepared to counter any landing anywhere.

Moreover, he had constantly to bear in mind that were he to send his forces across the St. Charles he would have to run the risk of sustaining heavy casualties. With six cannon ashore the enemy could have done a lot of damage to a massed body of troops and it

* There was another point up the St. Charles River where a crossing could have been made. It was used by de Monic with a party of one hundred men on the night of October 21–22 but, as Frontenac pointed out, it necessitated "a very long circuit," since it was far enough up-stream not to be made impassable by the tide To get a raiding party across was one thing, but to get a small army across in a hurry would have been at least difficult and probably impossible.

would have been difficult for Frontenac to get any field-pieces into action for counter-battery work. The only man on the French side able to lay a gun accurately was Ste Hélène le Moyne, [39] who received a fatal wound during the skirmishing on the twentieth. The French could not afford to risk heavy casualties; they had no reserves and their losses could not have been replaced by reinforcements from France until the following year. With war raging in Europe, Frontenac had no surety of receiving more troops no matter how desperate his need, and he needed every man to defend the colony against possible future attacks, not only from the English colonies but also from the Iroquois. It would have been poor policy to risk losing a war for the sake of winning a battle.

Throughout the assault Frontenac followed the established rules of seventeenth-century warfare for the defence of a besieged town.* He husbanded his forces to avoil heavy casualties, guarded against surprise moves by the enemy, and sat tight, waiting for the enemy to attack him, whereupon the odds would have been decidedly in his favour. This was tactically sound, for he could hardly have hoped, let alone anticipated, that the enemy, after undertaking such an ambitious enterprise, would suddenly abandon the assault after only five days of manoeuvring. A Condé or a Turenne might conceivably have surmised the enemy's capabilities and intentions accurately enough to throw caution to the winds and give battle, but Frontenac was not of their calibre; few men were. The fact remains that the New England forces failed to take Quebec and the French losses were slight. Frontenac thereby redeemed himself, to some extent, for the poor strategy of his raids on the border settlements of New York and New England. In fact, in the light of subsequent events these raids might almost seem to have had a touch of unwitting genius about them, for they caused the English colonies to organize great expeditions against Canada which accomplished nothing and resulted in their suffering heavy losses in both men and materials.

* An eminent military historian has put it very succinctly: "The wasting struggles of the Thirty Years War had encouraged a tendency to favour defensive methods of warfare. During the latter half of the 17th century the principle of offensive action as accepted today received little recognition; to be considered a successful commander it was less important to win victories than to guard against defeat." See Lieut-Col. G. W. C. Nicholson, *Marlborough and the War of the Spanish Succession*, Directorate of Military Training, Army Headquarters, Queen's Printer, Ottawa, 1955.

CHAPTER FIFTEEN

THE LITTLE WAR

ONCE the first jubilation at the ignominious withdrawal of the Boston fleet had subsided, the people of New France came face to face with the fact that their troubles were by no means over. The Iroquois were still as terrible a menace as ever, the colony's supplies of food and ammunition were almost exhausted, and the Massachusetts men had threatened to return the following year with a larger force. Only three out of eleven supply ships had reached Quebec before freeze-up;[1] the previous spring the king's storehouse at Montreal had burned down, destroying all that had remained of the year's supplies for the troops,[2] and the Iroquois and heavy rains had combined to ruin what should have been a good crop. The price of wheat rose to 12 to 15 *livres* a bushel and that of other foodstuffs proportionally even higher. When the snow left the ground in the spring the people grubbed for roots and gleanings; this and fish was all that stood between them and starvation.[3] As for such an essential as wine, there was none to be had. Frontenac wryly stated in November that he himself would be reduced to drinking water within a week.[4] All that the people could do was tighten their belts and wait for the ships to bring supplies from France.

Meanwhile, the colony's long-neglected defences had to be attended to: strong fortifications were needed at Quebec to guard against the threatened return of the New England fleet, Montreal and Trois Rivières required stronger defence works to guard against a possible combined assault by the Iroquois and the English colonists, and the exposed seigneuries at the head of the colony needed more forts where the people could take refuge. This meant that, for the time being at least, military operations had to be confined to continual watchfulness and the sending of small parties to counter Iroquois raids—in other words, *la petite guerre*.

Although the fortifications of Quebec had not been put to the test by Phips's forces, it was obvious that they were pitifully inadequate. The intendant's main aim was to build a strong stone wall with redoubts to protect the town on the landward side, platforms for batteries of cannon to command the river and the cove where Phips's ships had attempted to effect a landing, and a strong point on Cape Diamond, since this height dominated the whole of Upper Town.[5] Two things hindered him in this work: lack of funds, and Frontenac's determination to use a large part of what funds were available to restore his residence, the Château St. Louis, which had been reported crumbling into ruins for the past sixteen years. Frontenac was most insistent that the walls of this old fort should be made impregnable before anything else was done, regarding the work as imperative because, as he put it, "it was a shelter where I, and what this colony has by way of important people, would be secure."[6] Champigny's biting comments on the relative merits of fortifications to protect the town and a private bombardment-proof shelter for the governor and a few others did little to endear him to Frontenac. However, the work progressed; when reports reached the colony of a threatened English attack there would be a great acceleration of activity, but it was not until 1697, at the very end of the war, that Quebec was finally declared impregnable against any force the English colonies could conceivably throw against it.[7]

At Montreal and Trois Rivières the encircling palisades were repaired, but they were sufficient only to stop arrows and musket balls, little more being considered necessary.[8] It was the defence of the outlying seigneuries that posed the most urgent and difficult problem. The *habitants* had to get their land seeded and the crops harvested. Denonville and Champigny had made a strong effort to get them to live in villages rather than scattered about, each family in an isolated house, but they had met with stubborn resistance from the very people whose lives they were trying to save. Frontenac encountered the same difficulty, but largely as a result of pressure from the Five Nations the opposition of the Canadians was overcome.[9] Yet so long as the *habitants* had to work in the fields, they were a prey for marauding Iroquois.

The year following Phips's attack was one of the worst in the history of the colony. Owing to the shortage of supplies, no war parties were sent out during the winter, and no sooner had the ice gone out of the river than some nine hundred to a thousand Iroquois descended on the island of Montreal in two bands. Twenty-five to thirty farms were burned and several *habitants* killed at Pointe-aux-Trembles before the two parties linked up at Senneville at the western tip of the island. Afterwards they split up into bands of a hundred or so to ravage the island and the area from Repentigny to the Richelieu River. One of these bands surprised a group of Mission Indians in their fields on the very doorstep of Montreal, taking thirty-five women and children prisoners. To make matters worse the troops and militia could not take the field in force against the raiders because of the lack of food and ammunition. The shortage of the latter was so bad that Champigny was reduced to melting down the lead eavestroughs and window-mouldings on the houses for bullets.[10]

The Sieur de Vaudreuil, upon hearing of these attacks, rushed up from Quebec and organized a party of one hundred and twenty volunteers, officers, soldiers and *habitants*. He sent them from door to door in Montreal to beg a bit of bread, a piece of salt pork, anything that the people could spare. With these meagre supplies they paddled down river to the Repentigny shore and at night came upon some fifty unsuspecting Oneidas asleep in and about an abandoned farm-house. The first volley killed those sleeping outside. Three of those in the house dashed out. One was killed instantly, the two others got away, leaving trails of blood. The rest remained in the house to fight to the end. Some of the Canadians were too eager to get at them. They crept up to the very walls of the house; when an Iroquois appeared at a window to fire they tried to grab him and drag him out. Four or five of their number lost their lives in this fashion. Somewhat belatedly, Vaudreuil ordered the house set on fire; the Iroquois within then began their death chant. One of them called to the French to know who was killing them. To be sent into the next world by a foe with no reputation as a fighter would have been a galling thought for their last hour of life. Le Moyne de Bienville crept up to a window, fired his pistol at the defenders within, and called out the name given him in earlier days by the Iroquois. It was the last word he ever spoke. A musket ball dropped him dead on the spot.

Some of the enemy, perhaps badly wounded, remained in the house and were consumed in the flames. The remainder broke out in small groups and attempted to hack their way through the encircling French. One did break through and get away, five were taken alive, the rest were felled. Of the five prisoners, one, a boy of fourteen, had his life spared because his family had earlier saved Father Millet from the torture stake; one was given to the Ottawas to deal with in their fashion; the three others were distributed to the *habitants* at Pointe-aux-Trembles, at Boucherville and at Repentigny. They were all three burned to death. The *habitants* had suffered too much at the hands of this foe to accord them an easier end, and to have done so would have been construed as weakness by the Iroquois. Any satisfaction the Canadians might have derived from this *coup* was, however, obliterated by the loss of another of the le Moyne brothers. The news that the Sieur de Bienville was dead put the whole colony into mourning and the Iroquois, when they later learned that he had fallen, sent a delegation to Montreal under a flag of truce to express their condolences to the le Moyne family. This was the true measure of Bienville's stature. In the engagement the French had lost no more than eight of their own men, but before the rest of the Iroquois army finally retired, over a hundred men, women and children had been killed or captured.[11]

While the people in the settlements between Trois Rivières and Montreal saw their houses go up in flames and hardly dared go beyond musket range of the forts, below Trois Rivières the Iroquois menace was not great and at Quebec it concerned the people but little. There, in mid-July, the people were celebrating the arrival of the ships from France bringing the anxiously awaited supplies and the news that the armies of Louis XIV had won a great victory at Mons. A *Te Deum* was sung, salutes were fired from the ships in the river, a fireworks display was let off, and on Frontenac's orders all the houses in the town were illuminated. Frontenac himself held a reception and banquet at the Château St. Louis for the leading residents and their ladies. This gay affair was also attended by sixteen Ottawas, just down from Michilimackinac to complain of the high price of trade goods. They had never been to Quebec before and were amazed by all they saw: the large ships with their rows of cannon and sailors darting up and down the rigging, the wide-hooped gowns of the ladies at the reception, and particularly the coloured ices served at the banquet. When they left they were loaded with presents and were immeasurably impressed by all the evidence they had seen of French greatness.[12] The high price of trade goods perhaps faded from their minds in the light of all this.

The festivities and excitement at Quebec were barely over when word came from Montreal that an army was being mustered at

Albany for an attack on the colony. Frontenac immediately gathered up what men he could and advanced to Trois Rivières, where he remained, waiting for the enemy's intentions to become clear.[13] Callières, meanwhile, had mustered six hundred troops and militia, along with a detachment of allied Indians, at Prairie-de-la-Magdelaine, across the river from Montreal. A hundred and sixty men under the command of a French veteran officer, the Sieur de Vallerenne, were sent to guard the road leading to Chambly in case the enemy should attempt to capture the fort there or attack the adjacent settlements. For three days the army lay waiting for word of the enemy, scouting parties being sent out continually. The militia and some of the allied Indians were encamped near the river's edge to the left of a fort that Callières had made his headquarters and where he had been forced to take to his bed with an attack of gout. The regulars were on the right of the fort. The night of August 10–11 was very dark and wet, causing many of the militia, including their sentinels, to take shelter at the fort. An hour before daybreak a sentry at a nearby mill saw figures moving along the river-bank and gave the alarm. The enemy, consisting of 146 Mohawks and Mohicans and 266 Albany militia led by Major Peter Schuyler, were by this time on top of the Canadians. They rushed in and routed them, killing several. The regulars came up in good order, but in the bad light they did not realize that the horde in the militia camp were the enemy rather than their own men and failed to charge. As a result they received a heavy fusillade before realizing their mistake. The losses in the French ranks were heavy. Five officers fell, some of them veterans of several campaigns in Europe. But the survivors quickly recovered and charged in, putting the enemy to flight.

Schuyler's retiring forces had not bargained on encountering such strong French forces, and were congratulating themselves on having inflicted heavy losses at so little cost to themselves when they suddenly found their route blocked by Vallerenne's detachment. Vallerenne had barely time to arrange his men in three ranks behind two large tree trunks fallen across the roadway when the enemy, seeing that they had the advantage in numbers of over two to one, with a hideous clamour charged down on them. Vallerenne waited until the enemy were within pistol range before giving the order to fire. Some thirty fell at the first volley, and the Mohicans promptly drew back out of the fray. But the Albany militia and the Mohawks came in again. At the third charge the Canadians, all young lads who had never been in action before, turned tail. Their commander, the Sieur le Ber du Chesne, quickly rallied them. Thoroughly ashamed of themselves, they returned to the attack. By this time the fighting had become a general mêlée, men struggling hand to hand with sword, knife, hatchet or clubbed musket. For an hour and a half the grim, bloody struggle went on. Then Schuyler's men began to give ground and finally turned and fled, abandoning their equipment. Vallerenne's forces were too exhausted to pursue them; they had barely enough strength to tend to their wounded.[14] All the French accounts agree that it was Vallerenne who had saved the day for the French: "He was everywhere, his calm confidence and the coolness with which he gave his orders put heart into everyone," wrote Frontenac.[15]

The French and the English accounts of the casualties suffered are, as usual, widely at variance. Schuyler stated that their own losses were thirty-seven killed and thirty-one wounded all told.[16] The Sieur Benac claimed that the enemy had lost nearly 130 killed. His estimate of forty-five killed and sixty wounded for the French forces is probably closer to the truth.[17] Schuyler claimed that his men had killed some two hundred of the French.[18] Frontenac's claims are the most extravagant of all. In a dispatch to the king he claimed that the enemy had lost three hundred men, five or six of their principal chiefs, and a battle flag.[19] He was rather more modest in writing to the minister, claiming only something over 120 killed and left on the field.[20] In any event, the Albany men had been mauled badly enough and they did not venture near New France again until peace was declared, much to the disgust of their Iroquois allies.

The following October, 1691, Frontenac began organizing a force of five to six hundred troops, militia and Indian allies to strike back at the Mohawks; but it had been left until too late in the season and finally had to be abandoned.[21] In his dispatches to the minister Frontenac claimed that although the Iroquois had roamed about Montreal and vicinity for two months, they had been repulsed in every skirmish. He took full credit to himself for their failure to hinder the harvesting, stating that this had been "the thing to which I thought I should devote myself completely."[22] He failed to mention that the Iroquois had retired from the colony before harvest time and had had made no effort to hinder it.[23] Throughout, he minimized the grievous losses the colony had suffered and made it appear that a great deal had been accomplished by his own untiring efforts.

Others in the colony, however, did not see the situation in such a comforting light. Food had been so scarce all summer that Champigny had had to dole out rations of flour and pork that he had hoarded for emergencies not only to the troops, but to the *habitants* as well.[24] When he made a tour of the upper colony he was appalled by the conditions he found there. He wrote:

> I found the people living above Trois Rivières in a state of great misery and the whole countryside ruined by the enemy, with the exception of the area around Boucherville and the forts, to which all the families have been forced to retire, which prevents them working on their distant fields or raising cattle except in very small numbers because of the limited space available in the forts. They dare not venture out because of the enemy who appears from time to time. What is even more grievous is the number of *habitants* crippled in the war and the poor widows who, having lost their husbands in the fighting, have trouble in obtaining bread for their children.[25]

Nor was Champigny at all satisfied with Frontenac's direction of military affairs. He was very critical of the governor's having sent, at a time of acute shortage, a party of 128 men up country with presents for the Ottawas and another forty men with six officers to Acadia with a boat-load of supplies from the king's stores for the Indians there. These voyages kept the men involved out of the colony for at least a year and Champigny maintained that with the colony besieged by the Iroquois, neither men nor supplies could be spared for such ventures. The expedition to Acadia particularly annoyed him; he strongly suspected that it was merely a means to enrich members of Frontenac's following, since the leader of the party, the Sieur de Beaubassin, a captain in Frontenac's corps of guards, had a trading post in Acadia. He gave it as his opinion that they could hope for no peace with the Iroquois until they had carried the war to them; and for this, he stated, they would have to receive large reinforcements from France, as they had lost over five hundred men, regulars and militia, during the past two years.[26]

But the colony had made one great gain in that cruel year of

1691. The Canadians had become hardened guerilla fighters, as skilled at this savage warfare as the Iroquois themselves. Those who were not apt pupils in this harsh school had a short life expectancy. The results of this training made themselves apparent the following year. In April an Iroquois war party of 140 men, 40 women and 20 children encamped on the Ottawa to ambush the fur brigade coming down from Michilimackinac. By mid-July they had become tired of waiting and descended on the settlements at La Chesnaye, capturing three Indian boys and fourteen *habitants*. Vaudreuil immediately set off in pursuit with 200 Canadians and 120 Mission Iroquois. They caught up with the enemy as they were recrossing the Ottawa, killing ten men, capturing five more and thirteen of the women. They also managed to rescue six of the Canadian prisoners and the three Indian boys.[27]

Throughout the summer of 1692, Montreal and district were kept in a state of semi-siege, but the crops were got in and the Canadians gave as good as they received. Moreover, the war was now being carried to the enemy. Small war parties were sent out from Montreal to strike at the New York border settlements and to ambush any stray Iroquois they encountered.[28] This type of warfare was well described by Governor Fletcher of New York:

> The French Indians . . . have destroi'd some careless people nigh our garrisons. . . . They are wolves, lay so close, no man can discover them, a hare sitting is much easier found in England; the parties I send daily out, they lett pass—lurking close—but if a naked [unarmed] man, woman or child pass they kill them or take them. Our Indians act the same part and with greater success on the French plantations.[29]

The Ottawas and Hurons were also active, taking forty-two scalps. All told, 102 Iroquois were killed during the course of the year and forty-four prisoners were taken, thirty men, the rest women and children. In addition, five blond scalps were taken by the Mission Iroquois in the English settlements.*[30]

* Until 1694 the French were paying bounties of 60 *livres* for male prisoners, 30 *livres* for females, and 30 *livres* for scalps. In 1693 the minister, considering these sums exorbitant, ordered the bounties reduced to 6, 3 and 3 *livres* respectively. Frontenac and Champigny protested this parsimony, claiming that if 30,000 *livres* were spent for a thousand enemy scalps the war would quickly be

Many people in the colony now urged that the time had come to take the offensive, invade the Iroquois cantons in force and destroy their villages, but Frontenac at first refused to consider these proposals, arguing that it would strip the colony of its defenders and leave it exposed to attack by the English and Iroquois.[31] Then, early in the winter, he decided to send a strong force to attack the Mohawk villages and ravage the Albany area. The Iroquois themselves made war only when the leaves were on the trees; thus it was hoped to take them unawares. On January 25, 1693, the expedition, consisting of 625 men—one hundred Troupes de la Marine, two hundred allied Indians and the rest Canadian militia—left Montreal with orders to give no quarter to the Mohawk men and to bring back alive the women and children. Dragging their supplies on toboggans, they reached the two smaller of the Mohawk villages undetected on February 16. There was only a handful of men in each village, as the others were away hunting; they offered no resistance and were taken prisoner along with the women and children. The villages were burned and the small army then marched on the third and larger village. It too was taken by surprise, the attackers losing only one man killed and one of the Indian allies wounded. The Mohawks lost twenty or thirty men and several women, but many of these casualties occurred not during the attack, but later when the allied Indians found a supply of rum and went berserk. This village too, with its winter food stores and other supplies, was set ablaze, but it was the best part of two days before the allied Indians had shaken off the effects of their drunken orgy. The following day was spent in debating whether or not to go on to attack the Albany settlements. It was finally decided to return directly to Montreal because they were now encumbered with three hundred prisoners, two hundred of them women and children. The Mission Iroquois flatly refused to kill the Mohawk men in cold blood since they themselves were mostly of Mohawk origin and in some instances closely related to the prisoners. Moreover, three prisoners had escaped during the first assault and it was feared they would have reached Albany to give warning. In this supposition they were quite correct. Men were already being

over, but the minister remained adamant and in November, 1694, the bounties were reduced. In the English colonies, New York paid £6 for every Frenchman or French Indian killed within three miles of the frontier, and Massachusetts paid £12 for every enemy killed or taken prisoner.

mustered at Schenectady and Albany, and four days later 250 Dutch and English militia and 290 Mohawk warriors set off in pursuit of the French.

On the third day of the retreat an advance party of the Albany force caught up with the French and asked them to wait for the main party to arrive, as peace had been proclaimed in Europe. The French officers would have none of this, deeming it to be a ruse. Their allies, however, insisted on waiting, stating that if peace had been proclaimed all well and good, but if not, since they had come to fight in the first instance, they should wait for the English and give battle. This view finally prevailed. Trees were felled to form a rough defence work and there the men remained until the English and Mohawks reached them two days later. This force immediately built a barricade of trees within musket range and made it clear that a discussion of peace was the last thing they had in mind. The French and their allies launched three attacks and were beaten back each time. Some twenty-seven of their men were killed and seventeen wounded.

The French then broke off the engagement and the next morning withdrew, carrying their wounded on improvised stretchers. Schuyler ordered his men to follow the French but they refused, owing to lack of provisions. The French were themselves running dangerously short of food by this time. When provisions were brought up to the English force from Schenectady eighty men set off and caught up with the French once more, but the Mohawks refused to allow an attack to be made because the French threatened to kill their women and children if they did. This gave the French immunity from one foe, but they still had to contend with another adversary just as relentless as the Iroquois—hunger. A thaw had set in, rain had fallen, and when they reached the shores of Lake Champlain they found the ice submerged waist deep in places with slush and water. Most of the allied Indians skirted the shore in order to hunt, and all but fifty-eight of the prisoners were left behind, some of the women being too encumbered by their children to attempt to cross. When the French reached the far shore they found the food they had cached for the return journey almost entirely spoiled by the rain. This placed them in a desperate situation; they were over a hundred miles from the nearest French settlement, with no food and the wounded to transport through the wet, clinging snow which made the mere lifting of a snowshoed foot hard work. Four Indians and a Canadian were dispatched to bring aid and in five days they reached Montreal. Callières immediately sent 150 men with supplies on their backs to succour the stranded army. By this time the men were reduced to boiling their moccasins for broth. Two or three of them died of starvation and exposure and several others were *in extremis*. Those still able to walk struggled on; the wounded were left behind with two of the officers and 120 of the men who were too weak to move. Nineteen days after the fight with the Albany militia and the Mohawks the first survivors staggered into Montreal. Many of them had thrown away their muskets, blankets and parkas to lighten their load. Monseignat, Frontenac's secretary, wrote: "Everyone reached Montreal so exhausted by the fatigue of the march and by hunger that only those who saw them could understand what they had been through." What had seemed at first to be a decisive blow against the Iroquois had come dangerously close to being a disaster for New France.[32]

Frontenac could not be held to blame in any way for the disappointing outcome of this campaign. The fortunes of war had turned against the French in the guise of mild weather. In conception the raid had been very sound; there had been grave risks involved, but they had been calculated ones, and Frontenac had been quite justified in taking them. Moreover, despite its near-tragic ending, the expedition had accomplished a good deal. The Mohawks had been dealt a hard blow, having been reduced to destitution, dependent on the grudging charity of their English allies and the other Iroquois nations. The prestige of the French among the up-country tribes was raised considerably;[33] the Mohawk and English losses probably exceeded those of the French,* and in both northern New York and the Iroquois cantons fear and consternation had been spread. But it had been such a near thing that the French did not attempt any more winter campaigns, which was unfortunate, as it was at this time of year that the Iroquois were most vulnerable.

Even before this raid the Iroquois had begun to feel the effects of the war and were becoming very disgruntled at the failure of the English to take an active part in the fighting. In June, 1692, the

---

* Frontenac's account of this raid bears but slight resemblance to those of the other narrators and was obviously designed to heighten his own prestige at Versailles. He refers to the expedition as "*fort extraordinaire et très glorieuse*," claiming that four hundred prisoners had been taken, but omitting to mention that all but a few had escaped or been released.

chief sachem of the Mohawks spoke very plainly to Richard Ingoldsby in a conference at Albany. After complaining that his men lacked guns and ammunition, he demanded to know why only Virginia had offered aid in the war; why were not Maryland, Delaware and New England also engaged? Were they not all subjects of the same king, he asked, or had he sold them, or had they rebelled, or had the king ordered that only New York should engage in the fighting? How could they be subjects of the same king and queen and not engage in the same war? How came it that the king was at war but refused to destroy the enemy? And this could easily be done, he added, if the king's subjects would unite. The Iroquois would be glad to show them how.[34]

The following February when Governor Fletcher urged the Iroquois to attack New France, their answer was that they expected him to fulfil the many promises and engagements made to the Iroquois that Canada would be attacked by a great fleet going by sea "that the enemy being assaulted both ways may be overcome." They stated that they pressed this the harder because a great part of their strength was broken and it was impossible to take Canada by land alone. Once again they complained of their lack of arms. "Some of our men," a sachem stated, "have guns and no powder and ball; and some but bowes and arrowes, which Major Schuyler can testifye who see us when we came up to him : whereas the Govr of Canada supplyes his Indians with all sorts of armes and ammunicon, which we found when we engaged them." It was hard for them to invade Canada, they declared, because they feared the French would induce the Ottawas and Hurons to attack their villages while they were away.[35]

It must have been virtually impossible for Governor Fletcher to provide the Iroquois with a satisfactory explanation for the lack of support from the English. He was himself complaining to the Privy Council of these selfsame things. In February, 1693, he wrote to Blathwayt, the secretary : "It is utterly impossible for this poor decayed Province to defend themselves without help from our neighbours. Our Fur Trade is quite lost, our charge very great, the neighbouring Collonies acknowledge no Government from the Crown, but harbour all our deserters, rob us of all Trade, by employing no duties, the Act for Navigation not observed or valued."[36] In March of the preceding year the governor and Council of New York had ordered all the residents of Albany capable of bearing arms who had quit the district to return within a fortnight and had forbidden anyone to leave the area in future without permission,[37] but this had been to no avail—the people continued to leave for less exposed parts.[38] The following October the Privy Council had ordered that the colonies of New England, Virginia, Maryland and Pennsylvania had to send aid and assistance to Albany when called upon to do so to protect the frontier.[39] The answer of Governor Phips of Massachusetts was to seize Martha's Vineyard, which Fletcher claimed for New York, and to threaten war if New York attempted to take it by force.[40] As to the attitude of the other colonies, "the Republick of Connecticutt" quarrelled at the superscription of the New York Council's letter "for want of their proper Title."[41] Pennsylvania stated they could send nothing but their good wishes;[42] East Jersey sent £248;[43] Virginia sent £600 New York money; Maryland sent £300 sterling. These two last contributions were sent in the form of bills of exchange, which the merchants on whom they were drawn refused to honour.[44] Governor Fletcher was so disgusted by all this that he was tempted to turn the Iroquois loose to ravage Virginia and Maryland as they had done on another occasion.[45]

Under these conditions, with the English unwilling or unable to give them support and the French sending small parties to harass them, the Iroquois changed their tactics and began using subtler weapons than muskets and scalping knives. In mid-June Governor Fletcher wrote "that if our Canton Indians, who seem to stagger and are enclined to make peace with the French of Canada, through want of those usual supplys and presents which this poor Province cannot longer support itself under, and they should be induced to make up a separate peace, the ruin of the whole country would unavoidably ensue."[46] Had he but known it, a chief of the Oneidas was at that time in Quebec, sounding out Frontenac on the prospects for peace.[47]

For the following two months there was much coming and going of Iroquois ambassadors. Governor Fletcher soon learned of this and in July he met the chiefs of the Five Nations at Albany. This time the Iroquois were more impressed with what he had to say, for he accompanied his address with liberal presents: 86 muskets, 800 pounds of powder, 800 bars of lead, hatchets, knives, clothing, tobacco, 60 gallons of rum, bread, beer, salt and two bulls, as well as other presents for the sachems.[48] The following day, in his reply, the Iroquois spokesman admitted that they had been negotiating for peace, but he assured Fletcher that an end would be put to it, the Five Nations now being determined to press the war to a finish.[49] The Iroquois' peace talks had achieved one aim; the English allies had been frightened into providing some material aid.

In August the Oneida ambassador arrived once more at Quebec and coolly informed Frontenac that the French war parties had prevented the chiefs of each nation coming to discuss the peace terms as the governor had demanded. But, he said, if Frontenac would send two French officers with authority to negotiate a settlement not only with the Five Nations but with the English as well, then the Iroquois would be glad to give them safe conduct to Albany, where negotiations could be undertaken for a general peace between the French, the Iroquois and the English. Frontenac was enraged by this calculated insolence and the peace talks were abruptly ended.[50]

Callières claimed that the whole purpose of the peace proposals had been to frustrate any plans the French might have had of invading the Iroquois cantons in force that autumn. There had been talk of a campaign against the Onondagas, and considering the amazing way that news travelled between New France and the Iroquois country, they may well have heard of it; * but it is by no means certain that anything more than talk would have transpired had the Iroquois not waged their "peace offensive." In any event, Callières expressed the hope that Frontenac would not allow these peace proposals to deter him from a full-scale assault against the Onondagas the following year.[51]

Frontenac stated that only the lack of sufficient troops had prevented him waging the war more vigorously and in August, immediately after receiving the arrogant Iroquois offer of a peace conference at Albany, he asserted that the Onondagas were the main obstacles to a peace settlement. He declared that it was "absolutely necessary to go and attack them in their villages." [52] A few weeks later he received 426 recruits from France for the Troupes de la Marine, bringing their total number to something

---

* To prevent the Iroquois learning of their plans, when the French sent out war parties the members were not told of their objective; the officer in command received sealed orders which were opened only after the party was eight to ten miles out from Montreal. It had been learned from bitter experience that loose talk in Montreal cost lives.

over fifteen hundred officers and men. These, with the militia, brought the total forces in the colony to something over three thousand men.[53] At the same time Frontenac received word from the minister that he had no cause to fear a sea-borne attack from New England. Men and ships had been massed at Boston, and it had been feared that an expedition was intended for Quebec, but instead it had been sent to join an English assault on Martinique, where it had suffered heavy losses.[54] He now informed his friend de Lagny at the Ministry of Marine that he needed at least another five hundred men before he could undertake any large-scale campaigns, and he requested that his wife and all his friends should use their influence with the minister to this end, as they had done with success the preceding year. He assured de Lagny that if the minister were to send him these troops, circumstances permitting, he would invade the Iroquois cantons in force and most assuredly reduce them to accepting his terms.[55] And to the minister he declared that the only way to deal with the Iroquois was with force, for "there is no other way than to go into the heart of their country, arms in hand, and subdue them." He gave assurances that the necessary preparations would be made for this campaign during the winter months and expressed his confidence that it would result in a decisive victory—provided that he received more troops.[56]

Champigny, like Callières, was also convinced that they would have to strike hard at the Iroquois the following year to prevent the French alliance with the Ottawas and Hurons from disintegrating. These tribes had once again entered into peace negotiations with the Iroquois.[57] In Acadia the situation was as bad; reports had reached Quebec that the Indians there had entered into negotiations with the Massachusetts authorities.[58] This last was confirmed by Iberville, who sent a dispatch to the minister post-haste from the Belle Isle roadstead to report that one Acadian tribe had gone over to the English and another was about to follow suit.[59] The underlying cause of this defection of the Acadian tribes was indicated in a memoir from Louis XIV stating: "The person who was responsible, in the area of Beaubassin and Minas, for the distribution of the presents used the powder that was sent there for his private trade and profit."[60] This could refer only to the expedition of the Sieur de Beaubassin, the captain of Frontenac's guards, sent by Frontenac to Acadia in 1691, the expedition which at the time had aroused Champigny's suspicions.

During the winter Champigny had one hundred and fifty flat-boats built, ready for the campaign he ardently hoped Frontenac would undertake the following summer.[61] When word of this activity reached the Iroquois cantons they promptly sent two Onondaga chiefs to reopen the peace negotiations. They informed Frontenac that if he would receive their proposals, two chiefs from each nation, led by the great Onondaga chief, Tegannissorens, would come to Quebec to arrange a general peace settlement.[62] From then until the late autumn Iroquois ambassadors kept arriving at Quebec to arrange the details. As a result, no campaign was launched against them that year, a virtual cessation of hostilities being agreed to by Frontenac while the negotiations were in progress.[63] Both Callières and Champigny were convinced that the Iroquois were deceiving Frontenac,[64] and he was equally convinced that they were acting in good faith.[65]

At the same time, however, that one group of Iroquois ambassadors was negotiating for peace with Frontenac, the Five Nations were quietly sending other ambassadors to the Hurons and Ottawas to make a separate peace with these tribes. Callières declared that their whole aim was to keep the French inactive "in order to enable themselves to recommence the war against us more vigorously and garner a good stock of furs, while at the same time attempting to draw to themselves the trade of our Indians by making peace with them without our participation."[66] He was convinced of this because they had sent deputies to Michilimackinac during the winter to inform the Ottawas and Hurons that they had already made peace with the French. This was cunningly calculated to make these tribes distrust the French for arranging a peace without their having had any part in it—this being something that Frontenac, in 1690, had assured them he would never do—and so induce them to negotiate a separate peace themselves with the Iroquois. These deputies had arrived just as an Ottawa war party, eight hundred strong, was about to leave for the Iroquois country. This expedition was immediately abandoned. The Iroquois had thus obtained, at least temporarily, security from attacks from that quarter. Louvigny, the commander at Michilimackinac, did his best to dissuade the Ottawas from continuing their negotiations and he finally persuaded several of their chiefs to go down to Montreal to reassure themselves that Frontenac was not negotiating a peace that did not include them.[67] A few days after the Ottawa chiefs reached

Montreal a group of Iroquois deputies also arrived, bringing with them thirteen French prisoners to be exchanged as part of the peace settlement.[68] No clearer proof than this could have been afforded the Ottawas of Frontenac's apparent duplicity.

In his lengthy account of the events of the year Frontenac claimed that he had removed all suspicion from the minds of the allies and convinced them that he would never accept any peace in which they were not included. He then went on at great length about how devoted the allies had shown themselves to be and how impressed all the French officers had been with the way in which he had handled these delicate matters. It appears that he was convinced he fully deserved all the praise he heaped upon himself. There was no doubt in his mind that the Iroquois sincerely desired peace and would agree to his terms. He was full of scorn for "all these would-be fine statesmen" who remained unconvinced of his claims. He informed the minister that the only thing holding up a general peace settlement was the difficulty the Iroquois chiefs were having with "certain ill-advised souls who, won over by the presents of the English, stood in the way of their nation's good intentions." And this last remaining impediment would be overcome very shortly; of this he was sure.[69]

Champigny and Callières were still far from sharing Frontenac's views. The governor of Montreal gave it as his opinion that they would have to invade the Onondaga canton in force before the Iroquois would accept the French terms. At the same time he very shrewdly pointed out that they must not crush the Iroquois completely but should leave them too weak to threaten New France, yet strong enough "so that the fear that our Ottawas might have of them will always serve as a barrier to prevent their going to the English to obtain their cheaper merchandise."[70]

The previous year, in the king's memoir, the minister had manifested considerable impatience with Frontenac's failure to accomplish anything tangible in the war, and the governor had been informed that the king expected to hear in the very near future that an end had been put to the devastation of the colony by the Iroquois and these tribes had been forced to come to terms.[71] In the light of the 1694 dispatches from Canada, Pontchartrain and Louis XIV became convinced that Frontenac had allowed himself to be duped by the Iroquois. Moreover, Vaudreuil had returned to France in 1694 to attend to family affairs; he undoubtedly gave the minister the benefit of his views on Frontenac's direction of the war. The minister and the king now ordered Frontenac to press the war against the Iroquois with some show of vigour. He was told bluntly that he had to justify the large military appropriations given him year after year * by launching a full-scale assault on the Iroquois and not merely remaining on the defensive. The Indian allies, the troops, the *habitants*—all had to be employed to bring the war to a quick and successful conclusion.[72]

The minister did not know it, but Canada by this time no longer had any allies worth mentioning. The western tribes had been singularly unimpressed by Frontenac's assurances that he had no intention of making peace without their participation. They were also very disgruntled because the French *coureurs de bois*, whom Frontenac kept sending up country in large numbers, had begun voyaging far afield and obtaining furs at first hand from the Assiniboines. Previously, the Ottawas had acted as middlemen to these tribes, and they resented the loss of this valuable trade.[73] The basis of their alliance with the French was being undermined. And the Iroquois, their northern flank secure, now abandoned all pretence of desiring peace with the French. The protracted negotiations with Frontenac had served their purpose. Early in 1695 they began attacking the colony with renewed vigour.[74] Yet in spite of this, in spite of the orders received from the Court and the constant urging of the intendant, Frontenac still refused to launch a full-scale attack. He maintained that he did not have enough troops, that he was afraid of a major attack on the colony while the bulk of the forces were away, that Denonville's campaign had shown the futility of such enterprises, and that, since an all-out assault on the Iroquois villages might be defeated or only half-succeed, it was best not to undertake it, but instead to continue the *petite guerre*.[75]

One reason why Frontenac was not anxious to invade the Iroquois country at that time was that he had set his heart on first re-establishing his old fort at Cataracoui. In 1689, when Denonville had ordered Vallerenne, the officer commanding the garrison, to

---

* In 1692 the colony's annual military budget was 75,000 *livres*; by 1694 it had increased to 200,000 *livres*, and the minister complained that over the preceding few years the excess of expenditures over allotted funds totalled 550,000 *livres*. From 1685 to 1697 the Crown received 500,000 *livres* a year from the Company of the Farm for the monopoly on beaver and moose hides; in the latter year the lease was sold for 350,000 *livres*. Thus, despite the heavy war expenditures, the Crown still derived some profit from the colony.

blow up the fort, he had given him detailed instructions to lay heavy powder charges with long fuses under the walls, then to get his men embarked, light the fuses and get away from the vicinity as fast as possible, because when the charges exploded every Iroquois for miles around would rush over to investigate.[76] This had been done, but unknown to Vallerenne only one of the charges had gone off, damaging the palisade but little else. Subsequently, the Iroquois had made no attempt to complete the destruction but had left the buildings to the mercy of the rodents and the weather. When Frontenac reported this to the minister he received orders to have the fort razed to the ground for fear the English might occupy it. This he had silently declined to do, and in 1691 he had declared his intention to restore the fort at the first opportunity. The minister, however, had been strongly opposed to the idea and informed him that "everyone who believes he has any knowledge of the country does not regard the re-establishment of the fort as expedient, particularly at a time when, having few troops, you cannot send them out of the colony without weakening its defences. They also say that this scheme cannot be carried out without great expense, that it would serve no worthwhile purpose and that this is proven by everything that has happened during the time that the fort has been in existence. This is why I pray you on no account to undertake to go back there without having carefully weighed these factors." [77]

The minister had not wished to interfere with the governor's tactical direction of the war for obvious reasons, therefore he had stopped just short of forbidding Frontenac to carry out his plans. That loophole sufficed for Frontenac. In 1694 he organized an expedition to re-establish and garrison the post. Just as it was about to leave Montreal an order arrived from the king commanding Frontenac to provide the Sieur d'Iberville with over one hundred Canadians for an attack on Fort Nelson in Hudson Bay.[78] Although Frontenac detested Iberville on personal grounds he dared not disobey this order. The only Canadians readily available were the ones assembled for the trip to Cataracoui, and they were far more eager to follow Iberville to the Bay—or anywhere else for that matter—than to go to Lake Ontario at Frontenac's behest. This spoiled Frontenac's plan.

The following year, despite the renewal of hostilities by the Iroquois, Frontenac refused to let anything stand in his way. An expedition composed of 36 officers, 300 soldiers, 160 *habitants* and nearly 200 Indians was dispatched to re-establish the fort.[79] Champigny protested vigorously but to no avail.[80] The expedition had been gone only a day when an urgent dispatch arrived from the minister ordering Frontenac to abandon his plans to re-establish the fort for the time being and instead to attack the Iroquois. Some of the Indians forming the rearguard still had not left Montreal when this order arrived, but Frontenac refused to send them to recall the expedition. In a letter to his friend de Lagny he admitted that he had deliberately disregarded the minister's instructions.[81]

Champigny was very bitter over this. He pointed out that seven hundred men had been required for this expedition, merely to transport a year's supplies for a garrison of forty-eight. He maintained that the men and supplies used for the expedition could equally well have been employed to invade the Iroquois cantons and this at least would have proved to the western allies that the French were now in earnest when they declared that they intended to humble the Iroquois.[82] And certainly the situation in the west was little short of desperate. Seeing no sign of the French taking the offensive against the Iroquois, not only the Hurons and Ottawas but also the Renards and Mascoutins, who numbered some twelve hundred warriors and who had never been anything but friendly to the French, were now negotiating for peace with the Iroquois.[83] Another factor that was disrupting the alliance was that some of the French *coureurs de bois*, led by one named Le Sueur to whom Frontenac had given the command of a fur-trading post at Chagouamigon on the south-west side of Lake Superior, were now trading arms to the Sioux, the traditional enemies of the Algonquin nations. As a result, the French allies were being driven to seek an alliance with the Iroquois against the Sioux. They began pillaging any French canoes they encountered carrying arms to their enemies. It was now the French rather than the Iroquois who were regarded as the common enemy.[84] La Mothe Cadillac, one of Frontenac's following who had recently been appointed commander at Michilimackinac, wrote to Champigny to inform him that unless the French undertook a full-scale offensive against the Iroquois cantons, the alliance with the western tribes would be finished and the fur trade lost to the Iroquois and the English.[85]

In the face of this Champigny and others in the colony did their best to persuade Frontenac to abandon his feeble policy and adopt stronger measures before it was too late. Champigny informed the minister: "It is this that causes me to plead continually with M. de Frontenac to adopt an entirely different method of pursuing the war from that which he has followed in the past. Four days ago thirty of the enemy captured eight French and killed two others just a league away from this place [Montreal] and at the same time they attempted to capture a nearby fort. Our inaction in the midst of all this makes me fear that the consequences will be grievous. I hope that M. de Frontenac will take the proper measures and as I realize the gravity of the situation, I shall continue to urge them on him."[86]

Frontenac, in a long, verbose, self-laudatory report to his friends at the Court, did his best to make it appear that he had everything under control; but he was unable to avoid certain contradictions. On pages twenty and twenty-one of this memoir, after admitting that the Iroquois were attacking New France again and dismissing this with the comment, "We shall let the dead mourn the dead and think only of rejoicing with the living," he claimed that the allies, with the single exception of the Hurons, were continually attacking the Iroquois "and that actually there were over 900 of them at war." Then on pages eighty-five and eighty-six of this same document he states that "the alienation of all these nations from us has come about for just two reasons": low prices for the poorer grades of beaver and the Jesuits' continual interference with the brandy traffic.[87] To the minister he attempted to excuse his inaction on the grounds that the peace negotiations with the Iroquois had prevented him making large-scale attacks, which, he added, would probably have caused heavy and useless expenditures—the same excuse that he had used in very similar circumstances in 1682. For these reasons, he explained, he had contented himself with sending small parties from time to time to harass the Iroquois while they were hunting "and make them, as well as our allies, understand that all these peace talks notwithstanding, we were by no means ceasing to press the war against them."[88]

But in the face of renewed Iroquois attacks, the wholesale defection of the allies, pressure from Callières and Champigny, and specific orders from the minister, Frontenac was unable to procrastinate any longer. During the winter of 1695–96 preparations were made for a full-scale assault on the Onondagas. Orders were sent to La Mothe Cadillac at Michilimackinac instructing him to do everything possible to prevent the peace between the allies and the Iroquois being ratified. Some in the colony were afraid that to wait until midsummer to invade the Iroquois cantons would be too late. They advised a winter campaign, but Callières was opposed to the idea.[89] There was no doubt, however, that time was running dangerously short. The Hurons and Ottawas had agreed to ratify their treaty with the Five Nations, prisoners on both sides had been exchanged, and a party of Iroquois had spent the winter hunting with the Ottawas.[90]

Then the French received a stroke of unexpected good fortune. When this Iroquois hunting party left for their own country in the spring, the Ottawas were unable to resist the temptation to score an easy but treacherous victory over their erstwhile foes. They stealthily followed the Iroquois party for three or four days, then ambushed them, killing fifty-one and taking twenty-two prisoners. This put an end to the peace treaty.[91] Yet the Ottawas were still unwilling to obey Frontenac's orders to join his army at Cataracoui for the assault on the Onondagas. They pleaded that owing to a dispute with the Hurons, whom they did not trust, they dared not leave their women and children in their villages unguarded.[92] Callières declared that this was just an excuse, the real reason for their refusal being that they had no confidence whatsoever that the French really intended to undertake this campaign. They had been given the same assurances year after year, and the long-promised attack had never been forthcoming.[93]

Meanwhile, Champigny and Callières were hard at work making ready for the campaign. On July 4 the army, composed of troops, militia and Mission Indians, numbering in all approximately 2,150 men, left Montreal with Frontenac nominally in command. Twelve days later they arrived at Cataracoui without incident, and there the army remained for six days, ostensibly waiting for the Ottawas; but during those six days Frontenac put the men to work strengthening the fort, cutting a supply of firewood and timber and stocking it with enough provisions to last the garrison for at least two years. When the men began to get impatient Frontenac gave the order to cross the lake to the mouth of the Onondaga River. From this point on, the going was extremely arduous; canoes and flat-boats had to be portaged and dragged around rapids and waterfalls, and on one occasion Callières kept the men hard at it by the light of torches until ten at night. On August 1 the lake at the head of the river was reached and there two days had to be spent in constructing a stockade to protect the boats, canoes and provisions for the return journey. On the second night after their arrival at the lake, the sky in the direction of the Onondaga village was lit by a red glow. The next day, leaving 140 men to guard the boats and supplies, the army continued its march with Callières leading the vanguard mounted on a horse which he had had transported on a flat-boat—afterwards, he tersely remarked that he believed it was the first horse ever to have appeared in that part of the world. Frontenac, now in his seventy-fourth year, was carried in an armchair, surrounded by the members of his household.

After an all-day march the army arrived at the enemy village, only to find it completely deserted. The strong wooden stockade that had been built with English help and direction, and that had caused Frontenac some trepidation,[94] had been burned. The Onondagas had fled two days before the French appeared. They lost only one of their men, an ancient warrior, too old and feeble to flee, who was found near the village. Frontenac sanctioned his being put to death by the Mission Indians. Callières later commented that this man "displayed an extraordinary fortitude, not making a single cry while the red-hot irons were being applied all over his body, but telling our men and the Indians to learn from his example how to die without complaining so that they would know how to act when they were captured and received the same treatment."[95] In the afternoon an Oneida chief, accompanied by a French soldier captured by the Oneidas six years previously, appeared to request peace terms for his nation. Frontenac's answer was that the Oneidas must abandon their villages, destroy their crops and move to New France to live among the Mission Iroquois. The next day Vaudreuil with over six hundred men went to the Oneida village and destroyed both it and the crops in the fields. Meanwhile, Callières set the rest of the men to work destroying the Onondagas' standing corn and burning the supplies they found cached in and about the village. After three days of this the army began its return journey, reaching Montreal on August 20. The total French casualties were three men drowned and one man killed—the victim of a lurking Iroquois on the way down river.[96]

Despite the failure to come to grips with the enemy, the French were confident that the Iroquois power was broken. The Five Nations were not nomadic tribes; they were dependent on agriculture for much of their food. With their stocks destroyed the Onondagas and Oneidas were thrown back on the charity of the other three tribes and the English. They could not move far out of reach of their enemies as could the northern and western tribes; to the south of them were the English colonies, to the east were the Abenakis, to the north the French and Ottawas, and to the west the Illinois, Miamis and other Algonquin tribes. As the Mohawks had stated at the beginning of the war, "we intend to stay here and to live here and die here, for where can we run?" [97] When the Iroquois appealed to Albany for aid their appeals met with little response. The New York frontier was suffering from continued raids by the French Indians and Governor Fletcher still could get no help from the neighbouring colonies. [98] In August the Council at Albany stated that since the French had retired from Onondaga and the Iroquois had burned their own villages, there was nothing to be done. [99] At a meeting a few weeks later Governor Fletcher gave the Five Nations £300 in clothes, kettles and arms, but of food there was none to spare.* [100] A Mohawk sachem requested Fletcher to write to the king and have him send his great ships to attack Canada, in conjunction with all the English colonies. If the king could not do this then the Mohawks asked that they be informed, so that they could make peace with the French. [101]

Throughout the war the Iroquois had received little but broken promises from the English; the time was now past when they could be satisfied with anything less than substantial aid, and when this was not forthcoming they had no alternative but to make peace on the best terms they could get. After Denonville's campaign against the Senecas in 1687 the Iroquois had been able to reply two years later with a large-scale assault on Canada. But then the Five Nations had been at the peak of their strength and they had received considerable aid from Albany which, to some extent, had nullified the effects of Denonville's attack. By 1696 their strength was only a shadow of what it had been in 1687; nine years of war had taken a terrible toll among their ranks. The high hopes they had had of seducing the Ottawas and Hurons had vanished, and while their own losses could not be replaced, they saw no diminution in the ranks of their main antagonist, who received replacements from France. In 1696, 123 more recruits for the

---

* According to reports reaching Quebec, wheat was so scarce in New York that the price at Albany had reached 25 *livres* the bushel.

Troupes de la Marine arrived in New France; the following year another 87 were sent, though 21 of them died at sea. In all, 615 reinforcements reached the colony from 1693 to the end of hostilities.[102] In 1688 the white population of New France had been 10,523; in 1695, despite heavy losses from disease and war, the population had increased to 12,786.[103] In 1689, the men able to bear arms among the Iroquois and Mohicans were estimated at 2,800; by 1698 their numbers were estimated to have declined to 1,320.[104]

In 1697 an Oneida embassy arrived at Montreal to ask if peace ambassadors from the Onondagas, Cayugas, Oneidas and Senecas would be well received. Frontenac, at last grown wary of Iroquois overtures, regarded this embassy with great suspicion, and he informed the minister: "I do not believe that I am mistaken when I tell you that little confidence can be entertained in all their proposals."[105] Meanwhile, neither the French nor the Iroquois pressed the war with any vigour; in August, 1697, Champigny reported, "only a few small war parties have been sent out by the one side and the other which have killed a few people and taken the odd prisoner on either side."[106] But the French allies, their doubts resolved by the Onondaga campaign, now began harrying the Five Nations mercilessly, over 125 being killed by the Ottawas alone within the year.[107] When the Iroquois struck back at the Ottawas, Frontenac regarded this as evidence that they were insincere in their desire for peace. He gave orders to the commander at Cataracoui to entice into the fort any Iroquois chiefs who came near and then to seize them so that they could be used as hostages.*[108] And so the peace negotiations dragged on for another three years, neither side trusting the other, while in the forest men still fleshed their weapons. But to all intents and purposes this, the last and the greatest of the Iroquois wars, was over. Their attempt to wrest control of the western fur trade from the French had failed.

In February, 1698, a delegation from Albany arrived at Montreal to inform the French that peace had been signed in Europe. They had brought with them some French prisoners in order to effect an exchange, but greatly to the discomfiture of the Albany delegates —one of the Schuyler brothers and Delius, a Dutch pastor—all but

* Fortunately for Frontenac's reputation, this order was not carried out. If it had been, then he would have been guilty of the same act of "treachery" that he had so scathingly condemned Denonville for having committed ten years earlier.

two or three of the English prisoners held by the French refused to return to the English colonies. They had been well treated in Canada, cared for by the nuns if very young or else adopted into Canadian families. Most of them had been received into the Church of Rome, and it was mainly for this reason that they refused to return.[109] In the case of the children it is very likely that life among the easy-going Canadians, who did not regard all pleasure as essentially wicked, was far more to their liking than the bleak puritan atmosphere of New England and New York. To remove all doubts from the minds of Schuyler and Delius, Frontenac ordered the prisoners to appear before them and submit to interrogation, but the response was still the same. The Albany delegates then had to content themselves with demanding that the children under fourteen should be forced to return whether they wished to or not, on the grounds that they were too young to know their own minds in matters of religion. Frontenac and Champigny finally agreed that all the children under twelve would be handed over, whereupon most of them ran off and hid, but Frontenac reluctantly promised to have them rounded up and sent to Albany at the first opportunity.[110] Those allowed to remain were granted French naturalization papers by the Crown.[111]

Although the English colonists were quick to take advantage of the peace themselves in order to forestall any war parties the French had intended to send out against them, at the same time they did everything in their power to prevent the Iroquois breaking off hostilities with Canada. The Earl of Bellomont, recently appointed governor of New York, was determined that the Iroquois should not negotiate a peace settlement themselves but that he should negotiate it for them, which would have meant an admission on the part of the French that the Iroquois were under British suzerainty. Frontenac dismissed this claim as nonsense, but Bellomont made him pause by threatening that if the French were to make any hostile move against the Iroquois he would invade New France in force.[112] And there the matter rested at the time of Frontenac's death, the peace with the Iroquois hanging fire and a diplomatic duel in progress over the status of these nations. This last was a far more vital problem than at first might appear and it was fortunate for New France that at this critical point Callières succeeded Frontenac as governor. He was a far more capable man in any dealings with the Iroquois, in either war or diplomacy, than Frontenac had ever shown himself to be.*

During the war Frontenac rarely concerned himself with either the planning or the execution of military operations against the Iroquois. Montreal was the main base and theatre of operations and Frontenac spent little time there. He left the conduct of the *petite guerre* almost entirely to Callières, for which he is to be commended. Too often military operations are impeded by interference from headquarters with the men in the field. It was only the major strategic decisions that were made by Frontenac and it is here that he does not show himself to advantage. When account is taken of the forces at Frontenac's disposal, regular troops, militia—some 3,000 men in all—and the allied Indians, and the forces at the disposal of the enemy—which, in effect, were the Iroquois and the Albany militia—then the outcome of the war should never have been in doubt.

At the onset of the war, New France could not have hoped to conquer the English colonies, but they, had they mobilized all their available forces under effective leadership, could easily have overwhelmed New France. This, however, was a task quite beyond them as long as they remained disunited, suspicious and squabbling among themselves. The real and immediate threat to New France was clearly that of the Iroquois, whose aim it was to drive the French out of the west. Frontenac's strategy should, therefore, have been aimed at avoiding any actions that might have caused the New England colonies to unite with New York against Canada, and at the same time at curbing the Iroquois without destroying them completely, since they were needed to serve as a buffer state between the French allies in the west and the English fur traders at Albany, and possibly Pennsylvania and Virginia later on.

In his border raids of 1690 Frontenac made a strategic blunder that caused the northern colonies to unite in a combined assault. New France was spared what might have been the disastrous consequences mainly by the ineptitude of the enemy. Although in this

---

* The Court was not unaware of Callières's services; in 1694 he had been made a Chevalier of the coveted Order of St. Louis and given a gratuity of 1,000 *livres*. Frontenac had to wait until 1697, after the Onondaga campaign, before the king saw fit to grant him this award. When he did finally receive it he complained that it was a poor recognition of his services and that it should have been given him years earlier so that he might have enjoyed the seniority among the members of the order that he felt was his due.

instance Frontenac's initial strategy had been very poor, his tactics during the siege of Quebec were basically sound. In the war with the Iroquois, however, he had no clear idea of the best strategy to employ because he never really understood their strategy; consequently they held the military and diplomatic initiative down to 1696. His main objectives should have been the destruction of Albany, the Iroquois supply base, and the maintenance of close liaison with the allies to bring the maximum pressure to bear against the Iroquois, regardless of their diplomatic overtures, until he was certain that their fangs had been drawn. Such a policy would have made it very difficult for the Iroquois to launch large-scale attacks on the French settlements or the Indian allies, and it was this policy that Frontenac's subordinates continually urged him to adopt.

Yet Frontenac never launched an attack on Albany, although the authorities of New York lived in fear and trembling throughout the war lest he should. In 1698 the Earl of Bellomont stated that had the French attacked this key base "with half the number of men that they had provided at Montreal they could not (humanly speaking) have failed to take it . . . and it is more than probable that those [the Iroquois] would have revolted to them upon such a loss and disgrace. God be thanked for the province's escape." [113]

Throughout his career in Canada Frontenac always boasted of his great influence over the Indians, and later historians, with very few exceptions, have accepted this claim at face value. Yet it was in his relations with these tribes, Iroquois and allied alike, that he was at his weakest. He always under-estimated their intelligence and their guile because he always over-estimated his own, and his excessive vanity made it all too easy for the Iroquois to deceive him by the judicious use of flattery. The allied tribes, on the other hand, too often mistook for duplicity what was in reality nothing more than obtuseness. Consequently, whenever the Iroquois were in danger of losing their military ascendancy they quickly and effectively waged a diplomatic offensive to split the French from their allies and bring about a cessation of hostilities, during which time they were able to recoup their strength for a fresh onslaught. Had it not been for the pressure exerted on Frontenac by his subordinates and the minister, hostilities might well have dragged on indefinitely. As it was, he had to be forced in 1696 into undertaking the Onondaga campaign that caused the Iroquois finally to come to terms. In fact, throughout the war, Frontenac seldom led; most of the time he had to be pushed.

But when all this has been said, it is still true that under Frontenac's command New France was not conquered and the Iroquois were finally defeated. Had the reverse occurred he would most certainly have been held responsible; therefore he deserves credit for what was accomplished under his command. But this credit is largely reflected from the actions of his subordinates; the men who deserve most of the credit for the final victory over the Iroquois were Callières, Vaudreuil, Champigny, the officers' corps of the Troupes de la Marine, and the Canadian *habitants*: Callières, because the war was fought in the Montreal area and by small detachments sent out by him to harry the enemy on their own territory; Vaudreuil, because he led so many of these detachments; Champigny, because like all wars this one was dependent on supplies and good organization and he saw to it that the French forces lacked for nothing it was in his power to furnish, defying on occasion the wrath of the minister on this score; the officers' corps and the *habitants*, because in the final analysis it was the man with a musket in his hands who defeated the Iroquois, and during the entire course of the war it was these officers leading the Canadian militia who did most of the fighting.

CHAPTER SIXTEEN

WESTERN EXPANSION AND THE FUR TRADE

THROUGHOUT Frontenac's second administration the Ministry of Marine still adhered to Colbert's old policy of concentrating the Canadian population in the St. Lawrence valley between Montreal and Gaspé and inducing them by one means or another to devote their talents to farming, fishing, lumbering and other industries. The one thing that was officially frowned on above all else was allowing the Canadians to take to the woods as *coureurs de bois*. It was clearly enunciated that the twenty-five *congés* granted each year, allowing twenty-five canoes with three men in each to leave the settlements to trade, was a concession made in the hope that the Canadians would be satisfied to wait their turn for a *congé* and the rest of the time engage in useful work within the colony. The government at Versailles continued to declare that Montreal, not the western posts, should be the fur-trade centre, and that the Hurons and Ottawas had to be encouraged to bring their furs down to the Canadians in the colony, rather than the Canadians allowed to travel up country to obtain them.[1]

The mainstay of the fur trade was still beaver for the simple reason that the Company of the Farm had to accept this fur at fixed prices, assuring a good margin of profit to the traders regardless of the amount brought in or the state of the market in France. It was this factor, more than anything else, that undermined the colonial policy of the Ministry of Marine. As long as the profits in beaver were assured, the Canadians had little incentive to engage in other activities. Nor was it only the Canadians who took advantage of this situation; merchants from France came out to the colony in the spring with supplies of merchandise, hired *coureurs de bois* to take their goods up country to trade with the Indians, then returned to France in the autumn after their agents had returned with the furs.[2]

Having created these conditions by the policy of fixed prices for beaver, the Ministry of Marine relied on the governor and the intendant to prevent advantage being taken of them by enforcing the edicts which forbade all but the *congé* holders to engage in the fur trade outside the confines of the colony. These edicts would have been difficult to put into effect in any event, but they could have been enforced far more effectively, particularly in wartime, than they actually were. The main difficulty was that Frontenac was not in the least interested in furthering such a policy and de Lagny, who was in charge of Canadian affairs at Versailles, paid only lip service to it, if he did not actually connive at its evasion by Frontenac. Whereas to the minister in France and to the intendant in New France the up-country posts were merely a military expediency, a means to encourage the Indian allies to harass the Iroquois and by so doing take the pressure of Iroquois attacks off the central colony, to Frontenac and his followers the central colony was merely a base for exploiting the western fur trade and the western posts were of as great importance as the settlements along the St. Lawrence, if not greater.[3]

Thus within the body of officials in the colony there were two factions, the one consisting of the governor and his supporters, who would not let any restrictions stand in the way of private profit, and the other, led by the intendant and his subordinates, who made an honest attempt to carry out their orders and to implement the policy laid down at Versailles. Contrary to a widely held opinion, the French Crown in the late seventeenth century did not turn a blind eye towards officials who availed themselves of their opportunities to put money in their purses; witness the repeated instructions of the minister, and the summary dismissal of the intendant de Meulles. In contrast to the situation in the English colonies at this time, salaries, however inadequate, and the honour of serving Louis XIV were regarded as the sole reward of office. Perquisites were, most definitely, not considered right and proper.* Frontenac, however, considered himself above any such injunctions and allowed free rein to his rapacity. But the junior officials, from the intendant down, lacked his influence at the Court; they were essentially civil service career men whose futures were dependent on good behaviour, the efficient discharge of their duties,

---

* These relatively high moral standards were not, however, maintained in either France or New France. In fact, standards of both efficiency and probity declined drastically in French administrative circles during the eighteenth century, and those who deplored this condition complained that it had come to be generally regarded that to rob the Crown was not really robbery.

and the minister's opinion of them. They could not afford to be detected in malversations.

In the dispute over the western posts, the intendant and his subordinates received strong but embarrassing support from the Jesuits, who were extremely anxious to have the French remain in the central colony and not live among the western tribes, for the simple reason that too many of the *coureurs de bois* led debauched lives among the Indians. When the Jesuit missionaries tried to instruct their charges in the Christian way of life, the Indians asked why it was that the French, who professed to be Christians, did not follow these fine precepts. To this the missionaries had no satisfactory answer. It was, therefore, all too easy for Frontenac, when he found both the intendant and the Jesuits opposing his flouting of the royal edicts governing the fur trade, to brand Champigny as a tool of the Jesuits and so discredit him.

In his official instructions Frontenac had been warned specifically that he was not to engage, directly or indirectly, in the fur trade; his servants were not permitted to engage in the trade for their own accounts; no one was to make use of his name for purposes of trade and any men he might have occasion to send up country with military orders were forbidden to take furs from the Indians.[4] In addition, all *congés* and military permits issued by the governor for travel up country had to be countersigned by the intendant, who was to see to it that the king's regulations governing such voyages were carried out.[5] Frontenac quickly showed that he had no intention of submitting to any such restraints. He refused to allow Champigny to sign the twenty-five annual *congés* until the minister ordered that he was to conform to the royal ordinances.[6] As to the king's order that officers in the Troupes de la Marine, their men, or any *habitants* sent up country for military purposes were not to do any trading while there, this was a dead letter so far as Frontenac was concerned. It would, of course, have been impossible to prevent them from doing some trading in order to gain the means of subsistence, and Champigny was quite willing to allow the officers and men at the posts to take trade goods up country to the value of their annual pay and allowances—which were paid in advance—but he would not countenance their engaging in large-scale trade for their private profit. It was on this point that he and Frontenac were in violent disagreement.

Even while the colony was being devastated by the Iroquois,

Frontenac persisted in sending large detachments to the western posts, ostensibly with munitions and supplies for the Indian allies. In April, 1690, he recalled Durantaye, who was without a doubt one of the best officers in the colony, from the command of Michili-mackinac and replaced him by an ex-captain of his guards, the Sieur de Louvigny, to whom he had recently given a commission in the Troupes de la Marine. With Louvigny went a detachment of 143 men. Champigny charged that the real reason for this change in command was that Durantaye had not been a member of Fron-tenac's following in earlier days, and that the expedition was little more than an excuse for Frontenac's appointees to take trade goods up country, mostly from the king's stores, to trade for their personal profit. He maintained that there was no necessity to send such a large detachment, particularly at a time when every man was needed to defend the settlements against Iroquois attacks. This really reduces itself to a question of degree: if 143 men were too many, how many would have sufficed? With the Iroquois attempting to sever communications between Montreal and the west, a fairly large party was needed for security, and in 1688, when Denonville had sent a party as large, if not larger, to Michilimack-inac to bring the furs back to Montreal, Champigny had voiced no criticism whatsoever. What really aroused Champigny over the Louvigny detachment was his discovery that Louvigny, with Fron-tenac's connivance, had taken nearly 4,000 *livres* of contraband goods with him. The canoes, supposedly carrying munitions and supplies to the allies, had been so laden down with such goods as brandy that they had abandoned en route part of the ammunition from the king's stores. Within a month of his arrival at Michili-mackinac, Louvigny sent down 4,500 *livres* of beaver to his wife in Montreal and a short time later sent down ten bales of prime beaver robes.[7]

The following year Frontenac sent another detachment of 128 men with six officers to bring back the furs that had been traded in 1690. Champigny was under no delusions as to what these men would be doing among the Ottawas. He pointed out to the minister that during Denonville's term as governor no officers had been sent to this post and that Frontenac's six appointees had all taken as much trade goods as had the *congé* holders, despite the fact that as officers they were strictly forbidden to engage in trade while on duty up country.[8]

Then, in September, 1693, when 187 canoes of Ottawa Indians came down to Montreal loaded with beaver pelts, Frontenac informed Champigny that he intended to send 146 men back with the Ottawas in order to reinforce the existing posts in the west and to garrison new ones. Champigny remonstrated with him over sending so many men up country in disregard of the king's explicit orders of the previous year forbidding this practice,[9] and at a time when the men were sorely needed for the defence of the colony, but since Frontenac stated flatly that it was a matter of military expediency, Champigny had to concede the point. He was very disturbed, however, when he learned that the members of the detachment were treating their military permits as *congés*, selling them publicly in the streets of Montreal for 1,000 to 1,100 *livres* each, and that those actually going up country were loading their canoes with as much trade goods as they would hold. Champigny sent his secretary to ask Frontenac how this came about and the governor informed him that the members of the detachment had his permission to take as much trade goods as they could transport. As to his military permits being sold as *congés*, he declared that he only wished they could be sold for 40,000 *livres* instead of a mere 1,000.[10]

The intendant then drew up an ordinance which was nothing more than a repetition of the king's edicts governing military detachments going up country. Before promulgating it he showed it to Frontenac, who, after keeping it for four or five days, informed Champigny that he had no intention of enforcing any such terms. He particularly objected to the clause prohibiting the transport of brandy to the Indian villages, which the intendant had included in accordance with a strict interpretation of the king's ordinance of 1679. Champigny deleted or watered down some clauses to please Frontenac, but he stubbornly refused to remove the ban on brandy. He then promulgated this revised version of his ordinance.[11] Frontenac promptly riposted by publishing an ordinance of his own "to explain that of M. de Champigny of the 11th September 1693 concerning that which has to be observed by those who have obtained *congés* to go to the country of the Ottawas and other distant nations."[12] In this ordinance Frontenac stated that compliance with Champagny's orders would delay the departure of the detachment and on that account he felt obliged "to clarify the greater part of the clauses in the said ordinance and those of His Majesty and thereby remove any scruples that any one might have lest he should be disobeying the king's orders." As for the king's edict that the intendant be given a declaration of the quantity and type of goods being taken by the party, Frontenac stated that he would not forbid compliance with it but that in his opinion "it appears useless to us and could only result in delays greatly to the prejudice of trade and the king's service." Having effectively scuttled that royal edict, Frontenac next threw into discard the king's order forbidding officers and soldiers to engage in trade up country by declaring that "we find ourselves obliged to grant them a little more freedom than appears to be accorded in the king's order." The restrictions on the transporting of brandy to the Indian villages he abrogated completely, stating that he was sure His Majesty had never intended to deprive his subjects of the right to barter brandy with the Indians any more than any other commodity, although this was precisely what the king had intended.

Before the promulgation of Frontenac's ordinance, some members of the detachment had submitted to the intendant lists of the goods they were taking with them, but afterwards none of them would do so. When Champigny sent his deputy to Lachine to ask Tonty for a declaration of his merchandise he received no satisfaction whatsoever. All that Champigny could discover was that fifty-five canoes had gone up country, all loaded to the thwarts with trade goods, and that in addition the members of the detachment had contrived to load the Indians' canoes with a cargo of brandy. The canoes of the soldiers had been so laden with merchandise that they had had no room for the Indian presents and Frontenac was obliged to rush to Lachine in the middle of the night and work till dawn organizing two more canoes and rounding up *voyageurs* to transport these goods.[13]

Champigny took a very narrow view of Frontenac's habit of granting permits for voyages up country to a favoured few. In May of that same year, 1693, Frontenac had sent the Sieur d'Argenteuil to Michilimackinac with twenty-two men in four canoes. Champigny admitted that d'Argenteuil carried dispatches from the governor to the post commanders, but, he added bitingly, these were very pleasant dispatches for the bearer since they enabled him to make a profit of between twelve and eighteen thousand *livres* on the trip. And the following September this same officer received two more permits. "It is very annoying," wrote Champigny, "to see all these favours granted, for the most part, to a single family in the colony, that of the captain of M. de Frontenac's guards, to which three of the officers who went up country belong, while poor families have no share in them." [14]

A memoir written in 1697 lends substance to Champigny's statement:

> It is well known that it is not the poor families that have a share in the *congés* given out for trading with the Indians . . . thus they would lose nothing if these *congés* were done away with entirely. One has to have influence in order to get them; these favours are for those who either know how to get them by certain means, or attach themselves to those who can obtain them, or for private considerations obtain the favour of those who have everything, or at least a great deal, to do with their distribution. Some persons who are incomparably better off than the poor *habitants* obtain, and have obtained in the past, up to ten and eleven *congés*, at a time when the poorer families are in the lowest depths of poverty.[15]

Frontenac's habit of treating *congés* and military permits as little more than largesse to be distributed to his favourites is confirmed in a letter of his to de Lagny. After explaining that on orders from the Court he had had to grant some of the *congés* for that year, 1693, to the Montreal hospital and to two private parties, Denis Riverin and the Sieur de la Durantaye, he offhandedly remarked that "this would be of no consequence; if we have anyone else in such pressing need that we feel we should grant them some favour, we will let them go under the guise of a detachment." [16]

Once these detachments reached the up-country posts there was no check at all on how the goods sent from the king's stores were distributed to the Indians. There was nothing whatsoever to stop the officers at the posts from using these goods, or at any rate a large part of them, in trading for their own account, and, according to some well-founded reports, this was the common practice.[17] Moreover, it was the custom of the Indians to give presents in the shape of furs in return for those they received. In 1697, following a sharp query from the minister, Frontenac stated that in future all such presents would be claimed for the Crown, but when

Champigny tried to execute the order Frontenac refused to allow it.[18] The governor had also revived an old practice of his first administration; when parties of Indians came down to Montreal or Trois Rivières to trade their furs, they were not permitted to do so until they had obtained Frontenac's permission when he was there, or that of the local governor when he was not. Before this permission was accorded, the Indians were expected to make sizeable presents to the governor, who would then appoint some of his guards to protect the Indians from harm; in return for this "protection" the Indians were expected to give the guards a *pourboire* for their trouble. The governors also gave the Indians presents in return before the general trading began—presents which came from the king's stores, but those received by the governors they treated as a perquisite of their office.[19]

Frontenac's abuse of his authority in the issuing of *congés* and military permits was bad enough—even Lahontan declared that the governor general "ought not to sell Licenses for trading with the Savages of the Great Lakes"[20]—but a far more serious abuse was his granting of a monopoly of the trade of the entire Illinois country to Tonty and La Forest. Frontenac had been virtually a business partner of La Salle in the fur trade, and after La Salle was murdered by his own men during his ill-fated attempt to establish a colony at the mouth of the Mississippi, Tonty and La Forest took over his trading organization. With Frontenac's help, they were granted Fort St. Louis-des-Illinois by the Crown under the same terms and conditions that had been stipulated in La Salle's concession.[21] In a lengthy and revealing letter to de Lagny, Frontenac wrote: "I forgot to tell you that [Champigny] is greatly incensed with Messrs de la Forest and de Tonty. . . . He complains that in the *congés* that I have granted I have not agreed to omit a clause which I have always inserted, to the effect that the persons who receive them may trade with all the distant nations with the exception of those tribes that trade at Tadoussac—the trade there being in the domain of the king and the Farmers General—and in the district of Fort St. Louis-des-Illinois, on account of the privilege granted to the late M. de la Salle, whose rights Messieurs de la Forest and Tonty now enjoy."[22] Here Frontenac is clearly giving de Lagny to believe that La Salle had been granted a monopoly of the fur trade in this vast area, but by the terms of his concession the only monopoly granted to La Salle had been in buffalo hides, and it had been specifically stated that the trade in other furs was open to all the king's subjects.[23] In 1685 Denonville had informed the minister that Tonty was trying to exclude everyone but his own men from this trade and the minister had replied, "This claim appears ridiculous to His Majesty and he is writing to [the Sieur de Tonty] in strong terms on the subject, his intention being to grant to all his subjects the liberty to trade in the Illinois country"[24] Again in 1692 the king ordered, "Those who obtain the said *congés* can go to the countries of the allied nations as they see fit without exclusion under any pretext whatsoever. His Majesty does not desire that the Sieur de Frontenac should grant any permission or orders to the officers and others in the distant territories to exclude those having these *congés*, with the exception of the trade at Tadoussac."[25]

In his letter to de Lagny, Frontenac was patently trying to mislead when he wrote: "M. de Champigny claims that only the trade at Tadoussac is discussed in his orders, and therefore Fort St. Louis and the Illinois country must not be included with it, despite the fact that he knows that in the letter written to both of us last year, it was expressly stated that the king understood that these two gentlemen were to enjoy the same privileges as had been granted to the late M. de la Salle."[26] All that he had done here was to take the king's statement out of its context and twist its meaning. The king's dispatch had stated that Tonty and La Forest had been granted the Illinois concession on the same conditions that had applied to La Salle's original grant, with the added condition that they cause the Indian nations of the area to campaign actively against the Iroquois; Frontenac and Champigny had to see to it that this last condition was executed and an exact account sent to His Majesty.[27] Quite obviously, the minister did not have the granting of a monopoly in mind here, as Frontenac would have had de Lagny believe, but Frontenac counted on his influence at the Court to sustain his pretentions, and he wrote to de Lagny: "[Champigny] is again threatening [Tonty and La Forest] that he will reopen this question all over again but they hope that, being able to count on your protection, they will have little cause to worry. I would be obliged if you would inform *Monsieur le premier** and my

* The *Monsieur le premier* here referred to was probably M. Rose, the king's first secretary, a man of considerable power both by virtue of his position and through the strength of his character.

wife in detail of this incident in order that, should they hear talk of it, they can reply. I shall write about it only in general terms to them, and to M. de Pontchartrain I shall say even less."[28]

The following year the minister stated that in this matter Frontenac and Champigny were to govern themselves by "the tenor of the letters that Tonty and de la Forest have obtained and by that which was the practice in M. de la Salle's time."[29] De Lagny had done his work well, for in effect this meant that Frontenac had been given tacit permission to continue Tonty and La Forest's monopoly of the fur trade in the entire Illinois country, which encompassed the vast area south of the Great Lakes in the angle of the Ohio and Mississippi Rivers.

The minister, however, had begun to suspect that Frontenac's attitude towards the western posts was more concerned with his private financial interests than with the Iroquois war. In 1692 Pontchartrain warned him: "I must tell you there are several reports that the expenditures made to press the allies into taking the offensive serve that purpose far less than they do the commercial interests of certain individuals."[30] And in the king's memoir Frontenac and Champigny were bluntly told that if they did not put a stop to the illicit trading being carried on under cover of the war, they would receive little military aid from the allies, who would be spending all their time hunting beaver instead of Iroquois. The governor and intendant were once again ordered to use every possible means to prevent the officers and men at the western posts from engaging in the fur trade.[31] Frontenac, of course, repeatedly denied that there were any such abuses. He claimed that the detachments he sent up country with the king's presents were producing excellent results by encouraging the allies to harass the Iroquois continually; so much so, in fact, that the Senecas had been forced to abandon their villages, and he hoped for even greater things in the near future. He declared that the essential purpose of the western posts and the large detachments he sent to them each year was to keep a close check on the allies, press them into carrying the war to the Iroquois, and by so harassing the Five Nations prevent them from leaving their villages to attack the Montreal settlements. He also claimed that these posts and their garrisons were necessary to prevent the allies deserting the French and going over to the Iroquois in order to get cheaper English trade goods, and also to prevent them from warring among themselves.

By his sending troops and supplies up country, he maintained, the allies would have no need to make the long voyage down to Montreal or to spend so much time hunting beaver to get the wherewithal to support themselves and their families; consequently they would have more time for war parties. Moreover, the allies would be more inclined to wage war when they knew that their own villages were protected from Iroquois attacks by the French garrisons.[32]

If these assertions had been born out by events there could have been little to criticize in Frontenac's policy, but the truth is, not a single one of them will stand up under investigation. There is no evidence whatsoever to show that the presence of French garrisons at these posts caused any appreciable slackening of the Iroquois attacks on the central colony; if anything, they had just the opposite effect because they actually served to free the Iroquois from the threat of attacks on their villages by the allies. Nor was it a very logical argument that the allies would be pleased to have the French remain in their villages while they themselves went off to fight the common enemy. In fact, as Champigny pointed out, these men did not remain at the main posts, such as Michilimackinac or St. Louis, but scattered far and wide in twos and threes among the distant tribes to do their trading. The only time the garrisons were at the posts was upon their first arrival from Montreal and upon their reassembling to make the voyage back to the colony in convoy to be more secure from Iroquois attacks en route.[33] As for the allies being freed from the necessity of hunting by the supplies and munitions furnished by the Crown, this claim is invalidated by the tremendous increase in the amount of summer-killed beaver sent down to Montreal, indicating that they were far more occupied in this pursuit than heretofore and could hardly have been devoting much time to the Iroquois.[34] Moreover, it is very doubtful if they ever received any sizeable part of the king's supplies without having to offer furs to the post commanders in exchange.

A memoir written in 1695 points out that the Indians were placed in a greater necessity than ever before of obtaining furs by hunting or trading with more distant tribes, owing to the presence of so many *coureurs de bois* and garrison troops in their midst, all well supplied with trade goods and interested in little else but obtaining furs.[35] And finally, the presence of the French garrisons did not prevent the allies from treating for a separate peace with the Iroquois in 1694; in fact, it was one of the main causes of their defection. As we have seen, by the early 1690's, French traders had begun supplying firearms to the Sioux, one of the most ferocious enemies of the Algonquin tribes. One tribe, the Saulteurs, soon began pillaging any French canoes they encountered headed for the Sioux country and the other tribes quickly followed suit. In 1693 Frontenac sent a party of ten men with 12,000 *livres* worth of trade goods to the Sioux, ostensibly to try to effect a peace settlement between the warring nations, but it had no success whatsoever.[36] Then in 1695 Tonty went far to the north-west of Michilimackinac with a large party on a trading expedition to the Assiniboines.[37] Naturally enough, the Ottawa middlemen took an extremely poor view of the French supplying their enemies, the Sioux, with arms, and they were hardly less pleased by the attempts of the French to eliminate them from the trade with the distant tribes from whom they had always obtained the bulk of their furs. They expected the French to act as commercial partners, not as trade rivals, and these attempts to forestall them destroyed the basis of the alliance. By 1695 most of the French allies were more concerned with fighting the Sioux than the Iroquois, and this, combined with Frontenac's attempts to negotiate peace with the Five Nations without keeping the allies informed of what he was about, had led them to begin negotiations themselves for a separate peace and an alliance with the Five Nations against the Sioux.[38] Thus, far from encouraging the allies to press the war against the Iroquois, the French sent up country were actually contributing to their going over to the enemy.

Although this catastrophe was narrowly averted, the western allies, despite the large sums expended by the Crown to furnish them with supplies during the preceding six years, refused to lift a finger to aid Frontenac in the Onondaga campaign. This is in marked contrast to their participation in Denonville's campaign against the Senecas nine years earlier. The western posts could have served a very useful purpose during the war; that they did not do so is largely owing to the use Frontenac made of them and the type of men he sent up country, men who were primarily interested in their own trading ventures and who gave little thought to the consequences. The evidence all indicates that these posts, when commanded by Frontenac's appointees, were more a political and military liability than an asset.

These, then, were the political consequences of Frontenac's western policy. The economic effects were no whit less serious. In 1696 New France found itself face to face with a crisis that had been building up for several years. In August of that year, Frontenac, just back from the Onondaga campaign, received a dispatch from the minister that must have staggered him. This dispatch ordered that immediately upon its receipt the acceptance of beaver pelts at the office of the Company of the Farm was to be suspended until further orders. Frontenac was strictly forbidden to grant any *congés* or permits for the carrying of trade goods to the Indians under any pretext whatsoever, and, the minister added, the king had ordered him to inform Frontenac that he would be held personally responsible for any actions contrary to these instructions.[39]

The state of mind of Frontenac and the entire fur-trading fraternity can well be imagined as they waited for further dispatches to bring some clarification of these drastic orders. In October the king's dispatch finally arrived and Frontenac's worst fears must have been realized. The king ordered that all the western posts, including Fort Frontenac, were to be abandoned and destroyed, with the single exception of Fort St. Louis in the Illinois country, which was to be retained solely for military reasons and where no trading in beaver pelts whatsoever was to be allowed. There were to be no more *congés* or permits issued, but those having merchandise or furs at the posts were to be allowed to send canoes to bring their goods back, provided that precautions were taken that they did not use this as an excuse to send fresh supplies of trade goods up country.

Accompanying these orders was a rather disconcerting letter for Frontenac from the minister. After saying that he had nothing to add to the king's orders he warned his kinsman, "You must be careful that the regulations, both in general and in particular, which you have to execute are not used as a pretext to serve any private interests or schemes to the prejudice of the orders and the intentions of His Majesty, since were that to happen I would not be able to prevent His Majesty holding you personally responsible."[40] It is clear that Pontchartrain was warning Frontenac that he could no longer merely pay lip service to the king's orders and rely on his influence at the Court to protect and sustain him.

The king gave two main reasons for the new restrictive policy: the insupportable expense of supplying the Indian allies with munitions and other goods when they could not be relied on in the war, and secondly, his desire to concentrate all the French in the central colony in order that they should be available for its defence. As a consequence of this, trading in the depths of the bush by the *coureurs de bois* was to end once and for all. From now on, the king decreed, the Indians were to bring their furs down to Montreal, as had been their custom in years gone by, and the trade which had been usurped by the *coureurs de bois* for the sole benefit of a few would be restored to all the merchants and *habitants*, who would all have an opportunity to share in the profits.[41] What this really amounted to was nothing more than a pious restatement of Colbert's old policy which the government in recent years had neither officially abandoned nor made a real attempt to implement. In other words, Louis XIV had decided to give western North America back to the Indians.

This sudden change in attitude by the king and the minister had really been brought about by the inescapable fact that the French beaver trade was virtually bankrupt. The market in Europe was completely glutted with poor-grade, summer-killed, dry beaver. In 1695 the Company stated that it had in storage three and a half million *livres* worth of beaver which it could not dispose of.[42] During the previous six or seven years at least 140,000 *livres* weight had been received each year from Canada, whereas, prior to 1675, the annual receipts had been only about 50,000 *livres* weight, this being the maximum that the French and Dutch markets could absorb. The French hat makers, who were the principal users of beaver, used three greasy beaver to one dry-cured pelt in the making of hats, but at least two-thirds of the pelts received by the Company were dry, summer-killed beaver and the Farmers could not get rid of their huge surplus at any price.[43]

In 1695 Champigny had pointed out that the amount of dry beaver coming down to Montreal was four times what it had been before the French began to exploit the trade of the Illinois, Miamis and adjacent areas in the Ohio–Mississippi valley. He stated: "if one asks why in earlier times there were more greasy than dry beaver pelts, it is because the French did not go after it so avidly as they do today. There is not a single nation within five or six hundred leagues of here where there are not Frenchmen with their merchandise, waiting to trade as fast as the Indians kill the beaver ... if such a large proportion of poor-grade beaver is coming in today, it is only because they have been trading with the tribes to the south." [44] He then went on to explain that the beaver trapped in the southern areas did not have as heavy or as fine a fur as those in the north, and also, owing to the milder climate, the southern Indians did not make the pelts into robes and wear them next to their skin for months on end, as did northern Indians. As a result they could supply little or no greasy beaver, only poorly-dressed dry pelts.

In 1694, in a feeble attempt to stave off the economic crisis, the minister had tried to get the Canadian merchants to ship their beaver pelts direct to Holland, despite the fact that France and the Netherlands were at war at the time. This had brought no response from the merchants, and in any event the carrying trade was largely controlled by the merchants of La Rochelle.[45] The following year the Farmer-General asked the minister to be allowed to ship beaver direct from Quebec to the English colonies, but this request was rejected for political reasons.[46] Another suggested solution was that the Company should do as the Dutch did when the pepper market became glutted—burn or dump in the sea the entire surplus to ensure that supply did not exceed demand. The Company pointed out that there was no substitute for pepper but several for beaver, hence this solution would, if applied, only aggravate matters. Felt hats could be made not only from beaver fur but also from llama wool, sheep wool or rabbit fur, and, despite rigid government restrictions, the hat makers used these materials in preference to beaver at every opportunity because they were far cheaper. Moreover, the general public greatly preferred hats made of these materials, for the simple reason that they cost only ten or eleven *livres*, whereas beaver hats sold for twenty to twenty-four *livres*. Were the surplus of beaver to be burned, it was stated, the price to the hat makers would have to be increased greatly to compensate for the loss and as a result fewer hats would be sold, even more fur would have to be burned, the price of hats would rise still further, and so on in a vicious spiral.[47]

To curb the malpractices of the hat makers, more stringent laws were enacted to prevent them using anything but beaver, and when the hat makers' guild resisted too vigorously, the director-general of commerce, Daguesseau, authorized the Company of the Farm to enter into the manufacture of hats in the St. Antoine district of Paris, a section where, by tradition, goods could be manufactured free from the restraints of the guilds. He also induced some English hat makers to settle in Paris and begin the manufacture of beaver hats according to a new, improved, English method. It was hoped that if the French hat makers were given more competition they would be forced to improve the quality of their produce and reduce their prices.[48]

At the same time, it was fully realized that the main cause of the trouble was that four times as much beaver was being exported from Canada as the market could absorb, and that unless drastic action were taken, it would be difficult to get anyone to take over the Farm when Pointeau's lease expired in 1697. This would have meant an annual loss of half a million *livres* revenue to the Crown. The minister had finally been convinced that the beaver glut had been brought about mainly by Frontenac's sending so many men to the west on one pretext or another and his complete disregard for the edicts forbidding all but the twenty-five *congé* holders to engage in the fur trade up country. He realized now that as long as the posts were there, Frontenac would have an excuse to send men to them with trade goods, and each canoe that went up country meant three canoe loads of furs coming down the following year. The only solution appeared to be to abandon the posts altogether, and Frontenac was accordingly ordered to carry this out. To make doubly sure, he was ordered to raze all the forts and buildings to the ground.[49]

Frontenac was extremely bitter at this turn of events. One of his first acts after receiving the order was to forbid the Jesuits to go to their missions, on the specious grounds that they too were included in the king's ban on travel to the west, but the following year he was ordered to rescind this ban.[50] To the minister he declared that the new orders meant the ruin of New France, asserting that once the western posts were abandoned the Ottawas and Hurons would immediately make peace with the Iroquois and trade with the English at Albany.[51] Pontchartrain, however, was of the opinion that, far from preventing any such alliance, the western posts, under Frontenac's command, would be far more likely to cause it.*[52] And it was Frontenac himself who destroyed his own arguments when he wrote, in his and Champigny's joint dispatch, that if Tonty

* In the margin of Frontenac's dispatch Pontchartrain wrote: "*Je ne suis de son avis.*" And in the précis of the Canadian dispatches, he wrote: "*Il a bien fait de donner des ordres et fera mieux encore s'il les fait bien exécuter.*"

and La Forest were forbidden to engage in the beaver trade there would be no point in their retaining their post in the Illinois country and he had no doubt that, under those circumstances, they would abandon it,[53] as, in fact, they did four years later.[54]

The minister lost no time in making it plain to Frontenac what he thought of this argument. In the king's dispatch to the governor and intendant he wrote: "His Majesty was surprised to learn that after having insisted, as they have done, on the necessity of conserving the posts at Michilimackinac and Miamis, they are abandoning them on the grounds that the officers and soldiers cannot subsist there without engaging in the fur trade. This argument seems very weak to His Majesty and it, more than anything else, has convinced him of the truth of the reports he has received that these posts were established to satisfy the greed of some of the officers rather than for the preservation of the colony."[55]

Although it is clear that at that particular time these posts were a dubious asset to the French, to have suddenly abandoned them as the king demanded would have been a very risky undertaking. For years the Indians had been dependent on them for the supplies of goods which they could no longer do without; to demand that these tribes should suddenly reorganize their economy and base it on Montreal, a few hundred miles away, was to risk upsetting the entire relationship between the French and their savage allies. There was little danger of their trading with the English at Albany for, as one anonymous memoir writer pointed out: "The Iroquois, who are between them and our Indians, would never allow them to pass through their country to trade with our Indians; it is for this that they war with us and they would deal with the English in the same way."[56] And at the end of the war when Bellomont made strenuous efforts to induce the Ottawas to bring their furs to Albany, he found the chief obstacle to be the Iroquois.[57]

Although he had fought tooth and nail against the abuses in the western posts and had been frustrated at every turn by Frontenac, Champigny was too conscientious to waste much time in gloating over Frontenac's discomfiture. He wrote to the minister: "His Majesty's proclamation seems to me to be very sweeping in some respects and it could cause the ruin of this country; this is the reason why I am taking the liberty of telling you that a second course could be followed which would be to retain only two posts in the Ottawa country and to issue twenty-five *congés* as heretofore, but with several restrictions which I am not able to mention in our joint dispatch since M. de Frontenac would not hear of them." The two posts that Champigny advocated retaining were Michilimackinac and St. Joseph des Miamis. At each post he suggested there should be a garrison of ten or twelve soldiers with an officer in command, the latter to be appointed by the king, not by the governor. He also proposed that there should be a commissary at each post who would perform much the same functions as an intendant; it would be this official's duty to distribute and account for the king's presents, pay the garrison, maintain a close check on both the members of the garrison and the *congé* holders and adjudicate in any disputes that might arise between the French and the Indians. The main purpose of these posts and their small garrisons, Champigny explained, would be to keep a sharp watch over the Indian tribes and ensure that they remained in the French alliance by means of diplomacy and the king's presents. The *congé* holders would be required to transport a specified amount of supplies up country for the garrisons and the Indian presents, this being one means of reducing the cost to the Crown of maintaining the posts. At the same time it was to be made quite clear that the king desired the Indians to gain the full benefits of the trade with the more distant tribes, but that in order to achieve this they would have to bring the bulk of their furs down to Montreal where they would get far better prices than they had in the past when dealing with the *coureurs de bois*; the *congé* holders would be able to supply them with their more pressing immediate needs, but would not be permitted to forestall them by going far afield.[58] According to Champigny, were his scheme to be adopted, both the economic and political aspects of the vexing fur-trade problem would be settled. The effectiveness of this scheme would have depended entirely upon the appointment of men of probity as post commanders and commissaries, men who also had both skill and experience in dealing with the Indians, men of the stamp of Durantaye or Nicholas Perrot.

But the question of how effective Champigny's plan would have been is purely an academic one, since most of his recommendations were ignored by the Court. When the minister had digested the flood of memoirs that followed the first stringent edict he agreed to modify it somewhat, and in so doing he made a recurrence of the old abuses inevitable. He refused to modify his ban on the *congés* and up-country trading, but he sanctioned the retention of the posts at Michilimackinac and St. Joseph des Miamis, and also Fort Frontenac and St. Louis-des-Illinois. He forbade the garrisons to engage in trade under any pretext whatsoever and he warned both Frontenac and Champigny, "His Majesty gives them fair warning that he will hold them responsible if he learns that, by means which he cannot foresee, the execution of this order is evaded." He concluded be reiterating that Tonty and La Forest could retain their post in the Illinois country only on condition that no trade in beaver pelts was carried on there or in the vicinity.[59] At the same time the Company of the Farm was ordered to begin accepting beaver pelts again at fixed, if slightly lower, prices.[60] This, in conjunction with the fact that Frontenac's appointees were still in command of the western posts, made it inevitable that the old disorders would continue as rampant as ever.

On August 29, 1697, La Mothe Cadillac came down to Montreal from Michilimackinac accompanied by sixty-two canoes of *coureurs de bois* and thirty-five canoes of Ottawas, bringing with them the bulk of the 176,000 *livres* weight of beaver that was shipped to France that year.[61] Cadillac became involved in a lawsuit and was prevented from returning up country. To replace him Frontenac appointed the Sieur de Tonty, a half-pay captain and brother of Henri Tonty, of the Illinois post. Champigny was not informed of this move by Frontenac and he learned of Tonty's departure for the west only when his deputy at Montreal, the Sieur de la Touche, wrote to inform him that Tonty had left, accompanied by five Montreal merchant fur traders. Several other men in the town had promptly tried to follow their example, but had been prevented by the authorities. According to the king's orders of 1691 no permits were to be granted for travel up country without their first having been countersigned by the intendant. Champigny reported this case to Frontenac and asked him to order that this party be pursued and obliged to return to Montreal with their effects. He might as well have saved his breath, for Frontenac merely informed him that these men had gone up country by virtue of his orders and that that was all there was to it.[62]

At the time Champigny had no evidence that Tonty and his companions had taken any trade goods with them, but, he acidly remarked, it was contrary to all good sense to believe that five merchants would leave their families and their shop counters for the dubious pleasure of paddling a half-pay captain some three hundred leagues up country. He subsequently learned that the Recollet gate at Montreal had been left conveniently open by the guards one night and several wagon-loads of merchandise had been transported to Lachine under cover of darkness on the pretext that they were for the Ottawas, who could not take the goods by canoe because the river was too low. He also learned from a Montreal merchant named Dupré that twenty-five to thirty men, in addition to the five merchants, had accompanied Tonty. Dupré himself admitted that he had supplied Tonty with 3,000 *livres* worth of merchandise and that several other Montreal merchants had supplied him with six canoe-loads of trade goods. Some time later Champigny discovered that Tonty's merchant companions had taken with them well over 35,000 *livres* worth of goods, on which Tonty was to receive fifty per cent of the profits. Then, a month after Tonty's departure, the Sieur d'Argenteuil was sent up country as commander of a party of *voyageurs* who had been granted permission to return to Michilimackinac to bring back the peltries they had stored there. This party too had taken up several canoe-loads of trade goods, d'Argenteuil himself taking a full canoe-load, including a barrel of brandy. In the face of this, Champigny asked, was it any wonder that the king's edict banning all trade up country was now regarded by everyone as a dead letter? [63]

Frontenac had admitted that Henri Tonty and La Forest would not maintain their Illinois post if they had to forgo the beaver trade. Champigny declared that if these men and their associates were permitted to remain at the western posts they would have a virtual monopoly on the fur trade and would reap enormous profits. La Forest was at St. Louis-des-Illinois, his partner Henri Tonty had gone to the Assiniboine country where beaver was most abundant, Henri Tonty's brother was in command at Michilimackinac, and their cousin, de Liette, was in charge of their post at Chicago. Two of their canoes had been pillaged recently by the Illinois when they tried to take goods to the Sioux, who were at war with the Illinois and Miamis. Some of their *coureurs de bois* had aided the Sioux against the Miamis, which gave Champigny to fear that the latter tribe might well unite with the Iroquois against the French. In his view conditions in the west were as bad as, if not worse than, they had been before the king's edict banning all trade up country had been issued. [64]

Frontenac could have argued that it would take time for the Ottawas to take over from the *coureurs de bois* the task of transporting trade goods from Montreal to the west and that in the meantime the French had to maintain supplies of goods at the western posts. If this had been Frontenac's motive in flouting the king's edict there would have been something to be said in defence of his actions, but it obviously was not. Frontenac's control over the western fur trade was now tighter than ever, and he quickly made it clear that he intended to make the most of his opportunities, regardless of orders from the king and threats from the minister. In his edict ordering all the *coureurs de bois* to return to Montreal, the king had left it to Frontenac to decide how much time they should have in which to return, and the minister had warned him not to use this as a pretext for the furthering of his own interests.[65] Although Frontenac and Champigny issued an ordinance in 1697 ordering all the men up country to return by September of the following year at the latest, Frontenac found one excuse after another to avoid having it executed. He claimed that some of the *coureurs de bois* had threatened to rebel if they were ordered to return and others had demanded that they be allowed to remain up country until the following year, as they had not finished their trading.[66] Champigny maintained that this resulted from the large amounts of trade goods that had been smuggled up to them during the past year. He gave it as his opinion that the ordinance should be enforced, come what might; even if some of the men did refuse to obey and dispersed into the wilderness to avoid arrest, it would be far better to abandon them and force the rest to come back, rather than permit them all to flout the king's express orders. If a firm stand were not taken, he warned, and these men were allowed to go unpunished, then all hope of remedying the abuses and disorders of the past would be lost. As he phrased it: "The French who disobey and rebel do so only because they believe that their contravention of the orders will be tolerated, as has been the custom in the past. I may tell you that had I had sufficient authority, the king would not have these just grounds for dissatisfaction." [67]

A month almost to the day after Champigny wrote this dispatch, Frontenac was dead. Dead also was Colbert's policy for Canada which Pontchartrain had belatedly attempted to revive. There had been little chance that it could succeed because it had run counter to the basic factors of geography, climate, and man's acquisitive instincts. Moreover, the fixing of prices for beaver by the Ministry of Marine and a change in fashion for men's hats were what had been primarily responsible for the glutting of the beaver market in Europe. Frontenac was not responsible for these conditions, but at the same time his activities had aggravated the situation. Even after the problem had been made perfectly clear to him he made no attempt to alter his practices. The Company of the Farm was still accepting beaver at set prices, and therefore Frontenac's associates, with his full support, continued in their old ways while the glut of beaver continued to grow until by 1698 the surplus had reached the astronomical figure of one million *livres* weight, for which the company had paid over five million *livres* cash.[68] Had it been only the Farmer-General who suffered it might have been argued that he could well afford to, but the Crown too suffered a serious loss. In 1697 the Fur Farm was leased to Louis Guigues for a period of twelve years at an annual rental of 350,000 *livres*, or 150,000 a year less than the previous lease.[69] Nor was there any hope of disposing of the surplus beaver on foreign markets. In England beaver hats had gone out of fashion and the price of beaver skins dropped from fourteen to five shillings a pound.[70] In Canada the beaver trade steadily declined and the trade in other furs, the *menus pelleteries*, began to increase, until by 1700 the Canadians were telling the Iroquois to bring the latter furs to trade at Cataracoui and Montreal and to take their beaver to Albany.[71] And at Versailles the minister, almost at his wits' end, soon began to hope that this decline in the fur trade would result in the abandonment of the western posts, and with them French interests in the west, which seemed to entail nothing but colossal expense.[72]

Ironically enough, however, just two years after Frontenac's death French policy in North America underwent a revolution. Colbert's moribund policy was finally jettisoned and an avowedly imperialist policy, to prevent the English colonies from expanding beyond the Alleghanies, was adopted in its stead. From the moment that this decision was made, the western posts south of the Great Lakes assumed the importance that Frontenac had always attributed to them, but for quite different reasons. They now became of great value, not merely for the fur trade as formerly, but as bases to bar the English from the west. In fact, had these posts not already existed they would have had to be established. Frontenac had died just a little too soon.

CHAPTER SEVENTEEN

TARTUFFE

THE civil administration of New France was much less turbulent during Frontenac's second administration than during his first. But there were conflicts, and they were to have serious consequences for Frontenac. Within the first few months of his arrival he succeeded in humbling the Sovereign Council and with that he appears to have been satisfied. He bickered constantly with the intendant, but their disputes never resulted in the complete disruption of the civil government, as they had during the latter years of his first regime.

With the clergy too, for the first five years after his return, Frontenac's relations were without serious incident. The changed attitude of the king and the Court towards religion and the clergy made it politic for him to avoid trouble, and before leaving for Canada he had expressed the resolve to an eminent cleric to do so. At the same time, however, he informed this cleric, the Abbé de Brisacier, that his only quarrel with the Canadian clergy was that they were over-zealous; he suggested that it would be a good thing for all concerned were they not to desire the good with too great a display of fervour. This sound advice was duly passed on to the seminary at Quebec and they appear to have profited from it.[1] The Sulpicians at Montreal, on the other hand, refused to adopt a more moderate attitude towards the failings of their flock. Perhaps they saw a greater need to be strict. Montreal was a frontier town, with troops and *coureurs de bois* roistering in the all-too-numerous taverns, officers duelling and wenching, and young women eager to snare husbands with the coveted *de* in front of their names.[2]

Soon after his arrival Frontenac wrote to the Abbé Tronson in Paris to complain of some members of the Seminary at Montreal, and to the minister he wrote that they were making the lives of the women miserable by their puritanical strictures against elaborate coiffures, gay ribbons and fashionable low-cut gowns. One of the Sulpicians, Frontenac claimed, desired to establish an Inquisition worse than that of Spain.[3] The Abbé Tronson, accustomed to the more worldly atmosphere of the old Court, had earlier warned the members of his order at Montreal that the *curé* Comtois was causing trouble by his attitude towards feminine vanities.[4] Subsequently, Champigny wrote to warn him—he was a relative of the Abbé's—that he would be well advised to take firm measures with the members of the Montreal seminary before there was serious trouble. The Abbé Tronson was duly appreciative of this; he wrote to Dollier de Casson at Montreal, listing all the offences of the members of the seminary and ordering him to see to it that they ceased.[5] Many of the offences he mentioned were such that Frontenac had had every right to protest.

With Bishop St. Vallier, who had been appointed while Frontenac was in France, he was on quite amicable terms for the first few months. But this could not last, as the bishop was extremely stubborn, irascible, determined always to have his own way, and capable of believing anything of those who opposed him. His predecessor, Bishop Laval, soon came to regard him as a disaster likely to wreck the church in New France.[6] Events were to prove this estimate to be not far removed from the truth. The clergy themselves were none too happy under St. Vallier,[7] and in the early 1690's a controversy arose between the bishop and the members of the seminary at Quebec over the annual grant of 4,000 *livres* from the Crown. The bishop insisted that the money should be paid directly to him to dole out to the seminary as he saw fit. The intendant was unwilling to allow St. Vallier to have things all his own way and he requested the minister to decide how the funds should be apportioned.[8] Frontenac, upon seeing the bishop aligned against his own natural foes, immediately began espousing the cause of St. Vallier, in whom he now discovered hitherto unsuspected and estimable qualities. He informed the minister that the priests were no more anxious to see a strong bishop in the colony than a strong governor;[9] and while Champigny was complaining to the minister that the bishop was not only taking no steps whatsoever towards the establishment of permanent parish priests, but had actually refused to grant several *curés* of outstanding merit the royal funds which they had been accustomed to receive for several years,[10] Frontenac was at the same time writing: "I have no doubt whatsoever that the bishop is executing that which the king desires; I find him very disposed to do that which he believes to be the intention of His Majesty, to be for the advantage of the colony and for the good of his diocese." He placed all the blame for the dispute between the bishop and priests of the seminary on the latter, maintaining that he was doing all he could to reconcile the two parties; [11] but his actions actually consisted more in fishing in the troubled waters than in pouring oil on them.

The following year, 1694, the five-year period of civil calm was suddenly shattered by a violent clash of temperaments which threw the internal affairs of the colony into a great turmoil; and it was not Frontenac who was responsible for the trouble but the bishop. This turbulent prelate began it all by bringing before the Sovereign Council charges of blasphemy and impiety against the Sieur de Mareuil, whom Frontenac had recently commissioned in the Troupes de la Marine. Before the initial furore caused by this incident had begun to die down, St. Vallier, whose imagination appears to have run riot, began levelling serious charges against several others in the colony. Before long he was feuding fiercely with Callières, the Recollets of Montreal and Frontenac. Then, as a side issue, Frontenac was drawn into a controversy with the Sovereign Council which for a time looked as though it would develop into a repetition of the fracas of 1679–81.

During the early months of the winter of 1694 Frontenac and his entourage had amused themselves, and everyone in Quebec having the entrée to the governor's circle, by staging plays in which some of the local ladies had taken part.[12] At this period the more puritanical churchmen regarded the theatre as the work of the devil and maintained that no one could even attend a play without thereby falling into sin, but in France only the dévots, the extremely devout, paid any attention to the fulminations of the clergy on this topic.[13] One play, Molière's Tartuffe, which was an attack on religious hypocrisy in general and the alleged hypocrisy of the dévots in particular, was regarded as anathema by the clergy. When St. Vallier heard rumours that Frontenac and his players intended to perform this play he became convinced that the devil was loose among his flock. He therefore had a pastoral letter read in the parish church of Quebec declaring that plays such as Tartuffe could not be enacted without all concerned falling into mortal sin.[14] At the same time he issued another mandamus publicly denouncing the Sieur de Mareuil, who he had been led to believe was to play the leading role in the comedy, for blasphemies and impieties. In consequence, this officer was denied the sacraments of the church.[15]

Mareuil immediately countered by demanding that the bishop furnish him with a copy of the pastoral letter in which his honour and reputation had been impugned and that the names of his accusers be made known to him.[16]

Two weeks later, on the first of February, 1694, the bishop informed the Sovereign Council that he had certain knowledge of the Sieur de Mareuil's having on several occasions committed scandalous impieties and abominable blasphemies. He stated that he had had the offender warned privately to mend his ways, but to no avail, and therefore he had found it necessary to denounce him publicly and to warn him that if he continued to defy his bishop he would be excommunicated. Since blasphemy was a civil offence, the Council, over Frontenac's protests, instructed the attorney-general to investigate the case and Mareuil was taken into custody on March 15.[17] Frontenac was indirectly involved here, since Mareuil was a member of his household and enjoyed the protection of his friend de Lagny. The previous year Frontenac had apologized to de Lagny because he had not been able to do more for this influential official's protégé "than to let him take his meals at my table and give him some means of subsisting by a job as inspector of the work being done on the fortifications, to which last I had considerable difficulty in getting the intendant to agree." He added that he hoped to be able to find something more substantial for Mareuil before long.[18] A few months later he found occasion to give him a half-pay commission in the Troupes de la Marine.[19]

When the attorney-general began his investigation of the bishop's charges against Mareuil, Frontenac took violent exception to his manner of procedure; he maintained that the entire proceedings were highly irregular. During one altercation he became so incensed that he used the dread threat that he well knew how, as chief of the Council and governor-general of the country, to bring d'Auteuil to heel.[20] A statement such as this gave the attorney-general an opening to launch an attack on the governor and he was quite unable to let it pass. He declared that Frontenac had no right whatsoever to take the title of chief of the Council, quoting the king's *déclaration* of 1675 and the edict of the Council of State of 1680. Then, allowing his long-held feelings towards Frontenac to run away with him, he declared that, in any event, he took his orders from the Council, not from the governor. The remainder of that sitting degenerated into a very heated altercation between d'Auteuil and Frontenac. Later, when he had had time for sober reflection, d'Auteuil realized that he had gone too far and of his own volition he tendered an apology to the governor.[21]

The bishop then added fresh fuel to the flames; encountering Frontenac and Champigny in the street in Upper Town he pleaded with the governor not to allow *Tartuffe* to be produced, offering to pay him one hundred *pistoles*—approximately $1,200—if he would refrain. Greatly to Champigny's surprise, Frontenac accepted the offer without demur. St. Vallier wrote out a note for this sum on the spot and Frontenac redeemed it the following day.[22] Shortly afterwards, Frontenac submitted a memoir to the Sovereign Council stating that the king desired those to whom he had confided the government of his provinces to ensure that the church did not, by means of specious pretexts, extend its authority too far and inaugurate a form of Inquisition. To this end, he requested the Sovereign Council to appoint two of its members to a committee to investigate whether or not in the plays that had been enacted there was anything criminal, wicked or vicious, and whether particular circumstances had made them more dangerous, if such they were at any time, in order that the Council might judge whether or not these plays were prejudicial to the honour of God and his church or harmful to the colony. The Council had reluctantly to agree to consider the proposition.[23]

Meanwhile, the bishop, by now thoroughly aroused, had left Quebec for Montreal. On his way he stopped at Trois Rivières just long enough to stir up more trouble. Some years before, the Sieur Desjordy, an officer in the Troupes de la Marine, had been reported to be living in sin with a woman named Brieux, who lived at Batiscan near Trois Rivières and whose husband was out of the colony. St. Vallier had complained of this scandalous state of affairs to Frontenac and to Vaudreuil; the latter promised that Desjordy would be barred from going anywhere near Trois Rivières in future and the bishop thereupon agreed not to take the matter further. Then, while en route to Montreal, St. Vallier heard that Desjordy had revisited the scene of his moral crimes. Without waiting to discuss the matter with Vaudreuil, he placed both Desjordy and his *inamorata* under an interdict.[24]

When Desjordy learned of this he, accompanied by his uncle, the Sieur de Cabanac, went to the *curé* at Batiscan and demanded a copy of the bishop's mandamus. The *curé* later stated that on three occasions Desjordy and his friends had invaded his church during mass, obliging him to suspend the service and retire to the sacristy. Not satisfied with that, they followed him into the sacristy and threatened him with physical violence. Desjordy also petitioned the Sovereign Council to order the *curé* to produce the bishop's mandamus placing him under an interdict, to show good cause for his having obtained it, and to produce his proofs. To all of this the *curé* replied that he had acted merely as the agent of the bishop.[25]

On this issue, too, Frontenac came into conflict with the Sovereign Council. Both Desjordy and Cabanac were well connected at the Court, and Frontenac had been requested by de Lagny and *M. le premier*—probably M. Rose, the king's first secretary—to do all he could to advance the careers of these two men.[26] When this case came before the Council, Frontenac tried to force the councillors to state their opinions and to have them recorded individually in the register, apparently intending to make it quite clear to the minister what the attitude of each one of them had been. The Council absolutely refused to countenance any such innovation, and in view of the governor's obvious partiality in the case, they ordered it to be sent to the king.[27]

Soon after his arrival in Montreal the bishop was invited by the Recollets to a ceremony at their church. When St. Vallier entered, the first thing he did was to have the stool used by the governor of Montreal removed from its place of honour and his own installed in its stead. Just as the ceremony was about to begin, Callières walked in; he immediately saw what had happened, and without any ado he took his place at the *prie dieu* near the altar normally used by Frontenac when he attended mass there. St. Vallier immediately rose from his place, went over to Callières, and whispered that he had no right to occupy that place. Callières bristled and replied that he had every right to occupy it. At this the bishop declared that if Callières remained where he was, he himself would leave the church. Callières replied curtly that he was at perfect liberty to do so. St. Vallier then stalked out, leaving Callières in possession of the field, and the ceremony went on without him. Immediately afterwards, Callières, some of his officers and a few others retired to the refectory where they joined the friars at lunch. During the course of the meal several ladies, among them the sister of the superior of the Recollets, entered the refectory and went about the tables with beggars' pouches, imitating the mendicants in a spirit of good-humoured raillery. Having obtained food in this fashion they went out into the refectory garden, where they held an impromptu picnic.[28]

A few days later St. Vallier ordered the Recollets to remove both the stool and the *prie dieu* from the positions they had occupied. The Recollets complied with this order, but when Callières heard of it he had them replaced, declaring publicly that he would place a sentry over them if anyone raised any objections. At this, St. Vallier placed the church under his interdict. The Jesuits and Sulpicians, who had long resented the presence of the mendicants, now began to treat them like pariahs. For two months the Recollets complied with the bishop's harsh order, during which time the intendant did his best to effect a reconciliation; but before this could be done one or the other of the parties concerned had to be willing to give way, and neither of them would budge an inch. Champigny, realizing that it was impossible to reason with unreasonable people, gave up in despair. Then, to make matters worse, the Recollets defied the bishop, reopened their church and began celebrating mass for the public. The situation had now become really serious. Despite repeated warnings from both the bishop and the intendant, the Recollets persisted in their defiance, thereby placing themselves, regardless of any injustice they had suffered, definitely in the wrong. After a further delay of three months, St. Vallier placed them—not just their church, as formerly—under the interdict. To justify this serious step he published two letters of admonition. In one of these he asserted that the superior of the Recollets was linked with the governor of Montreal "by motives so scandalous . . . that they would curl the paper and therefore could not be mentioned in writing," that the superior had tried to compromise his bishop by inviting him to participate in a ceremony at which the governor of Montreal had been given the place of honour, and that this had been followed by an even greater disorder, namely, the scandalous behaviour of several women who had entered the refectory of the Recollets while the friars were there assembled.[29]

When this admonition was read out at mass in the parish church at Montreal, Callières was incensed to hear himself publicly accused by the bishop of having illicit relations with the sister of the superior of the Recollets. While Montreal was still buzzing with

this, the people suddenly heard the urgent beating of a drum rever-
berating through the narrow streets. Rushing out of their houses
they saw the town-major with his escort march to the parish
church, nail a document to the door and post a sentinel beside it to
make sure that it was not torn down. This was Callières' reply to
the bishop. In it he declared, for all who could to read, that the
accusations made against him were completely false. Not satisfied
with this denial he went on to accuse St. Vallier of having used these
false charges as an excuse for his unjust procedure against the
Recollets, and to declare that the interdict against them had been
issued without just cause and contrary to the order's ecclesiastical
privileges.[30]

After this, Callières went down to Quebec and petitioned the
Sovereign Council that reparation be made by the bishop for the
gross insults that he had suffered.[31] This last, however, was merely
a gesture on Callières's part, for there was little or nothing that the
Sovereign Council could do in any of the cases to which the bishop
was a party except to take cognizance of them and refer them to
the king. For his part, St. Vallier informed the Council that he
intended to take ship for France to inform the king of all that had
transpired and he offered to convey any documents the Sovereign
Council cared to entrust to him to the minister.[32] The Sovereign
Council hastily declined the offer, but when one of their own
number, the Sieur de la Martinière, stated that he also was going
to France on private business, the Council readily accepted his offer
to take all the documents pertaining to these cases and hand them
over to the minister.[33]

Then, as though to put the finishing touches to the fracas, the
Sieur de Mareuil, who was challenging the competence of the
Sovereign Council to try him on the grounds that certain of its
members had shown bias towards him, somehow escaped from
custody. Assisted by some of his friends, he then broke into the
seminary gardens, smashed the windows of the bishop's palace and
did other mischief which prudery forbids mentioning. He was
quickly recaptured and, along with one of his accomplices, hauled
before the Provost Court and fined three hundred *livres* and costs
for these acts of vandalism. The original charges against Mareuil
still remained to be adjudicated when the last ships sailed for
France. Then, on November 29, Frontenac intervened. By virtue of
his authority as governor he ordered Mareuil set free and sent the

captain of his guards to release him. In a statement read before the Sovereign Council he made it clear that he was not declaring Mareuil to be innocent of the charges against him and that he would cause the accused to be placed at the disposal of the Council of State when this body had investigated the charges, the evidence and Mareuil's appeal against the Sovereign Council. Champigny and the attorney-general protested, then declared that there was nothing they could do in the face of Frontenac's arbitrary use of his authority; and there the matter rested until the ships returned from France the following summer.[34]

In none of these affairs had Frontenac been directly involved. His clashes with the Sovereign Council had arisen from his not exactly vigorous attempts to protect Mareuil and Desjordy. Moreover, it rather looks as though he spoke the truth when he stated that, in Mareuil's case, the Sovereign Council was more incensed with the person charged than with his alleged crimes. Whether or not he would have intervened in these matters had Mareuil and Desjordy not had influence at the Court is difficult to say, but, in comparison with the lengths to which he was to go to protect his friend and associate, La Mothe Cadillac, three years later, he really had not bestirred himself very much in their behalf. He made no attempt to prevent Mareuil's being taken into custody in the first instance, or to quash his conviction in the Provost Court, and he felt obliged to apologize to de Lagny for not having been able to do more to protect either Mareuil or Desjordy.[35] In his dispute with the bishop over the production of amateur theatricals, it was the latter who had been the instigator of the discord—unless, of course, the bishop's views on the wickedness of the theatre are accepted as being justified at that time and place. In any event, both the minister and the Privy Council considered that Frontenac had behaved correctly in opposing the bishop on this issue.[36] His acceptance of the one hundred *pistoles* from the bishop was a rather more dubious affair. What makes it all the more puzzling is that the bishop later submitted a memoir to the minister requesting that he be reimbursed. He asked that the one hundred *pistoles* be deducted from Frontenac's salary or, failing this, either that he be given a grant by the king for a like amount or else that he be granted two of the twenty-five *congés* issued annually for trading in the Ottawa country which could be sold by the recipient for, at this time, ten to eleven hundred *livres*, one to go to the Hôtel Dieu at Montreal

and the other to the General Hospital.[37] There is no evidence whatsoever that Frontenac allowed *Tartuffe* to be produced, and negative evidence is very convincing in this instance.

When St. Vallier and the Sieur de la Martinière arrived at Versailles with their documents and verbal accounts of these strange
doings, the king ordered that all the evidence in the different cases
should be studied by the *Conseil des Parties*, or Privy Council, the
highest court in the land in civil matters.[38] Frontenac's friends and
relatives, not excluding the minister himself, were quick to rise to
his defence,[39] but they were unable to prevent his being censured.
The minister had to take him to task for not having worked in closer
harmony with the intendant to prevent things getting so completely out of hand. He informed him acidly that the question of
the one hundred *pistoles* "does not show you in any too favourable
a light." And Frontenac was at the same time warned that he
would have to act with more restraint towards the Sovereign
Council in future.[40] Louix XIV was also of the opinion that Frontenac was still far too high-handed in his attitude towards the
Sovereign Council. The minister stated that the king would have
contented himself with ordering both the governor and the attorney-general to keep silence on all that had occurred in the past,
but, out of respect for the royal authority vested in a governor-
general, he had decided to order d'Auteuil to apologize to Frontenac
in front of witnesses. "But I have no compunction in telling you,"
he added, "that His Majesty would take it very ill were you to
accept this with any semblance of its being a public apology and
you must indicate that you are satisfied by the first overtures made
by the attorney-general." As to Frontenac's having laid claim to the
title of chief and president of the Sovereign Council, Pontchartrain
stated bitterly that he had had to assure the king that this had been
merely a slip of the tongue. "I beg of you," he wrote, "be very
careful never to do anything like this again." [41]

Champigny, for his part, was informed that neither the king nor
the minister saw any reason to commend him for the role he had
played in the events of the previous year. He was severely criticized
for not having supported Frontenac with greater vigour in the
latter's attempts to keep the bishop within bounds and so prevent
his encroaching on the royal authority. This pill, however, was
coated with a little sweetening; the minister assured him that he
would call the king's attention, whenever occasion presented itself,

to the efficient and loyal manner in which he was performing his duties. "It is for you to furnish me with the occasions," he added.[42]

The attorney-general did not get off so lightly. Frontenac's supporters at the Court claimed that d'Auteuil had rebelled against the governor's authority and they demanded that he should be dismissed from his post and sent back to France in irons as a warning to others. But d'Auteuil was not without friends and they defended him very ably.[43] He was merely warned by the minister that he had come dangerously close to being dismissed from office, ordered to apologize to Frontenac and told never to behave with such disrespect for the governor's rank and person again.[44] Although Frontenac had been informed indirectly by the king that he was as much to blame as d'Auteuil and ordered to accept the attorney-general's apology without any ado whatsoever, he took advantage of the fact that no one in the colony was aware of his having received any such instructions. He gave it out that the king had placed the attorney-general at his mercy, and when d'Auteuil duly tendered his apology he informed him, with disturbing coolness, that the king had come to no decision in his case, having found the incidents in which he had been involved so serious that he required more time to study them. This left d'Auteuil in a state of great anxiety for the next twelve months, until the following year's dispatches arrived from the Court.[45] When they did arrive, not a word was contained in them concerning the affairs of 1694. At the time Frontenac was very pleased with himself at having scored off d'Auteuil in this fashion and he boasted to de Lagny of how cleverly he had engineered it.[46] But he was highly indignant at the reprimand that he himself had received from the minister, which he considered to be completely undeserved. He had anticipated that d'Autueil would be suspended from his functions for at least a few months, if not permanently, and the other members of the Sovereign Council disciplined for not having rejected out of hand the charges made by the bishop. He declared that the deliberations of the Sovereign Council on this issue should have been ordered removed from the register and officially destroyed to prevent their being used as a precedent in the future.[47]

Callières, for his part, was tersely informed that it would have been far better for him had he not carried things to such extremes.[48] The Sieur de Mareuil, the unwitting but unworthy cause of all the trouble, was ordered to be placed on the first ship sailing for France and the captain instructed to give him into the custody of the intendant at Rochefort, who would have been told what to do with him.[49] Mareuil now disappears from sight and it is doubtful if anyone regretted his passing.

As for Bishop St. Vallier, he quickly alienated everyone at the Court, including the clergy. The members of the Missions Etrangères, the parent order of the seminary at Quebec, would not even have him under their roof and he was obliged to stay with the Sulpicians, who were unable to find a good enough excuse to avoid extending him their hospitality.[50] François de Callières, brother of the governor of Montreal and one of the king's four private secretaries, tried to arrange a face-saving, amicable settlement of his brother's quarrel with the bishop, but when St. Vallier broke a verbal agreement they had made to this end, Callières threw all his considerable influence against him.[51] At the minister's suggestion, St. Vallier called on Mme de Frontenac, who had been making the loudest outcry of anyone, to try to make his peace with her, and through her with Frontenac. But she would have none of it and instead insulted him, whereat he delivered himself of a few choice comments on her husband's mode of life, and was then obliged to show himself to the door.[52]

The minister, the Archbishop of Paris and the king's confessor, Père de la Chaise, were by this time convinced that St. Vallier was completely unfitted for the See at Quebec. Rumours that the king would forbid him to return were picked up and published by newssheets in the Low Countries, which had a wide circulation in Paris and at the Court. This made St. Vallier all the more determined to return to Quebec and when some of his friends advised him not to, he declared that it was imperative he should, for not to do so would be a victory for Frontenac and anyone sent out as bishop in his place would be at a grave disadvantage. This put Louis XIV in a very awkward position; he did not wish to use his authority to prevent St. Vallier returning, but persuasion required both that St. Vallier be amenable, which he was not, and that he be given a post of equivalent rank in France, which the higher clergy would not agree to, pointing out that St. Vallier had proven himself completely unsuited for any position of authority. He had, in fact, made himself look ridiculous; so much so that Mme de Frontenac took a hint from the chancellor, Phélypeaux de Pontchartrain, and ceased agitating to prevent St. Vallier's return to Canada. She now began telling all and sundry at the Court that it would serve her and her husband's interests admirably were he to go back because he was completely without credit at the Court; his complaints would not be listened to, therefore he was no longer to be feared.[53] The minister managed to retain St. Vallier in France only until 1697. During his three-year absence from Quebec tempers cooled and the grand vicar was able to smooth over the trouble with the Recollets and to restore some semblance of peace among the clergy.[54]

Throughout this entire fracas Frontenac had behaved with exemplary restrain and moderation. The person mainly responsible for all the tumult had been the bishop, and Frontenac had suffered a good deal of abuse from this testy prelate without reciprocating in kind. In retrospect, however, the year 1695 is seen to have marked a turning-point in the career of Frontenac. He informed de Lagny he felt secure in the knowledge that he had the active support at the Court not only of his wife and his friends and de Lagny himself, but also of *"le patron et Mr son fils,"* * hence he was sure that he had little to fear from his critics.[55] But in actual fact his influence at the Court was already on the wane. During the previous five years his relations with the intendant had varied from chilly to acrimonious and Champigny had always had to bear the brunt of the blame for their lack of co-operation. The intendant's complaints concerning Frontenac's high-handed practices and his malversations had always been rejected and he had been severely censured for even making them.[56] Champigny had enemies among the senior officials of the Department of Marine who were doing everything they could to discredit him in the eyes of the minister, and his friends feared that no matter how adroit he was in his dealings with Frontenac, it would not be long before he was dismissed from his post.[57] But Champigny's enemies, influential though they were, could not compensate for the fact that Frontenac was, too often, his own worst enemy. By 1695 Pontchartrain had begun to entertain grave doubts that Champigny's assertions were inspired merely by malice; events had shown all too clearly that his reports on the governor's abuses in the fur trade and his inept direction of the war against the Iroquois were justified. The tone of the

* Most likely *le patron* was the chancellor and minister of marine, Louis Phély-peaux de Pontchartrain; *Mr son fils* would then be Jerome Phélypeaux, who succeeded his father as minister of marine in 1699, having acted as his assistant in this post for several years.

minister's letters that accompanied the royal decrees ordering the abandonment of the western posts make this very apparent.

One likely explanation for the change in the minister's attitude is the fact that after 1695 Pontchartrain and Louis XIV began to give their personal attention to the affairs of Canada instead of leaving all but the most important decisions to de Lagny as heretofore. Beginning with 1696, in the margins of the dispatches from Canada there are terse lead-pencilled notes in the hand of Pontchartrain. They clearly indicate that changes had been made in the Ministry of Marine. The most notable thing about these notes is the frequent recurrence of the two words *Au Roy*, indicating that all important questions were to be referred to Louis XIV. This meant, in effect, that from now on Frontenac had to answer to the king for his actions rather than to his kinsman, Pontchartrain.

CHAPTER EIGHTEEN

THE FEUDAL GOVERNOR'S END

IN 1696, after receiving the dispatches from the Court, Frontenac should have realized that from now on he would have to tread very warily indeed. The minister's instructions accompanying the sweeping decisions governing the western fur trade had been couched in uncompromising terms. Pontchartrain had given him notice that his influence at Court would avail him little should he continue to abuse his authority. Yet the following year Frontenac demonstrated that he was incapable of changing his ways. This was made clear by what can only be described as a barefaced attempt on Frontenac's part to cheat a Quebec sea-captain out of his share of a legitimate prize that he had captured on the high seas.

In October, 1696, the Sieur Aubert, son of Aubert de la Chesnaye, who had been one of Frontenac's chief rivals in the fur trade, had left Quebec in his ship, bound for Bayonne in France. Before leaving he had gone through the usual formalities of obtaining a commission and passport from the governor, by virtue of which he was empowered to cross to France and return, and also to attack any enemy ships he might encounter en route. During the return voyage the following summer he sighted an English brigantine, gave chase and captured it, then sailed the prize to Quebec. Immediately upon his arrival he submitted a report of the action to the governor, who sent it on to the intendant. Champigny in turn sent this report to the Sieur de Lotbinière, the lieutenant-general of the Provostship, as the Provost Court normally handled maritime cases. Then the trouble started.

The Sieur Noel, a naval superintendent and a very meddlesome individual, informed Champigny that the commission given Aubert by the governor was invalid because it had not been registered at the Quebec Admiralty Court and that the prize was not a prize at all but a derelict hulk. He also asserted that Aubert had transferred some of the cargo to his own ship and had likely landed part of it at a point down-river. For these reasons he submitted that Champigny should adjudge the prize as a salvaged derelict, one-third of its value to go to the king, one-third to the admiral in France and one-third to Aubert and his crew. Champigny called in Aubert and his men, and also the crew of the prize, for questioning. They all declared that the prize was no derelict, Aubert's ship having chased it for two days and obliged the captain to strike his colours only after several shots had been fired. This satisfied Champigny that the ship was a legitimate prize. As to the transfer of the cargo, Aubert admitted that he had had some of it transferred to his own vessel but stated that he had reported this in the declaration he had made upon his first arrival at Quebec. He denied having discharged any part of the cargo before reaching port.

Next, Champigny examined the validity of Noel's charge that Aubert's commission was invalid because it had not been registered at the Quebec Admiralty Court. He found that, on the contrary, it had been quite in order, and on the basis of this the public prosecutor had no hesitation in declaring the ship and its cargo to be a legitimate prize and that all except a tenth of its assessed value, which was the perquisite of the admiral, should be adjudged to Aubert. Noel then presented a second petition, demanding that the prize be adjudged one-third to the king, one-third to Aubert, one-third to Frontenac for having issued the commission, and nothing to the admiral. Champigny disregarded this and had the case heard before a prize court composed of himself, the three senior members of the Sovereign Council and the lieutenant-general of the Provostship, this being the custom laid down by the king's ordinance governing the adjudication of prizes in the French government of the Americas (*Isles de l'Amérique*) that the Quebec prize courts had always followed in the past. After studying all the evidence, the members of the court had no hesitation in awarding the prize to Aubert, and they ordered that the admiral's tenth should be paid to the clerk of the treasurer-general of the navy, to be held pending the king's instructions.

This done, on the ninth of July notices of sale were published. Three weeks later, just as the sale was about to take place, Frontenac's secretary appeared on the scene with an ordinance dated the previous day which he proceeded to read out to the assembled officials and prospective bidders. This ordinance stated that since the Sieur Noel had made a verbal complaint to the governor that the judgement of the prize court was contrary to the king's interests, the proceeds of the sale were to be paid over to an individual by the name of Louisière. The lieutenant-general immediately suspended the proceedings and went to confer with the intendant. Meanwhile, several merchants coming away from the abortive auction encountered Noel. They told him what had happened and accused him of being the cause of the trouble. Noel, whose main fault seems to have been that he was too officious, was very disturbed by this; he sought out the intendant and informed him that he had had no part in this move by Frontenac and very definitely had not made any complaint such as Frontenac had stated in his ordinance. To make quite certain that he would not be misrepresented further, he made a written statement on the spot, formally declaring that he had never made any such complaint as had been alleged by Frontenac, either verbally or in writing. Four days later Champigny convened the members of the prize court again and it was decided that the only thing they could do was refer the case to the king and advise the Sieur Aubert to appeal to Frontenac personally to rescind his ordinance.

Aubert was extremely loath to see Frontenac's nominee, Louisière, get his hands on the money, for, as Champigny remarked, this man was of no standing in the colony and without any assets, being merely a minor official in the Quebec office of the Company of the Farm with a salary of only six hundred *livres* a year. Aubert submitted written appeals to Frontenac offering to give any security the governor cared to name while the case was referred to the Court, provided that the proceeds of the ship's sale should be paid over to him. He also suggested that these funds could be handed over to the treasurer's clerk and letters of exchange issued, to be made out to whomsoever the king should decide. Frontenac did not even acknowledge Aubert's appeals; instead he forced the lieutenant of the Provostship to sell the prize and pay over the proceeds, which amounted to the tidy sum of 80,000 *livres*, to this shadowy individual, Louisière. At this, Aubert determined to cross to France and plead his case personally at Versailles, but when he asked for a passport and a commission for his ship, Frontenac, realizing full well what Aubert intended, refused the request. Thus Aubert was obliged to pay off his crew, lay up his ship and wait until he could get passage on a merchantman.

Champigny later gave it as his opinion that Frontenac was under the impression that the privileges of the admiral were his personal perquisite, and he may not have been far wrong; a few years earlier

Frontenac had asked de Lagny whether or not he could claim all the prizes brought into ports within his government, it being his belief that he could.[1] What de Lagny's answer was is not known. Champigny pointed out that Frontenac had, by annulling the judgement of the prize court, appointed himself sovereign judge over matters dealt with by a court duly constituted by the king; moreover, the very fact that Frontenac had undertaken to render judgement in a case in which he stood to make a sizeable profit was in itself highly irregular.[2] Both Frontenac and Champigny were apparently unaware of the fact that in 1684 the king had declared: "The governor and lieutenant-general has no authority whatsoever over admiralty cases nor any authority over the officers who render justice in such matters." [3]

Frontenac complained to the minister of Champigny's attitude over "a little dispute . . . concerning a judgement which he, with certain councillors of the Sovereign Council, rendered in the adjudication of a prize . . . and of which I felt obliged to suspend the execution." He maintained that he had taken this action only because the intendant had not made proper provision for the safeguarding of the king's and the admiral's shares of the proceeds of the sale of the prize. He also stated that some of the officials who had executed his own ordinance had been subjected to threats and calumnies by the intendant, but that despite Champigny's displays of rancour he had refused to be deterred from doing what he had felt to be his duty.[4]

The minister was singularly unimpressed by Frontenac's version of events. Before submitting the case to the king he wrote to the governor, warning him that his overruling the judgement of the prize court was completely *ultra vires* and that he had no doubt whatsoever that the king would disallow his ordinance.* He advised him to set about immediately to repair as best he could the damage he had done.[5] Two months later Pontchartrain wrote to Frontenac again; apparently the king had taken an even sterner view of the whole affair than the minister had expected, for this time he stated:

The dispute that you have had with M. de Champigny over the prize taken by the Sieur Aubert is very poorly founded and I

* It would seem safe to conclude from this, and from negative evidence, that Aubert finally received the proceeds of his prize. Had he not there undoubtedly would have been further correspondence about it, but the matter is not mentioned again.

must confess that I fail to grasp how you could have been the author of such an incident, the unpleasant reactions to which, in spite of all the good will I bear you, it will be impossible for me to prevent. It is, in truth, unfortunate both for you and for me that instead of being able to use my influence to obtain for you His Majesty's favour, you oblige me to make excuses for a wild behaviour which gains you nothing and which is very difficult to account for. I beg of you to be more careful in future and on no account to listen to persons who, for reasons of personal gain, commit and expose you to this sort of vexation. I have been obliged to issue an edict confirming that of M. de Champigny and removing the injunction which you had placed on it.[6]

In his reply Frontenac appeared no whit chastened. He declared that he had only been trying to do his duty as he saw it, his main regret being the trouble he had unwittingly caused the minister in the latter's efforts to excuse his actions to the king. But the minister's charge that he had been influenced by the counsels of others really flicked him on the raw and he hotly denied that anyone had any such influence over him. "I alone am the author," he declared, "and it is on me alone that the blame must fall if such be merited." He then went on to blame the entire episode on the machinations of the intendant and his supporters at the Court who were, he lamented, constantly seeking to slander him in every way possible.[7]

What the minister thought of this, and of Frontenac, is summed up in one brief sentence. In the margin of the abstract of Frontenac's dispatch occurs in Pontchartrain's hand the terse, exasperated phrase: "He has always done the wrong thing."[8]

The dust had barely had a chance to settle, following this conflict, when a fresh dispute arose which had legal and constitutional implications more serious than those at stake in the Aubert case. This time the trouble began with a civil action taken against La Mothe Cadillac, the commander at Michilimackinac, by two coureurs de bois named Moreau and Durand. This was its rather prosaic beginning, but it soon developed into an all-out constitutional struggle between Frontenac and Cadillac on one side and Champigny and the Sovereign Council on the other.

This man Cadillac was, without a shadow of a doubt, one of the worst scoundrels ever to set foot in New France. On several occasions he had run afoul of the intendant but each time Frontenac had intervened to prevent his being brought to account for his misdemeanours. Cadillac's antecedents were, to say the least, dubious. He was the son of a provincial judge in Gascony and his real name was Antoine Laumet. He first appeared on the Canadian scene in Acadia after having lived in the English colonies for a number of years. By this time he had assumed a name, a title of nobility, a family tree, a coat of arms * and a commission as lieutenant in the regular army, all of them false.[9] The Sieur de Meneval, governor of Acadia, described him in the following words: "This Cadillac, the most malicious type in the world, is a rattle-head, chased out of France for I know not what crimes." Meneval complained in the most vigorous terms of Cadillac's conduct, accusing him of continual plotting and scheming and of trying to embroil him in quarrels with the clergy; failing in this, Cadillac and his cronies had done everything they could to vilify both Meneval and the priests, the better to carry on their illegal sale of brandy to the Indians.[10] The Department of Marine was not unaware of Cadillac's character: in the margin of Meneval's dispatch an official wrote: "He has been recognized as being, in fact, very sharp and capable of the practices that M. de Meneval has observed. He is an adventurer who has travelled far and wide in North America and has thus acquired a first-hand knowledge of those parts. He is mentally well endowed, claims to be of the nobility and to have held a commission as captain in the infantry. Recently he settled in Acadia."[11] Persons having an exact knowledge of the English colonies were rare in the French service, and this asset, combined with a very glib tongue, gained Antoine Laumet, *alias* La Mothe de Cadillac, the support of the minister, who decided he would be a useful man to have around in the event an expedition were to be launched at some future date against New York or Boston.[12] And so it happened that Cadillac was sent to New France, Frontenac being requested to "give him some fitting employment and to assist him as much as possible."[13]

In the summer of 1691 he arrived at Quebec with his family but with not a penny to his name, whereupon Frontenac gave him a half-pay commission in the Troupes de la Marine.[14] He very quickly gained Frontenac's confidence and was soon one of his closest

* This coat of arms has endured far longer, and in more imposing company, than Cadillac could ever have envisaged. It serves today as the crest of a well-known make of automobile.

associates in the fur trade. In 1694 de Lagny was instrumental in obtaining for him a commission as captain and a naval ensign's warrant. Cadillac thought this last was inadequate for a man of his years and experience—he was then thirty-six—and requested that he be given the rank of naval lieutenant. He did, however, show his gratitude for past favours by sending his benefactor a barrel of maple syrup. This sweet gift, de Lagny commented, never arrived.[15] That same year Frontenac sent Cadillac to replace Louvigny as commandant at Michilimackinac, and in very short order the Jesuit missionaries were complaining bitterly of his conduct, particularly of his trading brandy wholesale to the Indians. Frontenac was obliged to warn de Lagny to be prepared to defend Cadillac when these complaints reached the Court.[16] Le Roy de la Potherie later remarked: "It is known that Cadillac does not exactly have an aura of sanctity and . . . that he made a great deal of money while he was at Michilimackinac by means of the brandy trade."[17] And the Sieur de la Touche, the intendant's deputy at Montreal, declared in 1697 that when the king's edict was published ordering all the *coureurs de bois* up country to return to Montreal, Cadillac had allowed all those who paid him a large enough amount of beaver pelts to disregard the order. "Never has a man amassed so much money in so short a time, nor caused so much commotion as a result of the injuries suffered by the individuals who advance the funds for this trade," wrote la Touche.[18] It was by such means that by 1705, fourteen years after his penniless arrival in New France, Cadillac was in a position to offer to pay 1,400,000 *livres* for a monopoly on the purchase of all the beaver pelts in Canada.[19]

By 1697 Champigny had received numerous verbal complaints from *congé* holders concerning Cadillac's abuses and had written to him several times ordering him to abide by the king's edicts governing up-country trading, but Cadillac had always denied that there was any basis to the complaints against him or that he was contravening the king's edicts, stating that he would easily be able to convince the intendant of this when he returned to the colony.[20] In September, 1697, he did return to Quebec, whereupon the *coureurs de bois* Moreau and Durand presented a petition against him to the intendant. In this petition they declared that they had been hired by Mme Cadillac for one hundred *livres* each to take a canoe-load of trade goods to her husband at Michilimackinac. Frontenac gave them a permit for the trip, allowing them to take one hundred *livres'* worth of merchandise for their own account, over and above the amount of their wages. Mme Cadillac, however, had them take not one but two canoes of trade goods and they added another four to five hundred *livres'* worth of contraband of their own. Then, while they were loading the canoes, the Sieur de la Touche, the intendant's deputy at Montreal, caught them in the act and seized part of the contraband. Three other canoes loaded with contraband for Cadillac managed to evade detection, and when Moreau and Durand reached Michilimackinac they bought 7,000 *livres'* worth of trade goods from him on credit at Michilimackinac prices; included in these goods were 198 jugs of brandy at twenty-five *livres* the jug that had cost Cadillac only three *livres* a jug in Montreal. It is easy to see from this transaction how a man in Cadillac's position could amass a fortune in a few years.

About a month after this transaction took place, Cadillac had Durand imprisoned for refusing to pay for an Indian's dog which it was claimed he had injured. At this, Durand told Cadillac that he no longer wished to buy the trade goods which he and Moreau had contracted for, and Moreau informed Cadillac that he would not take these goods just for his own account alone. Cadillac then threw Moreau into gaol too, on the pretext that he had threatened to shoot Durand. While the two of them were locked up, Cadillac seized not only the disputed trade goods but also all their personal belongings, including their arms, wine, canoes and food supplies. Not satisfied with this he broke open their strong-boxes. In Moreau's he found some I O U's and a promissory note as well as some other papers, all of which he seized on the grounds that they contained evidence that the prisoners had brought contraband goods up country. A few days later Cadillac set them free. When they found themselves fleeced of everything except the clothes on their backs, they were obliged to borrow a supply of trade goods from some of the other *coureurs de bois*, which they proceeded to trade in the Sioux country.

Upon their return to the colony they patiently waited for Cadillac to come down to Quebec so that they could demand justice. There is some evidence to indicate that this was regarded as a test case throughout the colony, and it may well be that persons of considerable influence and authority—the intendant, even—were urging these two lowly *coureurs de bois* to take their case to the Sovereign Council. The Sieur de la Touche remarked in a letter to the minister that many more who had suffered in similar fashion at the hands of Cadillac would have stepped forward to demand justice had it not been that because Cadillac was protected by Frontenac they were afraid to complain.[21]

In their petition to the intendant, Moreau and Durand demanded that Cadillac should pay them the two hundred *livres* he owed for their wages, and reimburse them for their property that he had seized, including the amount of Moreau's I O U's and promissory note since he could not collect from his debtors for lack of them, plus costs and damages with interest. Cadillac's claim that he had seized their property because they had smuggled contraband up country, they stated, should be disallowed since this contraband had been transported in the same canoes that had carried contraband for Cadillac himself, and, as they rather naïvely put it, they had as much right to smuggle trade goods up country as he had. In his defence Cadillac stated that the contraband which he had seized from the plaintiffs was his perquisite as post commander, that since they had broken their contract they were liable for some part of the 7,000 *livres'* worth of trade goods that he had sold them, and finally, that he could not be liable for debts owed to Moreau if the latter's debtors refused to pay.

Both parties having stated their case before the intendant and submitted their written statements to him, Champigny was about to take the issue before the Sovereign Council for hearing and judgement when the litigants decided to have the case settled by arbitration before two Quebec merchants. This procedure being quite in order, Champigny sent the arbitrators the documents on the case and asked them to return these documents to him once they had rendered their decision. During the course of this arbitration, however, Durand became afraid, for some reason that is not made clear in the evidence, and withdrew from the litigation. Then new disputes arose over certain points and the arbitrators asked that a court of inquiry be set up to clarify these particular issues. Champigny obliged by issuing an ordinance appointing the Sieur Dupuy of the Provost Court to hold this inquiry.

What Dupuy was required to establish was the price of trade goods at three specific places: Michilimackinac, Chagouamigon and the Sioux country. Although the arbitrators had not given any indication as to why they wished a judicial inquiry on this matter, Cadillac was quick to see its purpose. Moreau had traded the goods he had borrowed, upon his release from prison, with the Sioux, where their value was many times greater than at Michilimackinac. Cadillac now grew afraid that Moreau was going to demand reimbursement for his seized goods at Sioux prices. He voiced his opposition to any such inquiry on the grounds that as commanding officer at Michilimackinac he had forbidden trading in the Sioux country on orders from Frontenac. Moreau countered by maintaining that Frontenac's order had merely forbidden travel to the Sioux country through the lands of the Fox tribe, and that Cadillac himself had sent canoes to trade with the Sioux via the Illinois territory, as had several other traders. Dupuy then suspended the hearing to permit Cadillac to obtain proof of his allegation that Frontenac had forbidden all trading in the Sioux country. Cadillac failed to produce any statement from the governor on this point, submitting instead a written statement of his own to the effect that no one had been allowed to go to the Sioux country without first obtaining the governor's permission. At this, Dupuy reopened the inquiry, declaring that there was no cause for terminating it, since Cadillac had failed to produce any grounds for such action other than his personal statement, which was inadmissible since he was one of the parties in the case. The next day Frontenac sent for Dupuy and his clerk, read the record of their inquiry, then remarked that it had been established by virtue only of a decree issued by the arbitrators. Dupuy replied that he had been duly empowered to hold this court of inquiry by an ordinance issued by the intendant, whereat Frontenac is quoted by Champigny as having stated: "It is because of that that I am sending you to gaol," and Dupuy was thrown in the cells, where he remained for two days.

The two arbitrators, upon hearing of this and in the face of threats of being served in a similar fashion, retired from the case. Moreau, however, refused to be intimidated, and he immediately presented his petition anew to the intendant, who submitted the whole affair to the Sovereign Council for hearing and judgement.[22] This litigation now became far more than a civil suit between two private parties; it developed into a test of strength between the governor and the Sovereign Council to see whether or not the governor and his friends were above the law.

La Mothe Cadillac was under no delusions as to where the sympathies of the members of the Sovereign Council lay, and consequently he tried by every possible means to prevent their hearing the case. His opening gambit was to present two petitions, one demanding that the intendant should abstain from taking any part in judging the action on the grounds that he had shown prejudice, and the other that the case should be heard in the Provost Court and not before the Sovereign Council.[23] Champigny declared that the first petition could not be entertained because by the terms of his commission his authority to hear and judge cases could not be challenged, and that the litigation could not be heard by the Provost Court because the lieutenant-general of that court was a close relative of Cadillac's wife.[24] The attorney-general pointed out too that Frontenac had previously committed a judge of that court to gaol for merely complying with an ordinance of the intendant and such intimidation rendered impossible any thought of a fair trial being held there.[25]

Cadillac next began challenging various members of the Sovereign Council on technical grounds, declaring that they had shown partiality to Moreau in one way or another, but the attorney-general flatly declared all Cadillac's grounds for so doing to be invalid. Finding themselves checked at every turn and faced with a hostile court, Cadillac and Frontenac now resorted to a stratagem which, if it had been tolerated, would have established a very dangerous precedent. On March 10 Frontenac informed the Council that since Cadillac's demand that his case be heard in the Provost Court had been denied, and since all subjects of the king had the right to appeal against the decisions of the *Parlements* and superior courts to the king's Privy Council, he as governor could not permit the Sovereign Council to proceed with the case because Cadillac was going to take it before this court of last resort in France. He then stated that he had no wish to cause the assembled company any trouble, but desired only to conserve for the king's subjects the right to avail themselves of the privileges the king had seen fit to grant them, and he warned d'Auteuil that it was his duty as attorney-general to maintain these privileges so far as lay in his power.

This totally unexpected manoeuvre took the Council by surprise. D'Auteuil, however, was equal to the occasion. He replied that although it was perfectly true that he was bound to maintain the privileges of the king's subjects, it was also his bounden duty to watch that nothing should be undertaken contrary to the decrees of the Sovereign Council at Quebec. This rejoinder caused Frontenac to lose control of his temper; jumping up from his seat he shouted that if the Council did not pay heed to what it had been told it would quickly learn which way its duty lay. And with this threat he stalked out of the chamber.[26]

At a subsequent meeting of the Council, d'Auteuil, quoting precedents, gave his interpretation of the statutes and subsequent royal ordinances whereby the Sovereign Council had been established and its prerogatives defined, all of which, in his considered opinion, made it clear that Cadillac's petition and Frontenac's injunction in support of it were completely contrary to the letter and the spirit of the law, being, in fact, nothing more than legal chicanery. D'Auteuil and Champigny both stated that it was merely a trick to prevent Moreau bringing the case before any court of law, since the governor and Cadillac knew full well that Moreau lacked the means to plead his case in France. Although it was quite true that anyone could take his case to a higher court, it was unheard of for a case to be taken to an appeal court before it had even been heard in the lower courts. To permit such a procedure, they argued, would establish a precedent whereby in any litigation between a rich and a poor man, the former could always evade justice by having the case withdrawn to a court three thousand miles away.[27]

Had it not been that the Perrot case of 1674 had occurred before the time of d'Auteuil and Champigny,[28] they could have shown that Frontenac had not always held the views he expressed in 1698. At the time of that earlier dispute, Frontenac had strongly denied Perrot's claim that he could not be tried by the Sovereign Council but only by the king, on the grounds that this would mean anyone could evade justice in Canada by having his case sent to France.[29]

The Sovereign Council was now in a difficult position; iniquitous though they considered the governor's actions to be, there was little they could do about them. But they had to decide on some action, if only for the record; Frontenac and Champigny were requested to retire from the chamber while the Council discussed what best to do. At first Frontenac balked at this, but finally gave way, and he and the intendant retired. After some deliberation the Council decided to evade the issue by asking the intendant to grant them leave not to proceed with the case and at the same time they requested him in his official capacity to deal with it as best he saw fit. They also asked that all the records relating to the affair should be sent to the minister. This done, they requested Champigny and

Frontenac to return and informed them of their decision. Frontenac took it to mean that the Council had deferred to his demands, and he proceeded to congratulate them on having refrained from continuing a course of action that was highly irregular, quite contrary to the king's ordinances, and one which would have resulted in their being reprimanded severely by the king. He added, for good measure, that he would not fail to inform the king of the reprehensible conduct of the attorney-general who, instead of supporting him in his efforts to uphold the royal ordinances and prevent the Council contravening them, had pursued a contrary course.

But Frontenac had reckoned without the intendant. The moment that Frontenac concluded his remarks Champigny rose in his place and stated that in conformity with the edict of the Council just passed, he would himself hear the case of Moreau versus La Mothe Cadillac and render judgement on it by virtue of his commission as intendant of justice. For Frontenac's especial benefit he added that he would advise His Majesty of the excellent manner in which the Council had handled the affair, and particularly that it had done nothing that was not in strict accordance with the king's ordinances. At this, Frontenac, who was almost livid with rage, turned on the intendant and declared that if he judged the case he would have to answer to the king for his actions.[30] Champigny was not to be frightened so easily; in his dispatch to the minister he called Pontchartrain's particular attention to Frontenac's threat and asked that the governor be taken at his word, thereby making it quite clear that he would like nothing better than to have the whole matter brought to the attention of Louis XIV.

When Champigny called the case before him, Cadillac refused to appear. Champigny then rendered judgement in favour of Moreau, ordering Cadillac to pay the plaintiff the separate sums of 1,860 *livres* 4 *deniers*, 600 *livres* and 99 *livres*, approximately $2,560 in present-day currency. Considering all the turmoil that this case had caused, these amounts were not excessive, and their payment would certainly not have caused Cadillac any great financial distress. Then, the day after this judgement was handed down, Frontenac issued an ordinance forbidding its execution. Thus Moreau was still no better off than he had been when he first presented his petition to the intendant six months previously. In fact, he was in a worse position, for when he tried to sign on as a member of the crew on a fishing boat Frontenac ordered that he was not to leave the confines of Quebec. Whether this was done out of vindictiveness or from fear that Moreau might somehow manage to make his way to France is not known. But one thing had been made very clear to everyone in the colony: those who enjoyed Frontenac's protection were above the law.

In summing up this case in his report to the minister, Champigny quoted from the king's official instructions to the governor wherein it was clearly stated that Frontenac was not to interfere in any way in affairs of justice, but only to assist and support the intendant and the Sovereign Council in the execution of their duties. Instead of this, Champigny pointed out, Frontenac had done exactly the opposite, having thrown the Sieur Dupuy in gaol, threatened the arbitrators with similar treatment just when they were about to render their judgement, threatened at one point to ship the attorney-general to France, and, finally, having annulled a judgement handed down by the intendant. Nor was this all that Champigny had to say; he went on to make a strong plea that steps be taken to put an end to Frontenac's all-too-frequent interference in the rendering of justice. To Pontchartrain he wrote:

> There is not a single man in Canada who can render justice freely without being exposed to very grievous annoyances. I should add that anyone having a claim against a person in the Governor's favour is well advised to withhold all proceedings. Others have felt compelled to protest secretly against a course of conduct which they have been forced to follow at the instance of the Governor himself, in which matters recourse should have been had to the ordinary courts of justice. The mischief, my lord, is great and it is of the utmost importance that a remedy be found whereby justice may be rendered freely without its being dependent on, or subordinate to, the harsh authority of the Governor.[31]

Although he had been frustrated by Frontenac in the Moreau case, Champigny was by no means done with Cadillac. He now began to take action against him for his contravention of the king's edicts governing the trading of furs by officers in the Troupes de la Marine and the peddling of brandy to the Indians up country. Enough evidence had come to light in Moreau's and Cadillac's own testimony to warrant his taking such action; but once again Frontenac checked him by confirming Cadillac's statement in his own defence that he had had the governor's sanction for his entire conduct of affairs at Michilimackinac. To cap it all, feeling secure in the knowledge that with Frontenac giving him his unconditional support the intendant could do nothing, Cadillac sneeringly accused Champigny to his face of having himself been engaged in the brandy traffic with the Ottawas. This infuriated the long-suffering intendant almost beyond endurance.

Then, while Champigny was still smarting under this last slanderous insult, the entire affair was resolved in a manner so unexpected that Champigny found himself in a rather false position. The way in which this came about is rather mysterious. All that is known is that a certain Marquis de Coutré suddenly appeared on the scene and that he was probably a naval officer—Champigny mentions that he was greatly indebted to the marquis for his courtesy and kindness in affording Mme de Champigny passage over to France. One thing is certain, this Marquis de Coutré must have been a person with considerable prestige as well as a very gifted diplomat, for he not only induced Cadillac to apologize to Champigny in the presence of himself and the Chevalier de Vaudreuil, but he also prevailed upon Cadillac to make a just settlement of Moreau's claims. When this had been done Champigny, most likely at the marquis's instigation, included in his next dispatch to the minister a rather grudging request that Cadillac's past excesses be overlooked.

It would be very interesting indeed to know how the Marquis de Coutré managed to bring this about; but regardless of how it was done, it constituted in effect a moral victory for Champigny, Cadillac's settlement of Moreau's claims being a tacit acknowledgement that he had been in the wrong. The bitterness and rancour, however, were not entirely dispersed; the legal questions involved still remained at issue and Champigny, to prevent any repetition of such troubles, asked the minister to decide once and for all whether or not Frontenac could force the Sovereign Council to defer to his opinions and whether or not he had the right to veto the intendant's judgements and forbid their being executed. Since he could not believe that this was the case he requested the minister to remedy the existing state of affairs "so that I shall not be exposed to the contempt of the people." [32]

Cadillac, who crossed over to France on private business, took with him Frontenac's dispatches to the Department of Marine. In them, the governor said nothing of the disputes of the past year, contenting himself with recommending Cadillac to the minister in glowing terms.[33] But to his friend de Lagny he was very scathing in his denunciation of the intendant. He wrote:

> After having laboured for nine years to gain the friendship of M. de Champigny, and having, to that end, done all that a very passionate lover would have done in order to overcome the rigours of his mistress, and without success, I have finally resolved to console myself and to think only of defending myself against all the stratagems which he continually employs to involve me in fresh controversies by methods so black and so villainous that they would horrify anyone who had a scrap of honour or probity. But that does not prevent my being on terms of perfect civility with him and it will never cause me to do anything which could hinder or prejudice the king's service.[34]

A few weeks later Frontenac abruptly ceased his quarrelling and made his peace with the intendant. For some little time he had been suffering from asthma, which necessitated his sleeping propped up in an arm-chair. On November 16, remarking to one of his officers that he felt far from well, he sent for his physician and demanded to be told the truth concerning his condition. The doctor could only confirm Frontenac's worst fears. Each day now his strength ebbed a little. Finally, his confessor had to suggest that he should begin to search his conscience and prepare for the repose of his soul. Frontenac then requested that he be given the viaticum. Monsignor St. Vallier himself came to the château to administer it while the church bells began to toll. After receiving the eucharist, as so often is the case, Frontenac's strength appeared to revive, but an officer who was present remarked that "this change was rather like a lamp that, before going out, musters all its forces in one final effort."[35]

On November 22 Frontenac made his will. It is a very short document and not very revealing. He requested that his body should be interred in the church of the Recollets at Quebec, but that his heart should first be removed and placed in a lead or silver receptacle, then sent to the chapel of St. Nicholas des Champs in Paris where his sister and uncle had been interred. He bequeathed 1,500 *livres* to the Recollets to have a low mass celebrated every day for a year for the repose of his soul; at the end of the year a similar mass was to be said annually on the anniversary of his death, and upon the death of Mme de Frontenac for them jointly in perpetuity. His first secretary, Monseignat, and the Sieur Hazeur, a merchant of Quebec, were named executors of his estate and Champigny was requested to lend them the protection of his authority in the execution of their office. Champigny was also requested to make whatever arrangements he deemed necessary for the satisfaction of Frontenac's domestic staff. To his valet, Frontenac bequeathed his entire wardrobe and a small silver plaque. The residue of his estate, once his debts in Canada had been discharged, he requested should be paid into the hands of his wife.[36]

Champigny, when he first learned that Frontenac was dying, immediately expunged from his mind all the bitter feelings of the past and placed himself entirely at the governor's service. Frontenac was not unappreciative of this and he asked the intendant to accept a crucifix that he had received from his sister at the time of her death and which he had always treasured. To Mme de Champigny he bequeathed a reliquary which he described as "filled with the most rare and precious relics that could be found."[37] On November 28, 1698, after receiving extreme unction from the bishop, the old courtier departed this world.

This was the first time that a royal governor had died in the colony, and the people of that day greatly enjoyed the pomp and circumstance of a grand funeral. During the three days preceding the funeral, cannon were fired every half hour. On the day itself, troops lined the route from the Château St. Louis to the cathedral, where the bishop officiated at a high mass, and then lined the way from the cathedral to the Recollets' church, where the interment took place.[38] There, Father Olivier Goyer, the superior of the Recollets, delivered a funeral eulogy which was considered by some to have been far too fulsome for even such an occasion.[39]

There can be little doubt, however, that Champigny, for one, was deeply moved by the death of Frontenac, despite all that had passed between them. In a dispatch which, owing to the lateness of the season, he had to send by way of New England to inform the minister of the governor's demise, he wrote:

. . . the Comte de Frontenac died on the 28th of November last with the sentiments of a true Christian. You may perhaps find it hard to believe, my lord, that I was deeply moved by his death in spite of the strained relations that had existed between us. The truth of the matter is that our misunderstandings sprang solely from a divergence of opinion as to what was best for the king's service. As private persons, we never quarrelled. Also I must state that during his last illness he used me most civilly; it would be ungrateful of me not to acknowledge the fact. His last will and testament, in brief form, of which I enclose a copy, bears this out. I shall watch over its execution and pay special attention to the Comtesse de Frontenac's interests.[40]

Champigny was as good as his word. He saw to it that Mme de Frontenac received the monies that remained once her husband's estate had been settled. He also sequestered all Frontenac's official and private papers. When the town-major of Quebec expressed a desire to assist him in going through them, Champigny politely but firmly declined the offer. He later informed the minister that he had considered it prudent to deny the major because it would have done no good for everyone to know all about Frontenac's and the colony's affairs.[41] He undoubtedly showed commendable respect for the dead in acting thus, but at the same time he may well have deprived historians of a later age of much vital information.

Although surprised at the depth of his own feelings at the time of Frontenac's death, Champigny made it plain to the minister that he had no desire to endure again the sort of troubles that he had had to suffer during the preceding nine years; thus, he asked, "the foremost favour that I could ask of you, my lord, is that you send us a governor who has no other aim but to carry out the king's orders and enable me to act in concert with him with the deference that is his due, and always to abide by my instructions. In truth, my lord, it is hard on a man who wishes to serve the king well to see the contrary." [42]

The news of Frontenac's death reached the Court before the minister had drafted his own dispatches in reply to those of the previous year from Canada. Consequently, what the official reaction would have been to the events of 1698, the Cadillac case, and the reports of the continued abuses at the western posts can only be guessed at. A few clues, however, are provided by the minister's marginal comments in the abstracts of the 1698 correspondence; in that of Frontenac's dispatch there occurs little but the one word *Non* or a single large *N*, signifying opposition to or denial of his requests and suggestions. Interspersed among these negatives are terse but scathing comments which indicate clearly that Pontchartrain was by this time completely disgusted with Frontenac's conduct. By contrast, in the margin of Champigny's dispatches Pontchartrain's remarks consist of little but the one word *Bon* beside each paragraph.[43]

If Frontenac had lived it would have been impossible for Pontchartrain to keep Louis XIV in ignorance of the fact that the governor had been involved in further bitter disputes with the Sovereign Council and the intendant. In the Aubert case Pontchartrain had been hard put to it to defend Frontenac's actions before Louis. Had the king now perused the documents in the Cadillac case, containing as they did such clear-cut evidence not only of Frontenac's further abuse of his authority in the affairs of justice, but also of his total disregard for the recently issued royal edicts governing the fur trade, it is more than likely that the minister would have been ordered to recall Frontenac immediately. It was perhaps a blessing in disguise that death spared Louis XIV and Pontchartrain the necessity for this decision.

CHAPTER NINETEEN

WAR'S END

UPON the death of Frontenac, Callières, being the senior officer in the colony, took over the functions of governor. He wasted no time in sending an officer to Versailles, by way of New England, to inform the Court of Frontenac's demise and to submit his plea that he be given the permanent appointment to the post of governor-general.[1] Vaudreuil also sent an emissary for the same purpose.[2] Callières was in much the stronger position in this contest; he was the acting governor and his brother, François de Callières, was one of the king's private secretaries. Thus it is hardly surprising that he, rather than Vaudreuil, received the commission the following summer, and, all things considered, his appointment certainly was not unmerited.

By far the most important problem with which Callières now found himself faced was negotiating a treaty of peace between the French and their allies and the Iroquois. This task, which involved reconciling conflicts among some twenty-eight different tribes and expunging the hatreds and rancours that had existed beyond living memory, was made even more difficult by the fact that the English of New York were determined to prevent the Iroquois from acting as their own plenipotentiaries. The Earl of Bellomont maintained that the Iroquois were subjects of his Britannic Majesty and therefore he, as governor of New York, must negotiate for them.[3] Callières refused to entertain any such notion, and it is a measure of his skill as a diplomat that he finally succeeded in besting the English in this game of frontier power politics. He did so by playing on the pride of the Iroquois; he told them that he had been given to understand that they were subjects of the English and unable to negotiate for themselves. When taunted in this fashion, the Iroquois chiefs proudly declared that they were subjects neither of the French nor of the English, but were their own masters.[4] Callières also received unlooked-for assistance from the English; a clique of Albany merchants had recently attempted to defraud the Mohawks of a large tract of their lands. Although the royal officials in both New York and Whitehall quickly quashed the scheme, the damage had been done. The Iroquois were now anything but kindly disposed towards their former allies.[5]

It was, however, only after much haggling, which tried Callières's patience to the limit—at one point he declared his intention to invade the Iroquois cantons in force unless they changed their attitude [6]—that they entered seriously into negotiations. Throughout these discussions the governor was greatly assisted by three men who had won the respect of the Iroquois; they were the Jesuit, Father Bruyas, the Sieur le Moyne de Maricourt and the Sieur Jonquaire. The prestige of the Le Moyne family had always been great among the Iroquois; Charles le Moyne, father of Maricourt, had been adopted into the Onondaga nation and his sons were all revered as great warriors. Father Bruyas, who had frequently acted as Frontenac's interpreter, had won their respect through sheer strength of character, and the Sieur Jonquaire had been adopted into the Onondaga nation. During the war Jonquaire had been taken prisoner by the Onondagas; when he was brought before their council to determine his fate, a chief had begun to amuse himself by thrusting the prisoner's finger-tips into the glowing bowl of his pipe. Jonquaire had responded with a swift blow of his fist which smashed the chief's nose. The Iroquois, who admired nothing so much as courage, had been greatly impressed with this show of spirit; so much so, in fact, that they spared Jonquaire's life, adopted him into their tribe, and gave him one of their young women as wife.[7]

It was these three men who, at the request of the Iroquois, went to their cantons to thrash out the details of the treaty.[8] Neither the Earl of Bellomont nor the local authorities at Albany had men of this stature whom they could employ in their constant efforts to spoil the French plans. Thus, when an Albany representative rose in the council meeting at Onondaga and forbade the Iroquois to speak with the French, Father Bruyas taunted them, asking if they were the dogs of the English, or their prisoners, or did the English intend war again?[9] And when Bellomont, in order to hold the Iroquois to the English cause, tried to persuade them to allow him to build a fort at Onondaga with a garrison of one hundred troops and twenty-four guns, their council refused to hear of it.[10]

The most difficult question, the one that delayed the negotiations for over two years and came close to preventing any treaty from being negotiated at all, was that concerning the prisoners of war.

All the nations demanded that the enemy must return their prisoners, but it proved extremely difficult to obtain any satisfaction from the Iroquois. Each time their ambassadors came to Montreal they declared that they were doing all they could to satisfy Callières on this point, but, they stated, their prisoners had been adopted into Iroquois families who refused to relinquish them. Some of these prisoners were French, and although at liberty to return to Canada, some of them refused to do so, preferring the free, irresponsible life of the Indian to the restraints of a more civilized society. Callières was rather sceptical of all this and the French allies refused to hand over their prisoners until the Iroquois gave up theirs.[11]

Despite the fact that this matter was still not settled, Callières succeeded in the summer of 1700 in getting a peace treaty arranged between four of the Iroquois nations and the Ottawas, Hurons and Abenakis.[12] It was agreed that a general assembly of all the nations would be held at Montreal the following year to ratify the treaty which would include them all in its terms. Meanwhile, the Iroquois requested that the Sieur de Maricourt, Father Bruyas and Jonquaire should return with them and use their influence to try to obtain the release of the prisoners.[13] When these men arrived at Onondaga, Maricourt went from cabin to cabin and induced three French women and a boy to return with him. Another French boy he tried to remove forcibly, but when the boy began to struggle and scream two Iroquois warriors intervened and obliged him to let the boy go. The following day Tegannissorens declared that since the French were demanding that all prisoners be returned, even against their will, the French must themselves tie up all the Iroquois prisoners at the Jesuit mission of Caughnawaga and throw them into canoes to be brought back to the villages of the Five Nations, whether they wanted to or not. "You come and speak of peace," said Tegannissorens bitterly, "and are scarce set down to smoke a pipe, but talk of coming and knocking us on the head, and therefore I say, nobody knows your heart."[14] After this stern rebuke from one of the greatest of the Iroquois chiefs, the French had to adopt more conciliatory methods, for it was now quite clear that the Five Nations, who had already released some fifty to sixty French prisoners,[15] were honest enough in their motives.

The following summer some 1,300 Indians from all the nations, from as far apart as Acadia, the Mississippi valley, the Great Lakes area, and the Iroquois cantons, arrived at Montreal. Callières imposed the strictest ban on the sale of liquor; had he not done so Montreal might well have been the scene not of peace negotiations but of a terrible carnage, as ancient enemies mingled outside the town walls and in the narrow streets of the town itself. Day after day the speeches, with their interminable parables so dear to the Indian orator, went on and on. It must have seemed as though nothing better than an uneasy stalemate could result, for once again the Iroquois had failed to bring their Indian prisoners whereas the allies had brought over thirty of theirs. The Sakis, however, had brought only one prisoner and they were known to have taken many more. When the Iroquois demanded to know where the others were, Coluby, a Saki chief, rose and with commendable brevity declared: "I have brought you only one prisoner because, if you have shown a liking for my flesh, I also have liked yours, and I have eaten my prisoners just as you have eaten yours." Callières, by this time, may well have wished that this simple method of cutting the Gordian knot had been employed by them all.

Then, on August 3, 1701, a delegation of Hurons and Miamis waited on Callières. Quarante Sols, the Huron chief who acted as their spokesman, declared that they had brought their eleven Iroquois prisoners and would hand them over to the governor to do with as he saw fit. Quarante Sols stated that they would be willing to have these prisoners given back to the Iroquois, and if the Iroquois did not then reciprocate it would be plain for all to see that they were not sincere; but in any event neither his people nor the French would have any cause to reproach themselves. This course of action, Quarante Sols concluded, they were taking at the behest of their ancient war chief Kondiaronk, who was at that moment on his death bed. It was this same Kondiaronk who, thirteen years earlier, had tried to prevent a peace being negotiated between the French and the Iroquois by ambushing the Iroquois ambassadors and declaring that he had been ordered to do so by Denonville. The other allied tribes followed the example of the Hurons and Miamis and handed over their Iroquois prisoners to the governor. At a great assembly of all the delegates, Callières then gave them to the Iroquois, who for their part declared that it would now be much easier for them to obtain the release of the prisoners they still held from the families that had adopted them.[16] After a great feast and many speeches, the chiefs of each nation drew on the peace treaty document, which bore the signatures of all the senior French officials, a picture of their tribal emblem to signify their acceptance of the terms. Louis XIV and his ministers may well have been rather taken aback when they received this document and saw at its foot rather crudely drawn pictures of wild animals, for some of the Indian signatories had been unable to restrain their earthy penchant for boasting of their virility and did so symbolically in depicting the animal totems of their clans.[17]

It had been only by the exercise of great adroitness, patience and knowledge of the Indian mentality that Callières had finally succeeded in bringing these long-drawn-out negotiations to a most successful conclusion. Not a little credit must also go to Kondiaronk, and the French were duly appreciative of this chief's last great gesture; a solemn *Te Deum* was sung for the repose of his soul and he was given a state funeral rivalling in splendour that of Frontenac. It was no mean feat to have reconciled all the conflicting claims, charges, counterclaims and countercharges of these tribes who had been warring for as long as men could remember. This, however, was only a part of Callières's achievement, for he had also managed to persuade the Iroquois to remain neutral in any future conflict between England and France. This agreement was incorporated as one of the terms of the peace treaty[18] and the Iroquois adhered to it faithfully in the years that followed. Callières had thereby succeeded in inflicting a stinging diplomatic defeat on the English, for not only had the Iroquois refused, under Callières's prodding, to accept the status of British dependents and so recognize British sovereignty over their lands, but the English colonies had also thereby lost their greatest source of military strength. Callières had succeeded in stripping them of their first line of both defence and offence. With the Iroquois neutral and England and France once again on the brink of war, the colonies of New York and New England had to face unassisted the threat of full-scale assaults from Canada, and when this was realized in New York the frontier settlements became panic-stricken.[19] In view of the sorry military record of the English colonies in the past, the French had good cause to feel that the neutrality of the Iroquois gave them a decided military advantage over their old foes. As one French officer wrote in 1701 upon his return from a tour of the northern English colonies: "It is true that this country has twice the population of New France, but the people there are astonishingly cowardly, completely undisciplined, and without any experience in war. The smallest Indian party has always made them flee; moreover, they have no regular troops. It is not at all like that in Canada. There are twenty-eight companies of infantry, the Canadians are brave, much inured to war, and untiring in travel; two thousand of them will at all times and in all places thrash the people of New England." [20]

Another outstanding aspect of this peace settlement was that, although the Iroquois fangs had been drawn, they were still strong enough to act as a barrier between the French allies and the English of New York, thus ensuring that the fur trade of the up-country tribes would continue to pass through Montreal rather than through Albany. When all these factors are taken into account, Bégon, the intendant at Rochefort, was not exaggerating when he wrote to his friend Villermont: "A sort of assembly has been held at Montreal which was attended by thirty-three different Indian nations who had never before been there in such large numbers. Messieurs de Callières and Champigny have acquired an immortal glory in reconciling all the differing interests of these peoples who have arranged among themselves a peace which, in its results, will be very advantageous to our country." [21]

With the signing of this treaty an epoch had come to an end. The Iroquois had finally accepted defeat in their century-long struggle to wrest control of the western fur trade from the French. They had fought valiantly for high stakes against great odds, asking no quarter and giving none. Their rules of war were not those of the French, but there was no valid reason why they should have been. Their losses had been heavy, yet they accepted the final outcome of the struggle without a whimper.

CHAPTER TWENTY

CONCLUSION

In 1663 New France had been rescued from the inept administration of various private companies and placed under the direction of Colbert. For the ensuing thirty-eight years the French government adhered to Colbert's policy of concentrating French energies in the valley of the St. Lawrence. As long as Colbert was alive anything that tended to disrupt this policy was vigorously opposed by the Ministry of Marine; the sole exception to this was La Salle's activities in the west, and had Colbert known the true nature of La Salle's enterprises, they undoubtedly would have been curbed.[1] After the death of Colbert in 1684, his successors continued his policy, but without making any real attempt to implement it. The minister's attention was increasingly diverted away from Canada by events in Europe. Pontchartrain continued Colbert's policy, not because he particularly favoured or even understood it, but largely because he lacked both the time and the inclination to frame a new one, and mere lip-service was paid to it by de Lagny, who was actually in charge of Canadian affairs for several years.

Immediately after the treaty of Ryswick was signed, ending the War of the League of Augsburg, Louis XIV began sidling, crabwise, towards a radically new and openly imperialist policy in North America. In 1698 Iberville was sent to the mouth of the Mississippi to claim this territory for France, to build forts there, and to hold it against all comers.[2] The following year he was sent back to the Mississippi with secret instructions to destroy by covert means any establishments the English might have founded, or might be about to found, between Georgia, the Carolinas and the great river.[3] In 1695 Governor Nicholson of Virginia had urged the government at Whitehall to forestall the French by establishing a base at the mouth of the Mississippi and building combined forts and trading posts up the valley to prevent the French drawing the Indian tribes into a commercial and military alliance.[4] Although this plan was not acted upon by the English, reports soon began to reach the French that English traders were crossing the Alleghanies and it was feared that they intended to establish forts in the Ohio valley.[5] In October, 1699, and again the following February, Iberville confirmed reports that the English had begun to penetrate the Ohio country [6] and Callières reported that the Albany men were talking of building a fort at Niagara and penetrating to the Illinois.[7] Meanwhile, Louis XIV was gathering all the information he could on the vast unexplored regions of the south-west from Iberville and others before deciding what action to take.[8]

When the decision was finally made, however, it was events in Europe that dictated it. For two years the powers had been waiting for Charles II, the moribund king of Spain, to die. Since he had no children the problem was to arrange a succession to the throne that would not upset the balance of power. Finally, after months of involved diplomatic manoeuvreing, on October 2, 1700, Charles II willed the throne of Spain and all its possessions to Philip, Duc d'Anjou, a grandson of Louis XIV. On November the first Charles died, and on the ninth the Spanish ambassador was pressing Louis for an immediate decision whether or not Philip would take the Spanish throne; if the offer were to be declined, it would be made to a son of the Hapsburg emperor. After conferring with his council all that day and for four hours the next, Louis finally decided to accept. By so doing he made war with the other powers inevitable. Sometime between then and the following May he made a further decision, all the implications of which could not possibly have been foreseen, a decision which was to mark a turning point in the history of North America. In a memoir dated May 31, 1701, Louis informed Callières and Champigny at Quebec: "His Majesty has resolved to found a settlement at the mouth of the Mississippi . . . this has become an indispensable necessity to halt the advance which the English from the colony of New York have begun to make in the lands which lie between them and this river." [9]

It was not expected that this new colony, when established, would be of great benefit to France in the foreseeable future. It was to serve mainly as a base, an anchor, for a series of posts to be built on the rivers flowing westward into the Mississippi from the Great Lakes to the Gulf of Mexico. Just as Governor Nicholson had foreseen six years earlier, these posts were to be used to weld all the Indian tribes between the Alleghanies and the Mississippi into an alliance with the French to bar the English from the west. If this were not done, it was feared that the English would soon begin to press south and west until they came into conflict with the Spanish in Mexico; in order to secure his grandson's hold on the throne of Spain, Louis XIV had to demonstrate to the Spanish people that France was able and willing to protect their colonial possessions from a common enemy.* [10] The French now found themselves committed to occupying the entire western section of North America from Hudson Bay to the Gulf of Mexico and to holding the English colonials on the eastern side of the Alleghanies—this at a time when the population of the English colonies was doubling every twenty-five years.

Essentially, it was a dog-in-the-manger policy. In 1696 Denis Riverin, one of the leading *bourgeois* in the colony and a staunch believer in Colbert's policy, had advocated what amounted to the abandonment of the Illinois country to the English, on the grounds that this whole area produced only poor-grade furs which were a glut on the market. He observed that the English had relatively easy access to this region but that the country to the north of the Great Lakes, which produced the best furs, was inaccessible to them. Even though it was quite possible to exclude the English from the Mississippi valley, would it be wise, he queried, to strive, arms in hand and at excessive cost, to retain the very things that were proving to be a liability both to the economy and to the state? [11] Champigny had recognized the logic of this, and he too had suggested the abandonment of the south-west,[12] but his recommendations had gone unheeded and the authority of the king of France still extended, at least nominally, throughout the mid-west. It was this tenuous sovereignty that Louis XIV had now decided to strengthen.

The consequences of Louis XIV's decision were certainly to be

---

* In May, 1701, M. Tremblay, a cleric in Paris who was always well informed on developments at the Court, wrote to a friend at the Quebec seminary: "It is not at the moment seen how the Mississippi area can be of much value to France, therefore it is not intended to found anything very considerable there, but to let it develop slowly. But as Spain has now fallen to a son of France, it is believed necessary, by means of the colony of the Mississippi and by drawing all the Indian tribes along this river into the French alliance, to create a barrier against the English from Boston as far as Florida, or Carolina as they call it; this to prevent them expanding farther into these lands and extending from one of these nations to another as far as the Spanish colonies, which they would lay waste were they to reach so far. It is therefore desired to block them, and in order to succeed in this aim, it is intended to place as many missionaries as possible among all the Indian nations between the Mississippi and the English."

of great moment, not only for France and New France, but for England and her empire as well. Nothing is inevitable in history but what is made so by the decisions and acts of men. It may well be that had Louis not made this decision and had the French not attempted to hold western North America south of the Great Lakes, there would have been no conflict in the Ohio Valley, some fifty years later, between the French and the English colonials as the latter pressed on beyond the Alleghanies. Perhaps then the English would not have thrown their full weight against Canada in the Seven Years War and it would have remained under the French flag. Had this occurred it may well be that there would have been no American Revolution and what is now the United States of America would today be a member of the British Commonwealth. And Canada? The imagination boggles; one dare not even venture to guess what the French Revolution and Napoleon would have done to its history in such circumstances. Perhaps there would not then have been a French Revolution!

But all this is to venture dangerously far into the historian's no-man's-land of "if". In the light of events which did occur, however, the period from 1663 to 1701 in the history of New France can be said to have a certain unity, and might well be termed the "middle period". It was during this "middle period" that Frontenac dominated the Canadian scene and his career has to be judged in the light of both the official policy of the Ministry of Marine at that time and conditions in both the colony and France.

There can be no doubt that Frontenac's first administration was disastrous and was recognized as such by the king and the minister when they recalled him. But during his second regime the administration of civil affairs was far less troubled than during his first, and he deserves as much credit as anyone for this. In the final analysis, however, Frontenac's claims to greatness have rested on three things: under his leadership the English assault on Canada was repulsed, the Iroquois were finally humbled, and the French extended their power into the heart of the continent.

The English made only the one attempt, in 1690, to conquer New France during Frontenac's day; that the intended attack on Montreal failed to materialize was in no way the consequence of any action taken by Frontenac, and, although the forces under his command repulsed the English colonial militia's half-hearted attempt on Quebec, this can hardly be regarded as a great military feat. Frontenac's ringing phrase that he would answer Phips's summons from the mouths of his cannon was, however, sufficient by itself to gain him glory as the dauntless defender of Quebec.

So far as the defeat of the Iroquois was concerned, Frontenac has been given a good deal more credit by his biographers than he deserved. Perhaps the main reason for this is the nature of the primary source material. In civil affairs there is abundant evidence which contradicts Frontenac's exaggerated claims, his excuses and accusations. Towards the end of his first administration the Ministry of Marine was being deluged with charges and complaints against him. Even the most prejudiced historian could not dismiss this body of evidence out of hand; all that could be done was to seek to explain it away. But in military affairs and the field of Indian relations the evidence is very one-sided. Moreover, he had sole authority in these two fields; no other official had any right to interfere. As a result, before Frontenac's subordinates felt free to criticize his actions, things had to be in a desperate condition, and even then their criticism had to be rather guarded. If the Iroquois and the French allies had left written records in the shape of journals of their council meetings, memoirs, inter-tribal dispatches, et cetera, Frontenac's version of events would undoubtedly not have gone so long unchallenged. The records of the conferences held at Albany with the Five Nations allow a glimpse of the Iroquois attitude towards both the French and the English, and frequently they expose the misleading nature of Frontenac's dispatches and memoirs, which were designed to inform the Court of what he wanted the officials there to believe rather than to give an accurate picture of events.

Every year he sent a detailed account of all that had happened in the colony during the preceding twelve months to his wife and some of his friends for circulation in Court circles. At least three copies, and very likely more, of these journals, which ran to some ninety folio pages, were sent, and they were skilfully contrived to make everything redound to the greater glory of Frontenac; every success, no matter how ephemeral, was extolled, and every setback was plausibly explained away or at least minimized. Since Frontenac had a very gifted pen, merely to accept his accounts of events ensured a colourful narrative particularly pleasing to the romantic historians of the nineteenth century who subscribed to the "great man" concept of history. But when Frontenac's accounts are closely checked against all the available evidence from other sources, then the discrepancies, the subtle half-truths, the calculated omissions and the distortions are very apparent.

Fortuitous timing also aided considerably in the creation of the Frontenac myth. He was recalled in 1682 before his ineptitude in the face of the Iroquois threat became apparent to the minister, and, with a complete lack of scruples, he did his best to obscure the condition in which he had left the colony. His successors then had to grapple with the problems that he had shirked and that had been made worse by his refusal to face them. As a result, it was all too easy for these men to be made scapegoats. Frontenac subsequently boasted that he had kept the colony at peace during his first administration and that his successors had plunged recklessly into a needless war with the Iroquois which had resulted in severe losses.[13] The fact that he took over the reins of government from Denonville immediately after the Iroquois had inflicted a heavy blow on the colony, the first of many that were to follow, was also fortunate for Frontenac; it offered him an opportunity—which he was quick to take—to enhance his own reputation by greatly exaggerating the losses suffered by the colony and thereby make the immensity of the task with which he was faced appear all the greater. Nevertheless, under his command the Iroquois were eventually humbled, and this was no mean achievement. Finally, he had the good fortune to die at a time when the war with the English was ended and peace with the Iroquois was in sight. Nothing can be more conducive to the enhancing of a military commander's reputation than for him to expire at a time when victory is assured.

To arrive at any clear-cut conclusions with regard to the role played by Frontenac in French expansion in the west is very difficult. To avoid the many pitfalls which this problem poses, Frontenac's motives must always be kept in mind. Although Frontenac never openly espoused an imperialist policy such as Louis XIV embarked upon in 1701, and although he always stoutly maintained that he was doing everything in his power to implement the official policy of preventing the dispersion of the colony's meagre manpower resources into the wilderness, the fact remains that during his regime the French did expand into the west. In 1672 French sovereignty had extended little beyond the island of Montreal. At the time of Frontenac's death the French held several isolated posts scattered through the basin of the Great Lakes, along the Mississippi from its headwaters to below the Ohio, and French fur traders had made their way along the rivers to Hudson Bay, south to the Gulf of Mexico, and had penetrated as far west as Lake Winnipeg and perhaps even farther.[14]

All this was done in spite of the fact that the colony was fighting for its life against the Iroquois and in spite of the avowed policy of the Ministry of Marine. In fact, the war was used as a means to circumvent the official policy and to carry out this expansion. Under the pretext of holding the western tribes in the alliance against the Iroquois, Frontenac continually sent large parties to the western posts; he gave members of his following commissions in the Troupes de la Marine and sent them to these posts, at the king's expense, where they concerned themselves chiefly with the carrying on of a very profitable and illicit trade in furs for their own account. Moreover, these men could hardly be said to have occupied the territory in which the posts lay; they were actually little more than travelling salesmen operating out of Montreal with *entrepôts* in the west. Frontenac was not at all concerned with the problem of occupying and holding this vast territory for France; his only interest was the furs to be garnered from the western tribes. This was made quite clear by his admission that his associates, Tonty and La Forest, would abandon their post in the Illinois country if they were not allowed to continue trading for beaver pelts. It is therefore apparent that the western expansion that Frontenac covertly engaged in was not the same as that embarked upon by Louis XIV at the beginning of the eighteenth century. Despite the distinction in motives, however, it is still true that it was under Frontenac's regime that the French pressed on into the west and that orders could be transmitted from Versailles to French officers in these distant parts. To some extent, then, the authority of the King of France could be exercised in the west, and it was upon these foundations that Louis XIV's imperialist policy was subsequently constructed.

Although Frontenac was rather fortunate in the timing of many events in his career and was adept at turning these events to his own advantage, he was really a man born too late into this world. He was a product of a class, the old nobility of the sword, that was rapidly being converted into a caste with no other functions than to appear at Versailles, to provide an elite cannon fodder in Louis XIV's wars, and to act as figureheads in the provinces—of which

New France was one. The members of this class, the old feudal aristocracy, still remembered the days when they were the power in the land, when they dominated the provinces, and when the king had to walk warily lest he arouse their anger; but now they found themselves being pushed to one side by a new class, men of humble or obscure origins who had obtained vast wealth in strange ways, men of low birth but great ability, ambitious and clever men, the lawyers, the professional administrators, in short, the nobility of the robe.

The *grands seigneurs* could still hold their own in this contest, their prestige was still great, they could still command armies better than most men, and their voices still had to be heard in the king's councils; but the lower ranks of the old aristocracy lacked their prestige, and worse yet, they lacked the wealth that might have sustained them. This class, of which Frontenac was a good example —despite the origins of his mother's family—found itself being submerged and swept aside, forced to bend the knee before the new men of power and wealth, the Colberts and Pontchartrains. Worse still, what little authority they had left to them was being whittled away by other men of talent scrambling up the ladder: the Talons, the Duchesneaus, the Champignys. All that was left to Frontenac and his class was a few empty privileges and to these they clung tenaciously, struggling to maintain at least an appearance of their old power and prerogatives. But the tide was set against them and, in the case of Frontenac, his temperament made it impossible for him to give way gracefully. He was, in many ways, an anachronism, unable to understand or to reconcile himself to the changes that were taking place all about him. This, inevitably, led to clashes within the colony during a period of great conflict on the larger stage of Europe and North America. And these disputes caused Frontenac to dominate the Canadian scene during a very colourful epoch, one replete with momentous events. For it was during this period that the candle of New France began to burn at both ends; if its existence was thereby shortened, at least it gave a brilliant light. This brilliance is immediately apparent to all who study the period even cursorily. To many it has seemed that the brilliance emanated from Frontenac and was cast by him on New France, but in reality it was the other way around.

ABBREVIATIONS USED IN THE NOTES

In the notes, Roman numerals are used throughout to indicate volume numbers and the mediaeval devices of $\overline{X}$ and $\overline{V}$ are used to signify 10,000 and 5,000 respectively.

Aff. Et.—Archives du Ministère des Affaires Etrangères.
AN.—Archives Nationales.
Bib. Nat.—Bibliothèque Nationale.
BRH.—Le Bulletin des Recherches Historiques.
Can. Arch.—The Public Archives of Canada.
CSP—Calendar of State Papers Colonial, America and West Indies.
Doc. Hist. N.Y.—Documentary History of the State of New York.
Doc. Rel. N.F.—Collection des manuscrits contenant lettres, mémoires et autres documents historiques relatifs à la Nouvelle France.
Jes. Rel.—Jesuit Relations and Allied Documents.
Mass. Arch.—Massachusetts State Archives.
MG.—Dépot du Ministère de Guerre, Vincennes.
NYCD—Documents Relating to the Colonial History of New York.
Que. Arch.—Archives de la Province de Québec.
RAPQ—Rapport de l'Archiviste de la Province de Québec.
Rpt. Can. Arch.—Public Archives of Canada : Annual Reports.
Sem. Que.—Archives du Séminaire de Québec.

CHAPTER ONE

1 AN. B, VIII, 5–6, Colbert à Duchesneau, St. Germain, April 25, 1679.

2 Aff. Et. Series Amérique, V, 201–2, Ratification of the peace treaty by the Seneca ambassadors. Que., May 28, 1666; Ratification of the peace treaty by the Oneida ambassadors. Que., July 7, 1666.

3 RAPQ 1930–1931, 169, Colbert à Talon, [June 4, 1672].

4 *Chronological List of Canadian Censuses*, Canada, Bureau of Statistics, Demography Branch, Ottawa, 1942.

5 *Jes. Rel.*, L, 236–46, Relation de 1666–1667; LI, 167, Relation de 1667–1668.

6 AN. B, I, 81–2, Mémoire du Roy pour servir d'instruction au Sr Talon. Louis et Lionne, Paris, March 27, 1665; RAPQ 1930–1931, 111, Mémoire succinct des principaux poincts des intentions du Roy sur le pays de Canada que Sa Maté veut estre mis ez mains du Sr Talon, St. Germain-en-Laye, May 18, 1669.

7 AN. C11A, VII, De Meulles au Ministre, Que., Sept. 28, 1685; VI, Extrait du Mémoire du Roy envoyé par le Sr de la Barre le 13 nov., 1684.

8 *Jes. Rel.*, L, 169–70, Lettre du P. Beschefer à sa famille et au P. Antoine Chesne S.J. Que., Oct. 1, 1666.

9 RAPQ 1930–1931, 161, Talon au Ministre, Que., Nov. 2, 1671.

10 *Ibid.*; AN. B, IV, 61, Colbert à Talon, St. Germain-en-Laye, June 4, 1672.

11 AN. CiiA, III, 5, Mémoire . . . du Roy au Sr Talon, St. Germain-en-Laye, May 18, 1669.

12 RAPQ 1930–1931, 80, Talon au Ministre, Que., Oct. 27, 1667; 144, Colbert à Talon, Feb. 11, 1671; AN. B, III, Colbert à Talon, [1671]; CiiA, III, 40, Mémoire du Roy au Sr Talon, St. Germain-en-Laye, May 18, 1669.

13 AN. F3, Moreau de St. Méry, II, 5–6, Mémoire de Canada. M. de la Chesnaye à de Lagny, Que., Nov. 4, 1695.

14 RAPQ 1930–1931, 145, Colbert à Talon, Feb. 11, 1671.

15 AN. B, VII, 77–8, Colbert à Duchesneau, Paris, April 28, 1677.

16 G. N. Clark, *The Later Stuarts*, 57, n. 2; CSP 1700, 362, Gov. the Earl of Bellomont to the Council of Trade & Plantations, Boston, June 22, 1700; AN. CiiA, V, 63, Duchesneau au Ministre, Que., Nov. 10, 1679.

17 *Ibid.*

18 Can. Arch. AN. CiiA, XI, 512, Champigny au Ministre, Que., Oct. 12, 1691.

19 AN. F3, Moreau de St. Méry, II, 1–5, Mémoire de Canada. M. de la Chesnaye à de Lagny, Que., Nov. 4, 1695; IV, 75–6, Jean le Mire, sindiq, à Mgr le Gouverneur, Que., [1673]; RAPQ 1930–1931, 36, Talon à Colbert, Que., Oct. 4, 1665; 42, Colbert à Talon, Versailles, Jan. 5, 1666.

20 *Ibid.*, 70, Colbert à Talon, St. Germain-en-Laye, April 5. 1667.

21 AN. CiiA, XVII, 236, Mémoire sur la Ferme . . . 1699.

22 RAPQ 1930–1931, 63, Mémoire de Talon sur l'état présent du Canada, 1667.

23 AN. CiiA, XIII, 440–54, Mémoire de Canada. M. de la Chesnaye à de Lagny, Que., Nov. 4, 1695; 401, Commerce du Castor de Canada, fev^r 1695; RAPQ 1930–1931, 37, Talon à Colbert, Que., Oct. 4, 1665; Aff. Et. Series Amérique, V, 288–9, Au Roy. Mémoire sur le Canada. Talon, Que., Nov. 3, 1671.

24 R. Du Bois Cahall, *The Sovereign Council of New France*, 133; AN. CiiA, V, 50, Duchesneau au Ministre, Que., Nov. 10, 1679.

25 Aff. Et. Series Amérique, V, 339, Frontenac au Ministre, Que., Nov. 13, 1673; AN. B, IV, Le Roy à Frontenac, St. Germain-en-Laye, June 5, 1672. Marie Thérèse et Colbert.

26 AN. CiiA, XI, 192–3, Mémoire concernant le Canada pour Mgr le Marquis de Seignelay, Denonville, Jan., 1690.

27 *Ibid.*; VII, 89–95, Denonville au Ministre, Que., Nov. 13, 1685; IX, 31, Denonville au Ministre, Mtl., June 8, 1687; 69–70, Denonville au Ministre, Mtl., Aug. 25, 1687; XI, 196, Frontenac au Ministre, Que., Nov. 20, 1690; 143, Mémoire du Roy aux Srs Frontenac et Champigny 1690.

28 AN. CiiA, V, 51, Duchesneau au Ministre, Que., Nov. 10, 1679.

29 *Ibid.*, VIII, 141, Denonville au Ministre, Que., Nov. 10, 1686.

30 Aff. Et. Series Amérique, V, 343, Frontenac au Ministre, Que., Nov. 13, 1673.

31 RAPQ 1926–1927, 12, Frontenac au Ministre, Que., June 24, 1672; Can. Arch. AN. B, XII, 169–70, Ministre à Denonville, Versailles, April 9, 1687.

32 AN. CiiA, XI, 241, Frontenac au Ministre, Que., Oct. 20, 1691; XII, 9–10, Frontenac et Champigny au Ministre, Que., Sept. 15, 1692.

33 *Ibid.*, V, 292–3, Duchesneau à Seignelay, Que., Nov. 13, 1681.

34 *Ibid.*, XI, 467, Mémoire Instructif sur le Canada. Champigny, Que., May 10, 1691.

35 *Ibid.*, 294–6, Mémoire concernant le commerce de traitte entre les français et sauvages dans les pays esloignez des Outaouas, Islinois, Miamis et autres nations. Que., Oct. 12, 1691.

36 *Ibid.*, V, 297–8, Duchesneau à Seignelay, Que., Nov. 13, 1681.

37 *Ibid.*, VII, 89–95, Denonville au Ministre, Que., Nov. 13, 1685.

CHAPTER TWO

1 *Mémoires du Vicomte de Turenne*, 132–3, 203–4; *Mémoires de St. Simon*, VI, 166, n. 5.

2 Châteauroux. Departmental Archives. Series E, dossier 11, no. 2. Titres de Propriétés de la Seigneurie de Paluau. Sezie faite sur Claude Brachat adjugée par le parlement à Antoine de Buade, 78,000 livres quatre vingt une. 19 jan., 1606.

3 *Mémoires de St. Simon*, XIV, 268–71, 270 n. 3.

4 *Ibid.*, VI, 166, n. 2 and 3; *Mémoires de la Société Généalogique Canadienne-Française*, VI, No. 3, July, 1954, p. 155.

5 AN. CiiA, XIII, 267, Frontenac à de Lagny, Que., Nov. 2, 1695.

6 M. Pinard, *Chronologie Historique-Militaire*, VI, 216–17.

7 MG. Series A, XCVI, Brevet du Maréchal de Camp pour le Comte de Frontenac, Aug. 16, 1646.

8 Bib. Nat. Series fo. Factum 2505. Extrait des registres de parlement. Homologation de contrat passé entre . . . Frontenac et ses créanciers. Dec. 12, 1664.

9 *Mémoires de Mademoiselle de Montpensier*, II, 279; III, 16–17.

10 Aff. Et. Series France, Mémoires et Documents, MDXCI, 358, Sr Frucher au Comte de Chavigny, Paris, April 30, 1649.

11 *Mémoires de St. Simon*, VI, 166–9; XIV, 268–71.

12 *Les Historiettes de Tallemant des Réaux*, VII, 130–4; Aff. Et. Series France, Mémoires et Documents, MDXCII, 341–2, De Neufville à Chavigny, Paris, Sept. 25, 1650.

13 *Ibid.*, MDXCI, 320, Nouvelles du 14ᵉ avril à Paris; 161–3, De Neufville à Chavigny, Paris, Dec. 30, 1648.

14 *Ibid.*, 134–5, De Neufville à Chavigny, Paris, Dec. 13, 1648; 154, Nouvelles de Paris; Nouvelles de la Cour, Paris, April 24, 1649; 155–6, De

Neufville à Chavigny, Paris, Dec. 30, 1648; 349–50, De Neufville à Chavigny, Paris, April 25, 1649; MDXCII, 292–3, De Neufville à Chavigny, Paris, June 28, 1650; 341–2, De Neufville à Chavigny, Paris, Sept. 25, 1650.

15 *Ibid.*, 349–50, De Neufville à Chavigny, Paris, April 25, 1649; A. Jal, *Dictionnaire Critique de Biographie et d'Histoire*, 621–3.

16 Aff. Et. Series France, Mémoires et Documents, MDXCI, 367–8, De Neufville à Chavigny, Paris, May 12, 1649.

17 *Ibid.*, 358, Sr Frucher à Chavigny, Paris, April 30, 1649.

18 *Ibid.*, MDXCII, 42–3, Frontenac à Chavigny, Paris, July 26, 1649; 284, Chavigny à de Neufville, June 20, 1650; 292–3, De Neufville à Chavigny, Paris, June 28, 1650; 328–9, De Neufville à Chavigny, Paris, Sept. 14, 1650; 341–2, De Neufville à Chavigny, Paris, Sept. 25, 1650.

19 *Ibid.*; Bib. Nat. Collection Morel de Thoisy, CXXXII, 287–91, Factum pour Messire Buade-Frontenac.

20 *Les Historiettes de Tallemant des Réaux*, VII, 130–4.

21 Factum pour Messire Buade-Frontenac, *loc. cit.*

22 A. Jal, *loc. cit.*

23 *Mémoires de Mademoiselle de Montpensier*, II, 300.

24 *Ibid.*, II, 423; III, 16–17, 83–4.

25 *Ibid.*, III, 65, chaps. 31 and 32 *passim*; Bib. Nat. Mélanges Colbert, LII–A, 200, Mazarin à la Reine, Calais, Aug. 23, 1658.

26 *Historique des Corps de Troupe de l'Armée Française, 1569–1900*, 19.

27 Factum pour Messire Buade-Frontenac, *loc. cit.*

28 Bib. Nat. Series fo. Factum 2505, Extrait des registres de parlement.

29 Bib. Nat. Mélanges Colbert, CDIX, 294–5, M. Verjus à Colbert, Cologne, May 21, 1672.

30 Bib. Nat. Fonds Français, X̄MMMMCLXV, Relation de Candie.

31 Francis Parkman, *Frontenac and New France under Louis XIV*, 13.

32 Bib. Nat. Nouvelles Acquisitions, X̄XMMCXLIV, 300–5, Le Roy de la Potherye au comte de Maurepas, [Quebec, 1698–9].

33 Bib. Nat. Collection Morel de Thoisey, LII, 143–9, Plainte et Justification de Mr le comte de frontenac au Doge et Senat de Venice contre Mr le Capitaine Generale Morosini commandant dans cette isle, 1669.

34 W. Carew Hazlitt, *The Venetian Republic*, II, 276.

35 Plainte et Justification de Mr le comte de frontenac . . ., *loc. cit.*

36 *Ibid.*; Bib. Nat. Collection Dupuy, CCCLV, 48–9, Harangue prononcée en plein Collège par Monsr. le Comte de Frontenac Lieutenant Général des Armées de la Serenissime Republique de Venize le 7 febvrier, 1670.

37 *Mémoires de St. Simon*, XIV, 268–71.

38 Bib. Nat. Mélanges Colbert, CDIX, 294–5, M. Verjus au Ministre, Cologne, May 21, 1672.

39 *Ibid.*, CDX, 61, Colbert de Terron à Colbert, Rochefort, June 2, 1672; 196–7, Colbert de Terron à Colbert, Rochefort, June 6, 1672; 608, Colbert de Terron à Colbert, Rochefort, June 30, 1672; AN. B, IV, 55, Mémoire des hardes et vaisselles appertenans au Sr comte de Frontenac, Colbert et Marie Thérèse, St. Germain, May 19, 1672; 45, Ordonnance pour les Appointemens de Mr le comte de frontenac, Versailles, April 4, 1672, Louis, Colbert; 45–6, Ordonnance de Voyage pour led. Sr Comte de Frontenac, Versailles, April 4, 1672, Louis, Colbert.

40 *Mémoires de Mademoiselle de Montpensier*, II, 300; III, 65.

41 *Les Historiettes de Tallemant des Réaux*, VII, 132.

42 RAPQ 1926–1927, 84, Colbert à Frontenac, May 13, 1675.

43 Bib. Nat. Mélanges Colbert, CDIX, 294–5, M. Verjus au Ministre, Cologne, May 21, 1672; Series fo. Factum 2505, Extrait des registres de parlement. Homologation de contrat passé entre Louis de Buade Frontenac . . . et ses créanciers, Dec. 12, 1664; Fonds Français, Collection Dangeau, XXMMDCLXXII, 117, Annales. Du 16° Mars, 1686.

44 Bib. Nat. Mélanges Colbert, CDXVII, 353, Verjus au Ministre, Berlin, Feb. 20, 1674.

45 Bib. Nat. Series fo. Factum 2505, Extrait des registres de parlement . . . Dec. 12, 1664.

CHAPTER THREE

1 Bib. Nat. Mélanges Colbert, CLX, 829, Frontenac au Ministre, Du bord de la Grande Esperance à 200 lieues à l'ouest de la Rochelle, July 22, 1672; AN. CiiA, III, 234, Frontenac au Ministre, Que., Nov. 2, 1672.

2 *Ibid.*

3 AN. B, IV, 35, Provisions de gouverneur et Lieutenant General pour le Roy en Canada, pour Mr le Comte de Frontenac. Donné à Versailles le 6° avril 1672. Louis, Colbert.

4 AN. CiiA, III, 248–9, Frontenac au Ministre, Que., Nov. 2, 1672.

5 *Ibid.*

6 *Jugements et Délibérations du Conseil Souverain de Québec*, I, 700.

7 *Jes. Rel.*, L. 172–4, Lettre du P. Thierry Beschefer à sa Famille et au P. Antoine Chesne S. J. Kébec, Oct. 4, 1666.

8 Bib. Nat. Collection Clairambault, ID, 89–93, Harangue donné par M. le Comte de Frontenac en l'Assemblée tenu à Québec le 23 Oct., 1672.

9 AN. CiiA, III, 26–7, Frontenac au Ministre, Que., Nov. 2, 1672.

10 AN. B, V, 26–7, Colbert à Frontenac, Paris, June 13, 1673.

11 Francis Parkman, *Frontenac and New France under Louis XIV*, 19–20.

12 Aff. Et. Series Amérique, V, 346–7, Frontenac au Ministre, Que., Nov. 13, 1673.

13 *Jugements et Délibérations du Conseil Souverain de Québec*, I, 689.

14 Abbé de Belmont, *Histoire du Canada*, 13.

15 AN. C11A, III, 244–5, Frontenac au Ministre, Que., Nov. 2, 1672.

16 AN. B, V, 44, Mémoire du Roy pour servir d'instruction au S^r comte de Frontenac . . . Versailles, April 7, 1672.

17 *Jugements et Délibérations du Conseil Souverain de Québec*, I, 786.

18 Aff. Et. Series Amérique, V, 323, Frontenac au Ministre, Que., Nov. 13, 1673.

19 *Ibid.*

20 *Ibid.*, 321.

21 *Ibid.*

22 *Jugements et Délibérations du Conseil Souverain de Québec*, I, 637–8.

23 Aff. Et. Series Amérique, V, 319–20, Frontenac au Ministre, Que., Nov. 13, 1673.

24 *Ibid.*

25 AN. C11A, III, 275, Mémoire du Sr Patoulet demandé par Mgr. Paris, Jan. 25, 1672.

26 *Ibid.*, 249, Frontenac au Ministre, Que., Nov. 2, 1672.

27 AN. B, V, 27, Colbert à Frontenac, Paris, June 13, 1673.

28 Mémoire du Sr Patoulet . . . Paris, Jan. 25, 1672, *loc. cit.*

29 Aff. Et. Series Amérique, V, 347–8, Frontenac au Ministre, Que., Nov. 13, 1673.

30 RAPQ, 1926–1927, 59, Colbert à Frontenac, May 17, 1674.

31 AN. C11A, IV, 61–4, Frontenac au Ministre, Que., Nov. 12, 1674.

32 *Ibid.*, 64–7; *Jugements et Délibérations du Conseil Souverain de Québec*, I, 859–61.

33 RAPQ 1926–1927, 60, Colbert à Frontenac, May 17, 1674.

34 RAPQ 1921–1922, 129–38, Informations et déclarations faites au sujet d'un sermon du Sieur Abbé de Fénelon prononcé le jour de Paques, March 25, 1674.

35 AN. C11A, IV, 51–2, Frontenac au Ministre, Que., Feb. 16, 1674.

36 AN. B, III, 32, Colbert à Talon, 1671.

37 Informations et déclarations faites au sujet d'un sermon du Sieur Abbé de Fénelon prononcé le jour de Paques, March 25, 1674, *loc. cit.*

38 RAPQ 1926–1927, 43, Frontenac à Colbert, Que., Nov. 13, 1673.

39 Can. Arch. AN. F3, Moreau de St. Méry, IV, 294, Interrogatoire fait à M. Perrot commencé le dernier Janvier 1674.

40 *Ibid.*, 262.

41 *Ibid.*

42 Can. Arch. Documents St. Sulpice, III, Extrait des actes du greffe du Bailliage de l'isle de Montréal. Jan. 8, 1672.

43 *Ibid.*; AN. F3, Moreau de St. Méry, IV, 127–33, Mémoire des motifs qui ont obligé M. le comte de Frontenac de faire arrester M. Perrot gouverneur de Montreal.

44 *Ibid.*, 426–44, Requeste contenant les moyens de récusation contre Mgr le Gouverneur, Aug. 17, 1674.

45 Interrogatoire fait à M. Perrot . . ., *op. cit.*

46 Mémoire des motifs . . ., *op. cit.*

47 *Ibid.*; Interrogatoire fait à M. Perrot . . ., *op. cit.*

48 Mémoire des motifs . . ., *op. cit.*

49 *Ibid.*

50 Interrogatoire fait à M. Perrot . . ., *op. cit.*

51 *Ibid.*

52 Can. Arch. AN. F3, Moreau de St. Méry, IV, part I, 302–5, Proces-Verbal du reffus faict par le Sr Perrot de subir la continuation de l'Interrogatoire. Feb. 2, 1674.

53 *Jugements et Délibérations du Conseil Souverain de Québec*, I, 786.

54 AN. C11A, IV, 51–2, Frontenac au Ministre, Que., Feb. 16, 1674.

55 *Ibid.*, 70–7, Frontenac au Ministre, Que., Nov. 14, 1674.

56 RAPQ 1921–1922, 129–38, Informations et Déclarations faites au sujet d'un sermon du Sr Abbé de Fénelon . . . May 2, 1674.

57 Frontenac au Ministre, Que., Nov. 14, 1674, *op. cit.*

58 Informations et Déclarations . . ., *op. cit.*

59 *Ibid.*, 149, Déclarations des sieurs Ecclesiastiques de Montréal sur le Sermon du Sr abbé de Fénelon, May 12, 1674.

60 Informations et Déclarations . . ., *op. cit.*

61 *Ibid.*, 154–5, Comparution du Sr abbé de Fénelon devant le Conseil Souverain, Aug. 21, 1674; 163–4, Comparution au Conseil Souverain du Sr Abbé de Fénelon, Sept. 4, 1694; 169, Requête du Sr abbé de Fénelon au Conseil Souverain, Sept. 10, 1674; 175, Ordonnance du Conseil Souverain, Sept. 26, 1674; 177, Réponse du Sr abbé Pierre de Repentigny Francheville à l'assignation du Conseil Souverain, Oct. 6, 1674; 178–81, Ordonnance du Conseil Souverain, Oct. 15, 1674.

62 Can. Arch. AN. F3, Moreau de St. Méry, IV, part I, 426–44, Requeste contenant les moyens de récusation contre Mgr le Gouverneur. Perrot, Aug. 17, 1674.

63 *Ibid.*, 302–5, Proces-Verbal du reffus faict par le Sr Perrot de subir la continuation de l'Interrogatoire. Feb. 2, 1674.

64 Requeste contenant les moyens de récusation contre Mgr le Gouverneur. Perrot, Aug. 17, 1674, *op. cit.*

65 *Ibid.*

66 *Ibid.*

67 *Ibid.*, IV, part 2, 452–66, Requeste contenant des moyens de prise à partie Sept. 3, 1674, A Nos Seigneurs de Conseil Souverain de Quebec. Perrot.

68 *Ibid.*

69 *Ibid.*, 451, Extrait des Registres du Conseil Souverain, Aug. 29, 1674; 511, Extrait des Registres du Conseil Souverain, Sept. 3, 1674.

70 *Ibid.*, 523–6, Extrait des Registres du Conseil Souverain, Sept. 6, 1674.

71 AN. CiiA, IV, 70–7, Frontenac au Ministre, Que., Nov. 14, 1674.

72 RAPQ 1926–1927, 81, Le Roi à Frontenac, April 22, 1675.

73 *Ibid.*; Can. Arch. Lettres de l'Abbé Tronson, I, Abbé Tronson aux Messieurs du Séminaire de Montréal, May, 1675.

74 RAPQ 1926–1927, 80–1, Le Roi à Frontenac, April 22, 1675.

75 Can. Arch. AN. B, VI, 172–5, Provisions de con^{er} au Con^{el} Souverain de Québec pour le Sr de Villeray, May 26, 1675. *idem*, Le Gardeur de Tilly, Mathieu Damours, Nicholas Dupont, Réné Louis Chartier de Lobtinière [*sic*], Jean Baptiste de Peiras, Charles Denis.

76 AN. B, VI, 74, Estat des Conseillers au Conseil Souverain . . . suivant le rang que le Roy leur accorde. May 10, 1675.

77 AN. CiiA, IV, 104–5, Déclaration du Roy qui confirment et regle l'Etablissement du Conseil Souverain de Canada du 5 juin 1675.

78 RAPQ 1926–1927, 80–3, Le Roi au Gouverneur de Frontenac, April 22, 1675.

CHAPTER FOUR

1 Bib. Nat. Collection Clairambault, DCIIIL, 653, Mémoire sur les finances en 1700 et 1701.

2 Quoted in Ernest Lavisse, *Histoire de France*, VII–1, 172.

3 AN. B, IV, 42–3, Mémoire du Roy pour servir d'Instruction au Sr Comte de Frontenac. Louis, Colbert, Versailles, April 7, 1672.

4 RAPQ 1926–1927, 32, Frontenac au Ministre, Que., Nov. 13, 1673.

5 AN. CiiA, III, 246–8, Frontenac au Ministre, Que., Nov. 2, 1672.

6 Aff. Et. Series Amérique, V, 324–5, Frontenac au Ministre, Que., Nov. 13, 1673.

7 Can. Arch. Lettres de l'Abbé Tronson, IV, Abbé Tronson à M. de la Colombière, Paris, June 7, 1690; Abbé Tronson à M. Dollier de Casson, Paris, 1692; Abbé Tronson à Champigny, Paris, April 20, 1696; Abbé Tronson à Champigny, Paris, April 22, 1697.

8 AN. CiiA, III, 236, Frontenac au Ministre, Que., Nov. 2, 1672.

9 *Ibid.*, VI, 185, De Meulles au Ministre, Que., Nov. 4, 1683.

10 AN. B, III, 31, Colbert à Talon, 1671.

11 *Ibid.*, V, 28, Colbert à Frontenac, Paris, June 13, 1673.

12 Jean Delanglez, *Frontenac and the Jesuits*, 36–8.

13 Colbert à Frontenac, Paris, June 13, 1673, *loc. cit.*

14 Aff. Et. Series Amérique, V, 328–9, Frontenac au Ministre, Que., Nov. 13, 1673.

15 AN. CiiA, IV, 12–24, Harangue de M. le comte de Frontenac aux Iroquois, 1673.

16 *Ibid.*, 12–24, Voyage de M. le Comte de Frontenac au Lac Ontario en 1673.

17 *Ibid.*, 67–8, Frontenac au Ministre, Que., Nov. 14, 1674.

18 AN. F3, Moreau de St. Méry, II, 31, Père Milet à Mgr le Gouverneur,

[Onondaga,] Aug. 10, 1673; *Jes. Rel.*, LVII, 30, Père Lamberville à Mgr le gouverneur, Techiraguen, Sept. 9, 1673.

19 AN. CiiA, IV, 67–8, Frontenac au Ministre, Que., Nov. 14, 1674.

20 *Ibid.*, V, 68, Duchesneau au Ministre, Que., Nov. 10, 1679; 178–9, Duchesneau au Ministre, Que., Nov. 13, 1680.

21 *Jes. Rel.*, LXIII, 194, 198–200, Narration annuelle de la Mission du Sault depuis la fondation jusques à l'an 1686. R. P. Cauchetière.

22 AN. CiiA, IV, 83–4, Frontenac au Ministre, Que., Nov. 12, 1674.

23 AN. CiiA, V, 15, Frontenac au Ministre, Que., Nov. 6, 1679. [In this dispatch Frontenac recalls his earlier, more detailed one to the minister's attention.]

24 AN. B, VIII, 51–2, Le Roy à Frontenac, St. Germain, April 29, 1680.

25 AN. CiiA, VII, 89–95, Denonville au Ministre, Que., Nov. 13, 1685.

26 NYCD, III, 394, Gov. Dongan's Report on the state of the Province.

27 AN. CiiA, IV, 77, Frontenac au Ministre, Que., Nov. 14, 1674.

28 Aff. Et. Series Amérique, V, 327–8, Frontenac au Ministre, Que., Nov. 13, 1673.

29 RAPQ 1926–1927, 57–8, Colbert à Frontenac, May 17, 1674.

30 AN. B, VII, 29, Le Roy à Frontenac, St. Germain, April 16, 1676.

31 *Ibid.*, VIII, 9, Le Roy à Frontenac, St. Germain-en-Laye, April 25, 1679.

32 AN. CiiA, VI, 399–400, De Meulles au Ministre, Que., Nov. 12, 1684.

33 *Ibid.*, XII, 277, Champigny au Ministre, Que., Nov. 4, 1693; XVI, 114, Champigny au Ministre, Que., Oct. 14, 1698.

34 AN. B, XI, 5–6, Le Roy à La Barre, Versailles, April 10, 1684; AN. CiiA, VI, 59–60, La Barre au Ministre, [Que., 1682]; 140, La Barre au Ministre, Que., Nov. 4, 1683; XI, 137, Champigny au Ministre, Que., Nov. 14, 1690.

35 AN. B, VII, 82, Colbert à Duchesneau, Paris, May 1, 1677.

36 Can. Arch. Lettres de l'Abbé Tronson, I, Tronson à de Casson, May, 1679.

37 Sem. Que. Lettres, Carton N, No. 62, M. Dudouyt à Mgr de Laval, [Paris,] May 26, 1682.

38 AN. CiiA, XIX, 116, Callières au Ministre, Que., Oct. 4, 1701.

39 Pierre Boucher, *Histoire véritable et naturelle des moeurs et productions du pays de la Nouvelle France*, 118–19.

40 AN. CiiA, XII, 131, Attestation du Sr du Lhut . . . sur les desordres que cause l'ivrognerie des Sauvages de Canada.

41 W. B. Munro, "The Brandy Parliament of 1678," in *Canadian Historical Review*, June, 1921.

42 *Ibid.*

43 *Rpt. Can. Arch. 1885*, cviii, M. Dudouyt à Mgr Laval, 1677.

44 "Mémoire historique sur les mauvais effets de la réunion des castors dans une même main, 1705," in Emma Helen Blair, *The Indian*

Tribes of the Mississippi Valley and Region of the Great Lakes, I, 208–9, n. 148.

45 NYCD, III, 479, Peter Schuyler to Gov. Dongan, Sept. 2, 1687.

46 AN. CiiA, X, 72–3, Mémoire d'un des plus grands maux de la colonie. Denonville, Aug. 10, 1688; NYCD, IV, 15, Journal of Gov. Fletcher's expedition . . . to the frontiers against the French and Indians of Canada, New York, March 7, 1692/3.

47 Peter Wraxall, *An Abridgement of the New York Indian Records*, xli.

48 NYCD, IV, 24, Propositions made by four of the Chief Sachems of the Five Nations to his Excell., Benjamin Fletcher . . . in Albany, Feb. 26, 1692/3.

49 *Ibid.*, 123, Intelligence received from Onondaga, Albany, Feb. 18, 1694/5.

50 Wraxall, *op. cit.*, 31.

51 AN. F3, Moreau de St. Méry, VIII, 270–2, Assemblée faite par M. le Chev. de Callières . . . Mtl., Aug. 6, 1701.

52 AN. CiiA, XII, 380, Mémoire touchant les boissons. Charles Aubert de lachenaye. Oct. 24, 1693.

53 Bib. Nat. Mélanges Colbert, CLVIII, 60, Bellinzani à Colbert, Paris, Jan. 5, 1672.

54 AN. CiiA, XII, 281–7, Champigny au Ministre, Que., Nov. 4, 1693.

55 E. C. Pease and R. C. Werner, *The French Foundations*, 1680–1693, 43.

56 AN. CiiA, III, Arrest du Conseil Superieur [*sic*] de Quebec du 10 Nov. 1668.

57 *Ibid.*, XII, 380–1, Mémoire touchant les boissons. Charles Aubert de lachenaye. Oct. 24, 1693.

58 Aff. Et. Series Amérique, V, 323–7, Frontenac au Ministre, Que., Nov. 13, 1673.

59 AN. CiiA, IV, 91–2, Ordonnance du comte de Frontenac, Que., Feb. 17, 1674.

60 AN. B, VII, 80–1, Colbert à Duchesneau, Paris, May 1, 1677.

61 M. Dudouyt à Mgr Laval, 1677, *loc. cit.*

62 Colbert à Duchesneau, Paris, May 1, 1677, *op. cit.*

63 AN. CiiA, IX, 328, Vaudreuil au Ministre, Mtl., Oct. 1, 1701.

64 AN. B, VII, 166–7, Arrest du Conseil d'Etat du Roy, St. Germain-en-Laye, May 12, 1678.

65 *Ibid.*, 182–4, Mémoire fait par ordre du Roy sur la difficulté de la traitte des boissons aux Sauvages dans le Canada. . . . Sceaux, May 24, 1678.

66 Can. Arch. Documents St. Sulpice, III, Extrait de la lettre de M. de la Chesnaye escrite à Quebec 6 Nov. 1678.

67 W. B. Munro, "The Brandy Parliament of 1678," *op. cit.*

68 AN. B, VIII, Ordonnance du Roy, St. Germain, May 24, 1679.

69 AN. CiiA, V, 54, Duchesneau au Ministre, Que., Nov. 10, 1679.

70 Can. Arch. Lettres de l'Abbé Tronson, I, Tronson à M. le Fevre, April 5, 1677.

71 *Ibid.*, Tronson aux Messieurs du séminaire de Montréal, May, 1675.

72 Aff. Et. Series Amérique, V, 329, Frontenac au Ministre, Que., Nov. 13, 1673.

73 RAPQ 1921–1922, 186, Procès-verbal des declarations des Abbés Rémy et de Francheville devant MM. de Tilly et Dupont, Oct. 18, 1674.

74 *Ibid.*, 175, Assignation de comparution au sieur abbé de Francheville . . . avec le refus du dit sieur de Francheville de comparaitre à cause de son caractère, Oct. 5, 1674; 176, Ordonnance du Conseil Souverain qui condamne le sieur Rémy . . . à dix livres d'amende pour sa non comparance . . ., Oct. 8, 1674.

75 *Ibid.*, 182, Ordonnance du Conseil Souverain qui condamne à une amende de dix livres le sieur Pierre de Repentigny Francheville . . ., Oct. 15, 1674.

76 *Ibid.*, 179, Ordonnance du Conseil Souverain . . ., Oct. 15, 1674.

77 *Ibid.*, 159, Ordonnance du Conseil Souverain, Aug. 27, 1674; AN. CiiA, IV, 70–7, Frontenac au Ministre, Que., Nov. 14, 1674.

78 RAPQ 1921–1922, 179–81, Ordonnance du Conseil Souverain, Oct. 15, 1674.

79 Can. Arch. Documents St. Sulpice, XXI, M. l'abbé d'Urfé se plaint à M. Colbert de mauvais traitements qu'il a reçus de M. le comte de Frontenac.

80 RAPQ 1926–1927, 83–4, Colbert à Frontenac, May 13, 1675.

81 *Ibid.*, 82, Le Roi à Frontenac, April 22, 1675.

82 Can. Arch. Lettres de l'Abbé Tronson, I, Tronson aux MM. du Séminaire de Montréal, May, 1675.

83 *Ibid.*

84 AN. B, VII, 77, Colbert à Duchesneau, Paris, April 28, 1677.

85 Can. Arch. Documents St. Sulpice, XXI, Mémoire de quelques faits qui se sont passés dans l'ile de Montréal dont on se croit obligé de rendre compte à Mgr Colbert.

86 AN. CiiA, V, 172–3, 180, Duchesneau au Ministre, Que., Nov. 13, 1680.

87 *Rpt. Can. Arch. 1885*, cxi, cxx, M. Dudouyt à Mgr Laval, 1677.

88 Can. Arch. Lettres de l'Abbé Tronson, I, Tronson à M. de Casson, May, 1679.

89 *Ibid.*

90 *Ibid.*, II, Tronson à de Casson, April 7, 1681.

91 AN. B, V, 27–8, Colbert à Frontenac, Paris, June 13, 1673.

92 Aff. Et. Series Amérique, V, 350–1, Frontenac au Ministre, Que., Nov. 13, 1673.

93 AN. CiiA, VI, 377, Le Ministre à de Meulles, Versailles, April 10, 1684.

94 BRH, XLVI (1940), 71, Laval au Roy, Que., Nov. 10, 1683; AN. CIIA, VI, 329, Extrait du Mémoire au Roy envoyé par le Sr de la Barre le 13ᵉ Nov. 1684.

95 Bib. Nat. Nouvelles Acquisitions, X̄XMMCXLIV, 269–73; RAPQ 1926–1927, 129, Frontenac au Roy, Que., Nov. 2, 1681.

96 AN. CIIA, VI, 185–6, De Meulles au Ministre, Que., Nov. 4, 1683; 143–4, La Barre au Ministre, Que., Nov. 4, 1683.

97 *Ibid.*, 329, Extrait du Mémoire au Roy envoyé par le Sr de la Barre le 13ᵉ Nov. 1684.

98 Sem. Que. Lettres, Carton N, No. 62, M. Dudouyt à Mgr de Laval, May 26, 1682.

CHAPTER FIVE

1 AN. CIIA, XVI, 241, Mémoire généraux. Mr Saulger. Paris, May 27, 1698.

2 CSP 1700, 688, Journal of Col. Romer's Expedition to Onondaga, Oct. 5, 1700.

3 E. E. Rich, "Russia and the Colonial Fur Trade," in *Economic History Review*, VII, No. 3, April, 1955.

4 AN. CIIA, XVII, 236, Mémoire sur la Ferme . . ., 1699.

5 *Ibid.*, VI, 119–20, Remarques faites par Du Chesneau cy devant Intendant . . . dans la Nouvelle France . . . Sur le projet du bail de la ferme dud pays; IV, 169–70, Arrest du Roy, au camp de Condé, May 16, 1677; V, 174, Duchesneau au Ministre, Que., Nov. 13, 1680; 322–3, Mémoire de Duchesneau, Nov. 13, 1681.

6 AN. B, XXVII, Ministre à M. de Champigny, Versailles, June 2, 1706.

7 AN. CIIA, IX, 266, Colbert à Talon, March 30, 1666.

8 AN. B, IV, 61, Colbert à Talon, St. Germain-en-Laye, June 4, 1672.

9 RAPQ 1926–1927, 85, Colbert à Frontenac, May 30, 1675.

10 *Jes. Rel.*, LVII, 24–6, Père Bruyas S. J. au Gouverneur, Tionnontoguen, June 12, 1673; 26–8, Père Garnier S. J. à Mgr. le gouverneur Tsonnontouanan, July 6, 1673.

11 Peter Wraxall, *An Abridgement of the New York Indian Records*, lviii–lix.

12 RAPQ 1926–1927, 58, Colbert à Frontenac, May 17, 1674.

13 Aff. Et. Series Amérique, V, 330–40, Frontenac au Ministre, Que., Nov. 13, 1673.

14 RAPQ 1926–1927, 58, Colbert à Frontenac, May 17, 1674.

15 AN. CIIA, IV, 67–70, Frontenac au Ministre, Que., Nov. 14, 1674.

16 *Ibid.*, XI, 136, Champigny au Ministre, Que., Nov. 14, 1690; Bib. Nat. Collection Clairambault, MXVI, 51, Relation des découvertes et des Voyages du Sr de la Salle; Aff. Et. Series Amérique, V. 337, Frontenac au Ministre, Que., Nov. 13, 1673.

17 *Ibid.*; AN. CIIA, IV, 68–70, Frontenac au Ministre, Que., Nov. 14, 1674.

18 RAPQ 1926–1927, 78, Frontenac au Ministre, Que., Nov. 14, 1674; AN. F3, Moreau de St. Méry, IV, 402, Lettres patentes de concessions du fort de frontenac et terres adjacentes du Sr de la Salle. Donné à Compiègne, May 13, 1675.

19 Ibid.; AN. CiiA, XIX, 4, Callières et Champigny au Ministre, Que., Oct. 5, 1701.

20 Relation des descouvertes et des Voyages du Sr de la Salle, loc. cit.

21 Arthur H. Buffinton, "The Policy of Albany and English Westward Expansion," in Mississippi Valley Historical Review, 1921–22; Peter Wraxall, An Abridgement of the New York Indian Records, liii.

22 Buffinton, op. cit.

23 RAPQ 1926–1927, 58, Colbert à Frontenac, May 17, 1674.

24 AN. CiiA, IV, 82, Frontenac au Ministre, Que., Nov. 12, 1674.

25 AN. B, VII, 79, Colbert à Duchesneau, Paris, April 28, 1677.

26 AN. CiiA, XIII, 401–2, Commerce du Castor de Canada. Colonies fevr. 1695.

27 Jes. Rel., LX, 134, P. Jean Enjalran [to an unnamed correspondent], Sillery, Oct. 13, 1676.

28 AN. B, VII, 179–80, Permission au Sr de la Salle de descouvrir la partie occidentale de la Nouvelle France. St. Germain-en-Laye, May 12, 1678.

29 Bib. Nat. Nouvelles Acquisitions, $\overline{V}$MMCDLXXXV, 103, Mémoire de Henri Tonty; AN. CiiA, V, 39–40, Duchesneau au Ministre, Que., Nov. 13, 1680.

30 AN. B, VIII, 76, Le Roy à Frontenac, Versailles, April 30, 1681.

31 AN. CiiA, V, 387, Frontenac au Roy, Que., Nov. 2, 1681.

32 Bib. Nat. Collection Clairambault, DCCCLXXIX, 320–38, Frontenac à de Lagny, Que., Oct. 25, 1693.

33 De Bacqueville de la Potherie, Histoire de l'Amérique Septentrionale, II, 143.

34 RAPQ 1926–1927, 9, Lettre du Roy au Gouverneur de Frontenac, Marie Thérèse et Colbert., St. Germain-en-Laye, June 5, 1672.

35 AN. CiiA, III, 222–4, Ordonnance de M. le comte de Frontenac, Que., Sept. 27, 1672.

36 Aff. Et. Series Amérique, V, 341, Frontenac au Ministre, Que., Nov. 13, 1673.

37 AN. CiiA, IV, Frontenac [to the town-major of Quebec], Mtl., July 4, 1674; 70–7, Frontenac au Ministre, Que., Nov. 14, 1674.

38 RAPQ 1926–1927, 85, Colbert à Frontenac, May 30, 1675.

39 Ibid.; AN. B, VII, 160, Le Roy à Frontenac, St. Germain-en-Laye, May 12, 1678; VIII, 9, Le Roy à Frontenac, St. Germain-en-Laye, April 25, 1679; 55, Colbert à Frontenac, St. Germain-en-Laye, April 20, 1680.

40 AN. CiiA, IV, 82, Ordonnance du Roy, St. Germain-en-Laye, May 12, 1678; AN. B, VII, 160, Le Roy à Frontenac, St. Germain-en-Laye, May 12, 1678.

41 *Ibid.*, 30, Le Roy à Frontenac, St. Germain-en-Laye, April 16, 1676; 34, Colbert à Duchesneau, St. Germain-en-Laye, April 16, 1676.

42 AN. F3, Moreau de St. Méry, II, 76–7, Conduite du Sr Perrot . . . 1681; *Annales de l'Hôtel-Dieu de Montréal*, 24–5.

43 *Ibid.*, 228.

44 AN. F3, Moreau de St. Méry, II, 65, Proces verbal de M. Duchesneau, Aug. 2, 1680; AN. CiiA, V, 38–48, Duchesneau au Ministre, Que., Nov. 10, 1679; 172–3, Duchesneau au Ministre, Que., Nov. 13, 1680.

45 Conduite du Sr Perrot . . . 1681, *loc. cit.*

46 AN. CiiA, V, 299, Duchesneau à Seignelay, Que., Nov. 13, 1681.

47 *Ibid.*

48 *Ibid.*, 38–48, Duchesneau au Ministre, Que., Nov. 10, 1679.

49 *Ibid.*, 6–7, Frontenac au Ministre, Que., Oct. 9, 1679; 14, Frontenac au Roy, Que., Nov. 6, 1679.

50 Duchesneau au Ministre, Que., Nov. 10, 1679, *loc. cit.*

51 *Ibid.*

52 AN. CiiA, V, 8–10, Frontenac au Ministre, Que., Nov. 6, 1679.

53 *Ibid.*, 198–204, Lettre du Roi à Frontenac, St. Germain-en-Laye, April 29, 1680.

54 *Ibid.*, 359–62, Mémoire et preuves de la cause du désordre des coureurs de bois . . . Frontenac, Que., 1681.

55 AN. B, VIII, 55, Lettre à la main de Mgr Colbert à Frontenac, St. Germain-en-Laye, April 20, 1680.

56 *Ibid.*, 86–8, Edit du Roy, Versailles, May 2, 1681; 88–9, Ordonnance du Roy, Versailles, May 2, 1681.

57 AN. CiiA, VIII, 20–2, Denonville au Ministre, Que., May 8, 1686.

58 *Ibid.*, V, 384, Frontenac au Roy, Que., Nov. 2, 1681.

59 *Ibid.*, 297–8, Duchesneau à Seignelay, Que., Nov. 13, 1681.

60 *Ibid.*, VII, 131, Castors venus de Canada depuis 1675 jusqu'à 1685.

61 *Ibid.*, IX, 295–300, Mémoire touchant le commerce de Canada.

62 AN. CiiE, XVI, 2–5, Dulhut à Frontenac, Sault Ste. Marie, April 5, 1679.

63 *Ibid.*; AN. CiiA, VI, 216–25, Mémoire à messieurs les interessez en la société en commendite de la ferme et commerce de Canada.

64 *Ibid.*, IV, 95–6, Extrait de la lettre du Père Nouvel Jesuiste escrite de Ste. Marie du Sault à Mgr le Gouverneur le 29 mai 1673.

65 Aff. Et. Series Amérique, V, 350, Frontenac au Ministre, Que., Nov. 13, 1673.

66 *Publications of the Hudson's Bay Record Society*, XI, *Letters Outward*, 1679–1694, 71–2, Frontenac à Monsieur Commandant pour le Roy de Grande Bretagne à la Baye d'Hudson, Que., Oct. 8, 1673.

67 *Publications of the Hudson's Bay Record Society*, *Minutes of the Hudson's Bay Company*, 1671–1674, appendix G.

68 AN. CiiA, V, Mémoire du Sr Duchesneau, Que., Nov. 13, 1681.

69 *Rpt. Can. Arch.* *1895*, Relations des Voyages de Pierre Esprit Radisson dans les Années 1682, 3 et 4, p. 7.

70 RAPQ 1926–1927, 136, Frontenac au Ministre, Que., Nov. 2, 1681.

71 AN. CiiA, VI, 153, La Barre à Colbert, Que., Nov. 4, 1683; 196–7, De Meulles au Ministre, Que., Nov. 4, 1683.

72 AN. CiiE, I, 46, Memorial on the Rights of the English in Hudson's Bay, 7/17 March, 1698/9.

73 Relations des Voyages de Pierre Esprit Radisson, *op. cit.*

74 AN. CiiA, VI, 119–20, Remarques faites par Du Chesneau cy devant Intendant . . . dans la Nouvelle France . . . sur le projet du bail de la ferme dud pays; IV, 169–70, Arrest du Roy au camp de Condé, May 16, 1677; V, 174, Duchesneau au Ministre, Que., Nov. 13, 1680; 322–3, Mémoire de Duchesneau, Nov. 13, 1681.

75 *Ibid.*, V, 13, Frontenac au Roy, Que., Nov. 6, 1679; 384–5, Frontenac au Roy, Que., Dec. 2, 1681.

76 *Ibid.*, 322, Mémoire du Duchesneau, Nov. 13, 1681.

77 *Ibid.*, VI, 216, Mémoire à messieurs les interessez en la société en commendite de la ferme et commerce de Canada.

78 *Ibid.*

79 *Ibid.*, XII, 90–1, Champigny au Ministre, Que., Nov. 10, 1692; XIX, Champigny au Ministre, Que., Oct. 30, 1701.

80 *Ibid.*, V, 316–19, Mémoire de Duchesneau, Que., Nov. 13, 1681.

81 *Ibid.*, X, 65–7, Denonville à Seignelay, Que., Aug. 10, 1688.

82 AN. F3, Moreau de St. Méry, II, 76–7, Conduite du Sr. Perrot . . . 1681; Can. Arch. Lettres de l'Abbé Tronson, II, Abbé Tronson à Dollier de Casson, Feb. 21, 1683; Sem. Que. Lettres, Carton N, No. 71, M. Dudouyt à Mgr de Laval, May 28, 1683.

83 New York State Archives, N.Y. Col. Ms. XXVII, 19, A List of letters which Sergeant Champangie [*sic*] brought from Canida, bound to Boston. Ro. Livingston, [Albany,] Feb. 15, 1677/8.

CHAPTER SIX

1 AN. F3, Moreau de St. Méry, II, 6, Mémoire de Canada. M. de la Chesnaye à de Lagny, Que., Nov. 4, 1695.

2 P. Margry, *Découvertes et établissements* . . ., V, 93–101; Pierre Boucher, *Histoire véritable* . . ., 125–35; NYCD, III, 252, Wentworth Greenhalgh's Journal of a Tour to the Indians of Western New York, May–July 1677; *Jes. Rel.*, see index, Indians *captives*.

3 AN. CiiA, III, 97, Au Roy, Mémoire sur le Canada, Talon, Que., Nov. 10, 1670; 104–5, Addition au présent mémoire, Talon, Nov. 10, 1670; 240–1, Frontenac au Ministre, Que., Nov. 2, 1672.

4 AN. B, III, 28, Colbert à Talon, [1671].

5 AN. CiiA, IV, 12–24, Voyage de M. le Comte de Frontenac au Lac

Ontario en 1673; *Jes. Rel.*, LVII, 26–8, R. P. Garnier S. J., à Frontenac, Tsonnontouan, July 6, 1673.

6 AN. F3, Moreau de St. Méry, II, 30, Père Millet à Frontenac, Onondaga, Aug. 10, 1673; Aff. Et. Series Amérique, V, 341, Frontenac au Ministre, Que., Nov. 13, 1673.

7 AN. C11A, IV, 22, Harangue de M. le Comte de Frontenac aux Iroquois, 1673.

8 Aff. Et. Series Amérique, V, 335, Frontenac au Ministre, Que., Nov. 13, 1673.

9 Voyage de M. le Comte de Frontenac au Lac Ontario en 1673, *loc. cit.*

10 *Ibid.*

11 CSP 1675–1676, 398, Journal of the Lords of Trade & Plantations, May, 1676.

12 AN. C11A, VI, 517, Lamberville à La Barre, Onnontagué, Feb. 10, 1684.

13 NYCD, III, 277, Gov. Andros to Mr. Blathwayt, N. Yorck, March 25, 1679.

14 CSP 1700, 449, Propositions made by the River Indians to Lieut. Gov. Nanfan, Albany, July 18, 1700.

15 *Jes. Rel.*, LIX, 250, Etat présent des missions des Pères de la Compagnie de Jésus en la Nouvelle France pendant l'année 1675; LX, 172, Relation de 1676–1677.

16 *Ibid.*; Etat présent des missions . . ., *loc. cit.*

17 AN. C11A, V, 5, Frontenac au Ministre, Que., Oct. 9, 1679.

18 RAPQ 1926–1927, 90, Le Roy à Frontenac, Dunkerque, April 28, 1677.

19 *Ibid.*, 107, Frontenac au Ministre, Que., Oct 9, 1679.

20 *Ibid.*, 96, Le Roy à Frontenac, St. Germain-en-Laye, May 12, 1678.

21 *Ibid.*, 98, Le Roy à Frontenac, St. Germain-en-Laye, April 25, 1679.

22 AN. C11A, V, 12, Frontenac au Roy, Nov. 6, 1679.

23 P. Margry, *Découvertes et établissements* . . ., I, 585–92.

24 AN. C11A, V, 300–15, Mémoire du Sr Duchesneau, Que., Nov. 13, 1681; 386–7, Frontenac au Roy, Que., Nov. 2, 1681.

25 *Ibid.*

26 Mémoire du Sr Duchesneau, Que., Nov. 13, 1681, *loc. cit.*

27 AN. C11A, V, 390, Frontenac au Roy, Que., Nov. 2, 1681.

28 *Ibid.*, VI, 21–3, Mémoire pour éclaircir les dispositions dans lesquelles M. le comte de Frontenac a laissé le Canada à l'égard des Sauvages et principalement les Iroquois [Paris, 1683].

29 Mémoire du Sr Duchesneau, Que., Nov. 13, 1681, *loc. cit.*

30 AN. C11A, VI, 24–7, Extrait des avis donnés à la conférence tenus chez les PP. Jesuites au sujet des nouvelles venues des Iroquois. March 23, 1682.

31 *Ibid.*, 68–70, Assemblée tenue le 10ᵉ Oct. 1682, composée de M. le

Gouverneur, de M. l'Intendant, de M. l'Evesque de Québec, M. Dollier, Superieur du Séminaire de St. Sulpice à Montréal, des RR. PP. Beschefer Superieur, d'Ablon et Fremin Jesuittes, M. le Major de cette ville, Messieurs de Varenne, Gouverneur des Trois Rivières, de Brussy, Dalibout, Duguet, Le Moine, La Durantais, Bizard, Chailly, Vieuxpont, Duluth, de Sorel, de Repentigny, Berthier et Boucher.

32 Extrait des avis . . ., *op. cit.*

33 Aff. Et. Series Amérique, VI, Mémoire du chevalier de la Forest. Inventaire de production des pièces. Paris. Dec. 29, 1719.

34 AN. CiiA, VI, 28–9, Duchesneau à Frontenac, July 28, 1682.

35 Abbé de Belmont, *Histoire du Canada*, 14; AN. CiiA, VI, 4, Frontenac à Duchesneau, Mtl., Aug. 5, 1682.

36 *Ibid.*; Mémoire pour éclaircir les dispositions dans lesquelles M. le comte de Frontenac a laissé le Canada . . ., *loc. cit.*

37 Abbé de Belmont, *op. cit.*

38 AN. CiiA, VI, 5–13, Affaires traitées par M. le comte de Frontenac avec les Kiskakons, Tionontataez et Miamis. Aug. 13, 1682.

39 *Ibid.*, VII, 213–15, Mémoire concernant l'estat présent du Canada . . ., Denonville, Nov. 12, 1685; VIII, 59–63, Denonville au Ministre, Mtl., June 12, 1686.

40 RAPQ 1926–1927, 4, Mémoire du Roy pour servir d'instruction au Sr comte de Frontenac . . ., April 7, 1672.

41 Aff. Et. Series Amérique, V, 345–6, Frontenac au Ministre, Que., Nov. 13, 1673; AN. CiiA, IV, 63–4, Frontenac au Ministre, Que., Nov. 12, 1674.

42 RAPQ 1926–1927, 81, Le Roi à Frontenac, April 22, 1675.

43 AN. B, X, 3–5, Le Roy à la Barre, Fontainebleau, Aug. 5, 1683.

44 *Jes. Rel.*, LXII, 70–2, Lettre de Jean de Lamberville à R.P. Beschefer, Onnontagué, Aug. 25, 1682.

45 *Ibid.*, 92–4.

46 Mémoire pour éclaircir les dispositions dans lesquelles M. le comte de Frontenac a laissé le Canada . . ., *loc. cit.*

47 AN. CiiA, VI, 14, Conference de M. de Frontenac avec un deputé des Iroquois, Sept. 11, 1682; 33–6, Discours de M. de Frontenac au deputé des Iroquois, Sept. 12, 1682; 15, Paroles du deputé des Cinq Nations Iroquoises à M. le comte de Frontenac, Sept. 11, 1682; 37, Sr de la Forest à Frontenac, Fort Frontenac, Sept. 16, 1682.

48 *Ibid.*, 68–70, Assemblée tenue le 10ᵉ octobre 1682. . . .

49 *Ibid.*, 47–8, Père de Lamberville à Frontenac, d'Onnontagué, Sept. 20, 1682.

50 *Ibid.*, 60, La Barre au Ministre, Que., 1682.

51 *Ibid.*, V, 388, Frontenac au Roy, Que., Nov. 2, 1681.

52 Mémoire pour éclaircir les dispositions dans lesquelles M. le comte de Frontenac a laissé le Canada . . ., *loc. cit.*

53 Can. Arch. Lettres de l'Abbé Tronson, II, Tronson à de Casson,

May 25, 1681; Tronson à de Casson, April 7, 1681; Tronson à de Casson, Mar. 29, 1682; Sem. Que. Lettres, Carton N, No. 61, M. Dudouyt à Mgr de Laval, March 9, 1682.

54 AN. CIIA, XI, 5, Relation de ce qui s'est passé de plus remarquable en Canada depuis le départ des vaisseaux au mois de Nov. 1689 jusqu'au mois de Nov. 1690; 230–2, Frontenac au Ministre, Que., Oct. 20, 1691.

CHAPTER SEVEN

1 RAPQ 1926–1927, 80–3, Colbert à Frontenac, May 13, 1675.

2 Bib. Nat. Mélanges Colbert, CXXXV, 548, Colbert à Duchesneau, Trésorier de France à Tours, St. Germain-en-Laye, Jan. 27, 1666; CLXXbis, 379–80, Duchesneau à Colbert, Tours, Feb. 6, 1675; AN. CIIA, V, 73–4, Duchesneau au Ministre, Que., Nov. 10, 1679.

3 RAPQ 1926–1927, 88, Le Roi à Frontenac, April 15, 1676.

4 Ibid.

5 Ibid.

6 AN. B, VII, 45, Le Roy à Frontenac, Au Camp de hurtebise, May 20, 1676; idem à Duchesneau.

7 AN. CIIA, V, 27–8, Duchesneau au Ministre, Que., Oct. 6, 1679.

8 AN. B, VIII, 16–17, Colbert à Duchesneau, St. Germain, May 8, 1679.

9 AN. CIIA, V, 59, Duchesneau au Ministre, Que., Nov. 10, 1679.

10 AN. B, VIII, 52, Le Roy à Frontenac, St. Germain, April 29, 1680.

11 Ibid., VII, 161–2, Colbert à Duchesneau, Paris, May 15, 1678.

12 Ibid., VII, 80–1, Colbert à Duchesneau, Paris, May 1, 1677; 168, Colbert à Duchesneau, Paris, May 15, 1678.

13 AN. CIIA, V, 50, Duchesneau au Ministre, Que., Nov. 10, 1679.

14 Can. Arch. Lettres de l'Abbé Tronson, I, Abbé Tronson à M. de Casson, [Paris,] May, 1679; AN. F3, Moreau de St. Méry, II, 26–7, Extrait du mémoire pour les gens tenans le Conseil Souverain à Québec contre M. de Frontenac sur le sujet de l'Usurpation par luy fait de la qualité de Chef et Président du Conseil.

15 Ibid.

16 AN. CIIA, V, D'Auteuil au Ministre, Que., Nov. 10, 1679; 33–7, Duchesneau au Ministre, Que., Nov. 10, 1679.

17 Can. Arch. Lettres de l'Abbé Tronson, I, Abbé Tronson à Dollier de Casson, May, 1679.

18 AN. CIIA, V, 99, Ordonnance du Roy, St. Germain-en-Laye, May 7, 1679; AN. B, VIII, 18, Colbert à Frontenac, St. Germain, May 8, 1679.

19 AN. CIIA., V, 167, Duchesneau au Ministre, Que., Nov. 13, 1680.

20 Jugements et Délibérations du Conseil Souverain de Québec, II, 266.

21 Can. Arch. AN. F3, Moreau de St. Méry, V, 281–7, Requeste présentée par le Sr Peuvret, greffier en chef du Conseil portant plainte de l'imprisonment fait de sa personne et demande d'estre eslargy. A nos

seigneurs du Conseil Souverain de la Nouvelle France. Que., Feb. 21, 1679. [It appears that Peuvret was imprisoned on Feb. 20 since the case in question was heard by the Sovereign Council on that day, and he must have been released within a few days since he was present at a Council meeting on the 27th of that month. See *Jugements et Délibérations* . . ., II, 278-9.]

22 *Ibid.*, 311-13, Acte de déclaration du Sʳ Peuvret greffier contre M. le gouverneur . . ., April 17, 1679.

23 AN. CııA, IV, 104-5, Déclaration du Roi qui confirme et regle l'Etablissement du Conseil Souverain du Canada du 5 juin 1675. Louis, Colbert.

24 I can give no specific reference for this opinion; it rests largely on negative evidence. In the minutes of the Sovereign Council meetings, although the proceedings are reported in detail, nowhere is there any mention of a vote being taken, or a record of such a vote. Colbert stated in the *Déclaration du Roi* of June 5, 1675, that the intendant would "demande les avis, recueille les voix et prononce les arrêts." Clearly, he meant just that and not something else. It is interesting to note that in the British Cabinet today a very similar system is in vogue. See Herbert Morrison, *Government and Parliament* (London, 1954), 5-6.

25 AN. F3, Moreau de St. Méry, II, 47-8, Extrait des contestations arrivés entre M. le Comte de Frontenac et M. du Chesneau pour la qualité de chef et Président du Con.ᵉˡ Souverain de Québec. 1679.

26 *Ibid.*

27 *Ibid.*, 46-55; 26-7, Extraict du mémoire pour les gens tenans le Conseil Souverain à Québec.

28 AN. CııA, V, 5-6, Frontenac au Ministre, Que., Oct. 9, 1679.

29 AN. B, VII, 161, Le Roi à Frontenac, St. Germain-en-Laye, May 12, 1678.

30 RAPQ 1926-1927, 87, Le Roi à Frontenac, April 15, 1676; 80, Le Roi à Frontenac, April 22, 1675.

31 *Jugements et Délibérations du Conseil Souverain de Québec*, II, 279-83, 288-9, 295, 298, 300-2, 304; AN. F3, Moreau de St. Méry, II, 26-7, Extraict du mémoire pour les gens tenans le Conseil Souverain à Québec.

32 *Ibid.*; *Jugements et Délibérations* . . ., II, 304-6, 308.

33 AN. F3, Moreau de St. Méry, II, 48-51, Extrait des contestations arrivés entre M. le Comte de Frontenac et M. du Chesneau. . . .

34 *Ibid.*, 50.

35 *Ibid.*, 51-2.

36 AN. CııA, V, D'Auteuil au Ministre, Que., Nov. 10, 1679.

37 Extrait des contestations . . ., *op. cit.*, 50.

38 *Jugements et Délibérations* . . ., II, 304-6, 308; AN. CııA, V, D'Auteuil au Ministre, Que., Nov. 10, 1679.

39 Extrait des contestations . . ., *op. cit.*, 51-3.

40 AN. CɪɪA, V, D'Auteuil au Ministre, Que., Nov. 10, 1679.
41 *Ibid.*
42 *Ibid.*, V, 5–6, Frontenac au Ministre, Que., Oct. 9, 1679.
43 *Ibid.*, V, 99, Ordonnance du Roy, St. Germain-en-Laye, May 7, 1679; AN. B, VIII, 18, Colbert à Frontenac, St. Germain-en-Laye, May 8, 1679.
44 AN. CɪɪA, V, 33–7, Duchesneau au Ministre, Que., Nov. 10, 1679.
45 *Ibid.*
46 *Jugements et Délibérations* . . ., II, 318–19.
47 *Ibid.*; AN. CɪɪA, V, 33–7, Duchesneau au Ministre, Que., Nov. 10, 1679.
48 D'Auteuil au Ministre, Que., Nov. 10, 1679, *op. cit.*
49 AN. CɪɪA, V, 8–9, Frontenac au Ministre, Que., Nov. 6, 1679.
50 *Ibid.*
51 D'Auteuil an Ministre, Que., Nov. 10, 1679, *op. cit.*
52 AN. CɪɪA, V, 5–6, Frontenac au Ministre, Que., Oct. 9, 1679.
53 *Ibid.*, 8–9, Frontenac au Ministre, Que., Nov. 6, 1679.
54 *Ibid.*, 184, D'Auteuil [fils] au Ministre, [Que.,] 1680; 166, Duchesneau au Ministre, Que., Nov. 13, 1680.
55 *Ibid.*, 37–8, Duchesneau au Ministre, Que., Nov. 10, 1679.
56 *Jugements et Délibérations* . . ., II, 341–3; AN. CɪɪA, V, 166, Duchesneau au Ministre, Que., Nov. 13, 1680; 184, D'Auteuil [fils] au Ministre, [Que.,] 1680.
57 *Ibid.*; 166, Duchesneau au Ministre, Que., Nov. 13, 1680; *Jugements et Délibérations* . . ., II, 341–2.
58 *Ibid.*, 344–420.
59 AN. CɪɪA, V, 205–7, Lettre du Roi à M. le Comte de Frontenac, St. Germain-en-Laye, April 29, 1680.
60 AN. B, VIII, 53–5, Lettre à la main de Mgr. Colbert à M. le comte de Frontenac, St. Germain-en-Laye, April 20, 1680.
61 Bib. Nat. Fonds Français, XXMMDCCIC, 46, De Villermont à M. Denys, Paris, April 10, 1680.
62 AN. CɪɪA, V, 238–9, Le Roi à M. Duchesneau, June 2, 1680.
63 AN. B, VIII, 59, Lettre à la main de Mgr. Colbert au Sr Duchesneau, Fontainebleau, June 2, 1680.
64 AN. CɪɪA, V, 69–70, Duchesneau au Ministre, Que., Nov. 10, 1679.
65 *Ibid.*, 218–19, Arrêt du Conseil d'Etat, Sa Maté y étant, Fontainebleau, May 29, 1680. [Signed, Colbert]
66 D'Auteuil au Ministre, Que., Nov. 10, 1679, *op. cit.*
67 *Jugements et Délibérations* . . ., II, 422–3.
68 RAPQ, 1926–1927, 118, Frontenac au maréchal de Bellefonds, Que., Nov. 14, 1680.
69 AN. CɪɪA, V, 33–7, Duchesneau au Ministre, Que., Nov. 10, 1679.
70 AN. F3, Moreau de St. Méry, II, 76–7, Conduite du Sr Perrot . . . 1681; *Jugements et Délibérations* . . ., II, 441–5, 481 ff.

71 *Ibid.*, 606–7, 681–6; Conduite du S' Perrot . . . 1681, *op. cit.*

72 *Ibid.*; AN. C11A, V, 172–3, Duchesneau au Ministre, Que., Nov. 13, 1680; Can. Arch. Documents St. Sulpice, XXI, Mémoire de quelques faits qui se sont passés dans l'ile de Montréal. . . .

73 Can. Arch. Lettres de l'Abbé Tronson, II, Tronson à Dollier de Casson, [Paris,] Feb. 21, 1683.

74 *Jugements et Délibérations* . . ., II, 442–5.

75 *Ibid.*, 343, 358, 434.

76 *Ibid.*, 570–2.

77 *Ibid.*, 572–7.

78 AN. C11A, V, 302–4, Duchesneau au Ministre, Que., Nov. 13, 1681.

79 *Jugements et Délibérations* . . ., II, 596.

80 *Ibid.*, 596, 632–5, 696–701, 720–1, 726.

81 *Ibid.*; AN. C11A, V, 281, Frontenac au Ministre, Que., Nov. 13, 1681.

82 *Ibid.*, 357–8, Lettre du Roi à Frontenac, Versailles, April 30, 1681.

83 *Ibid.*, 271, Frontenac au Ministre, Que., Nov. 2, 1681.

84 *Ibid.*, D'Auteuil au Ministre, Que., Nov. 10, 1679.

85 *Ibid.*, 281, Frontenac au Ministre, Que., Nov. 13, 1681.

86 *Ibid.*; *Jugements et Délibérations* . . ., II, 551–4.

87 This was not the first time that Boisseau had been accused of such conduct. See *Jugements et Délibérations* . . ., II, 625–35, 721.

88 AN. C11A, V, 302–4, Duchesneau à Seignelay, Que., Nov. 13, 1681; 382–4, Frontenac au Roy, Que., Nov. 2, 1681; AN. F3, Moreau de St. Méry, II, 78–9; Mémoire de l'Evesque de Québec de ce qui s'est passé . . .; *Jugements et Délibérations* . . ., II, 528–30.

89 *Ibid.*, 534–5, 552–5.

90 AN. C11A, V, 283–5, [Mme de Frontenac] à Seignelay, [1681–2].

91 *Ibid.*; 382–4, Frontenac au Roy, Que., Nov. 2, 1681. [Duchesneau, in his account of events, conspicuously fails to mention his having barricaded his house and armed his servants.]

92 *Jugements et Délibérations* . . ., II, 635–51.

93 *Ibid.*, 640–1, 652.

94 *Ibid.*, 699.

95 Sem. Que. Carton N, No. 62, M. Dudouyt à Mgr. de Laval, [Paris,] May 26, 1682.

96 Can. Arch. Lettres de l'Abbé Tronson, II, Tronson à de Casson, [Paris,] March 29, 1682.

97 M. Dudouyt à Mgr de Laval, [Paris,] May 26, 1682, *op. cit.*

98 AN. B, VIII, 128, A M. le comte de Frontenac, Versailles, May 9, 1682; Au S' Duchesneau, Versailles, May 9, 1682.

99 AN. C11A, V, 205–7, Lettre du Roi à M. le Comte de Frontenac, St. Germain-en-Laye, April 29, 1680.

100 *Ibid.*, 198–204.

101 Francis Parkman, *Frontenac and New France under Louis XIV*, 74.

102 *Ibid.*, 75.

CHAPTER EIGHT

1 Bib. Nat. Fonds Français, XXMMDVC, 296, Dossier of La Barre; XXMMDCXXIII, 72, Gouvernement des Provinces; AN. CiiA, VI, 361–2, La Barre au Ministre, Que., Nov. 14, 1684.

2 Stewart L. Mims, *Colbert's West India Policy*, 129.

3 Sem. Que. Lettres, Carton N, No. 62, M. Dudouyt à Mgr de Laval, May 26, 1682.

4 AN. B. VIII, Instruction que le Roy veut estre mise es mains du Sr de Meulles . . ., Versailles, May 9, 1682; Instruction que le Roy veut estre mise es mains du Sr de la Barre . . ., Versailles, May 10, 1682; Can. Arch. Lettres de l'Abbé Tronson, II, Tronson à de Casson, May 15, 1682.

5 AN. CiiA, VI, 63, La Barre au Ministre [1682].

6 *Ibid.*, 242–3, Ministre à La Barre, Versailles, April 10, 1684; 289–90, Le Roy à la Barre, Versailles, April 10, 1684; 177–80, De Meulles au Ministre, Que., Nov. 4, 1683.

7 AN. B, XI, 47–8, Ministre à de Meulles, Versailles, July 31, 1684; AN. CiiA, VI, 379, Ministre à de Meulles, Versailles, April 10, 1684.

8 AN. B, VIII, 103–4, Instruction que le Roy veut estre mise es mains du Sr de la Barre . . ., Versailles, May 10, 1682.

9 AN. CiiA, VI, 68–70, Mémoire de l'Assemblée tenu le 10e Octobre 1682. Que., Le Febvre de la Barre; 85–6, De Meulles au Ministre, Que., Nov. 12, 1682.

10 *Ibid.*, VI, 66–7, La Barre au Roy, [1682]; 61, La Barre au Ministre, [1682]; 138, La Barre au Ministre, Que., Nov. 4, 1683; 227, Ordonnance de la Barre, Que., March 19, 1684.

11 *Ibid.*, 167–70, De Meulles au Ministre, Que., June 2, 1683.

12 *Ibid.*, 134, La Barre au Ministre, Que., Nov. 4, 1683.

13 *Ibid.*

14 *Ibid.*

15 Abbé de Belmont, *Histoire du Canada*, 15–16.

16 AN. CiiA, VI, 134–7, La Barre au Ministre, Que., Nov. 4, 1683.

17 *Ibid.*; 153, La Barre à Colbert, Que., Nov. 4, 1683.

18 Sem. Que. Lettres, Carton N, No. 71, Dudouyt à Mgr de Laval, Paris, May 28, 1683.

19 AN. B, X, 3–5, Le Roy à La Barre, Fontainebleau, Aug. 5, 1683.

20 AN. CiiA, VI, 273–7, La Barre au Ministre, Que., June 5, 1684.

21 *Ibid.*, Relation d'un voyage dans le Pays des Illinois par MM. Beauvais, Provost et Desrosiers, Que., May 28, 1684; 519, Chev. de Baugy à de la Durantaye, Aux Illinois, March 24, 1684; 273–7, La Barre au Ministre, Que., June 5, 1684.

22 Francis Parkman, *Frontenac and New France under Louis XIV*, Chap. 5, *passim*.

23 AN. CiiA, VI, 177–80, De Meulles au Ministre, Que., Nov. 4, 1683; Abbé de Belmont, *op. cit.*, 16–17; AN. F3, Moreau de St. Méry, II, Recueil de ce qui s'est passé en Canada . . . depuis l'année 1682. [Gédéon de Catalogne]; Lahontan, *New Voyages to North America*, I, 91.

24 AN. B, VIII, 107, Instruction que le Roy veut estre mise es mains du Sr de la Barre . . ., Versailles, May 10, 1682.

25 AN. CiiA, VI, 177–80, De Meulles au Ministre, Que., Nov. 4, 1683.

26 AN. B, X, 6, Le Roy à la Barre, Fontainebleau, Aug. 5, 1683.

27 Le Chevalier de Baugy, *Journal d'une expédition contre les Iroquois en 1687*, 183.

28 De Meulles au Ministre, Que., Nov. 4, 1683, *loc. cit.*; Lahontan, *op. cit.*, I, 91.

29 AN. B, XI, 15–16, Ministre à la Barre, Versailles, April 10, 1684.

30 AN. CiiA, VI, 361–2, La Barre au Ministre, Que., Nov. 14, 1684.

31 AN. F3, Moreau de St. Méry, II, Recueil de ce qui s'est passé en Canada au sujet de la guerre depuis l'année 1682. [Gédéon de Catalogne]

32 AN. CiiA, IX, Dongan à Denonville, Sept. 9, 1687.

33 *Ibid.*, VI, 348–9, Mémoire au Roy, La Barre, Que., Nov. 13, 1684.

34 Abbé de Belmont, *op. cit.*, 15–16.

35 *Ibid.*, 16–17; AN. CiiA, VI, 273–7, La Barre au Ministre, Que., June 5, 1684.

36 AN. CiiA, VI, 528–32, Boisguillot à la Barre, Missilimakinac, May 7, 1684; 522, Durantaye à la Barre, St. François Xavier, Baye des Puants, April 22, 1684; 525, R. P. Enjalran S. J. à la Barre, Missilimakinac, May 7, 1684; 523, R.P. Henry Nouvel S.J. à la Barre, St. François Xavier, Baye des Puants, April 23, 1684.

37 *Ibid.*, 273–7, La Barre au Ministre, Que., June 5, 1684; 388–93, De Meulles au Ministre, Que., Oct. 10, 1684.

38 *Ibid.*, 273–7, La Barre au Ministre, Que., June 5, 1684; 284–5, La Barre au Ministre, Que., July 9, 1684; 344–6, Mémoire au Roy, La Barre, Que., Nov. 13, 1684; 400, De Meulles au Ministre, Que., July, 1684.

39 Bib. Nat. Fonds Français, XXMMDCCIC, 179, De Machault Rougemont à M. de Villermont, Rochefort, July 22, 1684.

40 AN. CiiA, VI, 285, La Barre au Ministre, Que., July 9, 1684.

41 *Ibid.*, 309, La Barre au Ministre, Que., Oct. 1, 1684; 295, Revue des troupes qui ont accompagné M. de la Barre, Aug. 14, 1684.

42 *Ibid.*, 265, La Barre à Col. Dongan, Mtl., June 15, 1684; 266, Col. Dongan à la Barre, Manatte, June 25, 1684; 268, La Barre à Dongan, July 24, 1684; CSP 1681–1685, 688, Gov. de la Barre to the Gov. of Boston, Que., June 29, 1684.

43 AN. CiiA, VI, 291–2, De Meulles à la Barre, Que., July 15, 1684.

44 *Ibid.*, 382–5, De Meulles au Ministre, Que., July 8, 1684.

45 *Ibid.*, 534–8, R. P. Lamberville à la Barre, Onontagué, 10, 11 & 18 July, 1684.

46 *Ibid.*, 293–4, De Meulles au Ministre, Mtl., Aug. 14, 1684.

47 *Ibid.*, 309–13, La Barre au Ministre, Que., Oct. 1, 1684; 388–93, De Meulles au Ministre, Que., Oct. 10, 1684.

48 *Ibid.*, 299–300, Presens des Onontaguez à Onontio à la Famine le Cinq Septembre 1684. Le febvre de la barre.

49 *Ibid.*, 309–13, La Barre au Ministre, Que., Oct. 1, 1684.

50 *Ibid.*, 388–93, De Meulles au Ministre, Que., Oct. 1, 1684.

51 *Ibid.*, VIII, 139, Denonville au Ministre, Que., Nov. 10, 1686.

52 *Ibid.*, VI, 400–1, De Meulles au Ministre, Que., Nov. 12, 1684; 344, Mémoire au Roy . . . La Barre, Que., Nov. 13, 1684.

53 AN. B, XI, 43–4, Le Roy à la Barre, Versailles, July 31, 1684.

54 *Ibid.*, 96, Le Roy au Sr de Meulles, Versailles, March 10, 1685.

55 AN. CiiA, VII, 208, Mémoire des Interessez dans la Compagnie de la Baye d'Hudson, 1685.

56 *Ibid.*, VIII, 139, Denonville au Ministre, Que., Nov. 10, 1686.

CHAPTER NINE

1 *Bulletin de la Société Archéologique d'Eure-et-Loire*, 1er Semestre, 1951; AN. B, XI, 100–1, Ministre à de Meulles, Versailles, March 10, 1685.

2 *Ibid.*, 89, Instruction que le Roy veut estre mise es mains du Sr Marquis de Denonville, March 10, 1685.

3 Bib. Nat. Fonds Français, $\overline{\text{XX}}$MMDCLXXI, 233, Charges d'Emplois de Guerre. [To be strictly accurate, Louis XIV granted Denonville 20,000 *écus* for his regiment, then gave it to the Marquis de Murcé, Mme de Maintenon's nephew.]

4 AN. CiiA, VII, 18–19, Denonville au Ministre, La Rochelle, May 1, 1685; 37–8, Denonville au Ministre, La Rochelle, June 5, 1685; 43, Denonville au Ministre, La Rochelle, June 5, 1685.

5 *Ibid.*, V, 364–7, Mémoire que Denonville presente à Seignelay [1685]; Mémoire des choses qui praicent daventage Denonville de demander les ordres de Mgr de Seignelay [1685].

6 *Ibid.*, VII, 87–8, Denonville au Ministre, Que., Nov. 13, 1685.

7 *Ibid.*, 110–11; 56–7, Denonville au Ministre, Que., Aug. 20, 1685.

8 *Ibid.*; 146, De Meulles au Ministre, Que., Sept. 28, 1685; VIII, 25–6, Denonville au Ministre, Mtl., June 8, 1686; AN. B, XV, 20, Mémoire du Roy à Denonville et Champigny, Versailles, March 8, 1688.

9 AN. CiiA, VII, 110–11, Denonville au Ministre, Que., Nov. 13, 1685; 74, Extrait des lettres de M. de Denonville de 20 aoust, 3 sept., 12 & 13 nov. 1685.

10 *Ibid.*; 59–60, Denonville au Ministre, Que., Aug. 20, 1685; AN. B, XII, 38, Mémoire du Roy au Sr Marquis de Denonville, Versailles, May 31, 1686.

11 AN. C11A, XI, 192–3, Mémoire concernant le Canada pour Mgr le Marquis de Seignelay, Jan., 1690.

12 *Ibid.*, VII, 89, Denonville au Ministre, Que., Nov. 13, 1685; VIII, 21–2, Denonville au Ministre, Que., May 8, 1686; 23, Copie d'un passeport pour aller en traitte aux Outaouax, Denonville, Que., Jan. 29, 1686.

13 *Ibid.*, VII, 213–15, Mémoire concernant l'estat présent du Canada. Denonville, Nov. 12, 1685; VIII, 59–63, Denonville au Ministre, Mtl., June 12, 1686; CSP 1685–1688, 195, Dongan to Father Lamberville, Albany, May 20, 1686; 371, Gov. Dongan to the Earl of Sutherland, New York, May 20, 1687; NYCD, III, 394–5, Gov. Dongan to the Lords of Trade & Plantations, March, 1687.

14 AN. C11A, VI, 246, Le Roy à la Barre, Versailles, April 10, 1684; IX, 26, Denonville au Ministre, Mtl., June 8, 1686; 68–9, Denonville au Ministre, Mtl., June 8, 1686; L'Abbé Maxime de Godefroy, *Le Chevalier de Callières, Gouverneur de la Nouvelle France, 1648–1703*, 3.

15 AN. C11A, X, 256, Champigny au Ministre, Que., Nov. 16, 1689.

16 Can. Arch. Lettres de l'Abbé Tronson, III, 315, Abbé Tronson à M. de Casson, May 2, 1686; AN. C11A, X, Mémoire au Ministre, 1688.

17 *Ibid.*, VII, 213–15, Mémoire concernant l'estat présent de Canada. Denonville, Nov. 12, 1685.

18 *Ibid.*, 211, Mémoire de ce qui s'est passé dans le dernier voyage de la Baye d'Hudson. Envoyé par M. de Meules le 4 Oct. 1685; 208, Mémoire des Interessez dans la Compagnie de la Baye d'Hudson, 1685.

19 *Ibid.*, VII, 254, Contrat de Concession pour la Baye d'Hudson [1685–6]; AN. F3, Moreau de St. Méry, II, 163, Abstract of de Meulles' dispatch of June 6, 1684, with Seignelay's marginal comments.

20 AN. C11E, I, 114–15, Copie du Traité Provisionel concernant l'Amérique, 11 Dec. 1687; AN. B, XII, Lettre du Roy à Denonville, June 17, 1687.

21 AN. C11A, VIII, 154–5, Denonville au Ministre, Que., Nov. 10, 1686; IX, 76–7, Denonville au Ministre, Mtl., Aug. 25, 1687; 52–3, Nouvelles de ce qui a esté fait par les français dans le Baye d'Hudson; Nellis M. Crouse, *Lemoyne d'Iberville, Soldier of New France*, 14–39; AN. C11A, VIII, 264, Instructions pour M. de Troyes, Denonville, Que., Feb. 12, 1686.

22 NYCD, III, 341, Sir John Werden to Gov. Dongan, St. James, March 10, 1683/4.

23 CSP 1685–1688, 195, Dongan to Father Lamberville, Albany, May 20, 1686; 371, Gov. Dongan to the Earl of Sunderland, New York, May 20, 1687; NYCD, III, 394–5, Gov. Dongan to the Lords of Trade & Plantations, March, 1687.

24 *Ibid.*; AN. C11A, VIII, 8–9, Denonville au Ministre, Que., May 8, 1686; 168–9, Denonville au Ministre, Que., Nov. 16, 1686.

25 *Ibid.*, IX, 21–3, Denonville au Ministre, Mtl., June 8, 1687.

26 Gov. Dongan's Report to the Lords of Trade & Plantations, March, 1687, *loc. cit.*

27 AN. C11A, VIII, 168–9, Denonville au Ministre, Que., Nov. 16, 1686; 117–18, Mémoire de l'estat présent des affaires de Canada, Denonville, Que., Nov. 8, 1686.

28 *Ibid.*

29 *Ibid.*, 9–10, Denonville au Ministre, Que., May 8, 1686.

30 *Ibid.*, 120–1, Mémoire de l'estat présent des affaires de Canada. Denonville, Que., Nov. 8, 1686.

31 *Ibid.*; 59–63, Denonville au Ministre, Mtl., June 12, 1686.

32 *Ibid.*, 15–16, 20–1, Denonville au Ministre, Que., May 8, 1686.

33 *Ibid.*, 209, Extrait des Registres du Conseil Souverain de Québec, Jan. 14, 1686.

34 *Ibid.*, 8–11, Denonville au Ministre, Que., May 8, 1686; 53, Denonville à M. du Lhude, Mtl., June 6, 1686; 51–2, Denonville au Sr de la Durantaye, Mtl., June 6, 1686; 98–9, Denonville à M. de la Forest, Mtl., June 6, 1686; AN. F3, Moreau de St. Méry, II, 218–21, Mémoire Instructif . . . pour Messieurs de Tonty, la Durantaye, et du Lhut . . ., Denonville, Aug. 26, 1686; 222–3, Instruction de la part de M. de Denonville . . . pour Mrs de la Durantaye et Du Lhut pour addiction au mémoire qu'ils ont déja reçu . . ., Aug. 26, 1686.

35 AN. C11A, IX, 105–7, Mémoire du Voyage pour l'entreprise de M. le Marquis de Denonville contre les Sonontouans. Denonville.

36 *Ibid.*; 32–3, Champigny au Ministre, Que., July 16, 1687.

37 Can. Arch. Documents St. Sulpice, Registre 25, Campagne de M. le Marquis de Denonville dans le Pays des Iroquois.

38 *Jes. Rel.*, LXII, 102–4, Jean de Lamberville à R.P. Beschefer, Onondaga, Aug. 25, 1682.

39 AN. C11A, IX, 33–6, Champigny au Ministre, Que., July 16, 1687.

40 Le Chevalier de Baugy, *Journal d'une expédition contre les Iroquois en 1687,* 76–7.

41 *Jes. Rel.*, LI, 176, Relation de ce qui s'est passé dans la Nouvelle France es années 1667 & 1668.

42 Campagne de M. le Marquis de Denonville dans le Pays des Iroquois, *op. cit.*

43 AN. C11A, IX, 110–11, Mémoire du Voyage pour l'Entreprise de M. le Marquis de Denonville contre les Sonontouans. Denonville [Oct., 1687]; NYCD, III, 485, Propositions of the Onondagas to the Mayor & Common Council of Albany, Sept. 14, 1687; *Livingston Indian Records, 1666–1723,* 121–3, Propositions made by the Cayouges Sachims to ye Magistrates of Albany ye 27th day of June 1687.

44 Mémoire du Voyage pour l'Entreprise de M. le Marquis de Denonville contre les Sonontouans, *op. cit.*; AN. C11A, IX, 33–6; Aff. Et. Series Amérique, V, 283, Réponses aux lettres de Canada, March 30, 1687.

45 Mémoire du Voyage . . ., *op. cit.*

46 AN. F3, Moreau de St. Méry, II, 103, Recueuil de ce qui s'est passé en Canada au sujet de la guerre . . . depuis l'année 1682.

47 AN. C11A, VIII, 8, Denonville au Ministre, Que., May 8, 1686.

48 *Ibid.*, 33–6; 177–9, Denonville au Ministre, Que., Nov. 7, 1687; 64–8, Denonville au Ministre, Mtl., Aug. 25, 1687; Mémoire du Voyage . . ., *op. cit.*; De Baugy, *op. cit.*

CHAPTER TEN

1 AN. C11A, IX, 188, Champigny au Ministre, Mtl., Aug. 26, 1687; *Jes. Rel.*, LXIII, 281, R. P. Beschefer à M. Cabart de Villermont, Que., Sept. 19, 1687.

2 AN. B, XII, Mémoire du Roy aux Srs Denonville et Champigny, Versailles, March 30, 1687; AN. C11A, VI, 289, Le Roy à la Barre, Versailles, July 31, 1684.

3 AN. B, XII, Ministre à M. de Denonville, Versailles, March 8, 1688.

4 Ernest Lavisse, *Histoire de France*, VII–1, 306; W. H. Lewis, *The Splendid Century*, Chap. 10, *passim*.

5 Doc. Rel. N.F. I, 394, Ministre au R. P. Leroux à Marseilles, Paris, March 26, 1687; 426, Ministre à l'Intendant des Galères à Marseilles, 1688.

6 AN. C11A, IX, 70–1, Denonville au Ministre, Mtl., Aug. 25, 1687.

7 *Ibid.*, 134–5, Mémoire de l'Estat Présent des Affaires de Canada, Denonville, Oct. 27, 1687.

8 *Ibid.*, 136–43; 281–2, Mémoire du Chev. de Callières sur l'estat des affairs du Canada à Mgr le Marquis de Seignelay [Mtl., 1688].

9 Abbé de Belmont, *Histoire du Canada*, 20–1; Mémoire de l'Estat Présent des Affaires de Canada, Denonville, Oct. 27, 1687, *loc. cit.*

10 AN. C11A, X, 11, Denonville et Champigny au Ministre, Que., Nov. 6, 1688; 148, Mémoire du Chev. de Callières . . . à Mgr le Marquis de Seignelay, 1688.

11 *Ibid.*, IX, 73, Denonville au Ministre, Que., Aug. 25, 1687.

12 Bib. Nat. Fonds Français, XXMMDCCC, 181, Bégon à de Villermont, La Rochelle, Dec. 19, 1688; AN. C11A, X, 185, Extrait des Lettres du Sr de Denonville, Mtl., Aug. 16, Oct. 31, Nov. 6, 1688.

13 *Ibid.*; IX, 140–2, Mémoire de l'Estat Présent des Affairs de Canada sur la Guerre des Iroquois. Denonville, Oct. 27, 1687.

14 AN. F3, Moreau de St. Méry, II, 237–42, Mémoire succinct de ce qui s'est passé . . . depuis de 1er Nov. 1687.

15 AN. C11A, X, 63–4, Denonville à Seignelay, Aug. 10, 1688.

16 *Ibid.*

17 AN. B, XV, 25, Ministre à Denonville, Versailles, March 8, 1688.

18 AN. C11A, X, 70–1, Mémoire instructif de l'estat des affaires de la Nouvelle France, Denonville, Aug. 10, 1688; 281–2, Mémoire du Chev.

de Callières . . . sur l'estat des affaires de Canada à Mgr le Marquis de Seignelay [Versailles, 1689].

19 *Ibid.*, IX, 177–9, Denonville au Ministre, Que., Nov. 7, 1687.

20 Mémoire du Chev. de Callières . . ., *op. cit.*; 10, Denonville et Champigny au Ministre, Que., Nov. 6, 1688; 46, Denonville à Dongan, Mtl., May 12, 1688; AN. F3, Moreau de St. Méry, II, 240–2, Mémoire succinct de ce qui s'est passé de plus considérable sur le fait de la guerre depuis le premier Nov. 1687. A Mgr de la part de Denonville, Aug. 10, 1688.

21 *Ibid.*, 237–42; AN. C11A, IX, 142, Mémoire de l'estat présent des affaires de Canada sur la Guerre des Iroquois. Denonville, Oct. 27, 1687; CSP 1685–1688, 543, Minutes of the Council of New York, May 6 & 7, 1688.

22 AN. C11A, X, 50–1, Declaration des Iroquois devant M. de Denonville à Mtl., June 15, 1688.

23 Mémoire du Chev. de Callières . . ., *op. cit.*

24 AN. F3, Moreau de St. Méry, II, 237–42, Mémoire succinct de ce qui s'est passé de plus considérable sur le fait de la guerre depuis le premier Nov. 1687. A Mgr de la part de Denonville, Aug. 10, 1688; AN. C11A, X, 69–70, Mémoire instructif . . . Denonville à Seignelay, Aug. 10, 1688; 86–93, Recit et l'Etat des affaires de Canada. Que., Oct. 30, 1688.

25 *Ibid.*, 103–4, Mémoire de l'estate présent des affaires de ce pays depuis le 10ᵉ Aoust 1688 jusqu'au dernier Octobre de la mesme année. Denonville, 6 Nov. 1688.

26 Mémoire instructif . . . Denonville à Seignelay, Aug. 10, 1688, *op. cit.*, 70–1.

27 AN. C11A, VIII, 124, Champigny au Ministre, Mtl., Aug. 8, 1688.

28 *Ibid.*, X, 100–1, Mémoire de l'estat présent des affaires de ce pays depuis le 10ᵉ Aoust 1688 jusqu'au dernier Octobre de la mesme année. Denonville, 6 Nov. 1688; 281–2, Mémoire du Chev. de Callières . . . à Mgr le Marquis de Seignelay, [Versailles,] 1689; Bib. Nat. Collection Clairambault, MXVI, 290–2, Tonty to an unknown correspondent, Mtl., Oct. 27, 1689.

29 AN. C11A, X, 70, Mémoire instructif de l'estat des affaires de la Nouvelle France. Denonville à Seignelay, Aug. 10, 1688.

30 *Ibid.*, 194–8, Denonville à Vallerenne, Sept. 24, 1689.

31 *Ibid.*, XI, 190–2, Mémoire concernant le Canada pour Mgr le Marquis de Seignelay, [Denonville,] Jan., 1690; 200–1, Projet de M. de Denonville pour l'entreprise de la Nouvelle York, 4 Mai 1690; IX, 76, Denonville au Ministre, Que., Aug. 25, 1687; X, 282–5, Mémoire du Chev. de Callières sur l'estat présent du Canada. A Mgr le marquis de Seignelay, Nov. 8, 1689; VIII, 170, Denonville au Ministre, Que., Nov. 16, 1686; X, 265–6, Jan., 1689, Canada. Mémoire du Sr Chev. de Callières.

32 AN. F3, Moreau de St. Méry, II, 104–20, Recueil de ce qui s'est passé en Canada au sujet de la guerre . . . depuis l'année 1682.

33 Robert Lionel Seguin, "Le comportement de certains habitants de Lachine aux environs de 1689," in BRH, LX, no. 4, Oct.–Nov.–Dec. 1954, 187–93.

34 Abbé de Belmont, *op. cit.*, 50–1; AN. CiiA, X, 321, Observations sur l'estat des affaires de Canada au départ des vaisseaux le 18 Nov. 1689; Bib. Nat. Collection Clairambault, MXVI, 290–2, Tonty to an unknown correspondent, Mtl., Oct. 27, 1689; Désiré Girouard, *Lake St. Louis, Old and New*, 124, 135; AN. F3, Moreau de St. Méry, II, 104–20, Recueil de ce qui s'est passé en Canada au sujet de la guerre . . . depuis l'année 1682.

35 *Ibid.*, 237–42, Mémoire succinct . . . à Mgr de la part de Denonville, Aug. 10, 1687.

36 AN. CiiA, X, 265–6, Jan., 1689, Canada. Mémoire du Sr Chev. de Callières.

37 *Ibid.*, 194–8, Denonville à M. de Vallerenne, Sept. 24, 1689.

38 RAPQ 1927–1928, 21, Frontenac au Ministre, Que., Nov. 15, 1689.

39 AN. CiiA, X, 244, Champigny au Ministre, Que., Nov. 16, 1689.

40 AN. B, XV, 56–7, Mémoire du Roy aux Srs Denonville et Champigny, Versailles, May 1, 1689.

41 CSP 1685–1688, 368, Memorandum; CSP 1681–1684, 740, Sir John Werden to Gov. Dongan, Dec. 4, 1684; NYCD, III, 558, Proceedings between Gov. Andros & the Five Nations, Albany, Sept. 19, 1688; 428, Gov. Dongan to the Lord President, n.d.; 396, Gov. Dongan's Report on the State of the Province [1687].

42 NYCD, III, 472–5, Dongan to Denonville, Sept. 9, 1687; CSP 1685–1688, 645, Memorial for the French Ambassador.

43 *The Livingston Indian Records, 1666–1723*, 129, Propositions sent by his Excellentie Tho: Dongan gov: genl to ye Maquase . . . July 8, 1687; 127, Propos made by his Excel Tho Dongan . . . to Sadogaree ye gen¹. of ye Sinnekes & some of Cayouge . . . & onnondage Indians. N. Yorke, July 4, 1687; 133–5, Propositions to ye five nations westward sent by . . . Tho Dongan, Albany, July 19, 1687; 131, Propositions made by his Excell. Tho. Dongan . . . to ye Maquase, oneyde, onnondages, Cayouges & Sinnekes . . . Skinnectady, July 14, 1687; 114, Answer of ye Maquase & ye Rest of ye Indians westward to the Propositions of his Excell: Thomas Dongan . . . Albany, April/May 1687; Peter Wraxall, *An Abridgement of the New York Indian Records*, 13–14, Speech of Govr Dongan to the Five Nations, Court House, Albany, Aug. 5, 1687.

44 NYCD, III, 591, Stephen Van Cortlandt to Gov. Andros, N. Yorke, July 9, 1689.

45 *Ibid.*

46 CSP 1689–1692, 22, Earl of Shrewsbury to Lord Howard of Effingham, Whitehall, April 19, 1689.

47 AN. CiiA, X, 226–7, Champigny au Ministre, Mtl., July 6, 1689.

48 NYCD, III, 608, Messrs Philips & Van Cortland to Secretary Blathwayt, Aug. 5, 1689.

CHAPTER ELEVEN

1 Sem. Que. Lettres, Carton N, No. 69, M. Dudouyt à Mgr de Laval, April 28, 1683; No. 71, M. Dudouyt à Mgr de Laval, May 28, 1683.

2 *Ibid.*, No. 79, M. Dudouyt à Mgr de Laval, March 28, 1684.

3 Bib. Nat. Fonds Français, XXMMDCLXXI, 256, Gratifications et Pensions, Aoust '85.

4 M. Dudouyt à Mgr de Laval, March 28, 1684, *op. cit.*

5 Châteauroux. Departmental Archives. Series E, Dossier 13, Chartiers du Comté de Palluau, Extrait des Registres du Conseil d'Estat, Feb. 23, 1678.

6 *Ibid.*

7 AN. C11A, XI, 245–6, Frontenac au Ministre, Que., Oct. 20, 1691.

8 *Ibid.*, X, 189, Extrait des Lettres de Canada. 1688.

9 *Ibid.*, IX, 143–4, Mémoire de l'Estat Présent des Affaires de Canada. Oct. 27, 1687 [Denonville]; see also le chevalier de Baugy, *Journal d'une expédition contre les Iroquois en 1687*, 101–2, 113–14.

10 Can. Arch. Lettres de l'Abbé Tronson, III, Tronson à Dollier de Casson, May 1, 1689.

11 Bib. Nat. Collection Clairambault, DCCCLXXIX, 319, Denonville au Ministre, La Rochelle, Dec. 27, 1689; AN. C11A, XII, 383, Mémoire touschant les boisons Enyvrant les Sauvages de Canada. 1693.

12 AN. B, XV, Ministre à Denonville, Versailles, May 1, 1689; Mémoire du Roy aux Srs Denonville et Champigny, Versailles, May 1, 1689; see also Ministre à Denonville, Versailles, March 8, 1688.

13 C. W. Alvord, *The Illinois Country, 1673–1818*, 95; Mason Wade, *The French Canadians, 1760–1945*, 21–2; Edgar McInnis, *Canada, A Political and Social History*, 89; J. M. S. Careless, *Canada, A Story of Challenge*, 55–6; Morden H. Long, *A History of the Canadian People*, I, 320; A. M. Machar, *The Story of Old Kingston*, 40; A. G. Dorland, *Our Canada*, 67; A. M. Peck, *The Pageant of Canadian History*, 83; Gustave Lanctot, *Le Canada d'Hier et d'Aujourdhui*, 48.

14 Can. Arch. Lettres de l'Abbé Tronson, III, Tronson à Dollier de Casson, May 1, 1689.

15 AN. B, XV, 63, Ministre à Denonville, Versailles, May 1, 1689.

16 CSP 1689–1692, 22, Earl of Shrewsbury to Lord Howard of Effingham, Whitehall, April 19, 1689.

17 Philippe Sagnac and A. de Saint-Leger, *Louis XIV*, 386–7.

18 RAPQ 1927–1928, 12–16, Mémoire pour servir d'Instruction à M. le comte de Frontenac sur l'entreprise de la Nouvelle York, [June 7, 1689].

19 AN. C11A, XI, 81, Extrait de l'Instruction donnée au Sr de Fron-

tenac au sujet de l'entreprise à faire sur la Nouvelle York; XIII, 318–19, Mémoire de M. de Lagny sur l'expédition de Manath.

20 *Ibid.*; AN. C11D, II, 134, Le Sr Saccardy au Ministre, La Rochelle, Jan. 3, 1690; Bib. Nat. Fonds Français, XXMMDCCC, 258, Bégon à de Villermont, Rochefort, June 26, 1689.

21 AN. C11A, X, 217–19, Frontenac au Ministre, Que., Nov. 15, 1689.

22 *Ibid.*

23 AN. B, XV, 85, Instruction pour le Sr Comte de Frontenac . . ., June 7, 1689; Sem. Que. Lettres, Carton M, No. 7, L'abbé de Brisacier aux prêtres du Séminaire de Québec, [Paris,] June 19, 1689.

24 AN. C11A, XI, 245–6, Frontenac au Ministre, Que., Oct. 20, 1691; XII, 31, Frontenac au Ministre, Que., Sept. 15, 1692; 232, Frontenac au Ministre, Que., Oct. 25, 1693; XIII, Frontenac au Ministre, Que., Oct. 25, 1694; 15–16, Frontenac au Ministre, Que., Nov. 4, 1695.

25 Can. Arch. Lettres de l'Abbé Tronson, III, Tronson à M. Dollier de Casson, May 1, 1689.

26 Sem. Que. Lettres, Carton M, No. 7, L'abbé de Brisacier aux prêtres du Séminaire de Québec, [Paris,] June 19, 1689.

27 *Ibid.*

28 AN. C11A, XII, 267–9, 272–4, Champigny au Ministre, Que., Nov. 4, 1693.

29 Bib. Nat. Collection Clairambault, MXVI, 290–2, Tonty to an unknown correspondent, Mtl., Oct. 27, 1689; Abbé de Belmont, *Histoire du Canada,* 30–1.

30 AN. C11A, X, 219, 224, Frontenac au Ministre, Que., Nov. 15, 1689.

31 *Ibid.*, 219–22.

32 Tonty to an unidentified correspondent, Mtl., Oct. 27, 1689, *op. cit.*

33 AN. C11A, XI, 192, Mémoire concernant le Canada pour Mgr le Marquis de Seignelay, [Denonville,] Jan., 1690; XIV, 30–1, Mémoire concernant le Fort de Cataracouy. Champigny. Nov. 6, 1695; XI, 267, Mémoire Instructif sur le Canada. Champigny, Que., May 12, 1691.

34 *Ibid.*, 264.

35 *Ibid.*, VI, 182–3, De Meulles au Ministre, Que., Nov. 4, 1683.

36 Lahontan, *New Voyages to North America,* I, 225–6.

37 Tonty to an unidentified correspondent, Mtl., Oct. 27, 1689, *op. cit.*

38 AN. C11A, XI, 264–7, Mémoire instructif sur le Canada. Champigny, Que., May 12, 1691.

39 *Ibid.*, X, 221, Frontenac au Ministre, Que., Nov. 15, 1689.

40 *Ibid.*, 74, Denonville au Ministre, Mtl., Aug. 10, 1688.

41 *Ibid.*, XI, 233, Sauvages Outaouas. Conseils à leur donner, [Frontenac,] 1690 [Although purporting to be an address to the Ottawas, this "speech" was clearly designed to impress an audience at Versailles rather than one at Michilimackinac.]; 84–5, Frontenac au Ministre, Que.,

April 30, 1690; 7, Relation de . . . 1690, Monseignat à [Mme de Frontenac], Que., Nov. 17, 1690.

42 *Ibid.*

43 *Ibid.*; 84–5, Frontenac au Ministre, Que., April 30, 1690.

44 *Ibid.*, X, 246, Champigny au Ministre, Que., Nov. 16, 1689.

45 Peter Wraxall, *An Abridgement of the New York Indian Records*, 14–16, Meeting of the Five Nations, Onondaga, Feb. 3, 1689/90.

46 AN. C11A, X, 207, Frontenac au Ministre, Que., Nov. 17, 1689.

47 *Ibid.*, XI, Frontenac au Ministre, Que., April 30, 1690.

48 AN. F3, Moreau de St. Méry, VI, 360–4, Extrait des Registres du Conseil Souverain de Québec, 20 & 27 Febvrier, 6 & 15 Mars, 1690.

49 AN. C11A, XI, 266–7, Mémoire Instructif sur le Canada. Champigny. Que., May 12, 1691.

CHAPTER TWELVE

1 AN. C11A, XII, 267–9, Champigny au Ministre, Que., Nov. 4, 1693.

2 *Ibid.*, XI, Champigny au Ministre, Que., Oct. 12, 1691.

3 *Ibid.*, XII, Frontenac et Champigny au Ministre, Que., Nov. 4, 1693.

4 AN. B, XVI, 146, Ministre à M. de la Vogadre, Versailles, Jan. 21, 1693.

5 AN. C11A, IX, 177–9, Denonville au Ministre, Que., Nov. 7, 1687.

6 *Ibid.*, XIII, 302, Frontenac et Champigny au Ministre, Que . Nov. 10, 1695.

7 *Ibid.*, XVI, 106, Champigny au Ministre, Que., Oct. 14, 1698.

8 P.-G. Roy (ed.), *Ordonnances, Commissions, etc., etc., des Gouverneurs et Intendants*, II, 96–7, Ordonnance de M. de Meulles, Que., April 26, 1685.

9 *Ibid.*, 104–5, Ordonnance de M. de Meulles, May 15, 1685.

10 *Ibid.*, 112–15, Ordonnance de M. de Meulles, June 8, 1685.

11 Que. Arch. Manuscrits Relatifs à l'Histoire de la Nouvelle France, 2me série, VII, Mémoire concernant le paye et le décompte des troupes en Canada. Champigny, Nov. 10, 1695.

12 AN. C11A, XI, 291, Champigny au Ministre, Que., Nov. 12, 1691.

13 *Ibid.*, XV, 164, Sr de la Touche au Ministre, Mtl., Oct. 15, 1697.

14 *Ibid.*; XIII, 284, Frontenac au Ministre, Que., Nov. 4, 1695.

15 AN. B, X, 17–18, Reglement que le Roy veut estre observé pour le payement des officiers de marine . . . dans la Nouvelle France. Versailles, April 10, 1684; AN. C11A, XVII, Mémoire sur la réforme des Troupes en Canada. 1700.

16 *Ibid.*, XII, 90, Champigny au Ministre, Que., Nov. 10, 1692.

17 AN. F3, Moreau de St. Méry, VII, 358, Reglement du Roy pour la Conduite, Police et Discipline des Compagnies que Sa Maté entretient dans le Canada. Du 30 May 1695.

18 AN. C11A, XVI, 106–7, Champigny au Ministre, Que., Oct. 14, 1698; see also Lahontan, *New Voyages in North America*, I, 387.

19 AN. C11A, XII, 213, Frontenac et Champigny au Ministre, Que., Nov. 4, 1693; XIII, 15, Frontenac et Champigny au Ministre, Que., Nov. 5, 1694.

20 AN. B, XVII, 95, Ministre à M. l'Evesque de Québec, Versailles, May 8, 1694; 77–8, Mémoire du Roy aux Srs Frontenac et Champigny, [April, 1694].

21 AN. C11A, XIII, 15, Frontenac et Champigny au Ministre, Que., Nov. 5, 1694.

22 *Ibid.*, XI, 291, Champigny au Ministre, Que., Nov. 12, 1691.

23 *Ibid.*, XV, 135–6, Champigny au Ministre, Que., Oct. 13, 1697.

24 *Ibid.*, X, 230, Champigny au Ministre, Ville Marie, July 6, 1689; XI, 290, Champigny au Ministre, Que., Nov. 12, 1691; XIII, 309, Frontenac et Champigny au Ministre, Que., Nov. 10, 1695.

25 *Ibid.*, IX, 198, Champigny au Ministre, Que., Nov. 5, 1687.

26 Sem. Que. Lettres, Carton N, No. 123, M. Tremblay à Mgr de Laval, [Paris,] June 19, 1705.

27 AN. C11A, X, 85, Mémoire sur les habits des Soldats envoyez en Canada en 1688. Juin 1688.

28 AN. B, XVI, 97, Mémoire du Roy aux Srs Comte de Frontenac et de Champigny [1692].

29 P.-G. Roy (ed.), *op. cit.*, 126–8, Ordonnance de M. de Denonville au sujet des Soldats à Montréal, Oct. 5, 1685.

30 AN. B, XVII, 179–80, Mémoire du Roy aux Srs Comte de Frontenac et de Champigny, Versailles, June 14, 1695; AN. C11A, XIII, 302–3, Frontenac et Champigny au Ministre, Que., Nov. 10, 1695.

31 *Ibid.*, XII, Champigny au Ministre, Que., Sept. 21, 1692; XV, 125, Champigny au Ministre, Que., Oct. 13, 1697.

CHAPTER THIRTEEN

1 AN. F3, Moreau de St. Méry, II, 243–4, Mémoire de ce qui s'est passé en Canada au sujet de la guerre contre les Anglois et Iroquois durant l'année 1690. Champigny.

2 CSP 1689–1692, 165, Edward Randolph to the Bishop of London, From the common gaol in Algiers, Oct. 25, 1689; see also 163–4, Copy of a letter from Boston, Oct. 24, 1689; 170, Governor & Council of Massachusetts to the Earl of Shrewsbury, Boston, Oct. 30, 1689; 158, Edward Randolph to the Lords of Trade & Plantations, Common Gaol, Boston, Oct. 15, 1689.

3 CSP 1689–1692, 101, Edward Randolph to the Lords of Trade & Plantations, Common Gaol, Boston, July 23, 1689: 220, The Revolutionary Council of New York to the Governor of Connecticut. Jacob Milborne; *Doc. Hist. N.Y.*, I, 192, Jacob Leisler to Maryland, Fort William, March 4, 1689/90; 195, Mr. Livingston to Capt. Nicholson, June 7, 1690; Mass. Arch. Inter-Charter, 1689–1690, XXXV, 151, Council to Cptn. Bull, Boston, Dec. 26, 1689.

4 *Ibid.*, 236–7, Jonathan Bull to General Council of Massachusetts, Albany, Feb. 14, 1689/90; 239–46, Mayor Peter Schuyler to General Court of Massachusetts, Albany, Feb. 15, 1689/90.

5 *Ibid.*

6 AN. CiiA, XI, 10–13, Relation de ce qui s'est passé de plus remarquable en Canada depuis . . . Novembre 1689 jusqu'au . . . Novembre 1690. Monseignat.

7 *Ibid.*; AN. F3, Moreau de St. Méry, II, 243–7, Mémoire de ce qui s'est passé en Canada . . . durant l'année 1690 . . . Champigny; CSP 1689–1692, 247–9, Robert Livingston to Sir Edmund Andros, Hartford, April 19, 1690; 242–3, Jacob Leisler to the Bishop of Salisbury, New York, March 31, 1690; Mass. Arch. Inter-Charter 1689–1690, XXXV, 239–46, Mayor Peter Schuyler to General Court of Massachusetts, Albany, Feb. 15, 1689/90.

8 *Ibid.*, 362–3, Samuel Sewall in behalf of Council of Massachusetts to the Gov. of Connecticut, Boston, March 24, 1689/90; AN. CiiA, XI, 10–13, Relation de ce qui s'est passé de plus remarquable en Canada depuis . . . Novembre 1689 jusqu'au . . . Novembre 1690. Monseignat.

9 AN. B-II, Marine, CCVI, 58, Ministre à M. le duc de Perth, Versailles, Jan. 4, 1708; AN. F3, Moreau de St. Méry, VI, 346, Mémoire de ce qui s'est passé à la descente des Anglois devant Québec. . . . Monseignat; *Les Annales de l'Hôtel Dieu de Québec, 1636–1716*, 258; AN. CiiA, XI, 37–8, Monseignat à [Mme de Frontenac], Que., Nov. 17, 1690.

10 *Ibid.*, 10–13, Relation de ce qui s'est passé de plus remarquable en Canada depuis . . . Novembre 1689 jusqu'au . . . Novembre 1690. Monseignat.

11 *Ibid.*; AN. F3, Moreau de St. Méry, II, 244, Mémoire de ce qui s'est passé en Canada . . . durant l'année 1690. Champigny; CSP 1689–1692, 269, Thomas Newton to an unidentified correspondent, Boston, May 26, 1690; Mass. Arch. Inter-Charter 1690–1691, XXXVI, 77, Chas. Frost to Gen'l Court, Portsmouth, May 22, 1690.

12 *Ibid.*, 202–16, Narrative of Capt. Sylvanus Davis.

13 AN. CiiA, XI, 83–7, Frontenac au Ministre, Que., April 30, 1690.

14 AN. F3, Moreau de St. Méry, II, 244–5, Mémoire de ce qui s'est passé en Canada . . . durant l'année 1690. . . . Champigny.

15 CSP 1685–1688, 641, Gov. de la Barre of Canada [to the minister], Nov. 11, 1682.

16 AN. CiiA, IX, 76, Denonville au Ministre, Que., Aug. 25, 1687; XI, 190–2 Mémoire concernant le Canada pour Mgr le Marquis de Seignelay, Janvier 1690 [Denonville]; X, 265–6, Janvier 1689, Canada. Mémoire du Sr chevalier de Callières.

17 *Doc. Hist. N.Y.*, III, 784–6, Gov. Slaughter to the Governors of the several Provinces, Fort Will. Henry, July 11, 1691.

18 Mass. Arch. Inter-Charter 1689–1690, XXXV, 362–3, Samuel

Sewall in behalf of the Council of Massachusetts to the Governor of Connecticut, Boston, March 24, 1689/90.

19 Peter Wraxall, *An Abridgement of the New York Indian Records*, 11, Onondaga & Cajuga Sachems to Dongan and Lord Effingham Howard, Gov'r of Virginia, Albany, Aug. 2, 1684.

20 *Ibid.*, lviii–lix; NYCD, III, 797, Address of the Governor & Council of New York to the King, Aug. 6, 1691; 394, Governor Dongan's Report on the State of the Province. . . . [1687]; *Livingston Indian Records, 1666–1723*, 113, Gov. Dongan Propos : by akns [*sic*] to ye Maquase & Sinnekas, Albany, 25 apl 1687.

21 Onondaga & Cajuga Sachems to Dongan & Lord Effingham Howard, Gov'r of Virginia, Albany, Aug. 2, 1684, Peter Wraxall, *loc. cit.*; 13, Lord Effingham Howard & Dongan confer with the Senecas, Albany, Aug. 5, 1684; AN. CiiA, VI, 517–18, Lamberville à la Barre, Onnontagué, Feb. 10, 1684.

22 Deputy Gov. Danforth to Sir H. Ashurst, April 1, 1690, *in* Thomas Hutchinson, *The History of Massachusetts*, I, 353.

CHAPTER FOURTEEN

1 AN. CiiA, XI, 84–5, Frontenac au Ministre, Que., April 30, 1690.

2 AN. F3, Moreau de St. Méry, II, 243, Mémoire de ce qui s'est passé en Canada au sujet de la guerre . . . durant l'année 1690. . . . Champigny.

3 *Ibid.*, 460–1, Champigny au Ministre, Que., May 10, 1691; XII, 27, Frontenac au Ministre, Que., Sept. 15, 1692; CSP 1689–1692, 285–6, The Rev. Committee at New York to the Earl of Shrewsbury, New York, June 23, 1689.

4 Peter Wraxall, *An Abridgement of the New York Indian Records*, 14–16, Meeting of the Five Nations, Onondaga, Feb. 3, 1689/90.

5 AN. F3, Moreau de St. Méry, II, 243, Mémoire de ce qui s'est passé en Canada . . . durant l'année 1690. . . . Champigny; AN. CiiA, XI, 6 Relation de ce qui s'est passé . . . en Canada depuis . . . Novembre 1690. Monseignat.

6 *Ibid.*, 83, Frontenac au Ministre, Que., April 30, 1690.

7 *Jes. Rel.*, LXIV, 22–39, Lettre de Père Carheil à M. le Gouverneur. Reçue par M. le Comte de Frontenac, Que., Sept. 17, 1690.

8 AN. F3, Moreau de St. Méry, II, 243, Mémoire de ce qui s'est passé en Canada . . . durant l'année 1690. . . . Champigny; AN. CiiA, XI, 14–15, Relation de ce qui s'est passé . . . en Canada depuis . . . Novembre 1689 jusqu'au . . . Novembre 1690. Monseignat.

9 *Ibid.*, 86–7, Frontenac au Ministre, Que., Nov. 12, 1690.

10 Bacqueville de la Potherie, *Histoire de l'Amérique Septentrionale*, II, 235–8; AN. CiiA, XI, 14–15, Monseignat à Mme [de Frontenac], 1690.

11 *Ibid.*, 88–9, Frontenac au Ministre, Que., Nov. 12, 1690.

12 *Ibid.*, X, 219, Frontenac au Ministre, Que., Nov. 15, 1689.

13 *Ibid.*, XI, 14–15, 24–8, Relation de ce qui s'est passé de plus

remarquable en Canada depuis . . . Novembre 1689 jusqu'au . . . Novembre 1690. Monseignat.

14 *Ibid.*, 88–9, Frontenac au Ministre, Que., Nov. 12, 1690.

15 *Ibid.*; AN. F3, Moreau de St. Méry, II, 243–7, Mémoire de ce qui s'est passé en Canada . . . durant l'année 1690. . . . Champigny; AN. C11A, XI, 27, Relation de ce qui s'est passé en Canada . . . depuis Novembre 1689 . . . jusqu'au . . . Novembre 1690. Monseignat.

16 *Doc. Hist. N.Y.*, II, 285, Journal of Captain John Schuyler.

17 NYCD, III, 611–12, Col. Bayard to Cptn. Nicholson, New York, Aug. 5, 1689; 695–6, Memorial of the Agents from Albany to the Gov't of Massachusetts, Charles Towne, March 20, 1689/90; 692–4, Memorial of the Agents from Albany, etc., to the Gov't of Connecticut, Hartford, March 12, 1689/90; Mass. Arch. Inter-Charter, 1689–1690, XXXV, 277, Gov'r & Council of Mass., to Albany, Boston, Feb. 27, 1689/90; Resolution of the Gen'l Court, March 19, 1689/90; 308a, Henry Bull, Gov. of R.I. to Gen'l Court of Mass., Newport, March 14, 1689/90; 284, Gov. Bradstreet of Mass. to Gov. & Council of R.I., Boston, March 10, 1689/90; 289, Gov. Bradstreet to Gov. Hinckley of Plymouth Plantation, Boston, March 11, 1689/90; 239–46, Peter Schuyler, Mayor of Albany, to Gen'l Court of Mass., Albany, Feb. 15, 1689/90; 247, Gov. Rob't Treat of Connecticut to Gov. & Council of Mass., Milford, Feb. 17, 1689/90.

18 *Rpt. Can. Arch.* 1912, Appendix G, 77, Captain Nicholson to the Lords of Trade & Plantations, Virginia, James Citty, Nov. 4, 1690; 64–6, An Abstract of a Lre from Mr. James Lloyd Merch[t] in Boston dat. 8th Jany., 1690/1; NYCD, IV, 193–6, Majr Genll Winthrop's Journal of his march from Albany towards Canada in 1690. Rec'd Sept. 18, 1696; III, 731–3, Lieut. Gov. Leisler to the Earl of Shrewsbury, Fort William, June 23, 1690.

19 AN. C11A, XI, 23, Relation de ce qui s'est passé . . . Nov. 1689 jusqu'au Nov. 1690. Monseignat.

20 *Les Annales de l'Hôtel-Dieu de Québec*, 247.

21 *Ibid.*, 248.

22 AN. F3, Moreau de St. Méry, VI, 343–4, Mémoire de ce qui s'est passé à la descente des Anglois devant Québec. . . . Monseignat.

23 *Les Annales de l'Hôtel-Dieu de Québec*, 257–8; AN. C11A, XI, 39, Relation de ce qui s'est passé . . . Nov. 1689 jusqu'au Nov. 1690. Monseignat; AN. F3, Moreau de St. Méry, II, 247, Mémoire de ce qui s'est passé en Canada au sujet de la guerre contre les anglois et Iroquois durant l'année 1690. . . . Champigny; "Relation de Mgr de Laval," in Ernest Myrand, *1690: Sir William Phips devant Québec*, 121.

24 An Abstract of a Lre from Mr. James Lloyd Merch[t] in Boston dat. 8th Jany. 1690/1, *loc. cit.*

25 *Les Annales de l'Hôtel-Dieu de Québec*, 250.

26 AN. F3, Moreau de St. Méry, VII, 39–40, Sommation faite par Le General Anglois à Mr de Frontenac et le réponse dud Sr de Frontenac.

27 *Ibid.*

28 "Major Walley's Journal in the Expedition against Canada in 1692. A narrative of the proceedings to Canada so far as concerned the land army," in Thomas Hutchinson, *The History of Massachusetts*, II, 470–8.

29 *Ibid.*

30 I am greatly indebted to Colonel C. P. Stacey and his staff at the Historical Section, Canadian Army Headquarters, Ottawa, to Mr. M. M. Thomson and Mr. R. W. Tanner of the Dominion Observatory, and in particular to Mr. C. M. Cross, Chief of the Tidal and Current Survey, Canadian Hydrographic Service, Ottawa, for the information on the times, heights and rate of rise and fall of the tides at Quebec in October, 1690. No one could ask for more assistance than that which they so readily afforded me in this connection.

31 AN. C11A, XI, 90–3, Frontenac au Ministre, Que., Nov. 12, 1690.

32 Major Walley's Journal, *op. cit.*; An Abstract of a Lre from Mr. James Lloyd Mercht in Boston dat. 8th Jany. 1690/1, *loc. cit.*; Mass. Arch. Inter-Charter 1690–1691, XXXVI, 202–16, The Declaration of Sylvanus Davis; Thomas Savage, *An Account of the Late Action of the New Englanders, under the Command of Sir William Phips, against the French at Canada*; "A short account of Sir William Phips's Expedition into Accady, and that upon Quebeck in Canada," in Ernest Myrand, *1690: Sir William Phips devant Québec*, 35–6; AN. F3, Moreau de St. Méry, VI, 343–7, Mémoire de ce qui s'est passé à la descente des Anglois devant Quebec, et à leur retraitte [Frontenac]; II, 243–7, Mémoire de ce qui s'est passé en Canada au sujet de la guerre . . . 1690. . . . Champigny; AN. C11A, XI, 90–3, Frontenac au Ministre, Que., Nov. 12, 1690; 30–40, Relation de ce qui s'est passé . . . Nov. 1689 . . . Nov. 1690. Monseignat à Mme [de Frontenac], Nov. 17, 1690.

33 Col. C. P. Stacey, "Sir William Phips' Attack on Quebec," in *Canadian Army Journal*, V, No. 6, September, 1951; George F. G. Stanley, *Canada's Soldiers, 1604–1954*, 42–3.

34 AN. C11A, XI, 36–7, Relation de ce qui s'est passé de plus remarquable en Canada. . . . Monseignat à Mme [de Frontenac], Que., Nov. 17, 1690.

35 NYCD, III, 761, Governor Slaughter to Lord Nottingham, Fort William Henry, May 6, 1691; see also CSP 1689–1692, 368–9, Dec. 12, 1690, Abstract of a letter from Mr. Samuel Myles, Minister at Boston.

36 Stanley, *op. cit.*, 44; Stacey, *op. cit.*; Gerald S. Graham, *Empire of the North Atlantic* (Toronto, 1950), 75.

37 AN. F3, Moreau de St. Méry, VI, 343–4, Mémoire de ce qui s'est passé à la descente des Anglois devant Québec . . . [Frontenac].

38 *Ibid.*, 344–5; II, 246–7, Mémoire de ce qui s'est passé en Canada . . . durant l'année 1690. Champigny.

39 AN. C11A, XI, 35, Relation de ce qui s'est passé de plus remarquable en Canada. . . . Monseignat à Mme [de Frontenac], Nov. 17, 1690;

AN. F3, Moreau de St. Méry, II, 257, Le Roy de la Potherye à Mgr le Comte de Pontchartrain.

CHAPTER FIFTEEN

1 AN. C11A, XI, 40, Relation de ce qui s'est passé de plus remarquable en Canada. . . . Monseignat à Mme [de Frontenac], Que., Nov. 17, 1690.

2 *Ibid.*, 83–5, Frontenac au Ministre, Que., April 30, 1690.

3 *Ibid.*; 95, Frontenac au Ministre, Que., Nov. 12, 1690; Can. Arch. AN. C11A, XI, 100–2, Relation de ce qui s'est passé de plus considérable en Canada depuis le . . . 27 Nov. 1690 jusqu'au . . . [Nov.] 1691.

4 AN. C11A, XI, 95, Frontenac au Ministre, Que., Nov. 12, 1690.

5 *Ibid.*, 252, Champigny au Ministre, Que., May 10, 1691; XII, 88, Champigny au Ministre, Que., Nov. 10, 1692.

6 Bib. Nat. Collection Clairambault, DCCCLXXIX, 320–8, Frontenac à de Lagny, Que., Oct. 25, 1693; AN. C11A, XII, 28–9, Frontenac au Ministre, Que., Sept. 15, 1692; XI, 283, Champigny au Ministre, Que., Oct. 12, 1691.

7 *Ibid.*, XII, 259, Relation de ce qui s'est passé en Canada . . . depuis . . . Novembre 1692. Champigny, Aug. 17, 1693; XV, Relation de ce qui s'est passé de plus remarquable . . . 1696 . . . 1697.

8 *Ibid.*, XIII, 85, Champigny au Ministre, Que., Oct. 27, 1694.

9 *Ibid.*, XI, 96, Frontenac au Ministre, Que., Nov. 12, 1690; 241, Frontenac au Ministre, Que., Oct. 20, 1691; XII, 220, Frontenac et Champigny au Ministre, Que., Nov. 4, 1693.

10 *Ibid.*, XI, 251, Champigny au Ministre, Que., May 12, 1691; 299–300, Relation des actions qu'il y a eu cette campagne entre les françois et les sauvages Anglois. M. Benac, Sept. 2, 1691.

11 *Ibid.*; AN. F3, Moreau de St. Méry, VI, 384–404, Relation de ce qui s'est passé de plus Considérable en Canada depuis . . . le 27 Novembre 1690 [Frontenac].

12 *Ibid.*

13 *Ibid.*

14 *Ibid.*; AN. C11A, XI, 271–2, Champigny au Ministre, Que., Aug. 12, 1691; 299–300, Relation des actions qu'il y a eu cette campagne entre les françois et les sauvages Anglois. M. Benac, Sept. 2, 1691.

15 AN. F3, Moreau de St. Méry, VI, 398–9, Relation de ce qui s'est passé . . . en Canada depuis . . . le 27 Novembre 1690 [Frontenac].

16 NYCD, III, 800–5, Major Peter Schuyler's Journal of his Expedition to Canada, 1691.

17 AN. C11A, XI, 299–300, Relation des actions. . . . M. Benac, Sept. 2, 1691.

18 Major Peter Schuyler's Journal . . . 1691, *op. cit.*

19 RAPQ 1927–1928, 60, Frontenac au Roy, 1691.

20 AN. C11A, XI, 236, Frontenac au Ministre, Que., Oct 20, 1691.

21 *Ibid.*, 281–2, Champigny au Ministre, Que., Oct. 12, 1691; 291, Champigny au Ministre, Que., Nov. 12, 1691.

22 *Ibid.*, 213, Frontenac au Ministre, Que., Aug. 30, 1691.

23 *Ibid.*, 281–2, Champigny au Ministre, Que., Oct. 12, 1691.

24 *Ibid.*, 288.

25 *Ibid.*, 290–1, Champigny au Ministre, Que., Nov. 12, 1691.

26 *Ibid.*, 280–2, Champigny au Ministre, Que., Oct. 12, 1691.

27 *Ibid.*, XII, 98–9, Callières au Ministre, Mtl., Sept. 20, 1692.

28 *Ibid.*, 87–8, Champigny au Ministre, Que., Nov. 10, 1692; 25–6, Frontenac au Ministre, Que., Sept. 15, 1692; AN. F3, Moreau de St. Méry, VI, 384–404, Relation de ce qui s'est passé de plus Considérable en Canada depuis . . . le 27 Nov. 1690 [Frontenac].

29 NYCD, IV, 158, Gov. Fletcher to Mr. Blathwayte, New York, May 30, 1696.

30 AN. F3, Moreau de St. Méry, VII, 44–6, Champigny au Ministre, Que., Oct. 5, 1692.

31 AN. C11A, XII, 25–6, Frontenac au Ministre, Que., Sept. 15, 1692.

32 NYCD, IV, 16–19, Major Peter Schuyler's Report to Gov. Fletcher, Feb. 1692/3; AN. F3, Moreau de St. Méry, VII, 118–123, Relation de ce qui s'est passé en Canada depuis le mois de Septembre 1692 jusqu'au départ des Vaisseaux en 1693 [Monseignat]; AN. C11A, XII, 256–8, Relation de ce qui s'est passé en Canada . . . depuis le mois de Novembre 1692. Champigny, Aug. 17, 1693; 318–20, Callières au Ministre, Mtl., Sept. 30, 1693; 230, Frontenac au Ministre, Que., Oct. 25, 1693.

33 *Ibid.*, 318, Callières au Ministre, Mtl., Sept. 30, 1693.

34 NYCD, III, 842–4, Answer of the Five Nations . . . to Hon. Richard Ingoldsby, Albany, June 6, 1692.

35 *Ibid.*, IV, 22–3, Answer of the Five Nations to Gov. Fletcher, Albany, Feb. 25, 1692/3.

36 *Ibid.*, IV, 2, Gov. Fletcher to Mr. Blathwayt, New York, Feb. 14, 1692/3.

37 CSP 1689–1692, 614, March 19, 1692. New York, Proclamation of the C. in C. & Council of New York.

38 NYCD, IV, 337–8, Comparative population of Albany and of the Indians in 1689 and 1698.

39 *Ibid.*, VIII, 855–6, The Queen to Sir W. Phipps, Whitehall, Oct. 11, 1692.

40 *Ibid.*, IV, 2, Governor Fletcher to Mr. Blathwayt, New York, Feb. 14, 1692/3; 5–6, Sir Wm. Phips to Gov. Fletcher, Boston, Jan. 27, 1692/3; 8–9, Thomas Clarke's Account of an interview with Sir Wm. Phips, Jan. 1692/3.

41 *Ibid.*, 13, Gov. Fletcher to Mr. Blathwayt, New York, March 8, 1692/3.

42 *Ibid.*

43 *Ibid.*

44 *Ibid.*, 74, Gov. Fletcher to the Committee of Trade, New York, Jan. 22, 1693/4; 84, Gov. Fletcher to the Committee of Trade and Plantations, New York, March 28, 1693/4.

45 *Ibid.*, 37, Gov. Fletcher to Mr. Blathwayt, New York, Aug. 15, 1693; *Jes. Rel.*, LXII, 66, Jean de Lamberville à R. P. Beschefer, Onnontagué, Aug. 25, 1682; CSP 1681–1685, 93–4, Extracts from letters to Lord Culpeper from Virginia, July 26, 1681.

46 NYCD, IV, 33, Gov. Fletcher's Instructions to Col. Lodwick, June 13, 1693.

47 AN. CiiA, XII, 318–19, Callières au Ministre, Mtl., Sept. 30, 1693.

48 NYCD, IV, 40–3, Gov. Fletcher's address to the Five Nations, Albany, July 3, 1693.

49 *Ibid.*, 42, Answer of the Five Nations to Gov. Fletcher, Albany, July 4, 1693.

50 AN. F3, Moreau de St. Méry, VII, 137, Relation de ce qui s'est passé en Canada . . . 1692 . . . 1693; NYCD, IV, 77–8, Joseph, Christian Mohawk's report from Oneida, Dec. 2, 1692.

51 AN. CiiA, XII, 320, Callières au Ministre, Mtl., Sept. 30, 1693.

52 AN. F3, Moreau de St. Méry, VII, 144, Frontenac au Ministre, Que., Aug. 14, 1693.

53 AN. CiiA, XII, 212, Frontenac et Champigny au Ministre, Que., Nov. 4, 1693; 73, Champigny au Ministre, Que., Oct. 5, 1692; CSP 1693–1696, item 612–vi, Examination of a French prisoner taken 12th September 1693.

54 *Ibid.*, 13, The King to Sir Wm. Phips, Whitehall, Feb. 2, 1693; 124, Sir Francis Wheler to Sir Wm. Phips, New England, July 8, 1693; 128–9, Sir Wm. Phips to Sir Francis Wheler, Boston, July 12, 1693; 133, Sir Wm. Phips to Sir Francis Wheler, Boston, July 27, 1693; AN. B, XVI, 226, Mémoire du Roy aux Srs Frontenac et Champigny [March 1693]; AN. CiiA, XII, 251, Champigny au Ministre, Que., Aug. 12, 1693; AN. B, XVII, 87, Ministre à Frontenac, Versailles, May 8, 1694.

55 Bib. Nat. Collection Clairambault. DCCCLXXIX, 327, 335, Frontenac à de Lagny, Que., Oct. 25, 1693.

56 AN. CiiA, XII, 230, Frontenac au Ministre, Que., Oct. 25, 1693.

57 *Ibid.*, 272, 276–7, Champigny au Ministre, Que., Nov. 4, 1693.

58 *Ibid.*

59 *Ibid.*, 312–14, Iberville au Ministre, Belle Isle, Dec. 16, 1693.

60 RAPQ 1927–1928, 143, Mémoire du Roy à Frontenac et Champigny [April, 1693].

61 AN. CiiA, XII, 276–7, Champigny au Ministre, Que., Nov. 4, 1693.

62 *Ibid.*, XIII, 104, Callières au Ministre, Que., Oct. 19, 1694.

63 *Ibid.*, 61, Frontenac au Ministre, Que., Oct. 25, 1694; XIV, 213, Mémoire sur le Canada, 1696; Peter Wraxall, *An Abridgement of the New York Indian Records*, 22–3, A Speech of the Sachems of the Five

Nations to His Excell'y Benjn Fletcher Govr of New York, Pennsyl., etc. Albany, May 4, 1694.

64 AN. CiiA, XIII, 107, Callières au Ministre, Mtl., Oct. 19, 1694; 80, Champigny au Ministre, Que., Oct. 24, 1694.

65 Bib. Nat. Fonds Français, XXMMDCCCIV, 283, Frontenac à M. de Villermont, Que., Oct. 30, 1694.

66 AN. CiiA, XIV, 213, Mémoire sur le Canada, 1696; Callières au Ministre, Mtl., Oct. 19, 1694.

67 Ibid., 106.

68 AN. F3, Moreau de St. Méry, VII, 172–9, Relation de ce qui s'est passé de plus considérable en Canada depuis . . . Novembre 1693 jusqu'au 28 Novembre 1694 [Frontenac].

69 Ibid.; Bib. Nat. Fonds Français, XXMMDCCCIV, 283, Frontenac à M. de Villermont, Que., Oct. 30, 1694; AN. CiiA, XIII, 77, Frontenac au Ministre, Que., Nov. 4, 1694.

70 Ibid., 108, Callières au Ministre, Mtl., Oct. 19, 1694.

71 AN. B, XVII, 66, Mémoire du Roy aux Srs comte de Frontenac et de Champigny [April, 1694].

72 Ibid., 144–6, Ministre à Frontenac, Versailles, April 16, 1695; 173–5, Mémoire du Roy aux Srs comte de Frontenac et de Champigny, Versailles, June 14, 1695.

73 AN. CiiA, XIII, 354–5, Champigny au Ministre, Que., Nov. 6, 1695; XIV, 213, Mémoire sur le Canada, 1696.

74 Ibid., XIII, 339, Champigny au Ministre, Mtl., Aug. 11, 1695.

75 Ibid., 286–7, Frontenac au Ministre, Que., Nov. 4, 1695.

76 Ibid., X, 194–8, Denonville à M. de Vallerenne, Sept. 24, 1689.

77 AN. B, XVI, 101, Ministre à Frontenac, Versailles, April, 1692.

78 AN. CiiA, XIII, 53–4, Frontenac au Ministre, Que., Oct. 25, 1694.

79 Ibid., 379, Callières au Ministre, Que., Oct. 27, 1695.

80 Ibid., 339–40, Champigny au Ministre, Mtl., Aug. 11, 1695.

81 AN. B, XVII, 144–6, Ministre à Frontenac, Versailles, April 16, 1695; AN. CiiA, XIII, 328, Frontenac à de Lagny, Que., Nov. 2, 1695.

82 Ibid., Champigny au Ministre, Mtl., Aug. 17, 1695.

83 Ibid.; 383–6, Callières au Ministre, Mtl., Oct. 27, 1695; XIV, 213, Mémoire sur le Canada, 1696.

84 Ibid.; AN. F3, Moreau de St. Méry, VII, 311, 320, Relation de ce qui s'est passé de plus remarquable . . . 1694 . . . 1695 [Frontenac]; Bib. Nat. Collection Clairambault, DCCCLXXXII, 137, La Mothe Cadillac à [de Lagny,] Michilimackinac, 1695; AN. CiiA, XV, 13, 18, Relation de ce qui s'est passé de plus remarquable . . . 1696 . . . 1697 [Frontenac]; XVII, 37, Callières au Ministre, Que., Oct. 20, 1699; AN. C13A, I, 236, Iberville au Ministre, Des Bayogoula, Feb. 26, 1700.

85 AN. CiiA, XIV, 213, Mémoire sur le Canada, 1696; XIII, Champigny au Ministre, Mtl., Aug. 17, 1695.

86 Ibid.; XIV, 213, Mémoire sur le Canada, 1696.

87 AN. F3, Moreau de St. Méry, VII, 302–3, 335, Relation de ce qui s'est passé en Canada . . . 1694 . . . 1695 [Frontenac].

88 AN. CiiA, XIII, 298, Frontenac et Champigny au Ministre, Que., Nov. 10, 1695.

89 AN. F3, Moreau de St. Méry, VII, 402–3, Callières à de Lagny, Mtl., Nov. 13, 1696.

90 AN. CiiA, XIV, 183, Champigny au Ministre, Que., Aug. 18, 1696.

91 Ibid.

92 AN. F3, Moreau de St. Méry, VII, 394–401, Relation de ce qui s'est passé en Canada . . . en 1695 jusqu'au mois de Novembre 1696, Champigny.

93 Ibid., 402–3, Callières à de Lagny, Mtl., Nov. 13, 1696.

94 Ibid., 144, Frontenac au Ministre, Que., Aug. 14, 1693; 129, Relation de ce qui s'est passé en Canada . . . Sept. 1692 . . . Nov. 1693 [Frontenac].

95 Ibid., 406, Callières à de Lagny, Mtl., Nov. 13, 1696.

96 Ibid., 402–7; 394–401, Relation de ce qui s'est passé en Canada . . . en 1695 jusqu'au . . . Novembre 1696, Champigny; 370–82, Relation de ce qui s'est passé de plus remarquable en Canada . . . 1695–1696 [Frontenac].

97 The Livingston Indian Records, 1666–1723, 128, Mohawk Sachems to Dirck Wessels, Caignowage, July 4, 1687.

98 NYCD, IV, 158, Gov. Fletcher to Mr. Blathwayt, New York, May 30, 1696; 165, Gov. Fletcher to Mr. Blathwayt, New York, July 13, 1696.

99 Ibid., 175–6, Gov. Fletcher & Council, Albany, Aug. 7, 1696.

100 Ibid., 235–241, Meeting of the Sachems of the Five Nations, Albany, Sept. 29, Oct. 1, 1696.

101 Ibid.

102 AN. CiiA, XII, 212, Frontenac et Champigny au Ministre, Que., Nov. 4, 1693; XIV, 125, Frontenac et Champigny au Ministre, Que., Oct. 26, 1696; XV, 41, Frontenac et Champigny au Ministre, Que., Oct. 19, 1697.

103 Chronological List of Canadian Censuses, Canada, Bureau of Statistics, Demography Branch, Ottawa, 1942.

104 NYCD, IV, 337–8, Comparative population of Albany and of the Indians in 1689 and 1698; CSP 1697–1698, 522–3, Account of the Population of New York.

105 AN. CiiA, XV, 94, Frontenac au Ministre, Que., Oct. 15, 1697.

106 Ibid., 109–110, Champigny au Ministre, Que., Aug. 26, 1697.

107 Ibid., 96–7, Frontenac au Ministre, Que., Oct. 15, 1697; XVI, 97–8, Champigny au Ministre, Que., July 12, 1698; AN. F3, Moreau de St. Méry, VIII, 49, Relation de ce qui s'est passé de plus remarquable en Canada . . . 1697 . . . 1698 [Frontenac]; CSP 1697–1698, Propositions made by the Five Nations to the Earl of Bellomont at Albany, July 20, 1698; CSP 1699, 475, Copy of a message from the Onondaga Indians,

Sept. 21, 1699; CSP 1700, 615, Bellomont to the Council of Trade & Plantations, New York, Oct. 24, 1700.

108 AN. F3, Moreau de St. Méry, VIII, 49, Relation de ce qui s'est passé de plus remarquable en Canada . . . 1697 . . . 1698 [Frontenac].

109 AN. C11A, XVI, 2, Frontenac et Champigny au Ministre, Que., Oct. 15, 1698.

110 Ibid.; 99, Champigny au Ministre, Que., July 12, 1698; NYCD, IV, 350–1, Report of Messrs Schuyler & Delius' Negotiations in Canada, New York, July 2, 1698; 435, Lords of Trade to Secretary Vernon, Whitehall, Dec. 8, 1698; AN. B, XX, 207, Mémoire du Roy aux Callières et Champigny, Versailles, May 27, 1699.

111 Ibid.; AN. C11A, XVII, 3, Callières et Champigny au Ministre, Que., Oct. 20, 1699.

112 Ibid., XVI, 82–3, Bellomont to Frontenac, New York, April 22, 1698; 2–3, Frontenac et Champigny au Ministre, Que., Oct. 15, 1698; 50, Frontenac au Ministre, Que., Oct. 10, 1698; XV, 98–9, Champigny au Ministre, Que., July 12, 1698; XVI, 63–4, Frontenac et Champigny au Ministre, Que., Oct. 25, 1698; CSP 1697–1698, 453, Minutes of the Council of New York, Sept. 21, 1698; CSP 1699, 139, Magistrates of Albany to Col. Schuyler, Feb. 4, 1699; Peter Wraxall, An Abridgement of the New York Indian Records, 31–2, Conference with Onondaga & Oneida Sachems, Albany, Feb. 3, 1698/9; 32, Lieut. Gov. Nanfan's instructions to Commissioners at Albany, June 12, 1699.

113 CSP 1697–1698, 499, Bellomont to the Council of Trade and Plantations, New York, Oct. 24, 1698; see also CSP 1699, 71, Col. W. Romer to the Earl of Bellomont, Aug. 26, 1698.

CHAPTER SIXTEEN

1 AN. B, XVI, 89–92, Mémoire du Roy aux Srs Comte de Frontenac et de Champigny, 1692.

2 AN. C11A, XV, 166, Sr de la Touche au Ministre, Mtl., Oct. 15, 1697.

3 Ibid., XIV, 157–61, Frontenac au Ministre, Que., Oct. 25, 1696.

4 AN. B, XV, 94, Instruction pour le Sr le Comte de Frontenac. . . . Versailles, June 7, 1689.

5 AN. C11A, XI, 136, Champigny au Ministre, Que., Nov. 14, 1690.

6 AN. B, XVI, 37, Mémoire du Roy aux Srs Frontenac et Champigny, au Camp devant Mons, April 7, 1691.

7 AN. F3, Moreau de St. Méry, VI, Remarques faites par l'Intendant sur l'ordonnance de Frontenac, April 8, 1690; AN. C11A, XI, 262–8, Mémoire Instructif sur le Canada, Champigny, May 10, 1691.

8 Ibid., 285, Champigny au Ministre, Que., Oct. 12, 1691; AN. B, XVI, 37, Mémoire du Roy aux Srs Frontenac et Champigny, au Camp devant Mons, April 7, 1691.

9 *Ibid.*, 89–90, Mémoire du Roy aux Srs Comte de Frontenac et de Champigny, 1692.

10 AN. C11A, XII, 281–3, Champigny au Ministre, Que., Nov. 4, 1693.

11 *Ibid.*, 262, Ordonnance de M. de Champigny, Villemarie, Sept. 11, 1693.

12 AN. C11E, XIV, 3–4, Ordonnance de M. le Cte de Frontenac pour expliquer celle du Sr de Champigny. . . . Mtl., Sept. 12, 1693.

13 Bib. Nat. Collection Clairambault, DCCCLXXIX, 320–38, Frontenac à de Lagny, Que., Oct. 25, 1693; AN. C11A, XII, 281–7, Champigny au Ministre, Que., Nov. 4, 1693.

14 *Ibid.*; 258–9, Relation de ce qui s'est passé en Canada au sujet de la guerre . . . depuis . . . novembre 1692. Champigny, Aug. 17, 1693.

15 *Ibid.*, XV, 261–71, Mémoire par le P. La [Chaise?] 1697.

16 Frontenac à de Lagny, Que., Oct. 25, 1693, *loc. cit.*

17 AN. C11A, XIV, 202, Champigny au Ministre, Que., Oct. 25, 1696; *Jes. Rel.*, LXV, 188–252, Père Carheil à Champigny, Michilimackinac, Aug. 30, 1702; Nicholas Perrot, *Mémoire sur les moeurs, coustumes et relligion des sauvages de l'Amérique septentrionale*, 150.

18 *Ibid.*; AN. C11A, XIV, 202, Champigny au Ministre, Que., Oct. 25, 1696; XV, Frontenac et Champigny au Ministre, Que., Oct. 19, 1697; 134, Champigny au Ministre, Que., Oct. 13, 1697.

19 *Ibid.*, XIV, 202, Champigny au Ministre, Que., Oct. 25, 1696.

20 Lahontan, *New Voyages to North America*, I, 392.

21 Pease and Werner, *Illinois Historical Collection*, I, 230–4, Lettres Patentes de Sa Majesté. . . . Louis, Colbert, July 14, 1690.

22 Frontenac à de Lagny, Que., Oct. 25, 1693, *loc. cit.*

23 AN. B, VII, 179–80, Permission au Sr de la Salle de descouvrir la partie occidentale de la Nouvelle France, St. Germain-en-Laye, May 12, 1678; AN. C11A, XIX, 4, Mrs le Chevalier de Callières et Champigny au Ministre, Que., Oct. 5, 1701.

24 *Ibid.*, VII, 88, Denonville au Ministre, Que., Nov. 13, 1685; AN. B, XII, 31, Mémoire du Roy au Sr de Denonville, Versailles, May 31, 1686; 22, Ministre au Sr Tonty, Versailles, May 31, 1686.

25 *Ibid.*, XVI, 91–2, Mémoire du Roy aux Srs Frontenac et Champigny, April, 1692.

26 Frontenac à de Lagny, Que., Oct. 25, 1693, *loc. cit.*

27 RAPQ, 1927–1928, 83, Lettre du Roi au Gouverneur de Frontenac et à l'Intendant Champigny [April 7, 1692].

28 Frontenac à de Lagny, Que., Oct. 25, 1693, *loc. cit.*

29 RAPQ, 1927–1928, 96, Mémoire du Roy au Gouverneur de Frontenac et à l'Intendant Bochart Champigny, [April, 1694].

30 AN. B, XVI, 101, Ministre à M. de Frontenac, Versailles, April, 1692.

31 *Ibid.*, 91, Mémoire du Roy aux Srs Comte de Frontenac et de Champigny, 1692.

32 Frontenac à de Lagny, Que., Oct. 25, 1693, *loc. cit.*; AN. F3, Moreau de St. Méry, VII, 134–5, Relation de ce qui s'est passé en Canada depuis le mois de Septembre 1692 jusqu'au [Novembre] 1693, [Frontenac]; AN. C11A, XI, 234–5, Frontenac au Ministre, Que., Oct. 20, 1691; XII, 24–5, Frontenac au Ministre, Que., Sept. 15, 1692; 214, Frontenac et Champigny au Ministre, Que., Nov. 4, 1693; XI, 86–7, Frontenac au Ministre, Que., Nov. 12, 1690; XIII, Frontenac au Ministre, Que., Oct. 25, 1694; 20, Frontenac et Champigny au Ministre, Que., Nov. 5, 1694.

33 *Ibid.*, XII, 281–7, Champigny au Ministre, Que., Nov. 4, 1693.

34 *Ibid.*, XIII, 274–6, Mémoire pour le Castor, Champigny, Que., Oct. 26, 1694.

35 *Ibid.*, 433–4, Congés et permissions pour la traitte, commerce, réception et prix du Castor. June 4, 1695.

36 Relation de ce qui s'est passé en Canada depuis le mois de Septembre 1692 jusqu'au [Novembre] 1693, [Frontenac] *loc. cit.*; AN. C11A, XII, 281–7, Champigny au Ministre, Que., Nov. 4, 1693; XV, 18, Relation de ce qui s'est passé de plus remarquable en Canada . . . 1696 . . . 1697 . . . [Frontenac]; XVII, 37, Callières au Ministre, Que., Oct. 20, 1699.

37 *Ibid.*, XIII, 354–5, Champigny au Ministre, Que., Nov. 6, 1695.

38 Bib. Nat. Collection Clairambault, DCCCLXXXII, 137, La Mothe Cadillac à [de Lagny, Michilimackinac, 1695]; AN. F3, Moreau de St. Méry, VII, 320, Relation de ce qui s'est passé . . . 1694 . . . 1695, [Frontenac]; AN. C11A, XIV, 213, Mémoire sur le Canada, 1696.

39 AN. B, XIX, 65–6, Ministre à Frontenac, Versailles, April 4, 1696.

40 *Ibid.*, 98–9, Ministre à Frontenac, Versailles, May 26, 1696.

41 *Ibid.*, 91–2, Mémoire du Roy pour les Srs de Frontenac et de Champigny, Versailles, May 26, 1696; AN. F3, Moreau de St. Méry, VII, 387–8, Déclaration du Roy, Versailles, May 21, 1696.

42 AN. C11A, XIII, 399–408, Colonies, febvrier 1695. Commerce du Castor de Canada : de Lagny à Daguesseau.

43 *Ibid.*, 415–17, Congés et permissions pour la traitte, commerce, réception et prix du Castor. June 4, 1695.

44 *Ibid.*, 274–6, Mémoire pour le Castor. Champigny, Que., Oct. 26, 1694.

45 AN. B, XVII, 84–5, Mémoire du Roy à Frontenac et Champigny, April, 1694; AN. C11A, XII, 9–10, Frontenac et Champigny au Ministre, Que., Sept. 15, 1692.

46 *Ibid.*, XIII, 476–80, Mémoire de la Cie de la Ferme. Mars 17, 1695; 415–17, Congés et permissions pour la traitte, commerce, réception et prix du Castor. June 4, 1695.

47 *Ibid.*, XVI, 239–42, Mémoire generaux [*sic*] pour M. Saulger. Paris, May 27, 1698.

48 *Ibid.*, XVII, 122–31, D'Argenson à [Daguesseau], Paris, July 22,

1699; 121, Mémoire à Mgr [Daguesseau], 1699; 132–8, Maurepas à Daguesseau.

49 AN. B, XIX, 98–9, Ministre à Frontenac, Versailles, May 26, 1696.

50 AN. CiiA, XIV, 136, Extrait des Despesches, Mémoires, Estats etc touchant les affaires de Canada . . . 1696; XV, 42, Frontenac et Champigny au Ministre, Que., Oct. 19, 1697.

51 *Ibid.*, XIV, 157–61, Frontenac au Ministre, Que., Oct. 25, 1696.

52 AN. B, XX, 197–200, Ministre à M. de Frontenac, Versailles, May 21, 1698.

53 AN. CiiA, XV, 41, Frontenac et Champigny au Ministre, Que., Oct. 19, 1697; XVI, 9, Frontenac et Champigny au Ministre, Que., Oct. 15, 1698.

54 Can. Arch. AN. CiiA, XXXVI, 65–6, Vaudreuil au Ministre, Que., Oct. 31, 1716.

55 AN. B, XX, 74–5, Mémoire du Roy à Frontenac et Champigny, Versailles, May 21, 1698.

56 AN. CiiA, XIV, 304–8, Mémoire sur les affaires du Canada, 1696.

57 CSP 1700, 573, Bellomont to the Council of Trade & Plantations, New York, Oct. 17, 1700; Same to same, New York, Nov. 28, 1700.

58 AN. CiiA, XIV, 197–9, Champigny au Ministre, Que., Oct. 25, 1696.

59 AN. B, XIX, 240–2, Mémoire du Roy pour les Srs Comte de Frontenac et de Champigny, Versailles, April 27, 1697.

60 AN. CiiA, XIV, 208–9, Ordonnance du Sr de Champigny, Que., Sept. 27, 1696. [The new price scale was: *castor gras* reduced from 5 *livres* 10 *sols* to 5 *livres* 5 *sols* and the poorer grades reduced to 2 *livres* 12 *sols* 6 *deniers*. These prices did not go into effect until 1697.]

61 *Ibid.*, XV, 151, Callières au Ministre, Que., Oct. 15, 1697; AN. B, XX, 106, Ministre à M. de Champigny, Versailles, May 28, 1698.

62 AN. CiiA, XV, 126–30, Champigny au Ministre, Que., Oct. 13, 1697.

63 *Ibid.*, XVI, 131–5, Champigny au Ministre, Que., Oct. 27, 1698; XV, 126–30, Champigny au Ministre, Que., Oct. 13, 1697.

64 *Ibid.*

65 AN. B, XIX, 91–2, Mémoire du Roy pour les Srs de Frontenac et de Champigny, Versailles, May 26, 1696; 98–9, Ministre à Frontenac, Versailles, May 26, 1696.

66 AN. CiiA, XVI, 94–8, Champigny au Ministre, Que., July 12, 1698; 110–14, Champigny au Ministre, Que., Oct. 14, 1698; 131–5, Champigny au Ministre, Que., Oct. 27, 1698.

67 *Ibid.*

68 AN. B, XX, 106, Ministre à Champigny, Versailles, May 28, 1698.

69 AN. CiiA, XVII, 236, Mémoire sur la Ferme . . . 1699.

70 CSP 1700, 345, Bellomont to the Council of Trade & Plantations, New York, Jan. 16, 1700; 675–6, Same to same, New York, Nov. 28, 1700.

71 E. R. Adair, "Anglo-French Rivalry in the Fur Trade during the 18th Century," in *Culture*, VIII, 1947; CSP 1700, 688, Journal of Col. Romer's Expedition to Onondaga, Oct. 5, 1700.

72 AN. B, XIX, 234–7, Mémoire du Roy pour les Srs Comte de Frontenac et de Champigny, Versailles, April 27, 1697.

CHAPTER SEVENTEEN

1 Sem. Que. Lettres, Carton M, No. 7, L'abbé de Brisacier aux prêtres du Séminaire de Québec, June 19, 1689.

2 AN. C11A, XI, 193, Mémoire concernant le Canada pour Mgr le Marquis de Seignelay. Janvier 1690 [Denonville].

3 *Ibid.*, 242–3, Frontenac au Ministre, Que., Oct. 20, 1691; 97–8, Frontenac au Ministre, Que., Nov. 20, 1690.

4 Can. Arch. Lettres de l'Abbé Tronson, IV, Tronson à de la Columbière, [Paris,] June 7, 1690.

5 *Ibid.*, Abbé Tronson à Champigny, April 4, 1692; Abbé Tronson à Dollier de Casson, 1692.

6 BRH, XLVI, 1940, 82, Laval à Denonville, Nov. 20, 1690; and see M. Gosselin, *Vie de Mgr Laval*, II, 449.

7 Bib. Nat. Collection Clairambault, DCCCIL, 65, Placet pour faire retourner en Canada l'ancien Evesque de Québec. Feb. 25, 1688.

8 AN. C11A, XII, 89–90, Champigny au Ministre, Que., Nov. 10, 1692.

9 *Ibid.*, XI, 242–3, Frontenac au Ministre, Que., Oct. 20, 1691.

10 *Ibid.*, XII, 277, Champigny au Ministre, Que., Nov. 4, 1693.

11 *Ibid.*, 233, Frontenac au Ministre, Que., Oct. 25, 1693.

12 *Ibid.*, XIII, 178–91, Cadillac à de Lagny, Mtl., Sept. 28, 1694.

13 AN. F3, Moreau de St. Méry, VII, 198–270, Extrait concernant le mandement du Sr Evesque . . . contre la comédie.

14 AN. C11A, XIII, 95–8, Champigny au Ministre, Que., Oct. 27, 1694.

15 Cadillac à de Lagny, Mtl., Sept. 28, 1694, *loc. cit.*

16 AN. F3, Moreau de St. Méry, VII, 198–270, Extrait des procédures faites au Conseil Royal de Québec depuis le premier Febvrier 1694 jusques au 20ᵉ Octobre suivant.

17 *Ibid.*

18 Bib. Nat. Collection Clairambault, DCCCLXXIX, 320–38, Frontenac à de Lagny, Que., Oct. 25, 1693.

19 AN. C11A, XIII, 64–6, Frontenac à [de Lagny], Que., Oct. 25, 1694.

20 *Ibid.*, 144–50, D'Auteuil au Ministre, Que., Oct. 26, 1694; AN. F3, Moreau de St. Méry, VII, 198–270, Extrait des procédures faites au Conseil Royal de Québec, cotte E.

21 *Ibid.*, cottes F, G, Z; AN. B, XVII, 213–14, Ministre à Frontenac, Versailles, June 8, 1695.

22 AN. C11A, XIII, 95–8, Champigny au Ministre, Que., Oct. 27, 1694.

23 AN. F3, Moreau de St. Méry, VII, 198–270, Extrait concernant le mandement du Sr Evesque . . . contre la comédie.

24 AN. C11A, XIII, 95–8, Champigny au Ministre, Que., Oct. 27, 1694.

25 AN. F3, Moreau de St. Méry, VII, 198–270, Affaire du Sr Jourdy et de la nommée Des Brieux.

26 Frontenac à [de Lagny], Que., Oct. 25, 1694, *loc. cit.*

27 D'Auteuil au Ministre, Que., Oct. 26, 1694, *op. cit.*, 129–31.

28 Champigny au Ministre, Que., Oct. 27, 1694, *loc. cit.*

29 *Ibid.*; AN. F3, Moreau de St. Méry, VII, 198–270, Interdit de l'Eglise des Récollets de Ville Marie.

30 *Ibid.*; Champigny au Ministre, Que., Oct. 27, 1694, *loc. cit.*

31 *Ibid.*

32 AN. F3, Moreau de St. Méry, VII, 198–270, Extraits des procédures faites au Conseil Royal de Québec depuis le premier Febvrier 1694 jusques au 20ᵉ Octobre suivant. Cotte DDDD.

33 D'Auteuil au Ministre, Que., Oct. 26, 1694, *loc. cit.*

34 AN. F3, Moreau de St. Méry, VII, 198–270, Décret de prise de corps contre le Sr de Mareuil; 222, Extraits des procédures faites au Conseil Royal de Québec depuis le premier Febvrier 1694 jusques au 20ᵉ Octobre suivant; AN. C11A, XIII, 95–8, Champigny au Ministre, Que., Oct. 27, 1694; *Jugements et Délibérations du Conseil Souverain de Québec*, III, 946–55.

35 Frontenac à [de Lagny], Que., Oct. 25, 1694, *loc. cit.*

36 AN. B, XVII, 199–201, Ministre à Frontenac, Versailles, June 4, 1695; AN. F3, Moreau de St. Méry, VII, 198–270, Extrait concernant le mandement du Sr Evesque . . . contre la comédie.

37 *Ibid.*, 198–270, Conseil de Québec, Extrait, Spectacles et Assemblées [marginal note].

38 AN. B, XVII, 220–1, Ministre à Frontenac, Versailles, June 18, 1695; 217, Arrêt du Roy, Versailles, July 13, 1695.

39 AN. F3, Moreau de St. Méry, VII, 194–7, Réflection sur les affaires arrivez en Canada pendant l'année 1694 [marginal annotations by de Lagny]; AN. C11A, XIII, 323–4, Frontenac à de Lagny, Que., Nov. 2, 1695.

40 AN. B, XVII, 199–201, Ministre à Frontenac, Versailles, June 4, 1695.

41 *Ibid.*, 213–14, Ministre à Frontenac, Versailles, June 8, 1695.

42 *Ibid.*, 206–7, Ministre à Champigny, Versailles, June 4, 1695; 215–16, Ministre à Champigny, Versailles, June 8, 1695; 221, Ministre à Champigny, Versailles, June 18, 1695.

43 Sem. Que. Lettres, Carton O, No. 7, M. Tremblay à M. Glandelet, [Paris,] May 21, 1695.

44 AN. B, XVII, 216–17, Ministre à d'Auteuil, Versailles, June 8, 1695.

45 AN. C11A, XIII, 439, Aubert de la Chesnaye à [de Lagny], Que., Nov. 4, 1695.

46 *Ibid.*, 323–4, Frontenac à de Lagny, Que., Nov. 2, 1695.

47 *Ibid.*; 287–9, Frontenac au Ministre, Que., Nov. 4, 1695.

48 AN. B, XVII, 211, Ministre à Callières, Versailles, June 4, 1695.

49 *Ibid.*, De Par le Roy, Versailles, June 8, 1695, Louis.

50 Sem. Que. Lettres, Carton M, No. 20, M. Tremblay aux Officiers du Séminaire de Québec, May 15, 1695.

51 *Ibid.*, Carton N, No. 101, M. Tremblay à Mgr de Laval, May 10, 1695.

52 *Ibid.*, Carton M, No. 19, M. Tremblay aux Officiers du Séminaire de Québec, May 12, 1695.

53 *Ibid.*; No. 20, pp. 72–3, M. Tremblay aux Officiers du Séminaire de Québec, May 15, 1695; No. 21, M. Tremblay aux Officiers du Séminaire de Québec, March 29, 1696.

54 AN. C11A, XIII, 325, Frontenac à de Lagny, Que., Nov. 2, 1695.

55 *Ibid.*, 328.

56 Bib. Nat. Collection Clairambault, DCCCLXXIX, 320–38, Frontenac à de Lagny, Que., Oct. 25, 1693; AN. B, XVII, Ministre à Champigny, Versailles, May 8, 1694.

57 Sem. Que. Lettres, Carton O, No. 7, M. Tremblay à M. Glandelet, Paris, May 21, 1695.

CHAPTER EIGHTEEN

1 Bib. Nat. Collection Clairambault, DCCCLXXIX, 320–38, Frontenac à de Lagny, Que., Oct. 25, 1693.

2. P.-G. Roy, *Ordonnances, Commissions, etc. etc. des Gouverneurs et Intendants*, II, 254–69; AN. C11A, XV, 107–18, Champigny au Ministre, Que., Oct. 10, 1697.

3 *Ibid.*, VI, 241, Difficultés qu'il plaira à M. le marquis de Seignelay de décider sur les fonctions du Gouverneur et Intendant du Canada. Réponse du Roy du 10 avril 1684.

4 *Ibid.*, XV, 99–100, Frontenac au Ministre, Que., Oct. 15, 1697.

5 AN. B, XX, 39, Ministre à Frontenac, Versailles, March 12, 1698.

6 *Ibid.*, 88–9, Ministre à Frontenac, Versailles, May 21, 1698.

7 AN. C11A, XVI, 56–7, Frontenac au Ministre, Que., Oct. 10, 1698.

8 *Ibid.*, Extraits des lettres du Canada de l'année 1698. [The phrase used by Pontchartrain was: "*Il a tousjours mal fait.*" It is a difficult phrase to translate and convey Pontchartrain's exact meaning; his exasperated mood, and the context, have to be taken into account.]

9 Jean Delanglez, "Cadillac's Early Years in America," in *Mid-America*, XXVI, No. 1, Jan., 1944.

10 AN. C11D, II, 126–7, Mémoire Instructif de la Conduitte des Srs de Soulegre et desgoutins au Port Royal de l'Acadie par le Sr de Meneval, gouverneur : au Port Royal le 7e Septembre 1689.

11 *Ibid.*, 119, Un Mémoire de M. de Meneval sur la conduitte du Sr des Goutins Juge et Ecrivain au Port Royal.

12 *Ibid.*

13 AN. B, XVI, 39, Mémoire du Roy aux Srs Frontenac et Champigny, au Camp devant Mons, April 7, 1691.

14 AN. C11A, XI, 242, Frontenac au Ministre, Que., Oct. 20, 1691.

15 *Ibid.*, XIII, 191, Cadillac à [de Lagny], Mtl., Sept. 28, 1694 [with de Lagny's marginal comments].

16 *Ibid.*, Frontenac à de Lagny, Que., Nov. 2, 1695.

17 AN. F3, Moreau de St. Méry, II, 263, Mémoire de Le Roy de la Potherye à Mgr le Comte de Pontchartrain, [1702].

18 AN. CuA, XV, 162–7, De la Touche au Ministre, [Mtl.,] Oct. 13, 1697.

19 AN. F3, Moreau de St. Méry, VIII, Propositions du Sr de la Mothe Cadillac à Mrs les Interessés de la Compagnie de la Colonie, Que., Oct. 20, 1705; AN. B, XXVII, Ministre au Sr de la M. Cadillac, Versailles, June 9, 1706.

20 AN. C11A, XVI, 87–95, Champigny au Ministre, Que., July 3, 1698.

21 De la Touche au Ministre, [Mtl.,] Oct. 13, 1697, *loc. cit.*

22 Champigny au Ministre, Que., July 3, 1698, *loc. cit.*; AN. F3, Moreau de St. Méry, VIII, 70–81, Extrait des Registres du Conseil Souverain.

23 *Ibid.*

24 Champigny au Ministre, Que., July 3, 1698, *loc. cit.*

25 Extrait des Registres . . ., *op. cit.*

26 *Ibid.*

27 *Ibid.*

28 Champigny did not come to Canada until 1686 and in 1674 d'Auteuil was in Paris, studying at the University.

29 AN. C11A, IV, 70–7, Frontenac au Ministre, Que., Nov. 14, 1674.

30 Extrait des Registres . . ., *op. cit.*

31 AN. C11A, XVI, 87–95, Champigny au Ministre, Que., July 3, 1698.

32 *Ibid.*, 120–1, Champigny au Ministre, Que., Oct. 14, 1698.

33 *Ibid.*, 59, Frontenac au Ministre, Que., Oct. 10, 1698.

34 Bib. Nat. Collection Clairambault, DCCCLXXIII, 362, Frontenac à de Lagny, [Que.,] Oct., 1698.

35 Bib. Nat. Nouvelles Acquisitions, X̄X̄MMCXLIV, 269–73, Le Roy de la Potherye au Comte de Maurepas, [Que., 1699]

36 AN. F3, Moreau de St. Méry, VIII, 58–60, Last will and testament of Louis Buade, Comte de Frontenac.

37 *Ibid.*

38 Le Roy de la Potherye au Comte de Maurepas, *op. cit.*

39 BRH, I, 1895, 99–108, Remarques sur l'oraison funèbre de feu M. de

Frontenac prononcés en l'église des Récollets de Québec, le 19 Décembre 1698, par le P. Olivier Goyer, Commissaire des Récollets.

40 AN. CIIA, XVI, Champigny au Ministre, Que., Dec. 22, 1698.

41 *Ibid.*, XVII, 53, Champigny au Ministre, Que., May 26, 1699.

42 Champigny au Ministre, Que., Dec. 22, 1698, *loc. cit.*

43 *Ibid.*, XVI, Extraits des lettres du Canada de l'année 1698.

CHAPTER NINETEEN

1 AN. CIIA, XVII, 24, Callières au Ministre, Mtl., May 2, 1699.

2 Bib. Nat. Collection Clairambault, DCCCLXXIII, 359–60, Vaudreuil au Ministre, Que., Dec. 26, 1698.

3 AN. CIIA, XVI, 2–3, Frontenac et Champigny au Ministre, Que., Oct. 15, 1698.

4 AN. F3, Moreau de St. Méry, VIII, 140, Parolles des Iroquois à M. le Chevalier de Callières, Sept. 20, 1699.

5 CSP 1697–1698, 434, Propositions made by the Five Nations to the Earl of Bellomont at Albany, July 20, 1698; NYCD, IV, 345–7, Depositions of Henry & Joseph of the Mohawk Nation before Gov. Earl of Bellomont & the attorney general, New York, May 31, 1698; 362–4, Earl of Bellomont to the Board of Trade, New York, Sept. 14, 1698; CSP 1700, 382, Solicitor General to the Council of Trade & Plantations, June 27, 1700.

6 AN. CIIA, XVII, 76, Champigny au Ministre, Que., Oct. 20, 1699.

7 *Ibid.*, XVIII, 147, Le Roy de la Potherye, Que., Oct. 16, 1700.

8 *Ibid.*; 81–3, Discours des deputés des Iroquois, Mtl., July 18, 1700.

9 *The Livingston Indian Records, 1666–1723,* 179, John Baptist Van Eps's Report about ye Indians, Albany, Aug. 5, 1700.

10 CSP 1700, 459, Minutes of the Council in Assembly of New York, Aug. 2, 1700.

11 AN. F3, Moreau de St. Méry, VIII, 55, Rélation de ce qui s'est passé de plus remarquable en Canada depuis le départ des Vaisseaux en 1697 jusques au 20e Octobre 1698; 262–8, Pourparlez entre M. le chevalier de Callières . . . et les Sauvages descendus à Montréal pour parvenir à la ratiffication de la paix; AN. CIIA, XIX, 115–18, Callières au Ministre, Que., Oct. 4, 1701.

12 *Ibid.*, XVIII, 81–8, Discours des deputés des Iroquois, Mtl., July 18, 1700; 90, Champigny au Ministre, Mtl., July 22, 1700; John Baptist Van Eps's report about ye Indians, Albany, Aug. 5, 1700, *loc. cit.*

13 AN. CIIA, XIX, 116–17, Callières au Ministre, Que., Oct. 4, 1701.

14 CSP 1700, 443–4, Journal of Capt. Johannes Bleeker junr., & David Schuyler, Journey to Onondage, Albany, June 1700.

15 *Ibid.*

16 AN. CIIA, XIX, 115–18, Callières au Ministre, Que., Oct. 4, 1701; AN. F3, Moreau de St. Méry, VIII, 262–8, Pourparlez entre M. le Cheva-

lier de Callières . . . et les Sauvages descendus à Montréal pour parvenir à la ratiffication de la paix.

17 AN. CIIA, XIX, Ratification de la Paix . . . entre la Colonie de Canada, Les Sauvages ses alliez, et les iroquois dans une assemblée générale des chefs de chacune de ces nations. . . . A Montréal le 4e aoust 1701; 125, Callières au Ministre, Que., Oct. 31, 1701.

18 *Ibid.*; AN. F3, Moreau de St. Méry, VIII, 278–9, Assemblée faite par M. le chevalier de Callières . . . de tous les nations Iroquoises . . . Mtl., Aug. 7, 1701; 260, Instruction pour le P. Bruyas que nous Envoyons avec le Sr Maricourt, de Joncaire, et autres chez les Onnontaguez; CSP 1701, Journal of Capt. Johannes Bleeker junr., & David Schuyler's Journey to Onnondage, Aug. 27, 1701; 556, Lieut. Gov. Nanfan to Council of Trade & Plantations, New York, Oct. 2, 1701.

19 CSP 1700, 90–3, Governor the Earl of Bellomont to the Council of Trade & Plantations, Boston, Feb. 28, 1700.

20 AN. CIIA, XIX, 233–4, Projets sur la Nouvelle Angleterre. Canada, 1701.

21 Bib. Nat. Fonds Français, X̄X̄MMCCMX, 417–18, Bégon à M. de Villermont, Rochefort, Nov. 29, 1701.

CHAPTER TWENTY

1 By 1696 the Ministry of Marine had become aware of what La Salle's character, aims and methods had really been. See the *mémoire* submitted to Daguesseau, the *surintendant de commerce*, AN. CIIA, XIII, 399–408, Commerce du Castor de Canada. 1696. Mémoire remis à M. Daguesseau pour délibérer sur les affaires de Canada.

2 AN. B, XX, Mémoire pour servir d'Instruction au Sr d'Iberville . . . Versailles, Oct. 19, 1698.

3 *Ibid.*, 276, Le Ministre au Sr d'Iberville, Fontainebleau, Sept. 22, 1699.

4 CSP 1693–1696, 518, Memorial of Sir Thomas Lawrence, Whitehall, June 25, 1695.

5 AN. C13C, II, 47, Mémoire sur l'establissement de la mobille et du Misisipy; AN. C13A, I, 75–6, Mémoire sur le projet d'établir une nouvelle colonie au Mississipy ou Louisiane. Joint à la lettre de M. Argoud, Procureur de Prises du 10 dec. 1697.

6 *Ibid.*, 107, Iberville au Ministre, La Rochelle, Oct. 30, 1699; 288–33, Iberville au Ministre, Des Bayogoula, Feb. 26, 1700.

7 AN. CIIA, XVI, 29, Callières au Ministre, Mtl., June 2, 1699.

8 AN. C13C, II, 5–6, 12–13, Mémoire pour rendre compte au Roy de le découverte du fleuve de Mississipy. 1699; AN. B, XX, 265, Le Ministre au Sr d'Iberville, Versailles, Aug. 5, 1699.

9 *Ibid.*, XXII, Mémoire du Roy à Callières et Champigny, Versailles, May 31, 1701.

10 Sem. Que. Lettres, Carton O, No. 34, M. Tremblay à M. de Glandelet, [Paris,] May 28, 1701; M. A. Thompson, "Louis XIV and the Origins of the War of the Spanish Succession," in *Transactions of the Royal Historical Society*, IV, 1954, Fifth Series, IV, 111–34.

11 AN. C11A, XIV, 280–5, Mémoire du Sr Riverin sur la traitte et la Ferme des Castors de Canada, 1696.

12 AN. B, XIX, 234–7, Mémoire du Roy pour les Srs Comte de Frontenac et de Champigny, Versailles, April 27, 1697.

13 AN. C11A, XI, 230–2, Frontenac au Ministre, Que., Oct. 20, 1691.

14 AN. F3, Moreau de St. Méry, II, 11, Mémoire de Canada. De la Chesnaye, 1695.

SELECT BIBLIOGRAPHY

PRIMARY SOURCES—MANUSCRIPT

Paris: Archives Nationales—Series B; Series C11A (Colonies); Series C11C (Colonies); Series C11D (Colonies); Series C11E (Colonies); Series C11G (Colonies); Series C13A (Colonies); Series C13B (Colonies); Series C13C (Colonies); Series D2D; Series E; Series F2C; Series F3 Moreau de St. Méry.

Paris: Bibliothèque Nationale—Mélanges Colbert; Les Cinq Cents de Colbert; Fonds Français; Nouvelles Acquisitions; Collection Clairambault; Collection Dupuy; Collection Moreau; Collection de Baluze; Collection Duchesne; Factum 2505.

Paris: Archives du Ministère des Affaires Etrangères—Series France, Mémoires et Documents; Series Amérique.

Paris: Bibliothèque Mazarine—Manuscrits, vol. 1963.

Vincennes: Dépot du Ministère de la Guerre—Series A.

Châteauroux: Archives Départementale Indre-et-Loire–Series E.

Ottawa: Public Archives of Canada—Lettres de l'Abbé Tronson.

Boston: Massachusetts Archives—Inter-Charter, vol. 35–6; Legislative Records of the Council, 1689–1698; Minutes of the Council, 1689–1732; Military, vol. 70.

Quebec: Archives du Séminaire de Québec—Lettres, Carton M; Lettres, Carton N; Lettres, Carton S; Lettres, Carton O.

Albany: New York State Archives—New York Colonial Manuscripts.

PRIMARY SOURCES—TRANSCRIPTS

Ottawa: Public Archives of Canada—Archives Nationales (Colonies) Paris; Series B; Series C11A; Series F3 Moreau de St. Méry.

Bibliothèque St. Sulpice, Montreal—Documents de St. Sulpice.

PRIMARY SOURCES—PRINTED

Annales de l'Hôtel-Dieu de Montréal, written by Sister Morin, edited by A.-E. Fauteux, E.-Z. Massicotte, and C. Bertrand, Montreal, 1921.

Annales de l'Hôtel-Dieu de Québec, written by Mère de St. Ignace Juchereau, edited by A. Jamet, Quebec, 1939.

BAUGY, le chevalier de: *Journal d'une expédition contre les Iroquois en 1687*, Paris, 1883.

BELMONT, Abbé de: "Histoire du Canada" in *Manuscripts Relating to the Early History of Canada*. Published by the Literary and Historical Society of Quebec, Quebec, 1868.

BOUCHER, Pierre, sieur de Boucherville: *Histoire véritable et naturelle des moeurs et productions du pays de la Nouvelle France*. (First published 1664.) Edited by G. Coffin, Montreal, 1882.

Calendar of State Papers Colonial, America and West Indies, 1660–1702, London, 1862–1912.

CHARLEVOIX, Père P.-F.-X. de: *Histoire et description générale de la Nouvelle France, avec le journal historique d'une voyage fait par ordre du roi dans l'Amérique Septentrionale*, Paris, 1744, 3 vols.

CLEMENT, Pierre (editor): *Lettres, instructions et mémoires de Colbert*, Paris, 1861–73, 7 vols.

Collection des manuscrits contenant lettres, mémoires et autres documents historiques relatifs à la Nouvelle France. Published by order of the Quebec Legislature, Quebec, 1883–85, 4 vols.

Edits, ordonnances royaux, déclarations d'état du Roi concernant le Canada, edited by W. B. Lindsay, Quebec, 1854, 3 vols.

Jesuit Relations and Allied Documents, edited by R. G. Thwaites, Cleveland, 1896–1901, 73 vols.

Jugements et délibérations du Conseil Souverain de la Nouvelle France. Published by order of the Quebec Legislature, Quebec, 1885, 6 vols.

LAHONTAN, Louis Armand de Lom d'Arce, baron de: *Nouveaux voyages de Mr le baron de Lahontan dans l'Amérique Septentrionale*, La Haye, 1703, 2 vols.

— *New Voyages to North America*, edited by R. G. Thwaites, Chicago, 1905, 2 vols.

LECLERCQ, P. Chrétien: *Premier Etablissement de la Foy dans la Nouvelle France*, Paris, 1691.

The Livingston Indian Records, 1666–1723, edited by Lawrence H. Leder, The Pennsylvania Historical Association, Gettysburg, 1956.

MARGRY, P. (editor): *Mémoires et documents pour servir à l'histoire des origines françaises des pays d'outre mer: Découvertes et établissements des Français dans l'ouest et dans le sud de l'Amérique septentrionale*, Paris, 1876, 6 vols.

MONTPENSIER, Mademoiselle de: *Mémoires de Mademoiselle de Montpensier, petite-fille de Henri IV*, edited by A. Chéruel, Paris, 1858, 4 vols.

New York—*Documentary History of the State of New York*, edited by E. B. O'Callaghan, Albany, 1850, 4 vols.

—*Documents Relating to the Colonial History of New York*, edited by E. B. O'Callaghan & J. R. Brodhead, Albany, 1856-83, 15 vols.

PEASE, E. C., and WERNER, R. C. (editors): *The French Foundations, 1680-1693*, Collection of the Illinois State Historical Library, vol. I, Springfield, 1934.

PERROT, Nicholas: *Mémoire sur les moeurs, coustumes et relligion des sauvages de l'Amérique septentrionale*, Tailhan edition, Leipzig and Paris, 1864.

POTHERIE, M. de Bacqueville de la: *Histoire de l'Amérique septentrionale*, Paris, 1753.

Quebec—*Rapport de l'archiviste de la province de Québec*, 1922-55.

—*Literary and Historical Society of Quebec, Historical Documents*, Series 1-9, Quebec, 1868-1915.

ROY, P.-G. (editor): *Ordonnances, Commissions etc., etc., des Gouverneurs et Intendants de la Nouvelle France, 1639-1760*, Beauceville, 1924, 2 vols.

SAVAGE, Thomas: *An Account of the Late Action of the New Englanders, under the Command of Sir William Phips, against the French at Canada*, London, 1691.

ST. SIMON, le duc de: *Mémoires de St. Simon*, edited by A. de Boislisle, Paris, 1879, 41 vols.

ST. VALLIER, Bishop Jean de la Croix: *Etat présent de l'Eglise et de la colonie française dans la Nouvelle France*, Paris, 1686.

TAC, Père Sixte le: *Histoire chronologique de la Nouvelle France*, edited by E. Réveillaud, Paris, 1888.

TURENNE, Vicomte de: *Mémoires du vicomte de Turenne*, Paris, 1901.

WRAXALL, Peter: *An Abridgement of the New York Indian Records*, edited by C. H. McIlwain, Cambridge, Mass., 1915.

SECONDARY SOURCES—PRINTED

ADAIR, E. R.: "Anglo-French Rivalry in the Fur Trade during the 18th Century," in *Culture*, vol. VIII, 1947.

ALVORD, Clarence W.: *The Illinois Country, 1673-1818*, Springfield, Ill., 1920.

ANSELME, P.: *Histoire généalogique et chronologique de la maison royale de France*, Paris, 1733, vol. VIII.

BEAUCHAMP, W. M.: *History of the New York Iroquois*, University of the State of New York, 1904.

BEDARD, T.: *La comtesse de Frontenac, 1632–1717*, Lévis, 1904.

BUFFINTON, Arthur H.: "The Policy of Albany and English Westward Expansion," in *Mississippi Valley Historical Review*, vol. VIII, March, 1922.

Bulletin de la Société Archéologique d'Eure-et-Loire, 1er semestre, 1951.

BURTON, F. W.: "The Wheat Supply of New France," in *Proceedings and Transactions of the Royal Society of Canada*, 3rd series, vol. XXX.

BUSSEROLLE, J.–X. Carré de: *Dictionnaire historique, géographique et biographique d'Indre-et-Loire et de l'ancienne province de Touraine*, Tours, 1878–84, 6 vols.

CAHALL, R. du Bois: *The Sovereign Council of New France*, New York, 1915.

Canadian Archives Report, Ottawa, 1872–1953.

CHAPAIS, Sir Thomas: *Jean Talon, intendant de la Nouvelle France*, Quebec, 1904.

COLBY, C. W.: *The Fighting Governor*, Toronto, 1922.

COLDEN, Cadwallader: *History of the Five Nations of Canada*, London, 1747.

COLE, C. W.: *French Mercantilism, 1683–1700*, New York, 1943.

— *Colbert and a Century of French Mercantilism*, New York, 1939, 2 vols.

CROUSE, Nellis M.: *Lemoyne d'Iberville; Soldier of New France*, Ithaca, New York, 1954.

DELALANDE, J.: *Le Conseil Souverain de la Nouvelle France*, Quebec, 1927.

DELANGLEZ, Jean, S.J.: *Frontenac and the Jesuits*, Chicago, 1939.

— *Louis Jolliet, vie et voyages (1645–1700)*, Montreal, 1950.

— *Some La Salle Journeys*, Chicago, 1938.

— "Cadillac's Early Years in America," in *Mid-America*, January, 1944.

— "Antoine Laumet, *alias* Cadillac, Commandant at Michilimackinac: 1694–1697," in *Mid-America*, April, July, October, 1945.

DOUCET, R.: *Les institutions de la France au XVI siècle*, Paris, 1948, 2 vols.

EASTMAN, Mack: *Church and State in Early Canada*, Edinburgh, 1915.

FLICK, A. C. (editor): *History of the State of New York*, New York, 1933, 10 vols.

FREGAULT, Guy: *Iberville le conquérant*, Montreal, 1944.

GIPSON, L. H.: *The British Empire before the American Revolution*, New York, 1942, vols. IV and V.

GIRAUD, Marcel: *Histoire de la Louisiane Française. Vol. I. Le règne de Louis XIV, 1698–1715*, Paris, 1953.

GIROUARD, Désiré: *Lake St. Louis, Old and New*, Montreal, 1895.

— *Les Anciens Postes de Lac St. Louis*, Montreal, 1895.

— "L'expédition de marquis de Denonville," in *Proceedings and Transac-*

tions of the Royal Society of Canada, 2nd series, vol. V, 1899.

GOSSELIN, Abbé Auguste: *L'Eglise du Canada*, Quebec, 1911, 3 vols.

GRAHAM, G. S.: *Empire of the North Atlantic*, Toronto, 1950.

GROULX, Abbé Lionel: "Denonville et les galériens Iroquois," in *L'Action Universitaire*, Vol. VII, no. 8, April, 1941.

HAMMANG, F. H.: *The Marquis de Vaudreuil*, Bibliothèque de l'Université Louvain, Bruges, 1938.

HAZLITT, H. Carew: *The Venetian Republic: Its Rise, its Growth, and its Fall, 421–1797*, London, 1900.

HUNT, G. T.: *The Wars of the Iroquois*, Madison, Wisc., 1940.

HUTCHINSON, Thomas: *The History of Massachusetts, from the first settlement thereof in 1628, until the year 1750*, third edition, Boston, 1795, 2 vols.

INNIS, H. A.: *The Fur Trade of Canada*, London, 1930.

KELLOGG, Louise Phelps: *The French Régime in Wisconsin and the North-west*, Madison, Wisc., 1925.

KENNEDY, J. H.: *Jesuit and Savage in New France*, New Haven, 1950.

LALANNE, Ludovic: *Dictionnaire historique de la France*, Paris, 1872.

LANCTOT, G: *L'administration de la Nouvelle France*, Paris, 1929.

— *Réalisations françaises de Cartier à Montcalm*, Montreal, 1951.

LAVISSE, Ernest: *Histoire de France*, Paris, 1908, 9 vols.

LESUEUR, W.: *Count Frontenac*, Toronto, 1906.

LEWIS, W. H.: *The Splendid Century*, London, 1953.

LORIN, H.: *Le comte de Frontenac*, Paris, 1895.

MALCHELOSSE, D.: "La Salle et le Fort Saint-Joseph des Miamis," in *Cahier des Dix*, No. 22, 1957.

MARION, Marcel: *Dictionnaire des institutions de la France aux 17e et 18e siècles*, Paris, 1923.

MIMS, S. L.: *Colbert's West India Policy*, New Haven, 1912.

MORGAN, Lewis H.: *League of the Iroquois*, Rochester, N.Y., 1851.

MUNRO, W. B.: "The Brandy Parliament of 1678," in *Canadian Historical Review*, vol. II, June, 1921.

MURPHY, E. R. M.: *Henry de Tonty, Fur Trader of the Mississippi*, Baltimore, 1941.

MYRAND, E.: *Frontenac et ses amis*, Quebec, 1902.

— *Sir William Phips devant Québec*, Quebec, 1895.

NUTE, Grace Lee: *Caesars of the Wilderness*, New York, 1943.

PARKMAN, Francis: *Count Frontenac and New France under Louis XIV*, Frontenac edition, Toronto, 1899.

PINARD, M.: *Chronologie historique-militaire*, Paris, 1763, vol. VI.

REAUX, Tallement des: *Les Historiettes de Tallement des Réaux*, Paris, 1858, vol. VII.

RICH, E. E.: "Russia and the Colonial Fur Trade," in *Economic History Review*, vol. VII, no. 3, April, 1955.

ROCHEMONTEIX, Le R. P. Camille de : *Les Jesuittes de la Nouvelle France au XVII siècle*, Paris, 1896, 3 vols.

SAGNAC, P., and SAINT-LEGER, A. de : *La prépondérance française: Louis XIV (1661–1715)*, Paris, 1949.

SEGUIN, Robert-Lionel : "Le comportement de certains habitants de Lachine aux environs de 1689," in *Le Bulletin des Recherches Historiques*, vol. LX, no. 4, Oct.-Nov.-Dec., 1954.

STANLEY, G. F. G. : *Canada's Soldiers, 1604–1954*, Toronto, 1954.

WATKINS, W. K. : *Soldiers in the Expedition to Canada in 1690*, Boston, 1898.

INDEX